THE LAW OF SCOTLAND RELATING TO DEBT

W.D.—1

THE LAW OF SCOTLAND RELATING TO DEBT

W. A. WILSON, M.A., LL.B.
Lord President Reid Professor of Law
University of Edinburgh

EDINBURGH

W. GREEN & SON LTD.

Law Publishers

1982

First published in 1982

ISBN 0 414 00682 8

PRINTED IN GREAT BRITAIN BY
McQUEEN PRINTERS LTD.
GALASHIELS, SCOTLAND

PREFACE

MUCH of this book was drafted 20 or so years ago when, having recently had experience of practice, I thought there was room for a work which collected together, in relatively brief compass, the law on a number of topics relating to debt which seemed to crop up frequently in ordinary legal practice. I had in mind such matters as arrestment on the dependence, compensation, prescription, fraudulent preferences, preferential claims and the suing of partnerships. Something has been included about the particular contracts out of which debts commonly arise, such as sale, hire-purchase, and contracts for services but the treatment of these is not full and is intended only to show the ways in which the pecuniary obligations come into existence. Similarly, the various types of security are discussed in outline. The chapters on diligence and insolvency are designed to state how the individual creditor stands in these processes and do not give a detailed description of how diligence should be executed or how a sequestration or liquidation should be conducted. Information on these matters can be obtained from other works such as Mr G. Maher's admirable *Textbook of Diligence*. Obviously it is not possible in a volume of this size to produce modernised versions of Goudy, Graham Stewart and Gloag and Irvine; selection and compression have been necessary and no doubt there will be differences of view on how a new swathe should be cut through the law.

Many decisions of the sheriff court have been cited as much of the relevant law has been developed in that court rather than in the Court of Session; great respect must be accorded to such names as Fyfe and, in more recent times, Dobie, N. M. L. Walker, Prain and Sir Allan Walker.

An effort has been made to integrate the Consumer Credit Act 1974 into the general law by setting out the more general provisions of the Act in Chapter 3 and then including the rules relating to particular contracts in Chapter 4, which deals with credit transactions, and in other appropriate sections. It must be emphasised that this is a subject in which paraphrase can easily mislead and, where a question arises, reference to the text of the Act is always necessary.

An attempt has been made to state the law at 1 January 1981 but delays in the publication of reports and legislation are nowadays such that the attempt is unlikely to prove successful. It has been assumed that the Consumer Credit Act 1974 is completely in operation but a note is appended to this preface stating the sections which were in force at 1 July 1981. It has been possible to note the increase of the summary cause jurisdiction to £1,000 and the important effect of the Local Government (Miscellaneous Provisions) (Scotland) Act 1981, s.12, in relation to poinding of goods on hire-purchase. In footnotes, some indications have been given of the effect of registration of title. Similar indications are given of the changes in the ordinary sheriff court rules proposed in a draft of June 1980 circulated by the Sheriff Court Rules Council. Unfortunately, it has not been possible to predict the result of the convoluted course of the Companies Bill 1981 and much of what has been written as to the Registration of Business Names Act 1916 may be useless.

I am deeply indebted to Mr N. R. Whitty who put his vast knowledge of the law of diligence at my disposal and commented in detail on the chapters dealing with that subject. I am also grateful to my colleague Mr Kenneth Reid who commented on a part of the text and to other colleagues who helped in various ways. I am solely responsible for the errors which remain. My thanks are also due to Mrs June McIntyre who typed the manuscript with punctilious care, Mrs Dilly Emslie, who efficiently compiled the tables of cases and statutes, Mr R. R. Shaw, formerly of W. Green & Son Ltd., with whom the project of publication was first discussed, and Miss Iris Stewart, General Manager of that firm, for her help, patience and efficiency during the publishing process.

Edinburgh, W. A. W.
1 December 1981

CONTENTS

NOTE—COMMENCEMENT OF CONSUMER CREDIT ACT 1974

THE sections brought into force to some extent by the various commencement orders are:

No. 1—(S.I. 1975/2123 (C.62))—21, 35, 36, 148.
No. 2—(S.I. 1977/325 (C.11))—21, 56, 82, 137-140, 157, 158.
No. 3—(S.I. 1977/802 (C.30))—49, 50, 51, 75.
No. 4—(S.I. 1977/2163 (C.73))—21, 148, 149.
No. 5—(S.I. 1979/1685 (C.42))—Repeals, etc.
No. 6—(S.I. 1980/50 (C.3))—Part IV, 151.
No. 7—(S.I. 1981/280 (C.6))—Repeals, etc.

The provisions of the Act, except as mentioned in Schedule 3 thereto, came into operation on 31 July 1974. The provisions which have still to be brought into force are those mentioned in the Schedule other than those specified in the commencement orders above, that is to say, ss. 19(3), 57-59, 61-73, 76-81, 83-104, 105, 107-110, 111, 114-122, 123-125, 126, 127-136, 141-144.

TABLE OF CASES

TABLE OF STATUTES

PRINCIPAL AUTHORITIES CITED AND ABBREVIATIONS THEREOF

Bankton ....Andrew McDouall, Lord Bankton, *Institute of the Laws of Scotland in Civil Rights,* 3 vols., 1751-3.

Bell, *Comm.* ....Professor G. J. Bell, *Commentaries on the Law of Scotland and the Principles of Mercantile Jurisprudence,* 7th ed., 1870.

Bell, *Prin.* ....Professor G. J. Bell, *Principles of the Law of Scotland,* 10th ed., 1899.

Bell, *Lects.* ....*Lectures on Conveyancing* by A. M. Bell, 3rd ed., 1882.

Byles ....*Byles on Bills of Exchange,* 24th ed., by M. Megrah and F. R. Ryder, 1979.

Chalmers ....*Chalmers on Bills of Exchange,* 13th ed., by David L. Smout, 1964.

Ersk. ....Professor John Erskine of Carnock, *An Institute Of the Law of Scotland,* 8th ed., 2 vols., 1871.

Finlayson ....*Law Lectures to Bankers,* by Robert Finlayson, 1939.

Gloag ....*The Law of Contract,* by W. M. Gloag, 2nd ed., 1929.

Gloag & Henderson ....*Introduction to the Law of Scotland,* by W. M. Gloag and R. C. Henderson, 8th ed., by A. B. Wilkinson and Others, 1980.

Gloag & Irvine ....*Law of Rights in Security,* by W. M. Gloag and J. M. Irvine, 1897.

Goudy ....*A Treatise on the Law of Bankruptcy in Scotland,* by Henry Goudy, 4th ed., by T. A. Fyfe, 1914.

Graham Stewart ....*A Treatise on the Law of Diligence,* by J. Graham Stewart, 1898.

Paget ....*Paget's Law of Banking,* 8th ed., by Maurice Megrah and F. R. Ryder, 1972.

Thomson ....*A Treatise on the Law of Bills of Exchange,* by Robert Thomson, 3rd ed., 1865.

Thorburn ....*Commentary on the Bills of Exchange Act 1882,* by W. D. Thorburn, 1882.

Wallace & McNeil ....Wallace and McNeil's *Banking Law,* 8th ed., by Thomas Chalmers, 1949.

Wardhaugh ....*The Scottish Bankruptcy Manual,* by John B. Wardhaugh, 1955.

A.S. ....Act of Sederunt.

B.A. ....Bankruptcy (Scotland) Act 1913.

C.A.S. ....Codifying Act of Sederunt.

R.C. ....Rules of the Court of Session 1965.

S.C.R. ....Sheriff Court Rules.

CHAPTER 1

THE NATURE OF DEBT

1. Definition

Debts are "mere rights to demand payment of money at a stipulated time."[1] They are sometimes called *nomina debitorum*. "*Nomina debitorum* are not accounted *res*; nor yet are they mere *entia rationis*: But in plain Scots, are Debts."[2]

A debt can be distinguished from an obligation to account. "In the case of a debt proper there is an obligation to pay, and an obligation to pay necessarily includes an obligation to account. But there may be an obligation to account when at the moment there is no obligation to pay."[3] A debt is a species of *jus crediti*, defined in terms of English law as "a right which the holder of it cannot make available, if it is resisted, without a suit, to compel persons to do something else in order to make the right perfect."[4] Thus, the insured under a life insurance policy has a *jus crediti*. "He was vested in the *jus crediti* or right to recover when the policy matured—a *jus crediti* which would not be enforced by him, because *ex hypothesi* he would be dead, but which would fall to, and be enforced by his personal representatives for the benefit of his estate."[5]

A "debt" may be a sum the amount of which is not ascertained.[6] But a right to the price of shares fixed by reference to the market price on the first day of dealing after a flotation of the company if a flotation should occur was held not to be a "debt"; it was merely "a contingent right . . . to receive an unascertainable amount of money at an unknown date."[7]

There may be degrees of obligation. Lord Dunedin made this classification:

(1) an ordinary debt "which you are bound to pay the moment that you are sued upon it";

---

1 Bell, *Comm.*, II, 15.
2 *Stuart's Answers to Dirleton's Doubts, s.v. Nomina Debitorum.*
3 *Per* L.P. Dunedin, *Riley* v. *Ellis,* 1910 S.C.934 at 941.
4 *Per* Lord Cranworth, *Edmond* v. *Gordon* (1858) 3 Macq. 116 at 122.
5 *Per* L.P. Normand, *Tennant's Trs.* v. *Lord Advocate,* 1938 S.C.224 at 231.
6 *O'Driscoll* v. *Manchester Insurance Committee* [1915] 3 K.B.499.
7 *Marren* v. *Ingles* [1980] 1 W.L.R.983.

(2) a debt which is good against the debtor but which cannot come into competition with his ordinary creditors;
(3) a quasi-obligation "which is truly no obligation at all, which simply says 'I promise to pay if I like to pay' ".[8]

In the case[9] cited by Lord Dunedin as an example of the second type, the words "I shall be happy to pay . . . as soon as I have it in my power" were held to justify a decree against the grantor's executor.

2. Currency

The denominations of money in the currency of the United Kingdom are the pound sterling and the new penny, the new penny being one-hundredth part of a pound sterling.[10] Bank balances and periodical payments in so far as they were expressed in shillings and pence before 15 February 1971 are to be converted in accordance with Schedule 1 to the Decimal Currency Act 1969.[11] There are special provisions for friendly society and industrial assurance company contracts.[12]

A creditor is entitled to insist on payment in legal tender. The following are legal tender[13]:— coins of bronze, for payment of any amount not exceeding 20 new pence; coins of cupro-nickel or silver of denominations of not more than 10 new pence, for payment of any amount not exceeding five pounds; coins of cupro-nickel or silver of denominations of more than 10 new pence, for payment of any amount not exceeding 10 pounds; gold coins of appropriate weight and Bank of England notes[14] of denomination of less than five pounds for payment of any amount. It is open to the creditor and debtor to agree that gold sovereigns tendered in payment are to be treated as having a value greater than their nominal value.[15]

The pound Scots is one twelfth of the pound sterling so 100 pounds Scots is £8·33p.

---

[8] *Mackinnon's Trs.* v. *Dunlop,* 1913 S.C.232 at 239. See, as to the use of *"ex gratia", Wick Harbour Trs.* v. *Admiralty,* 1921 2 S.L.T.109.

[9] *Fair* v. *Hunter* (1861) 24 D.1.

[10] Decimal Currency Act 1967, s.1.

[11] Decimal Currency Act 1969, ss.4, 5.

[12] ss.6, 7; Friendly Societies (Halfpenny) Regulations 1969 (S.I. 1969/886); Friendly Societies (Decimal Currency) Regulations 1970 (S.I. 1970/932); Industrial Assurance (Halfpenny) Regulations 1969 (S.I. 1969/887); Industrial Assurance (Premium Receipt Books) (Decimal Currency) Regulations 1970 (S.I. 1970/1012).

[13] Coinage Act 1971, s.2.

[14] Currency and Bank Notes Act 1954, s.1(2). Scottish bank-notes were legal tender for the war period but are not now: Currency (Defence) Act 1939, s.2(2); Order in Council dated 20 December 1945, S.R. & O. 1945 No. 1631.

[15] *Jenkins* v. *Horn* [1979] 2 All E.R.1141.

3. International Units

In legislation giving effect to international conventions, the practice, apart from the unfortunate use of "gold value" in the Carriage of Goods by Sea Act 1924,[16] was to express sums in currency units of 65½ milligrammes of gold of millesimal fineness 900[17] (the franc Poincaré) or gold francs weighing 10/31 of a gramme and being of millesimal fineness 900[18] (the franc de germinal), the sterling equivalent being determined in each case by statutory instruments made from time to time. The legislation is now being amended to express the sums in special drawing rights as defined by the International Monetary Fund, the sterling equivalent for a particular day being determined by a certificate by the Treasury.[19]

In legislation of the European Economic Community, sums were originally fixed in units of account (u.a.), the unit being the value of ·88867088 grammes of fine gold;[20] more recently, there has been a process of conversion to the European Unit of Account (EUA) which is based on the value of a "basket" of currencies published daily.[21]

4. Gold Clauses

The effect of a clause requiring payment in gold or gold coin depends on a construction of the clause but where the proper law of the contract is English it will usually be construed to import an obligation to pay sterling representing the value of the gold specified and not to pay in gold itself.[22] Such a clause is known as a gold clause and is "intended to afford a definite standard or measure of value, and thus to protect against a depreciation of the currency and against the discharge of the obligation by a payment of lesser value than that prescribed."[23] A clause may, however, be construed,

---

16 Sched., art. IX.

17 *E.g.* Carriage by Air Act 1961, 1st Sched., art. 22(5).

18 *E.g.* Carriage of Goods by Road Act 1965, Sched., art. 23.3.

19 See Carriage by Air and Road Act 1979, ss.4, 5.

20 Council Regulation 129 of 30 October 1962.

21 H. Joly Dixon, "The European Unit of Account" (1977) 14 C.M.L. Rev.191.

22 *Feist* v. *Societé Intercommunale Belge D'Electricité* [1934] A.C.161; *New Brunswick Ry. Co.* v. *British and French Trust Corporation Ltd.* [1939] A.C.1.

23 *Norman* v. *Baltimore and Ohio Railroad Co.*, 294 U.S.240, quoted by Lord Maugham, *Rex.* v. *International Trustee for the Protection of Bondholders Aktiengesellschaft* [1937] A.C.500 at 562.

albeit that it contains a reference to gold, as an obligation to pay in lawful currency.[24]

A money obligation index-linked by reference to the rate of exchange between the Swiss franc and sterling has been held in England not to be contrary to public policy.[25]

5. Foreign Currency

A reference to a currency in an obligation may be to a "money of account" or a "money of payment". "The *money of account* is the currency in which an obligation is measured. It tells the debtor *how much* he has to pay. The *money of payment* is the currency in which the obligation is to be discharged. It tells the debtor *by what means* he is to pay."[26]

Decree can competently be granted in a foreign currency: conversion to sterling can be at the date of the extract decree but it may be that it could be later.[27] But decree in a foreign currency is not competent if the contract provides for payment in sterling.

A foreign debt falls to be converted into British currency at the rate of exchange current at the date it became payable and not that at the date of decree.

6. Sources of Debt

The principal sources of obligation to pay money are: (a) contracts and promises, (b) unjustified enrichment, (c) other quasi-contractual situations, (d) delict, (e) natural relationship, (f) trust, (g) succession, (h) statute.

The distinction between a debt due under the contract and a claim for damages for breach of contract may be important in that in the case of damages, firstly, the claimant must take steps to minimise his loss and, secondly, it may be argued that a claim for liquidated damages is a penalty.[28]

---

[24] *Treseder-Griffin* v. *Co-operative Insurance Society* [1956] 2 Q.B.127; *Campos* v. *Kentucky & Indiana Terminal Railroad Co.* [1962] 2 Lloyd's Rep.459.

[25] *Multiservice Bookbinding Ltd.* v. *Marden* [1979] Ch.84.

[26] *Per* Lord Denning M.R., *Woodhouse Ltd.* v. *Nigerian Produce Ltd.* [1971] 2 Q.B.23 at 54.

[27] *Commerzbank Aktiengesellschaft* v. *Large,* 1977 S.C. 375. See Marshall, 1978 S.L.T.(News)77; *L/F Foroya Fiskasola* v. *Charles Mauritzen Ltd.,* 1978 S.L.T. (Sh.Ct.)27; *Macfie's J.F.* v. *Macfie,* 1932 S.L.T.460; Extracts Department Regulations, reg. 5A, *Parliament House Book,* Division C.

[28] *Bell Brothers (H.P.) Ltd.* v. *Aitken,* 1939 S.C.577; *Bridge* v. *Campbell Discount Co. Ltd.* [1962] A.C.600; *White & Carter (Councils) Ltd.* v. *McGregor,* 1962 S.C. (H.L.)1.

Many cases refer to actions of relief. "Now, relief means, of course that A is bound to relieve B of a liability which has been found against B".[29] It would seem that apart from statutory provisions for relief[30] the right of relief arises from a contractual relationship.[31] The action is limited to cases where the liability of the party from whom relief is claimed is exactly commensurate with that of the party claiming the relief and the action must be founded on the same type of liability as that of the party claiming relief:[32] "where the Pursuer and the Defender were under a common obligation, which ought first to have been performed by the Defender, and which, by his neglect, was cast upon the Pursuer, so that the Pursuer, having been sued, was forced to pay damages, together with the costs of his adversary and his own costs in the suit."[33] Where B is found liable under a statute to pay compensation to C in respect of damage caused to C's property, B's action against his professional advisers whose negligence caused the damage is not an action of relief.[34]

Obligations arising from unjustified enrichment are sometimes classified as quasi-contractual obligations. The *condictio indebiti,* or repetition, is the appropriate remedy to recover money paid under an error of fact. "The action of *condictio indebiti* implies *indebiti solutio.* It is a peculiar action well known in our law. It depends not on contract but on *quasi* contract. When a payment is made which is supposed to be due, but which is not due, the law makes a contract between the parties such as they would have made had the real truth been known."[35] The claim is not to be sustained unless it appears that retention of the money would be inequitable.[36]

The payment must have been made in error; a payment made by a person in full knowledge of his legal rights where there was no

---

29 *Per* L.P. Dunedin, *Wood & Co.* v. *A. & A.Y. Mackay* (1906) 8 F.625 at 633.

30 *E.g.* Law Reform (Miscellaneous Provisions) (Scotland) Act 1940, s.3(2).

31 *Buchanan & Carswell* v. *Eugene Ltd.,* 1936 S.C.160, *per* Lord Murray at p.181; *National Coal Board* v. *Thomson,* 1959 S.C.353.

32 *Caledonian Rlwy Co.* v. *Colt* (1860) 3 Macq.833, *per* Lord Chelmsford at p.848; *Ovington* v. *McVicar* (1864) 2 M.1066.

33 *Caledonian Rlwy. Co.* v. *Colt, supra, per* Lord Campbell L.C. at p.840.

34 *British Railways Board* v. *Ross and Cromarty C.C.,* 1974 S.L.T.274.

35 *Per* Lord Neaves, *Masters and Seamen of Dundee* v. *Cockerill* (1869) 8 M.278 at 281.

36 *Bell* v. *Thomson* (1867) 6 M.64, *per* L.J.-C. Patton at p.67; *Henderson & Co. Ltd.* v. *Turnbull & Co.,* 1909 S.C.510; *Agnew* v. *Ferguson* (1903) 5 F.879; *Haggarty* v. *Scottish Transport and General Workers Union,* 1955 S.C.109; *Unigate Food* v. *Scottish Milk Marketing Board,* 1972 S.L.T.137.

liability to pay cannot be recovered;[37] but, to bar recovery, it must be shown that the knowledge that the sum was not due was, or should have been, present to his mind.[38] The error must be excusable,[39] as where it is due to the conduct of the other party.[40] It is not a bar to recovery that the payer had means of discovering the true facts.[41] The error must be as to fact and not law; an error as to the construction of a statute is an error of law for this purpose[42] but an error as to the construction of a private commercial contract is not, it seems.[43] It is an equitable defence that the payee had reasonable ground for believing that the money was his and acted upon his belief so as to alter his position in such a way as to make repetition unjust.[44] The doctrine has no application where there is an attempt to recover from an innocent party funds which have been improperly paid through the fraud of an intermediary.[45] There is a separate doctrine that excess charges exacted by a public body and later found unwarranted can be recovered;[46] *a fortiori,* if payment has been made under reservation.[47] It is not enough that the payment has been found to be unreasonable.[48]

The *condictio causa data causa non secuta* is appropriate where money has been paid by one of the parties to a contractual obligation and there has been a subsequent failure of consideration.[49]

The principle of recompense is that "where one has gained by the lawful act of another, done without any intention of donation, he is bound to recompense or indemnify that other to the extent of the

---

37 *Balfour Melville* v. *Duncan* (1903) 5 F.1079.

38 *Dalmellington Iron Co.* v. *Glasgow and South-Western Rlwy. Co.* (1889) 16 R.523.

39 *Taylor* v. *Wilson's Trs.,* 1979 S.L.T.105.

40 *Duncan, Galloway & Co.* v. *Duncan, Falconer & Co.,* 1913 S.C.265.

41 *Balfour* v. *Smith and Logan* (1877) 4 R.454.

42 *Glasgow Corporation* v. *Lord Advocate,* 1959 S.C.203; *Unigate Food Ltd.* v. *Scottish Milk Marketing Board,* 1972 S.L.T.137; *Taylor* v. *Wilson's Trs., supra.*

43 *Baird's Trs.* v. *Baird & Co.* (1877) 4 R.1005; *British Hydro-Carbon Chemicals Ltd. and British Transport Commission, Petrs.,* 1961 S.L.T.280; *cf. Rowan's Trs.* v. *Rowan,* 1940 S.C.30.

44 *Credit Lyonnais* v. *George Stevenson & Co. Ltd.* (1901) 9 S.L.T.93.

45 *G.M. Scott (Willowbank Cooperage) Ltd.* v. *York Trailer Co. Ltd.,* 1969 S.L.T.87.

46 *British Oxygen Co.* v. *South West Scotland Electricity Board,* 1958 S.C.53, esp. *per* Lord Patrick at p.79.

47 *British Railways Board* v. *Glasgow Corporation,* 1976 S.C.224.

48 *Lanarkshire Steel Co. Ltd.* v. *Caledonian Rlwy. Co.* (1903) 6 F.47.

49 *Cantiere San Rocco* v. *Clyde Shipbuilding and Engineering Co.,* 1923 S.C. (H.L.)105.

gain."[50] The party making the demand must have been put to some expense or disadvantage which resulted in a benefit to the other party which cannot be undone.[51] The remedy is excluded when the expenditure is incurred in the expectation of benefit to the spender.[52] It is not decided whether the claim can succeed where there is no error of fact.[53] Recompense cannot be invoked if another legal remedy is available.[54] Examples of the operation of the principle are:

(a) where employers had paid a workman's fare from Kuwait to Scotland when they were under no contractual obligation to do so;[55]
(b) where executors were held liable to repay with interest a bank overdraft which had been arranged by their law agent without authority;[56]
(c) where a lender was allowed to recover a loan which, to his knowledge, was *ultra vires* of the borrower;[57]
(d) where assignees had paid premiums on a policy which had been invalidly assigned;[58]
(e) where a builder has deviated from the plans to such an extent that he cannot recover the contract price;[59]
(f) where a person has expended money on melioration on a house in a bona fide belief that he was the owner;[60]
(g) where a person had made payments over a period for the maintenance of a deceased person;[61]
(h) where suppliers have provided clothes for a wife to the benefit of her husband.[62]

With regard to (f), it has been held that the relationship of a

---

50 Bell, *Prin.*, § 538.

51 *Buchanan* v. *Stewart* (1874) 2 R.78; *Stewart* v. *Steuart* (1878) 6 R.145; *Edinburgh and District Tramways Co. Ltd.* v. *Courtenay*, 1909 S.C.99; *Exchange Telegraph Co. Ltd.* v. *Giulianotti*, 1959 S.L.T.293.

52 *Rankin* v. *Wither* (1886) 13 R.903.

53 See *Rankin* v. *Wither* (1886) 13 R.903, *per* Lord Young at p.908; *Gray* v. *Johnston*, 1928 S.C.659, *per* L.J.-C. Alness at p.681.

54 *Varney (Scotland) Ltd.* v. *Burgh of Lanark*, 1976 S.L.T.46.

55 *Duncan* v. *Motherwell Bridge & Engineering Co.*, 1952 S.C.131.

56 *Commercial Bank of Scotland* v. *Biggar*, 1958 S.L.T.(Notes)46.

57 *Mags. of Stonehaven* v. *Kincardineshire County Council*, 1939 S.C.760.

58 *Edinburgh Life Assurance Co.* v. *Balderston*, 1909 2 S.L.T.323.

59 *Ramsay & Son* v. *Brand* (1898) 25 R.1212. See Chap. 2, para. 10.

60 *Newton* v. *Newton*, 1925 S.C.715. *Cf. Rankin* v. *Wither* (1886) 13 R.903.

61 *Horne* v. *Horne's Exrs.* 1963 S.L.T.(Sh.Ct.)37; but see *Gray* v. *Johnston*, 1928 S.C.659.

62 *Neilson* v. *Guthrie and Gairn* (1672) Mor.5878.

sub-lessee to the heritable creditor of the lessor cannot give rise to a claim of recompense.[63]

Under the heading of "other quasi-contractual situations" can be placed *negotiorum gestio,* salvage and general average.

The principle of *negotiorum gestio* is that where a person, acting without authority, undertakes the management of the affairs of another who is absent or incapacitated he has a right to be reimbursed for any expenditure incurred in the course of administration.[64] Salvage is "a reward or recompense given to those by means of whose labour, intrepidity, or perseverance, a ship, or goods . . . have been saved from shipwreck, fire or capture".[65] "Salvage in its true sense is suitable reward for services voluntarily rendered in circumstances where by the services offered on the one hand and accepted on the other there is saving of what otherwise was in risk of perishing or being lost".[66] The claim to salvage does not rest upon contract.[67]

The principle of general average is that "where in the danger of shipwreck or capture it is thought by those on board advisable to sacrifice any part of the cargo, or of the ship . . . for the general safety, the loss is to be adjusted by a contribution from all who have partaken of the benefit".[68] The liability does not depend on contract.[69]

Aliment has distinctive features. "A claim for aliment has many distinguishing characteristics from the ordinary claim of debt. It is in the first place rejected if the alleged debtor be unable to satisfy the demand, if he reserve enough for his own subsistence. It is in the next place rejected if the claimant have means of his own, which though contingent may be turned into money. It is also rejected if he have brains and hands enabling him to labour, accompanied by good health; and lastly, there is no claim for arrears, even although the destitute individual may have been supported by the charity of others."[70]

---

63 *Trade Development Bank* v. *Warriner & Mason (Scotland) Ltd.,* 1980 S.L.T.223.

64 Bell, *Prin.,* § 540.

65 Bell, *Prin.,* § 443.

66 *Clan Steam Trawling Co. Ltd.* v. *Aberdeen Steam Trawling and Fishing Co. Ltd.,* 1908 S.C.651, *per* L.J.-C. Macdonald at p.657.

67 *The Hestia* [1895] P.193.

68 Bell, *Comm.,* I, 631.

69 *Milburn & Co.* v. *Jamaica Fruit Importing and Trading Co. of London* [1900] 2 Q.B.540.

70 *Smith* v. *Smith's Trs.* (1882) 19 S.L.R.552, *per* Lord Fraser at p.555. See also *Oncken's J.F.* v. *Reimers* (1892) 19 R.519.

A decree for aliment can never be made for all time coming.[71]

Succession as a source of obligation presents some analytical difficulties. Obviously, a vitious intromitter may become liable for the debts of the deceased and an executor in respect of legacies; similarly, a person acquiring heritage is liable *quanto lucratus* under the personal obligation in a security affecting the subjects. But legal rights are described as being in the nature of debts which attach to the free succession after the claims of onerous creditors (and, in intestacy, the prior rights of the spouse) have been satisfied and they exist as debts from the date of death.[72]

7. Debitum Fundi

A *debitum fundi* is "a real debt or lien over land, which attaches to the land itself, into whose hands soever it may come."[73] A *debitum fundi* must appear on the face of the feudal title and, except where there is a disposition of land burdened with a particular debt in favour of a third party, the creditor's right must rest upon infeftment.[74] The chief examples are feuduties, real money burdens, bonds and dispositions in security, standard securities, ground-annuals and heritably secured annuities. The *debitum fundi* affects not only the land itself but also the moveables thereon, the remedy for enforcing this right against the moveables being a poinding of the ground.[75] The nature of a *debitum fundi* is illustrated by the form of this action. It contains no personal conclusions except for expenses and the persons called as defenders—normally the proprietor of the ground and the tenants—are called, not in respect of a conclusion directed against them, but in respect of their interest in the ground. Similarly, while an adjudication on a personal obligation covers all the debtor's heritage, an adjudication on a *debitum fundi* is restricted to the security subjects. A liability for a share of the common maintenance charges of a tenement imposed by a deed of conditions is a personal obligation.[76]

---

71 *Duncan* v. *Forbes* (1878) 15 S.L.R.371.

72 *McMurray* v. *McMurray's Trs.* (1852) 14 D.1048; *Russel* v. *Attorney-General,* 1917 S.C.28; *Sanderson* v. *Lockhart-Mure,* 1946 S.C.298.

73 Bell's *Dictionary, s.v. Debitum Fundi.*

74 *Scottish Heritable Security Co.* v. *Allan Campbell & Co.* (1876) 3 R.333, *per* Lord Deas at p.343; *Scottish Heritages Co. Ltd.* v. *North British Property Investment Co. Ltd.* (1885) 12 R.550, *per* Lord Lee at p.555.

75 *Bell* v. *Cadell* (1831) 10 S.100; *Royal Bank* v. *Bain* (1877) 4 R.985, *per* Lord Deas at p.989.

76 *Wells* v. *New House Purchasers Ltd.* (1963) 79 Sh.Ct.Rep.185.

8. Personal Liability

The question of personal liability may arise in three principal ways. Firstly, where an individual is acting in a representative capacity—as a trustee, for example—a question may arise as to whether a transaction has rendered the individual liable personally—in which case, of course, his whole property may be attached for the debt—or whether he is liable only as trustee—in which case he is liable only to the extent of the trust funds which he holds.[77] Trustees, for example, are personally liable on contracts which they make unless there is some clear stipulation that their liability is limited.[78] "Whenever a man means to bind another and not himself he should take care to say so. I think this is never to be implied. Even if a trust character is mentioned it will be held in general that this is merely descriptive of the obligant, but does not exempt him from personal liability. A trustee who does not mean to be personally bound should take care to use words which will exclude his personal liability,—for example, 'I bind not myself, but the trust-estate'; 'I bind not myself, but my constituent, or my client, for whom I act'. If he binds 'himself' it will not in general limit his responsibility that he adds, 'as agent for so and so', or 'as trustee'. This may indicate that he claims relief, but, in general, he himself will be liable in the first place."[79] Secondly, in the case of certain debts connected in some way with land a question arises as to whether the proprietor of the land can be sued personally for the debt or whether the creditor's only remedy is to seize the land by a legal process. For example, in the case of feuduty the proprietor of the land became personally liable when the disposition in his favour was recorded;[80] he was not personally liable for the amount of a heritable security over the subjects granted by his authors unless he had signed the conveyance in his favour.[81] But the heritable creditor can, of course, operate various remedies such as an action of maills and duties or his power of sale in order to recover the amount of his bond. Debts which are recoverable from the land itself are termed *"debita fundi"*. The third type of question which arises is whether the debtor's estate is

---

77 See *Kilmarnock Theatre Co.* v. *Buchanan,* 1911 S.C.607.

78 *Lumsden* v. *Buchanan* (1865) 3 M.(H.L.)89.

79 *Brown* v. *Sutherland* (1875) 2 R.615, *per* Lord Gifford at p.621. See also *Mackenzie* v. *Macalister* (1925) 41 Sh.Ct.Rep.163.

80 Conveyancing (Scotland) Act 1874, s.4.

81 Conveyancing (Scotland) Act 1874, s.47; Conveyancing (Scotland) Act 1924, s.15.

liable in respect of a debt for which the deceased was personally liable. This is dealt with elsewhere.[82]

9. Liquidity

The concept of a liquid debt is not altogether clear. The first characteristic of a liquid debt is that the amount should be clear: "a clear settled thing by itself[83]." "To liquidate a debt is only to make appear *quid, quale, quantum*."[84] So a claim for damages[85] and a claim for an accounting[86] are not liquid. It has often been said that the amount must be fixed by an obligatory document or decree: "To render a claim liquid it is necessary that it should be constituted, and that its exact amount should be fixed either by an obligatory writing or by the judgment of a competent Court."[87] But there has to be some relaxation of this in some contexts because the price of goods fixed by an oral contract is regarded as liquid as is rent;[88] Lord Deas speaks of a claim for a price as "not what is called a liquid claim in the correct sense in which bonds, bills and leases constitute liquid claims," but goes on to treat it as liquid.[89] Of rent, Lord Fullerton said: "Rent is not liquid in the sense that a sum due by bond is. It is matter of contract in consideration for something to be done. It is paid for possession of the subject let . . . But the amount of the rent being mentioned in the lease does not make it liquid in the strict sense. It is only part of a contract."[90] The second characteristic is that it must be due and not future or contingent: "A debt is deemed liquid when it is actually due and the amount ascertained, *cum certum an et quantum debeatur*."[91] So a future or contingent debt[92] is not liquid. The third characteristic is that the debt must be proved or admitted: "Pure and Uncontroverted and Instantly Verified."[93] Erskine says liquid debts must be "ascertained either by a written

---

[82] See Chap. 26, para. 5.
[83] *Per* Lord Cockburn, *Lawson* v. *Drysdale* (1884) 7 D.153 at 155.
[84] *McDowal* v. *Agnew* (1707) Mor.2568.
[85] *Smart* v. *Wilkinson*, 1928 S.C.383.
[86] *Lawson* v. *Drysdale, supra.*
[87] *Per* Lord Kinnear, *Robertson & Co.* v. *Bird & Co.* (1897) 24 R.1076 at 1078.
[88] *Alexander* v. *Campbell's Trs.* (1903) 5 F.634.
[89] *Mackie* v. *Riddell* (1874) 2 R.115 at 117.
[90] *Graham* v. *Gordon* (1843) 5 D.1207 at 1211; see also *Lovie* v. *Baird's Trs.* (1895) 23 R.1, *per* Lord Kinnear at p.4.
[91] Bell, *Comm.*, II, 122.
[92] See *infra,* paras. 10 and 11.
[93] Bankton, I, 24, 25.

obligation, the oath of the adverse party, or the sentence of a judge."[94]

10. Future Debts

Debts are classified as pure, to a day or contingent.[95] A pure or simple debt is one which is presently due and can be exacted immediately. The obligation of a banker to his customer in respect of sums on current account is "from the first substantially operative and enforceable" and is properly classified as pure.[96] An obligation to a day, or *in diem,* or *ex die,* is one in which payment is to be made on a certain day in the future or on the occurrence of an event which must occur—*dies statim cedit, sed non venit.* The debt although it is not payable until a future time is nonetheless, in one sense of the word, "due"; it is *debitum in praesenti solvendum in futuro.* "A proper debt exists from the moment of completion of the engagement; the execution only is suspended till the arrival of the appointed day".[97] An action cannot be raised for such a debt before the date for payment.[98] Bell, in his *Commentaries,*[99] calls debts to a day "future debts" and this has been followed by later writers[1] and some judicial usage can be found to support this terminology.[2] In his *Principles,*[3] however, Bell states that debts to a day are "improperly" termed "future debts".

"Future" has been applied to the following:

(1) "a debt that is not contracted until after the date of the arrestment";[4]

(2) the obligation of a third party liability insurer to the insured prior to decree being granted against the insured (future *and* contingent);[5]

---

94 III, 4, 16.

95 Stair, I, 3, 7; Erskine III, 1, 6; Bell, *Prin.*, §§ 45-47.

96 *Macdonald* v. *North of Scotland Bank,* 1942 S.C.369.

97 Bell, *Prin.*, § 46.

98 *Crear* v. *Morrison* (1882) 9 R.890; *Hodgmac Ltd.* v. *Gardiners of Prestwick Ltd.*, 1980 S.L.T.(Sh.Ct.)68.

99 I, 332.

1 *E.g.* Graham Stewart, pp.15, 81, 528; Gloag, p.271; *cf.* Smith, *Short Commentary,* p.617.

2 *Smith* v. *Cameron* (1879) 6 R.1107; *Palace Billiard Rooms Ltd.* v. *City Property Investment Trust Corporation Ltd.,* 1912 S.C.5; *Strathdee* v. *Paterson,* 1913 1 S.L.T.498.

3 S.46. Graham Stewart, p.81, n.2, points out that Stair (III, 1, 31), Bankton (III, 1, 35), and Erskine (III, 6, 8), use "future" when they mean contingent.

4 *Marshall* v. *Nimmo & Co.*, (1847) 10 D.328 at 329 (sheriff's note).

5 *Kerr* v. *R. & W. Ferguson,* 1931 S.C.736 at 743. In *Smith* v. *Lord Advocate* (No.2), 1981 S.L.T.19, a guarantee was held to be a contingent and not a future debt.

(3) "(an obligation) the existence, and not merely the enforceability, of which depends on an event which must certainly happen, though when it will do so remains uncertain, such as an agreement to offer to sell the house to another, when the promisor's mother dies."[6]

Then there is statutory usage. The Debtors (Scotland) Act 1838, s.22, provides that arrestments upon a "future or contingent debt" will prescribe in three years "from the time when the debt shall become due and the contingency be purified." In *Jameson* v. *Sharp*[7] the arrestment of a vested interest in a trust was held to be prescribed and it does not seem to have been suggested that the 1838 Act had any application. Perhaps the "or" is exegetical and "future" is used to mean "contingent"; that would explain the "and" between "due" and "the contingency".

The existence of the category of obligations to a day gives rise to the double signification of the word "due". " 'Due' is often employed as synonymous with 'payable', but it has another meaning as referring to the creation of an obligation. A debt in this sense is often 'due' before it is 'payable'. A man is a creditor who holds a bill at three months, although he cannot enforce the obligation till the three months expire. The debt is due from the first when it is created; the relation of debtor and creditor is constituted from the date of the contract."[8]

11. Contingent Debts

A contingent debt is one which depends on the occurrence of an uncertain future event—an event which may or may not happen. *Dies nec cedit nec venit.* Whether a debt is contingent can be important: a petition for sequestration cannot proceed on a contingent debt;[9] in a sequestration there is provision for the valuation of claims depending on a contingency;[10] a *spes successionis* is not arrestable.[11]

Graham Stewart[12] makes a distinction in discussing what debts are arrestable: "Debts and claims which are truly contingent, that is, debts and claims to which at the time of arrestment the common

6 Walker, *Contracts,* p.306.
7 (1887) 14 R.643.
8 *Per* Lord Neaves, *McFarlane* v. *Robb & Co.* (1870) 9 M.370 at 375.
9 Bankruptcy (Scotland) Act 1913, s.12. See Chap. 18, para. 1.
10 *Ibid.*, s.49.
11 *Trappes* v. *Meredith* (1871) 10 M.38.
12 p.81.

debtor has no vested right, which exist only *in spe,* are not arrestable. Where, however, the right has vested in the common debtor, although it is not yet prestable or is liable to be defeated by the occurrence or non-occurrence of some event before payment, arrestment will be sustained for what it may ultimately prove to be worth."

In an English Revenue appeal, Lord Reid said: " . . . conditional obligation and contingent liability have no different significance. I would, therefore, find it impossible to hold that in Scots Law a contingent liability is merely a species of existing liability. It is a liability which, by reason of something done by the person bound, will necessarily arise or come into being if one or more of certain events occur or do not occur."[13]

Consider the following:

(1) a "right" of a person to a legacy *if* someone makes a will in his favour. This is clearly not a right of any kind although it may be a liability in the Hohfeldian analysis.[14]

(2) a right to a legacy if the testator does not alter his testament; this may be called a *spes successionis.*[15]

(3) a right of a beneficiary under a discretionary trust to be considered as a potential recipient of benefit by the trustees who must exercise their discretion properly; this has been said to be more than a mere *spes,*[16] but was held not to be an "interest" for purposes of estate duty. Similar, perhaps, is the right to have a request for financial assistance fairly considered.[17] It cannot amount to a contingent debt.

(4) a right of a beneficiary to income of a trust if the trustees do not exercise a power of accumulation; this has been held not to be an "interest in possession" in the sense of a present right to present enjoyment.[18] Similarly trustees may have a discretion to reduce an interest to a liferent or to reduce revenue payments.[19] It might be said that the beneficiary has a contingent debt due to him.

(5) a right of a party who holds an award of expenses and had

---

13 *Re Sutherland decd.* [1963] A.C.235 at 249.

14 Paton, *Textbook of Jurisprudence,* 4th ed., p.292.

15 *Reid* v. *Morison* (1893) 20 R.510, *per* Lord Rutherfurd Clark at pp.512-514; *Wright* v. *Bryson,* 1935 S.C.(H.L.)49, *per* Lord Alness at p.54. See *infra,* (9).

16 *Gartside* v. *I.R.C.* [1968] A.C.553.

17 *Medical Defence Union* v. *Dept. of Trade* [1980] Ch.82.

18 *Pearson* v. *I.R.C.* [1980] 2 W.L.R.872.

19 *Train* v. *Buchanan's Tr.,* 1908 S.C.(H.L.)26.

obtained a decree for interim execution pending an appeal to the House of Lords; this was held to be "contingent" for purposes of a sequestration petition—"Contingency may be of this nature that the debt may never become due or payable."[20] Where decree had been extracted and no appeal had been taken but appeal was still competent the debt was held not to be contingent.[21]

(6) a right of a person injured by delict to obtain payment of damages once these are assessed by a court; this has been said not to be contingent because if the claim is good it accrued from the date of the delict.[22]

(7) a right of an insured against his insurer to be indemnified against a third party claim which has not yet been the subject of an action; this has been held to be contingent for purposes of arrestment as it is both future and contingent.[23]

(8) the right of an insured against whom decree has been obtained to be indemnified by the insurers, the right being subject to arbitration; this is arrestable.[24]

(9) the right of a beneficiary to a legacy if he survives another person; this is regarded as a contingent right and is sometimes called a *spes successionis* but in the law relating to the revocation of trusts it is called a *jus quaesitum* as distinct from a mere *spes*.[25] ("It is necessary to distinguish between two meanings which may attach to the term *spes successionis.* It may mean that A hopes to benefit by the will of B who is still alive, or it may mean, as here, that A has a right under the will of B, who is dead, subject to a certain contingency."[26]).

(10) the right of the creditor against a cautioner before the debtor is in default or the right of the holder of a bill against the drawer before the bill is dishonoured by the acceptor; these are contingent.[27]

---

20 *Forbes* v. *Whyte* (1890) 18 R.182.

21 *Mags. of Falkirk* v. *Lundie* (1892) 8 Sh.Ct.Rep.272.

22 *Riley* v. *Ellis,* 1910 S.C.934, *per* Lord Johnston at p.938.

23 *Kerr* v. *R. & W. Ferguson,* 1931 S.C.736.

24 *Boland* v. *White Cross Insurance Association,* 1926 S.C.1066.

25 *Scott* v. *Scott,* 1930 S.C.903, *per* L.P. Clyde at p.916; *Parker* v. *Lord Advocate,* 1958 S.C.426, *per* Lord Mackintosh at p.437.

26 *Per* Lord Mackenzie, *Salaman* v. *Tod,* 1911 S.C.1214 at 1223. *Cf.* Stair, I, 3, 7: "Conditional obligations are such as depend upon a condition: and so are but obligations in hope, till the condition be existent."

27 *Morrison* v. *Turnbull* (1832) 10 S.259; *Gordon* v. *McCubbin* (1851) 13 D.1154; *Stuart & Stuart* v. *Macleod* (1891) 19 R.223; *Smith* v. *Lord Advocate (No.2),* 1981 S.L.T.19.

(11) the right of a creditor against his debtor who has given a cheque for the amount due if the cheque is not honoured; the correlative of this is described as a contingent liability which is not arrestable.[28]

(12) the right of a contractor to payment if he completes the contract work; this is a conditional obligation and is arrestable.[29]

(13) a wife's claim to future aliment if the parties do not resume co-habitation; this is not even a contingent debt in a sequestration.[30]

(14) the right of the holder of a document of debt which was to be retained as a voucher for a current account until final adjustment but could not be used for suing the debtor or for diligence; this is not a contingent debt in petitioning for sequestration: "a contingent debt . . . is a debt which has no existence now but will only emerge and become due upon the occurrence of some future event."[31] Similarly, where a duty of accounting is owed to a person, his right to payment of any balance found due is not contingent and is arrestable.[32]

In cases (1) and (2) the right depends on the unrestricted volition of a party other than the possessor of the right. In (3) and (4) the right depends on the decision of persons subject to fiduciary and other duties and it is between the two cases that the line between a right which is not even a contingent right to payment and a right which is of that character is drawn. Cases (5) to (8) depend on the decision of a court or arbiter. It seems that a claim which has yet to be litigated in order to quantify it is pure and not contingent but, once it has been successfully brought to litigation, a pending appeal renders it contingent. The result in case (7) is perhaps suspect but its facts differ from the others in that there are two claims to be decided. In cases (9) to (11), the right depends on the occurrence of an event independent of the will of the parties and that makes it a contingent right. Case (12) involves only the future actings of the creditor but it is obviously contingent in some sense. It has been suggested that, to render an obligation contingent, the condition attaching to it must be casual or mixed, and not potestative.[33]

---

28 *Leggat Brothers* v. *Gray*, 1908 S.C.67, *per* Lord Kinnear at p.76.

29 *Marshall* v. *Nimmo & Co.* (1847) 10 D.328; *Park, Dobson & Co.* v. *William Taylor & Son*, 1929 S.C.571.

30 *Matthew* v. *Matthew's Tr.* (1907) 15 S.L.T.326.

31 *Fleming* v. *Yeaman* (1884) 9 App. Cas. 966, *per* Lord Watson at p.976.

32 *American Mortgage Co. of Scotland Ltd.* v. *Sidway*, 1908 S.C.500.

33 *Per* Lord Jamieson, *Macdonald* v. *North of Scotland Bank*, 1942 S.C.369 at 382.

Future aliment (case (13)) is obviously special as, for one thing, it involves the future actings of both creditor and debtor. The accounting situation in case (14) stands apart from the others as the existence of liability does not depend on future events or actings; it is not known whether the liability exists or not.

12. Vesting

Another distinction is between a right to payment of money which has vested and one which has not vested. Vesting means "a right of property in the thing vested transmissible by, or through, and in right of the person in whom it is vested."[34] "The fair meaning of vesting is nothing more than that the subject goes to a man's heirs and assignees."[35] A debt may be vested although the date of payment has not yet arrived and the essence of vesting is that, if the person in whom the debt is vested predeceases the date of payment, the debt is transmitted in accordance with his will if he dies testate and passes to his heirs *ab intestato* if he dies intestate. A right which has not vested is sometimes said to be a mere *spes successionis*.[36]

---

34 *Per* Lord Young, *Haldane's Trs.* v. *Murphy* (1881) 9 R.269 at 295.
35 *Per* Lord Mackenzie, *Kilgour* v. *Kilgour* (1845) 7 D.451 at 456.
36 But see, *supra*, para. 11, n.26.

Chapter 2

COMMON DEBTS

1. Sale: Price

A contract of sale of goods is a contract by which the seller transfers or agrees to transfer the property in goods to the buyer for a money consideration, called the price.[1]

The price may be fixed in the contract or may be left to be fixed in a manner agreed or it may be determined by the course of dealing between the parties.[2] If the price is not determined in any of those ways the buyer must pay a reasonable price and this is a question of fact dependent on the circumstances of each particular case.[3]

If, after the contract is made, and before the goods are supplied, there is a change in the amount of value added tax charged, or a change to or from tax being charged on the transaction, unless the contract otherwise provides, there shall be added to or deducted from the price, an amount equal to the change.[4]

An order for goods which includes the words "contra account" may in some circumstances bear the meaning that the seller if he implements the order is obliged to order goods in exchange and he is not entitled to demand payment in cash.[5]

Where the contract is cancelled a question may arise as to whether a sum already paid to the seller is a forfeitable deposit or an instalment which should be returned to the buyer.[6] Where it is a deposit, and the contract is terminated by the buyer's repudiation, it cannot be recovered and the law as to penalties has no application.[7]

2. Failure to Pay

The seller may raise an action for the price if the property has passed to the buyer and the buyer wrongfully neglects or refuses to pay according to the contract.[8] Unless otherwise agreed, the price is

---

1 Sale of Goods Act 1979, s.2(1).

2 s.8(1).

3 s.8(2); *Lennox* v. *Rennie,* 1951 S.L.T.(Notes) 78. See, as to prices to be fixed by a third party, s.9.

4 Finance Act 1972, s.42.

5 *Mitchell & Sons* v. *Sirdar Rubber Co. Ltd.* (1911) 27 Sh.Ct.Rep.334.

6 *Rohtas Industries Ltd.* v. *Urquhart Lindsay and Robertson Orchar Ltd.*, 1950 S.L.T.(Notes) 5.

7 *Roberts & Cooper Ltd.* v. *Salvesen & Co.*, 1918 S.C.794.

8 s.49(1).

payable on delivery of the goods.[9] Where a period of credit has been agreed upon, the closure of the account does not affect the period of credit for past transactions.[10] The seller can also raise an action for the price if it is payable on a day certain irrespective of delivery although the property has not passed and the goods have not been appropriated to the contract.[11] A day certain is a fixed day and not, for example, a day determined by the sending of an invoice.[12]

In the common case, when the question arises, the goods are in the possession of the buyer and the property has passed to him. The seller's only remedy is to sue for the price. He cannot recover the goods unless he can rescind the contract on the ground that the buyer induced him to enter into it by fraudulent misrepresentations and had no intention of making payment.[13] If the goods are in the buyer's possession but the property has not passed, the seller can bring an action for re-delivery.

If the goods are in the seller's possession and the property has passed to the buyer and the price is due, the seller can either sue for the price or claim damages for non-acceptance.[14] He may also, under his right of lien, retain possession of the goods until payment or tender of the price and he does not lose this right by reason only that he has obtained decree for the price of the goods.[15] Where the goods are of a perishable nature, or where the seller gives notice of his intention to resell and the buyer does not within a reasonable time pay or tender the price, the seller may resell the goods and recover from the buyer damages for any loss occasioned.[16] He need not account to the buyer for any profit on the resale.[17] Where the seller sues for damages for non-acceptance the conclusion in the action is normally to ordain the defender to pay the price to the pursuer in exchange for the goods with an alternative conclusion for damages for breach of contract. Such an action is not for a decree *ad factum praestandum* and an extract of the decree given cannot be

---

[9] s.28.

[10] *Hodgmac Ltd.* v. *Gardiners of Prestwick Ltd.*, 1980 S.L.T.(Sh.Ct.)68.

[11] s.49(2).

[12] *Henderson & Keay Ltd.* v. *A.M. Carmichael Ltd.*, 1956 S.L.T.(Notes)58.

[13] *Gamage* v. *Charlesworth's Tr.*, 1910 S.C.257.

[14] s.50.

[15] ss.41-43.

[16] s.48(3).

[17] *R. V. Ward Ltd.* v. *Bignall* [1967] 1 Q.B.534.

used to enforce payment of the price. Its operative effect is to permit recovery of the damages for breach of contract.[18]

If the goods are in the seller's possession and the property has not yet passed to the buyer, the seller's normal remedy is to claim damages for non-acceptance[19] but he may alternatively sue for the price if it is payable on a day certain irrespective of delivery. If, while the goods are in the seller's possession, the buyer becomes insolvent or fails to pay the price when it is due, the seller can retain the goods until the price is paid or tendered.[20] Failing payment he can sell the goods after giving notice.[21]

3. Reservation of Title

A contractual provision that the property in the goods will not pass to the buyer until the price (or all sums due to the seller) has been paid will be given effect. On the sequestration of the buyer before payment, the goods, as they are still the seller's property, can be recovered from the trustee in the sequestration.[22] If the goods have been sold by the buyer the sub-purchaser gets a good title[23] and the original seller can recover the proceeds in the hands of the sub-purchaser or, if they can be identified, from the bankrupt's estate.[24] It is thought that a clause of reservation of title which purports to extend the seller's rights to a product made from, *inter alia,* the sold goods would not be given effect in Scotland as it would be an

---

[18] *R. S. Leigh & Co.* v. *Berger & Co.*, 1958 S.L.T.(Sh.Ct.)21.

[19] s.50; *Brown* v. *Carron Co.* (1898) 6 S.L.T.231; the conclusion will be the one mentioned in the last paragraph.

[20] s.39(2).

[21] *Scott* v. *Marshall,* 1949 S.L.T.(Notes)35.

[22] *Aluminium Industrie B.V.* v. *Romalpa Ltd.* [1976] 1 W.L.R.676. In *Re Bond Worth Ltd.* [1980] Ch.228, the clause was not apt to retain title in the sellers.

[23] Sale of Goods Act 1979, s.25(1), which does not, however, apply to conditional sales regulated by statute: see Chap. 4, para. 10.

[24] See *Macadam* v. *Martin's Tr.* (1872) 11 M.33. If the arrangement is a "sale and return" the buyer sells as a principal and the proceeds are not recoverable by the original seller in the buyer's sequestration: *Michelin Tyre Co. Ltd.* v. *Macfarlane (Glasgow) Ltd.*, 1917 2 S.L.T.205. Where there is an ordinary reservation of title, on the other hand, the buyer, in a question with the original seller, sells as an agent (*Aluminium B.V.* v. *Romalpa Ltd., supra, per* Roskill L.J. at p.690) and the proceeds are recoverable by the original seller: if they are identifiable: *Michelin supra.* That result cannot be obtained in Scotland, it seems, by the creation of a trust: *Export Credits Guarantee Department* v. *Turner,* 1981 S.L.T.286; *Clark Taylor & Co. Ltd.* v. *Quality Site Development (Edinburgh) Ltd.* (First Division, 8 January 1981, unreported).

attempt to create a security over corporeal moveables *retenta possessione*.[25]

4. Representations and Warranties

Not infrequently the reason for the purchaser's failure to pay the price is that a statement made by or on behalf of the seller at or about the time the contract of sale was made was untrue. Whether the falsity of the statement provides a defence to an action for the price depends on whether the statement was a warranty (a term of the contract), a representation inducing the purchaser to enter the contract, or merely an expression of opinion. If the statement was a term of the contract, the purchaser's remedy is to claim damages for breach of contract and in some circumstances he may also reject the goods.[26] If the statement was an innocent misrepresentation the remedy is rescission of the contract provided that *restitutio in integrum* is possible.[27] If the misrepresentation was fraudulent the remedy is damages and the purchaser may in his option also rescind the contract.[28] Expressions of opinion honestly held and *verba jactantia* cannot be founded on by the purchaser.[29]

The principal difficulty is to distinguish a representation from a warranty. Whether a statement is a warranty depends on whether it appears on the evidence that it was intended and understood to be a warranty.[30] Generally a statement as to a collateral matter is not a warranty.[31] It seems that a verbal statement can be a warranty even although the remainder of the contract is in writing but the presumption is against this result.[32]

---

25 See *Borden (U.K.) Ltd.* v. *Scottish Timber Products Ltd.* [1979] 3 W.L.R.672. The point taken there as to failure to register a charge under Companies Act 1948, s.95, would not arise in Scotland as a fixed security over corporeal moveables is not listed in s.106A(2) of the 1948 Act.

26 See next paragraph.

27 *Stewart* v. *Kennedy* (1890) 17 R.(H.L.)25; *Menzies* v. *Menzies* (1893) 20 R. (H.L.)108; *Manners* v. *Whitehead* (1898) 1 F.171; *Westville Shipping Co. Ltd.* v. *Abram Steamship Co. Ltd.*, 1922 S.C.571; 1923 S.C.(H.L.)68. The possibility of *restitutio in integrum* is a question of circumstances: *McGuiness* v. *Anderson*, 1953 S.L.T. (Notes) 1.

28 *Spence* v. *Crawford*, 1939 S.C.(H.L.)52; *Smith* v. *Sim*, 1954 S.C.357; *McGuiness* v. *Anderson*, 1953 S.L.T.(Notes) 1: as to the measure of damages see Walker, *Civil Remedies*, p.689.

29 *Hamilton* v. *Duke of Montrose* (1906) 8 F.1026; *City of Edinburgh Brewery Co.* v. *Gibson's Tr.* (1869) 7 M.886; *Flynn* v. *Scott*, 1949 S.C.442.

30 *Heilbut Symons & Co.* v. *Buckleton* [1913] A.C.30; *Hyslop* v. *Shirlaw* (1905) 7 F.875.

31 Gloag, p.467.

32 Gloag, p.467; *Oscar Chess Ltd.* v. *Williams* [1957] 1 All E.R.325.

5. Breach of Contract

Breach of a condition or a warranty implied by the Sale of Goods Act 1979 constitutes a material breach of the contract.[33] In *Millars of Falkirk Ltd.* v. *Turpie*,[34] the First Division suggested, *obiter,* that breach of an implied condition, if it is minor and remediable, may not justify rescission of the contract. It is suggested, with respect, that this doubt is unfounded. The common law was that breach of a material part of the contract justified rejection of the goods. This position was preserved in 1893 by what is now s.11(5) of the 1979 Act which provides that "failure by the seller to perform any material part of a contract of sale is a breach of contract, which entitles the buyer either within a reasonable time after delivery to reject the goods and treat the contract as repudiated, or to retain the goods and treat the failure to perform such material part as a breach which may give rise to a claim for compensation or damages." The 1893 Act had, however, introduced certain implied conditions breach of which in England gave rise to a right to treat the contract as repudiated, and certain implied warranties breach of which gave rise to a claim for damages but not to a right to reject the goods and treat the contract as repudiated. To make the Scottish position clear it was provided in s.62(1) that breach of a warranty was deemed a failure to perform a material part of the contract. This is not a definition of a warranty but a direction as to the legal effect of a breach of warranty, leading the inquirer from the implied warranties in ss.12 and 14 to the remedies in s.11. There was no need for similar clarification with regard to breach of implied conditions, because the remedy provided for England was the remedy under Scots common law. Breach of a condition is undoubtedly a breach of a material part of the contract.

If the buyer maintains that there has been a material breach of contract he can either reject the goods and claim damages for non-delivery or retain the goods and claim damages for breach of contract.[35] If he wishes to reject he must do so within a reasonable time[36] and before he does any act in relation to the goods which is inconsistent with the seller's ownership;[37] if he has intimated accept-

---

[33] s.61(2).

[34] 1976 S.L.T.(Notes)66.

[35] s.11(5).

[36] s.35; what is a reasonable time is a question of fact; the Scottish case law is collected in Walker, *Civil Remedies,* pp.668-669.

[37] s.35; *Mechan & Sons Ltd.* v. *Bow McLachlan & Co. Ltd.*, 1910 S.C.758.

ance of them he cannot later reject them.[38] He can reject them even if the property has passed to him[39] and even if the defect has resulted in the destruction of the goods.[40]

On rejection the buyer can retain the goods in security for the repayment of the price but not in security of a claim for damages.[41] If he intimates rejection to the seller, he is not bound to return the goods but if the goods are perishable he may be bound to sell them on the seller's behalf.[42] If the seller refuses to accept the rejection the buyer should place the goods in neutral custody and obtain a warrant for sale from the sheriff.[43] Continued use of the goods after rejection is intimated may render the rejection ineffectual.[44]

A buyer who, having paid the price, later rejects the goods, can sue the seller for repetition of the price and for damages. It seems that the claim for damages may be either in respect of a material breach under s.53 or in respect of non-delivery of goods under s.51.[45] If a buyer who has rejected goods is sued for the price his course of action is to deny liability for the price as the contract has been repudiated and to counter-claim for damages.

An ineffectual rejection does not bar a subsequent claim to retain the goods and recover damages but this alternative claim must be stated in the pleadings.[46]

If the buyer, having paid the price, wishes to retain the goods and claim damages, he must raise an action for damages. If he has not paid the price, he can set off his claim for damages against the seller's claim for the price.[47] He may, however, be required, in the discretion of the court, to consign or pay into court the price or part thereof or to give reasonable security for due payment thereof.[48] It has been said that this provision applies primarily to cases where a

---

[38] s.35; *Mechans Ltd.* v. *Highland Marine Charters Ltd.*, 1964 S.C.48.

[39] *Nelson* v. *Wm. Chalmers & Co.*, 1913 S.C.441.

[40] *Kinnear* v. *Brodie* (1901) 3 F.540.

[41] *Laing* v. *Westren* (1858) 20 D.519; *Lupton & Co.* v. *Schulze & Co.* (1900) 2 F.1118.

[42] s.36; *Pommer* v. *Mowat* (1906) 14 S.L.T.373.

[43] *Malcolm* v. *Cross* (1898) 25 R.1089.

[44] *Electric Construction Co.* v. *Hurry & Young* (1897) 24 R.312.

[45] Brown, *Sale*, p.388.

[46] *Pollock* v. *McCrae*, 1922 S.C.(H.L.)192; *Mechans Ltd.* v. *Highland Marine Charters Ltd.*, 1964 S.C.48.

[47] s.53(1).

[48] s.58; in *George Cohen, Sons & Co. Ltd.* v. *Jamieson & Paterson*, 1963 S.L.T.35, it was held that s.58 had no application where the buyer was relying on s.53(1) and could be used only where the buyer relied on s.11(5). The decision is suspect but in any event it was held that there was a common law discretion to order consignation.

doubt has been raised as to the buyer's financial stability but its application is not restricted to such cases.[49] If the claim for damages exceeds the amount of the price the excess can be recovered by bringing the claim for damages in the form of a counter claim. Even if the buyer's claim has been set off against the price, he may raise an action for damages if further damage is sustained.[50]

It seems that where the buyer alleges a non-material breach of contract his only remedy is to retain the goods and claim damages.[51] In the case of machinery and similar goods, if there are only slight breakages or defects, the buyer should give the seller an opportunity to remedy them.[52]

If the seller fails to deliver the goods, the buyer's remedy is to claim damages for non-delivery.[53]

6. Hire-Purchase

A contract of hire-purchase is one in which an article is let on hire and the hirer, after making a certain number of payments of hire, has an option to purchase the goods on payment of a further sum.[54] The effects of the agreement are:

(1) the article does not become the property of the hirer until the final payment has been paid; delivery of a cheque which was subsequently dishonoured is not payment for this purpose;[55]

(2) during the period of hire, the article is not subject to the diligence of the hirer's creditors[56] except diligence for[57] the landlord's hypothec;[58]

(3) during the period of hire, the hirer cannot give a good title to someone who purchases the article from him,[59] except in the case of a motor vehicle which can be effectually conveyed to a "private purchaser";[60]

---

49 *Porter Spiers (Leicester) Ltd.* v. *Cameron* [1950] C.L.Y. 5329.

50 s.53(4).

51 Gloag, p.609; the discussion in *Robey* v. *Stein* (1900) 3 F.278 is confusing.

52 *Morrison & Mason* v. *Clarkson Bros.* (1898) 25 R.427.

53 s.51.

54 For the statutory definition see Chap. 4, para. 10.

55 *McLaren's Tr.* v. *Argylls Ltd.*, 1915 2 S.L.T.241.

56 *George Hopkinson Ltd.* v. *N. G. Napier & Son*, 1953 S.C.139.

57 Not now for rates: Local Government (Miscellaneous Provisions) (Scotland) Act 1981, s.12.

58 *Rudman* v. *Jay*, 1908 S.C.552.

59 *Helby* v. *Matthews* [1895] A.C.471.

60 Hire Purchase Act 1964, Pt.III., now set out in Consumer Credit Act 1974, Sched. 4, para. 22.

(4) on the sequestration of the hirer during the period of hire the article does not pass to the trustee.[61]

There are implied terms as to the title to, and as to the description, quality and fitness for purpose of the article hired.[62] The extent to which it is possible to exclude these terms or restrict liability for breach of them is restricted.[63] The hirer has a title to sue for recovery of the goods from a third party.[64]

At common law, the following debts due to the owner may arise:

(1) a claim for arrears of hire payments;

(2) a claim for an amount payable in terms of the contract if the hirer exercises his option to terminate the contract; this claim cannot be treated as a penalty;[65]

(3) a claim for damages; on repudiation of the contract by the hirer, the damages recoverable are the hire-purchase price under deduction of (i) instalments already paid, (ii) the value of the goods repossessed, (iii) the amount payable on exercise of the option to purchase, (iv) a discount for the earlier return to the owner of his capital outlay.[66] In England it has been held that failure to pay two instalments is not a repudiation by the hirer and the owner could only recover the arrears on retaking the goods.[67] There is no doubt that the owner can retake possession and sue for arrears.[68]

7. Professional Services

If there is an express agreement as to the remuneration for the services, this must rule[69] even if it does not conform to the scale laid down by the professional institute.[70] If there is no express agreement, there is no presumption that the services have been rendered

---

61 *McLaren's Tr.* v. *Argylls Ltd., supra.*

62 Supply of Goods (Implied Terms) Act 1973, ss.8-11 (as amended by Consumer Credit Act 1974, Sched.4, para. 35). As to the common law, see *Brown* v. *Brecknell, Munro & Rogers (1928) Ltd.* (1938) 54 Sh.Ct.Rep.254.

63 Unfair Contract Terms Act 1977, s.20.

64 *McArthur* v. *O'Donnell,* 1969 S.L.T.(Sh.Ct.)24.

65 *Bell Brothers (H.P.) Ltd.* v. *Aitken,* 1939 S.C.577; *Granor Finance Ltd.* v. *Liqr. of Eastore Ltd.*, 1974 S.L.T.296.

66 *Yeoman Credit Ltd.* v. *Waragowski* [1961] 1 W.L.R.1124; *Overstone Ltd.* v. *Shipway* [1962] 1 W.L.R.117; *Yeoman Credit Ltd.* v. *McLean* [1962] 1 W.L.R.131.

67 *Financings Ltd.* v. *Baldock* [1963] 2 Q.B.104.

68 *Bowmaker (Commercial) Ltd.* v. *Dunnigan,* 1976 S.L.T.(Sh.Ct.)54.

69 *Arthur Duthie & Co. Ltd.* v. *Merson & Gerry,* 1947 S.C.43. But, as to solicitors, see the next paragraph.

70 *Wilkie* v. *Scottish Aviation Ltd.*, 1956 S.C.198.

gratuitously.[71] If there has been a usage between the parties of payment at a certain rate this will rule.[72] If there is no such usage, the matter is regulated by the custom of the profession if this is reasonable, certain and notorious.[73] It is not necessary to prove that the employer knew of the custom if it is so well recognised that it ought to have been known.[74] A scale of charges fixed by a general consensus of the profession concerned has "very high authority"[75] but the court need not adopt such a scale if it regards the charges as unreasonable.[76] If there is no acceptable custom, the court fixes a reasonable remuneration.[77] The test is "what a man of business, having knowledge of the question, would fix as fair remuneration."[78]

A charge for medical advice or attendance or for the performance of an operation or for a medicine which the pursuer has both prescribed and supplied cannot be recovered unless the pursuer proves that he is a fully registered medical practitioner.[79] If a fellow of a college of physicians is prohibited by bye-law from recovering his charges, the bye-law may be pleaded in bar of proceedings.

8. Solicitor's Account

In an action by a solicitor or his representatives for payment of an account of expenses due by a client, the court must remit the account for taxation and no decree shall be pronounced either in absence or after hearing parties, without a report having been made by the auditor.[80] The table of fees of the Law Society of Scotland is not the full and final test by which the auditor is bound to fix the fee.[81] It seems that an agreement between solicitor and client for remuneration in excess of the authorised scale is unenforceable.[82]

---

71 *Landless* v. *Wilson* (1880) 8 R.289; *Macintyre Bros.* v. *Smith,* 1913 S.C.129.

72 *Eunson* v. *Johnson & Greig,* 1940 S.C.49.

73 *Hogarth & Sons* v. *Leith Cotton Seed Oil Co.,* 1909 S.C.955; *Wilkie* v. *Scottish Aviation Ltd., supra.*

74 *"Strathlorne" S.S. Co.* v. *Baird & Sons Ltd.,* 1916 S.C.(H.L.)134.

75 *Per* L.P. Dunedin, *Welsh & Forbes* v. *Johnston* (1906) 8 F.453 at 456.

76 *Wilkie* v. *Scottish Aviation Ltd., supra.*

77 Gloag, p.294; *Clyde Air Extraction Ltd.* v. *Helmville Ltd.,* 1964 S.L.T. (Sh.Ct.)49.

78 *Brownlie, Watson & Beckett* v. *Caledonian Rlwy. Co.,* 1907 S.C.617.

79 Medical Act 1956, s.27.

80 R.C.350(*c*); Dobie, *Sheriff Court Practice,* p.338.

81 *Davidson & Syme, W.S.,* v. *Booth,* 1972 S.L.T.122.

82 *Anstruther* v. *Wilkie* (1856) 18 D.405; *Moir* v. *Robertson,* 1924 S.L.T.435.

This applies to remuneration in respect of criminal business as well as civil.[83]

9. Contracts for Repairs etc.

The contract may be made even although the identity of the person giving the order is not disclosed.[84] Where the owner of a damaged car has it taken to a garage and the cost of repairs is subsequently agreed by the owner's insurers before the work is done, the contract for repairs is between the insurers and the garage.[85] There is no general rule that the insurer acts as agent of the owner in instructing the repairs.[86] An "estimate" will be regarded as an offer.[87] A request for an estimate for repairs does not create a liability for work involved in putting the article in a state for inspection.[88] But there may be circumstances in which preparatory work for a contract may be the subject of a *quantum meruit* claim.[89] Additional work of an extensive and costly nature should be preceded by a further estimate and instruction by the employer.[90] If there is no estimate the account must be on a "time and materials" basis.[91] It is not enough for the contractors to prove the number of man-hours actually spent on the job; they must prove what would have been a reasonable charge for the time normally spent in carrying out the job.[92] If the evidence is sketchy the court must do its best on the material available.[93] A custom of trade can be relied upon only if it is certain, uniform, reasonable and notorious.[94] Interest is allowed on a *quantum meruit* claim from the date of citation.[95] A tradesman has an obligation to carry out the contract work properly unless he either makes it known to the employer before making the contract that the job requires more special skill than he commands or can

---

83 *Y* v. *Z*, 1927 S.L.T.(Sh.Ct.)74; *McKay* v. *McIntosh*, 1952 S.L.T.(Sh.Ct.)88.

84 *Craik* v. *Glasgow Taxicab Co. Ltd.* (1911) 27 Sh.Ct.Rep.157.

85 *McCallum* v. *Wilson*. 1974 S.L.T.(Sh.Ct.)72.

86 *Kirklands Garage (Kinross) Ltd.* v. *Clark*, 1967 S.L.T.(Sh.Ct.)60.

87 *Croshaw* v. *Pritchard and Renwick* (1899) 16 T.L.R.45.

88 *Murray* v. *Fairlie Yacht Slip Ltd.*, 1975 S.L.T.(Sh.Ct.)62.

89 *Pillans & Wilson* v. *Castlecary Fireclay Co. Ltd.*, 1931 S.L.T.532. But see *Site Preparations Ltd.* v. *Secretary of State for Scotland*, 1975 S.L.T.(Notes)41.

90 *Walter Wright & Co. Ltd.* v. *Cowdray*, 1973 S.L.T.(Sh.Ct.)56.

91 *James Erskine* v. *Weibye*, 1976 S.L.T.(Sh.Ct.)14.

92 *Scottish Motor Traction Co.* v. *Murphy*, 1949 S.L.T.(Notes)39.

93 *Mellor* v. *Wm. Beardmore & Co.*, 1927 S.C.597; *Sinclair* v. *Logan*, 1961 S.L.T.(Sh.Ct.)10; *Robert Allan and Partners* v. *McKinstray*, 1975 S.L.T.(Sh.Ct.)63.

94 *Dalblair Motors Ltd.* v. *J. Forrest & Son (Ayr) Ltd.* (1954) 70 Sh.Ct.Rep.107.

95 *Keir Ltd.* v. *East of Scotland Water Board*, 1976 S.L.T. (Notes) 72.

show that the customer was aware of that when contracting with him.[96] Where, under the contract, work is to be done to the satisfaction of a specified person, in an action for the price there must be an averment that the person is satisfied or his judgment must be impugned in some way.[97] In the repair of machinery, the employer cannot recover the account of other repairers as damages unless he gave the original repairers an opportunity to remedy the defect.[98] Failure to pay a part of the contract price at the stipulated time may entitle the contractor to rescind the contract.[99]

10. Building Contracts

Where there has been defective performance of a building contract, the legal position is not clear. A distinction is made between lump sum contracts and measure and value contracts. A contract which sets figures against certain branches of the work, the aggregate of which makes up the total contract price, is a lump sum contract.[1] If the contractor does not complete a lump sum contract, he cannot sue for the price. If the work has been completed but there has been an unauthorised material deviation from the terms of the contract, the contractor cannot recover the price; the employer can either call upon the contractor to remove his materials from the ground or retain them subject to the contractor's claim against him *in quantum lucratus est*.[2] If, in a lump sum contract, the deviation is not material and can be remedied, the contractor can recover the price under deduction of the cost of bringing the work into conformity with the contract.[2] If the deviation is not material but cannot be remedied, the position is doubtful; it may be that the contractor can recover the price under deduction of the damage sustained by the employer.[3] If the parties have agreed to a material alteration in a lump sum contract, it is treated on a time and material basis.[4]

---

96 *Brett* v. *Williamson,* 1980 S.L.T.(Sh.Ct.)56.

97 *Kidd and Sons* v. *Bain* (1913) 29 Sh.Ct.Rep.123.

98 *Brown* v. *Nisbet & Co. Ltd.* (1941) 57 Sh.Ct.Rep.202.

99 *Fixby Engineering Co. Ltd.* v. *Auchlochan Sand and Gravel Co. Ltd.,* 1974 S.L.T.(Sh.Ct.)58.

1 *Gray & Son Ltd.* v. *Stern,* 1953 S.L.T.(Sh.Ct.)34.

2 *Ramsay* v. *Brand* (1898) 25 R.1212; *Spiers* v. *Peterson,* 1924 S.C.428; *McKillop* v. *Mutual Securities Ltd.,* 1945 S.C.166; *Franco-British Electrical Co.* v. *Jean Dougall Macdonald Ltd.* (1949) 65 Sh.Ct.Rep.82; *Stewart Roofing Co. Ltd.* v. *Shanlin* (1958) 74 Sh.Ct.Rep.134.

3 Gloag & Henderson, p.132; *Anderson* v. *Dow* (1907) 23 Sh.Ct.Rep.51.

4 *Mercer* v. *Wright* (1953) 69 Sh.Ct.Rep.39.

In the case of a measure and value contract, the contractor can recover the appropriate sums due for items completed conform to contract even although there are other defective items.[5] It seems, however, that the employer can deduct or set off any damage sustained by him in respect of the defective items.

In prime cost contracts, the employer should challenge any item in a monthly account at the time he receives it and once he has made payment of the monthly account, if he later challenges an item in it, the onus is on him to show why it should not stand.[6]

In a lump sum contract, if the parties agree on major modifications which are so fundamental that they result in frustration of the contract, the contractor can recover on a *quantum meruit* basis.[7]

11. Sale of Heritage

The terms of the missives may show that a provision that the price is payable on a particular date is an essential stipulation, breach of which entitles the seller to resile from the contract. Normally, however, such a provision is not an essential stipulation; if there is unnecessary or unjustifiable delay in paying the price the seller's remedy is to intimate to the buyer a reasonable time within which payment must be made; failure to pay in the period entitles the seller to rescind.[8] His duty to mitigate his loss arises at the expiry of the period.[9] There may be circumstances in which the seller can rescind after the elapse of a reasonable time even although no limit was imposed.[10]

If the price is payable on a fixed date the seller can sue for the price provided that he is able and willing to give the buyer a good title.[11]

If the buyer has been given entry to the subjects of sale, the seller may raise an action for payment of the price with alternative conclusions for declarator that the buyer is in material breach of the

---

5 *Forrest* v. *Scottish County Investment Co.*, 1916 S.C.(H.L.)28, *per* Lord Parmoor at p.36. *Steel* v. *Young*, 1907 S.C.360, must now be doubted—see the authorities cited in *Stewart Roofing Co. Ltd.* v. *Shanlin*, *supra*.

6 *Johnston* v. *Greenock Corporation*, 1951 S.L.T.(Notes)57.

7 *Head Wrightson Aluminium Ltd.* v. *Aberdeen Harbour Commissioners*, 1958 S.L.T.(Notes)12.

8 *Burns* v. *Garscadden* (1901) 8 S.L.T.321; *Rodger (Builders) Ltd.* v. *Fawdry*, 1950 S.C.483, *per* Lord Sorn at p.492; *Inveresk Paper Co.* v. *Pembry Machinery Co. Ltd.*, 1972 S.L.T.(Notes)63; *Lloyds Bank Ltd.* v. *Bauld*, 1976 S.L.T. (Notes)53.

9 *Johnstone* v. *Harris*, 1977 S.C.365.

10 *George Packman & Sons* v. *Dunbar's Trs.*, 1977 S.L.T.140.

11 *British Railways Board* v. *Birrell*, 1971 S.L.T.(Notes)17.

contract, decree of removal and damages representing the loss on resale. It is competent to take decree for payment of the price and subsequently to obtain decree in terms of the alternative conclusions.[12]

Where a contract of sale is subject to a suspensive condition, purification of which is not within the power of the parties, the contract is terminated if the condition is not fulfilled within a reasonable time, there being in this situation, of course, no breach of contract.[13] The contract may fix a date for fulfilment of the condition. A condition may be waived if it is purely in the interest of one party.[14] A claim to recover sums paid to account of the price of a house must be founded on a probative writ.[15] A stipulation in a contract for purchase of heritage by instalments that if an instalment was unpaid when the next fell due, the buyer would lose all right to acquire the house and to recover instalments already paid, has been held not to be a penalty.[16]

The buyer may refuse to implement the contract if the seller cannot grant a disposition in compliance with the missives; he can resile from the contract and recover the price if it has been paid.[17] If the seller fails to implement the contract, the buyer may bring an action for implement of the missives together with an alternative conclusion for damages.[18]

If there is a defect in the subjects as set forth in the disposition after delivery of the disposition the buyer's only remedy is to claim damages under the warrandice clause.[19] If the disposition does not convey what is in the missives the buyer's remedy is to raise an action for reduction of the disposition and implement of the missives.[20] Where there is a breach of a collateral obligation in the missives, an obligation in respect of which the disposition does not

---

12 *Bosco Design Services Ltd.* v. *Plastic Sealant Services Ltd.*, 1979 S.C.189.

13 *T. Boland & Co. Ltd.* v. *Dundas's Trs.*, 1975 S.L.T.(Notes)80.

14 See, *e.g. Gilchrist* v. *Paton,* 1979 S.L.T.135.

15 *Cord* v. *Gormley,* 1971 S.L.T.(Sh.Ct.)19.

16 *Reid* v. *Campbell,* 1958 S.L.T.(Sh.Ct.)45. But see, now, Chap. 4, para. 12.

17 *Crofts* v. *Stewart's Trs.*, 1927 S.C.(H.L.)65 (minerals); *Campbell* v. *McCutcheon,* 1963 S.C.505 (minerals); *Armia Ltd.* v. *Daejan Developments Ltd.*, 1979 S.C.(H.L.)56 (undisclosed right of access); *Stuart* v. *Lort-Phillips,* 1977 S.C.244 (vacant possession); *Kelly* v. *A. & J. Clark Ltd.*, 1967 S.L.T.(Notes)115 (undisclosed restrictions).

18 *Mackay* v. *Campbell,* 1967 S.C.(H.L.)53.

19 *Welsh* v. *Russell* (1894) 21 R.769.

20 *Equitable Loan Company of Scotland Ltd.* v. *Storie,* 1972 S.L.T.(Notes)20.

supersede the missives, an action for damages resembling the *actio quanti minoris* is competent.[21]

12. Electricity and Gas

Where gas is supplied through a meter, the register of the meter is *prima facie* evidence of the quantity of gas supplied.[22]

A consumer of electricity must give 24 hours' notice in writing before he quits premises supplied with electricity. If he fails to do so he is liable to the Electricity Board for sums in respect of supply up to next usual meter reading or the date when the subsequent occupier requires the board to supply electricity to the premises, whichever shall first occur.[23] There is a similar provision for gas.[24] If the occupier of premises supplied by gas quits the premises without paying amounts due for supply, the Gas Corporation is not entitled to require payment from the next occupier unless he has undertaken with the former occupier to pay or exonerate him for payment of that amount.[25]

If a person neglects to pay a charge for electricity or any other sum due in respect of the supply of electricity, the Electricity Board may cut off the supply until payment of the sums due together with the expenses of cutting off the supply.[26]

If a person has not, 28 days after a demand in writing, made payment of charges due by him in respect of the supply of gas, the Gas Corporation, after seven days' notice, may cut off the supply of gas to the premises and the expense thus incurred is recoverable in like manner as charges for gas. There is no obligation to restore the supply until payment has been made of all sums due and of the expenses of reconnection.[27] These remedies cannot be used after sequestration.[28]

A code of practice regulates the operation of these provisions.

---

21 *McKillop* v. *Mutual Securities Ltd.*, 1945 S.C.166; *Bradley* v. *Scott*, 1966 S.L.T. (Sh.Ct.)25; *Hoey* v. *Butler*, 1975 S.C.87.
22 Gas Act 1972, Sched. 4, para. 10.
23 Electric Lighting Act 1909, s.17.
24 Gas Act 1972, Sched. 4, para. 15.
25 Para. 14.
26 Electricity Lighting Act 1882, s.21; Electric Lighting Act 1909, s.18.
27 Gas Act 1972, Sched. 4, para. 17.
28 *McCulloch* v. *Ardrossan Commissioners* (1895) 11 Sh.Ct.Rep.55.

CHAPTER 3

THE CONSUMER CREDIT ACT

1. Credit

Credit has been regarded as a species of trust: "Trust, in the vulgar acceptation, comprehends all personal obligations for paying, delivering or performing, anything where the creditor has no real right in security; for thereby he trusts more to the faithfulness of his debtors, that they did not engage to what they were not able to perform, and that they would not disappoint their performance by disposing of their means in the creditor's prejudice."[1]

A person obtains credit if he obtains an immediate benefit or advantage in consideration of an obligation to pay money at a future date. The benefit may be the use of cash, the use and possession of goods which at some time are to become his property, or services. It has been held in a matter of statutory interpretation that the receipt of money on a promise to render services or deliver goods in the future is not credit.[2]

2. Extortionate Credit Bargains

One of the most important provisions of the Consumer Credit Act 1974 is that the court is given power, if it finds a "credit bargain" to be extortionate, to reopen the credit agreement so as to do justice between the parties.[3] The operation of this power is not restricted to regulated consumer credit agreements; it is not subject to a financial limit; "exempt" agreements[4] are affected by it.

A "credit agreement" is an agreement between an individual and any other person by which that person provides credit of any amount. A "credit bargain" is the credit agreement if no other transaction is to be taken into account in computing the total charge for credit; otherwise it means the credit agreement and those other transactions taken together.[5]

---

[1] Stair, IV, 6, 1.

[2] *Fisher* v. *Raven* [1964] A.C.210.

[3] s.137(1). Agreements whenever made are affected: Sched. 3, para. 42; S.I.1977/325.

[4] See *infra*, para. 4.

[5] s.137(2). As to the total charge for credit, see *infra*, para. 3.

A credit bargain is extortionate if it requires the debtor or a relative of his to make payments (whether unconditionally, or on certain contingencies) which are grossly exorbitant or if it otherwise grossly contravenes ordinary principles of fair dealing.[6] In considering whether the bargain is extortionate, regard is to be had to such evidence as is adduced concerning: interest rates prevailing when the bargain was made; the debtor's age, experience, business capacity and state of health; the degree to which, at the time of making the bargain, he was under financial pressure, and the nature of that pressure; the degree of risk accepted by the creditor, having regard to the value of any security provided; the creditor's relationship to the debtor; whether or not a colourable cash price was quoted for any goods or services included in the credit bargain; in relation to a linked transaction, how far the transaction was reasonably required for the protection of the debtor or creditor or was in the interest of the debtor; any other relevant considerations.[7] If the debtor or any "surety" alleges that the bargain is extortionate it is for the creditor to prove the contrary.[8] A "surety" is the person by whom any security is provided, or the person to whom his rights and duties in relation to the security have passed by assignation or operation of law.[9]

The credit agreement may be reopened, if the court "thinks just" on the ground that the credit bargain is extortionate: (a) on any application by the debtor or any surety to the Court of Session or sheriff court (which may be the sheriff court for the district in which the debtor or surety resides or carries on business); or (b) at the instance of the debtor or surety in any proceedings to which the debtor and creditor are parties, being proceedings to enforce the credit agreement, any security relating to it, or any linked transaction; or (c) at the instance of the debtor or surety in other proceedings in any court where the amount paid or payable under the credit agreement is relevant.[10]

In reopening the agreement the court may, to relieve the debtor or surety from payment of any sum in excess of that fairly due and reasonable, direct an accounting to be made, set aside obligations, require the creditor to make repayments, direct the return of the

[6] s.138(1). See Wilkinson (1979) 8 Anglo-American Law Review, 240.
[7] s.138(2)-(5). See *A. Ketley Ltd.* v. *Scott, The Times*, 24 June 1980.
[8] s.171(7).
[9] s.189(1).
[10] s.139(1).

property to the surety or alter the terms of the credit agreement or of any security instrument.[11] These measures may be taken notwithstanding that their effect is to place a burden on the creditor in respect of an advantage unfairly enjoyed by another person who is a party to a linked transaction. The terms of the statute do not seem to allow the court to adjust a linked transaction entered into by a relative of the debtor.[12]

3. Consumer Credit Act: definitions

A *personal credit agreement* is "an agreement between an individual ('the debtor') and any other person ('the creditor') by which the creditor provides the debtor with credit of any amount".[13] An "individual" includes a partnership or other unincorporated body of persons not consisting entirely of bodies corporate.[14] "Credit" includes a cash loan and any other form of financial accommodation;[15] where it is provided otherwise than in sterling it is treated as provided in sterling of an equivalent amount.[16] A hire-purchase agreement is regarded as a provision of a fixed-sum credit to finance the transaction of an amount equal to the total price of the goods less the aggregate of the deposit (if any) and the total charge for credit.[17] An item entering into the total charge for credit is not treated as credit even though time is allowed for its payment.[18] The amounts of the following charges are included in the total charge for credit:[19] (a) the total amount of the interest on the credit, and (b) other charges at any time payable under the transaction by or on behalf of the debtor or a relative of his whether to the creditor or any other person, notwithstanding that the whole or part of the charge may be repayable at any time or that the consideration therefor may include matters not within the transaction or subsisting at a time not within the duration of the agreement. The following are excluded from the total charge for credit:

11 s.139(2).

12 Bennion (1977) 121 S.J.822.

13 s.8(1). There is a question as to whether a cheque card agreement is a personal credit agreement (notwithstanding Sched. 2 Ex.21) as the bank does not agree to the creation of an overdraft although it must honour cheques drawn by use of the card: Dobson [1977] J.B.L.126.

14 s.189(1).

15 s.9(1).

16 s.9(2).

17 s.9(3).

18 s.9(4).

19 s.20; Consumer Credit (Total Charge for Credit) Regulations, 1980 (S.I.1980/51) regs 4, 5.

(a) charges payable to the creditor upon failure by the debtor or his relative to do or refrain from doing anything which he is required to do or to refrain from doing;
(b) any charge relating to an agreement to finance a transaction between the debtor and the creditor, or between the debtor and a person other than the creditor, being a charge which would be payable if the transaction were for cash;
(c) any charge not within (b) which relates to services or benefits incidental to the agreement and also to other services or benefits which may be supplied to the debtor and which is payable under an obligation under arrangements effected before the debtor applied to enter into the agreement, not being arrangements under which the debtor is bound to enter into any personal credit agreement;
(d) certain charges for the care, maintenance or protection of any land or goods;
(e) certain charges for money transmission services;
(f) certain insurance premiums.

A *consumer credit agreement* is a personal credit agreement by which the creditor provides the debtor with credit not exceeding £5,000.[20] (There is power to alter this amount[21]). A consumer credit agreement is a *regulated agreement* if it is not an "exempt agreement."[22] A consumer hire agreement is a regulated agreement if it is not an exempt agreement.[23] A *consumer hire agreement* is an agreement for the hiring of goods to an individual, which is not a hire-purchase agreement, which is capable of subsisting for more than three months and which does not require the hirer to make payments exceeding £5,000.[24]

A *running-account credit* is a facility under a personal credit agreement whereby the debtor can receive cash, goods and services to a value such that taking repayments by the debtor into account the credit limit is not exceeded, the credit limit being in any period the maximum debit balance permissible in the period, disregarding any term of the agreement which allows the maximum to be

---

[20] s.8(2).
[21] s.181(1).
[22] s.8(3). An agreement made before 1 April 1977 is not a regulated agreement: Sched. 3, para. 1: S.I. 1977/325.
[23] s.15(2).
[24] s.15(1).

exceeded temporarily.[25] For purposes of the £5,000 limit in the definition of a consumer credit agreement, the running-account credit is taken not to exceed £5,000 if the credit limit does not exceed £5,000; but even if there is no credit limit or a limit exceeding £5,000 the credit may be taken not to exceed £5,000 if the debtor cannot draw more than £5,000 at one time *or* if the credit charge increases or the agreement otherwise becomes more onerous when the debit balance rises above a given amount less than £5,000, *or* if "at the time the agreement is made it is probable, having regard to the terms of the agreement and any other relevant considerations, that the debit balance will not at any time rise above" £5,000.[26] If the agreement contains a term signifying that in the opinion of the parties that condition is not satisfied it shall be taken not to be satisfied unless the contrary is proved.[27] A bank overdraft is an example of a running-account credit.[28] A *fixed-sum credit* is any facility other than a running-account credit under a personal credit agreement whereby the debtor is enabled to receive credit in one amount or by instalments.[29] An ordinary loan granted in a number of instalments is a fixed-sum credit[30] and so is a hire-purchase agreement.[31]

A *restricted-use credit agreement* is a regulated consumer credit agreement:

(a) to finance a transaction between the debtor and the creditor, or

(b) to finance a transaction between the debtor and a person (the "supplier") other than the creditor, or

(c) to refinance any existing indebtedness of the debtor's whether to the creditor or another person.[32]

If the credit is supplied in such a way in fact that the debtor is free to use it as he chooses, even though certain uses would contravene the agreement or any other agreement, it is not a restricted-use agreement.[33] An *unrestricted-use credit agreement* is a regulated consumer credit agreement which is not a restricted-use agreement.[34]

25 s.10.
26 s.10(3).
27 s.171(1).
28 Sched. 2, Exs.18, 23.
29 s.10(1)(*b*).
30 Ex.9.
31 Ex.10.
32 s.11(1).
33 s.11(3).
34 s.11(2).

A *debtor-creditor-supplier agreement*[35] is a regulated consumer credit agreement in which the creditor has a connection with the goods or services supplied. There are three kinds:

(i) an agreement of type (a) *supra,* such as a hire-purchase transaction;

(ii) an agreement of type (b) *supra* made by the creditor under pre-existing arrangements,[36] or in contemplation of future arrangements, between himself and the supplier, *e.g.* a credit card agreement;

(iii) an unrestricted-use agreement made by the creditor under pre-existing arrangements between himself and a supplier in the knowledge that the credit is to be used to finance a transaction between the debtor and the supplier.

A *debtor-creditor agreement*[37] is a regulated consumer credit agreement where the creditor has no connection with the goods or services supplied. There are three kinds:

(i) an agreement of type (b) *supra,* not made by the creditor under arrangements or in contemplation of future arrangements between himself and the supplier;

(ii) an agreement of type (c) *supra*;

(iii) an unrestricted use agreement where there are no pre-existing arrangements between the creditor and a supplier.

4. Exempt Agreements

Exempt agreements are defined partly by s.16 of the Act and partly by an order made thereunder. It may be helpful to state at this point that, of the following 18 categories of exempt agreement, (1), (2) and (3) relate to agreements secured on land where the creditor is a local authority or building society, (4), (5), (6) and (7) relate

---

35 s.12. There is a circuity in the definitions in that the debtor-creditor-supplier and debtor-creditor agreements are defined as regulated agreements. Consumer credit agreements which are not exempt agreements are regulated agreements. Some exempt agreements are defined as debtor-creditor-supplier or debtor-creditor agreements.

36 An agreement is made under pre-existing arrangements if it is made in accordance with, or in furtherance of, arrangements previously made between the creditor or his associate and the supplier or his associate: s.187(1). Associates are, broadly, relatives, partners and controlled bodies corporate: s.184. An agreement is entered into in contemplation of future arrangements if it is entered into in the expectation that arrangements will subsequently be made between the creditor or his associates and a supplier or his associates for the supply of cash, goods and services to be financed by the agreement: s.187(2).

37 s.13. See also *supra,* note 35.

to agreements secured on land where the creditor is a specified insurance company, friendly society or charity (9), (10), (11), (12) and (13) are defined by a reference to the number of payments to be made by the debtor, and (14), (15) and (16) are defined by reference to the rate of charge for the credit:

(1) debtor-creditor-supplier agreements where the creditor is a local authority or building society and the agreement finances the purchase of land or the provision of dwellings on any land and is secured on that land.[38]

(2) debtor-creditor agreements where the creditor is a local authority or building society and the agreement is secured on land.[39]

(3) debtor-creditor-supplier agreements secured on land where the creditor is a local authority or building society and the agreement finances a linked transaction relating to an agreement which is of the type described in (1) *supra* and relates to the security subjects or which is of the type described in (2) *supra* and finances the purchase of the security subjects or the provision of dwellings thereon.[40]

(4) debtor-creditor-supplier agreements where the creditor is a specified[41] insurance company, friendly society or charity, and the agreement finances the purchase of land or the provision of dwellings on any land and is secured on that land.[42]

(5) debtor-creditor agreements secured on land where the creditor is a specified[41] insurance company, friendly society, or charity and the agreement finances the purchase of land or the provision of dwellings or business premises on any land.[43]

(6) debtor-creditor agreements secured on land where (a) the creditor is a specified[41] insurance company, friendly society or charity; (b) the agreement finances the alteration, enlarging, repair or improvement of a dwelling or business premises on any land; (c) the creditor is a creditor under either (i) an agreement (whenever made) secured on that

---

[38] s.16(1), (2)(*a*).

[39] s.16(1), (2)(*b*).

[40] s.16(1), (2)(*c*).

[41] s.16(1); Consumer Credit (Exempt Agreements) Order 1980 (S.I.1980/52), Sched., Pt.I.

[42] *Ibid.*, art.2(2)(*a*).

[43] *Ibid.*, art.2(2)(*b*).

land by which the debtor was provided with credit for the purchase of that land or the provision of dwellings or business premises thereon or (ii) an agreement refinancing such an agreement, and secured on that land (it should be noted that the land on which the "alteration credit agreement" is secured need not be the land on which the alterations are made[44]).

(7) debtor-creditor agreements secured on land where the creditor is a specified[41] insurance company, friendly society or charity and the agreement refinances any existing indebtedness of the debtor's, whether to the creditor or another person, under an agreement by which the debtor was provided with credit for the purchase of land or the provision of dwellings or business premises on any land or the alteration, enlarging, repair or improvement of a dwelling or business premises on any land.[45]

(8) an agreement secured on land where the creditor is a specified[46] body and the agreement is of a description specified in relation to that body.[47]

(9) debtor-creditor-supplier agreements for a fixed-sum credit where the number of payments[48] to be made by the debtor does not exceed four with the exception of (a) agreements financing the purchase of land; (b) conditional sale agreements and hire-purchase agreements; and (c) agreements secured by a pledge (other than a pledge of documents of title or of bearer bonds).[49] This will cover the normal credit given by, say, a department store.

(10) debtor-creditor-supplier agreements for running-account credit providing for payments by the debtor in relation to specified periods and requiring that the number of payments[48] to be made in repayment of the whole amount of the credit provided in each such period shall not exceed one.[50] There are the same exceptions as in (9). This will cover the monthly bills for milk and newspapers and some types of credit card.

---

41 s.16(1); Consumer Credit (Exempt Agreements) Order 1980 (S.I.1980/52), Sched., Pt.I.

44 *Ibid.*, art.2(2)(*b*), 2(3).

45 Art.2(2)(*c*).

46 Sched., Pt.II (public corporations).

47 Art.2(1), 2(4).

48 "Payment" means a payment comprising an amount in respect of credit with or without any other amount.

49 Art.3(1)(*a*)(i).

50 Art.3(1)(*a*)(ii).

(11) debtor-creditor-supplier agreements financing the purchase of land where the number of payments[51] to be made by the debtor does not exceed four.[52]

(12) debtor-creditor-supplier agreements for fixed-sum credit to finance a premium under an insurance contract relating to land or to any thing thereon where: (a) the creditor is the creditor under an agreement secured on that land which is exempt under (1)-(8) *supra* or would be so exempt if the credit did not exceed £5,000, (b) the credit is to be repaid within the period to which the premium relates, not being a period exceeding 12 months, (c) there is no charge for credit other than interest not exceeding the rate charged under the agreement mentioned in (a) *supra,* (d) the number of payments[51] to be made by the debtor does not exceed 12.[53]

(13) debtor-creditor-supplier agreements for fixed-sum credit where (a) the creditor is the creditor under an agreement secured on land which is exempt under (1)-(8) *supra* or would be so exempt if the credit did not exceed £5,000, (b) the agreement is to finance a premium under a life insurance contract which provides for payment on the death of the life insured of a sum not exceeding the amount sufficient to defray the sums which immediately after the credit under the agreement referred to in (a) *supra* had been advanced would have been payable to the creditor in respect of the credit and the total charge therefor, (c) there is no charge for the credit other than interest at a rate not exceeding the rate charged under the agreement referred to in (a) *supra,* and (d) the number of payments[51] to be made by the debtor does not exceed 12.[54]

(14) debtor-creditor agreements where the rate of the total charge for credit does not exceed the higher of (i) one per cent above the Bank of England minimum lending rate being the latest rate in operation on the date 28 days before the date on which the agreement is made, and (ii) 13 per cent, but excluding (a) agreements providing for an increase in, or permitting the creditor to increase, the amount or rate of any item of

---

[51] "Payment" means a payment comprising or including an amount in respect of credit or the total charge for credit (if any).

[52] Art.3(1)(*b*).

[53] Art.3(1)(*c*).

[54] Art.3(1)(*d*).

the total charge for credit after the agreement is in operation except by reference to the level of any index or of any other factor in accordance with any formula specified in the agreement, and (b) any agreements under which the total amount to be repaid by the debtor to discharge his indebtedness in respect of the amount of credit provided may vary according to any formula specified in the agreement having effect by reference to movements in the level of any index or to any other factor.[55]

(15) debtor-creditor-supplier agreements satisfying conditions (a), (b) and (c) specified in (13) *supra* where the rate of the total charge for credit does not exceed the rate specified in (14) *supra* but excluding agreements specified in exception (b) to (14) *supra*.[56]

(16) debtor-creditor agreements where the only amount included in the total charge for credit is interest[57] which cannot under the agreement at any time exceed the higher of (i) one per cent above the Bank of England minimum lending rate in operation at that time and (ii) 13 per cent, but excluding exception (b) in (14) *supra*.[58]

(17) agreements made in connection with trade in goods or services between the U.K. and other countries or within a country or between countries outside the U.K. being agreements under which credit is provided to the debtor in the course of a business carried on by him.[59]

(18) consumer hire agreements for meters or metering equipment owned by electricity, gas or water suppliers or for some types of telecommunications apparatus.[60]

5. Further Definitions

A *small agreement* is (a) a regulated consumer agreement for credit not exceeding £30 other than a hire purchase or conditional sale agreement or (b) a regulated consumer hire agreement which does not require the hirer to make payments exceeding £30, being,

---

55 Art.4(1)(*a*), (2), (3), (4).

56 Art.4(1)(*b*), (3), (4).

57 Interest is to be determined by the formula of reg. 7 of the Consumer Credit (Total Charge for Credit) Regulations 1980 (S.I. 1980/51); "period rate of charge" in the formula having the meaning given by reg.7(2).

58 Art.4(1)(*c*), (3), (4).

59 Art.5.

60 Art.6.

in either case, an agreement which is unsecured or secured only by a guarantee or indemnity.[61] There are provisions to avoid evasion by the splitting of an agreement into several small agreements.[62]

A *non-commercial agreement* is a consumer credit agreement or consumer hire agreement not made by the creditor or owner in the course of a business carried on by him.[63]

A *multiple agreement* is an agreement part of which falls within one category of agreement and part in another or an agreement which, or part of which, falls within two or more categories of agreement mentioned in the Act.[64] A part of a multiple agreement is to be treated as a separate agreement.

A transaction entered into by the debtor or his relatives other than one for the provision of a security may be a *linked transaction* in relation to an actual or prospective regulated agreement (the "principal agreement").[65] There are three types. The first is where the transaction is entered into in compliance with a term of the principal agreement, *e.g.* an insurance policy over goods. The second is where the transaction is financed by a principal debtor-creditor-supplier agreement, *e.g.* a purchase made with credit card. The third is where the other party to the transaction is a person of a specified class and the transaction is suggested by a person of a specified class. There are three sub-classes of this type. The first sub-class is where the transaction is entered into to induce the creditor to enter into the principal agreement. The second sub-class is where the transaction is for another purpose related to the principal agreement. The third sub-class is where the principal agreement is a restricted-use credit agreement and the transaction is for a purpose related to a transaction financed, or to be financed, by the principal agreement. It has been suggested that a contract for the purchase of food to stock a deep-freeze acquired on credit would fall into this third sub-class.[66] The specified classes of persons are the creditor, his associate, a person who knows that the principal agreement has been made or who contemplated that it might be made and a person who, in the negotiation of the transaction, is

---

61 s.17(1).
62 s.17(3), (4).
63 s.189(1).
64 s.18.
65 s.19.
66 Goode, *The Consumer Credit Act* (1979), p.292; Bennion, *Consumer Credit Control*, I, §1880C.

represented by a credit-broker who is also a negotiator in antecedent negotiations for the principal agreement.

A linked transaction has no effect until the regulated agreement is made.[67] Cancellation of the regulated agreement cancels the linked transaction.[68] Where, for any reason, the debtor's indebtedness under a regulated agreement is discharged before the time fixed by the agreement, he and his relatives are discharged from any liability under a linked transaction other than a debt which has already become payable.[69]

A *modifying agreement* is an agreement varying or supplementing an earlier agreement.[70] It is treated as revoking the earlier agreement and as containing provisions reproducing the combined effect of the two agreements. If the earlier agreement is a regulated one but the modifying one is not, the modifying one is to be treated as a regulated agreement unless it is for a running-account credit. The modifying agreement is treated as cancellable only in certain circumstances.

6. Total Charge for Credit: Assumptions

The total charge for credit is to be calculated in accordance with regulations. As the information required for the calculation will not always be available at the time the agreement is made, certain assumptions have to be made.

Unknown	Assumption
Amount of credit to be provided[71]	(a) In a running-account credit with a credit limit, the credit limit (b) In any other case, £100 (this assumption must be applied before any other)
Period for which credit is provided[72]	One year beginning with the relevant date

[67] s.19(3).
[68] s.69(1).
[69] s.96.
[70] s.82(2).
[71] Consumer Credit (Total Charge for Credit) Regulations 1980 (S.I.1980/51), reg. 13.
[72] Reg. 14. The relevant date is the earliest specified or determinable date on which the debtor is entitled to require provision of anything under the agreement and, where there is no such date, the date of making the agreement: Reg 1(2).

Unknown	Assumption
Level of index or factor by which rate or amount of item in total charge for credit or amount of any repayment of credit is calculated[73]	Level at date of making agreement
Rate or amount of item in total charge for credit which will change within one year beginning with the relevant date (where the period for which credit is to be provided cannot be ascertained)[74]	Highest rate or amount at any time obtaining under the transaction in that year
Earliest date on which credit is to be provided[75]	Date of making of agreement
Time of payment of one charge[76]	Relevant date or, where it may reasonably be expected that a debtor will not make payment on that date, the earliest date on which it may reasonably be expected that he will make payment
Times of payment of several charges of the same description[77]	The first as in the preceding entry, the last at the end of the period for which credit is provided, and the others at equal intervals between these times

The following assumptions have also to be made in the calculations[78]:

---

73 Reg.15.
74 Reg.16.
75 Reg.17.
76 Reg.18(*a*).
77 Reg.18(*b*).
78 Reg.2.

(1) the debtor will not be entitled to any income tax relief other than relief in respect of certain insurance premiums under Income and Corporation Taxes Act 1970, s.19, and Finance Act 1974, Sched. 4.
(2) no assistance is given under the Home Purchase Assistance and Housing Corporation Guarantee Act 1978.
(3) in a transaction providing for repayment at specified times, the creditor will not exercise any right under the transaction to require repayment at other times if the debtor performs his obligations under the transaction.
(4) in a transaction without such a provision, the creditor will not exercise any right under the transaction to require repayment if the debtor performs his obligations.
(5) where the rate or amount of any item in the total charge for credit is to vary on the occurrence of any event, that that event will not occur (but this does not apply to an event which is certain to occur and of which the date of occurrence, or the earliest date of occurrence, can be ascertained at the date of the making of the agreement).
(6) each provision of credit and each repayment is made at the specified time or, if there is no time specified, at the earliest time provided under the transaction.
(7) any repayment to be made before the relevant date is to be taken to be made on the relevant date.
(8) in a running-account credit or a fixed-sum credit where credit is not repayable at specified intervals or in specified amounts where, in either case, a constant period rate of charge in respect of periods of equal or nearly equal length is charged:
    (i) the amount of credit outstanding at the beginning of the period is to remain outstanding throughout the period;
    (ii) the amount of any credit provided during a period is provided immediately after the end of the period;
    (iii) any repayment made during a period is made immediately after the end of the period.
(9) any repayment of the credit or total charge for credit will, at the time when the repayment is made, be the smallest for which the agreement provides.

In determining the amount of the total of the interest on the credit which may be provided under the agreement, any subsidy receivable under Housing Subsidies Act 1967, Pt. II, is deducted.

7. Time

Then there are provisions as to the way in which periods of time are to be treated.[79]

Period	Counted
Not a whole number of calendar months and not a whole number of weeks	In years and days
Whole number of calendar months but not a whole number of weeks	In calendar months
Whole number of weeks but not a whole number of calendar months	In weeks
Whole number of calendar months and a whole number of weeks where only one repayment is to be made	In calendar months
Whole number of calendar months and a whole number of weeks where more than one repayment is to be made at intervals from the relevant date of one or more weeks	In weeks
Whole number of calendar months and a whole number of weeks where more than one repayment is to be made but not at intervals of one or more weeks	In calendar months
Calendar months	Relevant number of twelfth parts of a year

[79] Reg.11.

Period	Counted
Weeks	Relevant number of fifty-second parts of a year
Day	One three hundred and sixty-fifth part of a year
Every day	A working day

8. Computations

The "total charge for credit" is the total of the interest on the credit to be provided and all other charges at any time payable under the transaction by the debtor or his relative to the creditor or any other person.[80] Items to be included in, and items to be excluded from, the total charge have already been specified.[81]

The rate of the total charge for credit is the "annual percentage rate of charge" (A.P.R.C.) determined in accordance with the regulations to one decimal place, further decimal places being disregarded.[82]

The simplest case[83] is where a percentage rate of charge (x) comprising all charges in the total charge for credit is charged and the agreement is:

(a) an agreement under which the only charge for credit is a constant period rate of charge in respect of periods of equal length (y in a year) being either (i) an agreement for running-account credit, or (ii) an agreement for fixed-sum credit where the credit is not repayable at specified intervals or in specified amounts; or

(b) an agreement for fixed-sum credit under which (i) the only charge for credit is a constant period rate of charge in respect of periods of equal length, (ii) credit is outstanding throughout one or more such periods, and (iii) every repayment of credit and of the total charge is made at the end of such a period.

All that needs to be done here is to adjust the percentage rate if the period in respect of which it is charged is not a year; obviously, a

80 Reg.4.
81 *Supra*, para. 3.
82 Reg.6.
83 Reg.7.

10% rate charged for a six month period represents an annual rate of a little over 20%. The A.P.R.C. in this case is defined as:

$$100\left[\left(1+\frac{x}{100}\right)^{y}-1\right]$$

The second simple situation[84] is where a fixed-sum credit is provided in a lump sum (P) repayable at the end of a specified period (*t* in years) in a lump sum (P + C) where C is the total charge for credit. The A.P.R.C. is

$$100\left[\left(1+\frac{C}{P}\right)^{1/t}-1\right]$$

The third definition of the A.P.R.C. is applicable to any agreement.[85] It is "the rate per annum compounding annually expressed as a percentage such that: (a) the sum of the present values as at the relevant date of all repayments of credit and of the total charge for credit, and (b) the sum of the present values as at the relevant date of all credit under the agreement, would when calculated at that rate, be equal." The relevant date is, broadly, that on which the debtor can require provision of the credit. The present value at the relevant date of a sum to be paid on or before that date, is that sum; the present value of a sum A to be paid at a later date (*t* years later) is:

$$\frac{A}{\left(1+\frac{r}{100}\right)^{t}}$$

where *r* is the rate per annum expressed as a percentage. Where this method gives more than one rate, the A.P.R.C. is the positive rate nearest to zero, or, if there is none, the negative rate nearest to zero. This calculation will require the solution of an equation of the form:

$$P=\frac{a}{\left(1+\frac{r}{100}\right)^{1}}+\frac{b}{\left(1+\frac{r}{100}\right)^{2}}+\frac{c}{\left(1+\frac{r}{100}\right)^{3}}\quad\ldots$$

In most cases, the value of *r* can be found only by trial and error, or by the use of a computer.

In the case of an agreement to which an entry in *Consumer Credit Tables* published in 1977 by H.M.S.O. exactly applies, the applicable rate in the table is to be taken to be the rate determined in accordance with the regulations.[86]

---

[84] Reg.8.
[85] Reg.9.
[86] Reg.10.

9. Consumer Credit Tables

The tables are in 15 parts. Parts 1 to 7 deal with the case where under a fixed-sum credit agreement a single advance of credit is made, the sum of the credit and the total charge for credit is to be repaid in equal instalments at equal intervals throughout the period over which the credit is to be repaid and the first instalment is payable one such interval after the credit is advanced. The user of the tables must first calculate the "charge per pound lent", which is the total charge for credit, in pounds, divided by the amount of credit to be advanced, in pounds. The user then finds the table for the appropriate interval; for example, Part 2 covers weekly intervals for 52 to 111 instalments; Part 5 covers monthly instalments for three years or over. The next step is to find in the table the column for the appropriate number of instalments and go down it until the figure for the charge per pound lent is found; reference to the end of the row then gives the annual percentage rate of charge. If there is no entry in the table for the exact rate of charge per pound lent to the fourth decimal place, the tables cannot be used.

Parts 8 and 9 deal with the case of credit repaid with the total charge in a single sum after a specified interval. The charge per pound lent is found in the column for the appropriate length of transaction and the A.P.R.C. is again found at the end of the row.

Part 10 covers weekly instalment (4 to 113 weeks), monthly instalment (3 to 32 months) and single repayment (4 to 53 weeks and 1 to 10 months) cases where the A.P.R.C. is 100 or over.

Parts 11 to 13 cover transactions of the same types as are covered by Parts 1 to 7. Here the calculation begins with the computation of the "annual flat rate" which is:

$$\frac{C \times 100 \times 52}{P \times t}$$

where C is the total charge for credit in pounds, P is the amount of credit in pounds and t is the period, in weeks, over which the credit is to be repaid. The next step differs from the method used in the earlier parts. The columns are for numbers of instalments as before but the rows are the annual flat rates at intervals of a quarter of a per cent. The row for the appropriate annual flat rate is found and then the user moves along it to the column for the number of instalments and the figure at that point is the A.P.R.C. If the intervals are monthly the formula for the annual flat rate is

$$\frac{C \times 100 \times 12}{P \times t}$$

where t is the repayment period in months; if the intervals are quarterly, half yearly or yearly the formula is

$$\frac{C \times 100}{P \times t}$$

where t is the repayment period in years. Parts 11 to 13 are thus to some extent an alternative to Parts 1 to 7 but the range of transactions covered is slightly different.

Part 14 deals with single repayment transactions where an annual flat rate can be calculated by the formula:

$$\frac{C \times 100}{P \times t}$$

where t is the length of the transaction in years. Again the columns are lengths of transaction and the rows are annual flat rates; the A.P.R.C. is the figure in the appropriate row and column.

Part 15 applies where there is a "constant period rate of charge" (*i.e.* a percentage rate of charge for a period comprising all the charges included in the total charge for credit) and the agreement is a running-account credit agreement *or* a fixed-sum credit agreement where the credit is not repayable at specified intervals or in specified amounts *or* a fixed-sum credit agreement where the credit is repayable at the end of a specified period in a single lump sum comprising the credit and the total charge for credit. The page for the period for which the period rate of charge is charged is found and there each period rate has the appropriate A.P.R.C. opposite it.

10. Licensing

A person who carries on a business consisting of the provision of credit under regulated consumer credit agreements or the hiring of goods under regulated consumer hire agreements is required to have a licence.[87] A person is not treated as carrying on a particular type of business merely because occasionally he enters into transactions belonging to a business of that type.[88] If a regulated agreement, other than a non-commercial agreement, is made when the creditor or owner is unlicensed, it is enforceable against the debtor or hirer only where the Director of Fair Trading has made an order

[87] s.21. The Consumer Credit Act 1974 (Commencement No. 2) Order 1977 (S.I. 1977/325) exempts from the licensing requirement a business carried on by an individual in the course of which the only agreements made are for fixed-sum credit not exceeding £30 or for running-account credit where the credit limit does not exceed £30.

[88] s.189(2).

that the agreement is to be treated as if the trader had been licensed.[89]

A person carrying on an ancillary credit business (*i.e.* credit brokerage, debt-adjusting, debt counselling, debt-collecting or a credit reference agency) also requires a licence.[90] An agreement for the services of such a person made when he is unlicensed is enforceable against the customer only where the Director has made an appropriate order[91] and a regulated agreement made by a debtor who was introduced to the creditor by an unlicensed credit-broker is in the same position.[92] Credit brokerage is the effecting of introductions of individuals desiring credit or goods on hire to persons carrying on the appropriate business or to other credit-brokers.[93]

11. Advertising and Quotations

There is regulation of the contents of advertisements and quotations issued by a person carrying on a consumer credit business, a consumer hire business, a business in the course of which individuals are provided with credit secured on land, or certain other types of business.[94] The regulations allow for some relaxation of the rules applying to the calculation of the rate of the total charge for credit.

12. General Requirements

The following general requirements apply to the making of regulated agreements:[95]

(1) specified information must be given to the debtor or hirer in a prescribed manner;[96]

---

[89] s.40.

[90] s.147. Certain exceptions are made in the Consumer Credit Act 1974 (Commencement No. 4) Order 1977 (S.I. 1977/2163).

[91] s.148.

[92] s.149.

[93] s.145(2).

[94] ss.43, 52; Consumer Credit (Advertisements) Regulations 1980 (S.I.1980/54); Consumer Credit (Advertisements) (Amendment) Regulations 1980 (S.I. 1980/1360); Consumer Credit (Exempt Advertisements) Order 1980 (S.I.1980/53) Consumer Credit (Exempt Advertisements) (Amendment) Order 1980 (S.I. 1980/1359); Consumer Credit (Quotations) Regulations 1980 (S.I.1980/55).

[95] They do not apply to non-commercial agreements nor to a debtor-creditor agreement enabling the debtor to overdraw on a current account: s.74(1). Requirements (2)-(5) do not apply to a small debtor-creditor-supplier agreement for restricted-use credit unless a term is expressed in writing in which case requirement (2) applies: s.74(4) amended by Banking Act 1979, s. 38.

[96] s.55.

(2) the agreement must have the specified content and be in the specified form;[97]
(3) a document embodying all the terms of the agreement other than implied terms, the terms being readily legible, must be signed by the debtor or hirer and by or on behalf of the creditor or owner;[98]
(4) the debtor or hirer must be given a copy or copies of the agreement;[99]
(5) the debtor or hirer must be given notice of his right (if any) to cancel the agreement.[1]

If these requirements are not satisfied the agreement is not properly executed and it is enforceable against the debtor or hirer on an order of the court only.[2]

13. Cancellation

A regulated agreement may be cancelled if the antecedent negotiations included oral representations made in the debtor's presence by the negotiator unless (a) the agreement is secured on land, or is a restricted use agreement to finance the purchase of land or an agreement for a bridging loan in connection with the purchase of land, or (b) the unexecuted agreement is signed by the debtor at the business premises of the creditor, owner or negotiator or of a party to a linked transaction (other than the debtor or his relative).[3] The cancellation may normally be made before the end of the fifth day following the completion of the documentation.[4] The general effect of cancellation is that sums paid by the debtor are repayable, any credit extended is repayable and goods must be returned.[5] An unscrupulous consumer may take unfair advantage of these provisions where a car has been taken in part-exchange at a "written-up" value; a borrower may obtain a month's interest-free credit.[6]

---

[97] s.60.
[98] s.61.
[99] ss.62-63. As to "sent", see *V. L. Skuce & Co.* v. *Cooper* [1975] 1 W.L.R.593.
[1] s.64. See next paragraph.
[2] s.65(1).
[3] s.67.
[4] s.68.
[5] ss.70-73.
[6] Dobson (1978) 128 N.L.J.56.

14. Agency

"Antecedent negotiations" are negotiations with the debtor conducted by the creditor in relation to the making of an agreement, *or* by a credit-broker in relation to goods to be sold to the creditor who will then enter an agreement with the debtor relating to the goods *or* by the supplier in relation to a transaction to be financed by a debtor-creditor-supplier agreement. The person conducting the negotiations on behalf of the credit-broker or supplier is deemed to be conducting them as agent of the creditor as well as in his actual capacity.[7]

15. Currency of Agreement

During the currency of the regulated agreement, the creditor must give the debtor and the surety information as to the state of the transaction if requested to do so.[8] The creditor cannot during the specified term of duration of the agreement, without giving seven days' notice in the prescribed form, enforce a term of the agreement (other than one arising from the debtor's breach of the agreement) by demanding earlier payment of any sum, recovering possession of any goods or land, or treating any right conferred on the debtor as terminated, restricted or deferred;[9] this does not prevent the creditor treating a right to draw on credit as restricted or deferred.

If the creditor varies the agreement under a power therein, the variation does not take effect until notice is given in the prescribed manner.[10]

The debtor under a regulated consumer credit agreement is not liable for any loss arising from the use of the credit facility by someone not acting, or to be treated as acting, as his agent but this does not apply to a non-commercial agreement nor to a loss arising from misuse of a cheque or banker's draft.[11]

The debtor under a regulated consumer hire agreement is entitled to make payment to discharge his indebtedness under the agreement at any time.[12] Regulations may provide for the allowance of a

---

[7] s.56.

[8] ss.77-79, 107-109.

[9] s.76.

[10] s.82; Consumer Credit (Notice of Variation of Agreements) Regulations 1977 (S.I.1977/328).

[11] s.83.

[12] s.94.

rebate by the creditor.[13] This discharge of indebtedness has the effect of discharging him from liability under a linked transaction other than a debt which has already become payable.[14]

The creditor cannot terminate an agreement during its specified period of duration under a power in the agreement unless he gives the debtor seven days' notice in the prescribed manner.[15]

16. Default

On breach of a regulated agreement by the debtor, the creditor must serve a default notice before he is entitled:

(a) to terminate the agreement;
(b) to demand earlier payment of any sum;
(c) to recover possession of goods or land;
(d) to treat any of the debtor's rights as terminated, restricted or deferred;
(e) to enforce any security (an act by which a floating charge becomes fixed is not enforcement).[16]

The default notice must be in the prescribed form and must specify the breach and the action required to remedy it before a specified date not earlier than seven days after service of the notice, or, if the breach is not capable of remedy, the sum required to be paid as compensation before a specified date. If the action is taken or the sum paid before the specified date the breach is treated as not having occurred.[17]

On service of the notice the debtor may apply to the court for a time order.[18]

The debtor in a regulated consumer credit agreement cannot be obliged to pay interest on sums unpaid in breach of the agreement at a rate exceeding any rate of interest included in the total charge for credit or, if no interest is so included, what would be the rate of the total charge for credit if amounts payable under linked transactions were not included in the total charge.[19]

---

[13] s.95.
[14] s.96.
[15] s.98.
[16] s.87.
[17] ss.88, 89. See *Eshun* v. *Moorgate Mercantile Co. Ltd.* [1971] 1 W.L.R.722. (Hire-Purchase Act 1965).
[18] s.129. See *infra*, para. 19.
[19] s.93.

17. Debtor's Death

The creditor is not entitled to do the acts (a) to (e) specified in the preceding paragraph by reason of the death of the debtor if at the death the agreement is fully secured. If it is unsecured or partly secured, the creditor can do these acts on an order of the court only.[20] The creditor is not prevented from treating the right to draw on any credit as restricted or deferred. Nor is there anything to prevent the payment of sums due under the agreement out of the proceeds of a policy of assurance on the debtor's life. The restraint on terminating the agreement applies only where there is specified in the agreement a period of duration which has not ended when the creditor purports to terminate the agreement.

18. Enforcement Orders

The Act frequently provides that in certain circumstances an agreement is enforceable against the debtor on an order of the court only.[21] Apart from the possibility of resorting to summary diligence, which does proceed on a decree of the court,[22] the creditor must apply for an enforcement order. The court cannot make an enforcement order if there was failure to comply with certain provisions as to notice of the right to cancel, as to the giving of a copy agreement to the debtor, or as to the signing of the agreement.[23] Where the debtor has died an order can be made only if the creditor proves that he has been unable to satisfy himself that the present and future obligations of the debtor are likely to be discharged.[24] The court may dismiss the application if it considers it just to do so having regard to the prejudice caused to any person by the contravention in question and the degree of culpability for it and having regard also to the court's powers to make conditional or suspended orders or to vary the terms of the agreement.[25] In an enforcement order the court may reduce or discharge any sum payable by the debtor or by a surety to compensate him for any loss suffered as a result of the contravention.[26] Where the agreement is not in the correct form but

---

[20] s.86.

[21] ss.65(1), 86(2), 105(7)(*a*), (*b*), 111(2), 124(1), (2).

[22] *Taylor, Petr.*, 1931 S.L.T.260; *Smith Ltd.* v. *Hutchison* (1926) 42 Sh.Ct. Rep.183.

[23] s.127.

[24] s.128.

[25] s.127(1).

[26] s.127(2).

the debtor did sign a document containing all the prescribed terms, the order may direct that the agreement is to have effect as if it did not include a term omitted from that document.[27]

19. Time Orders

A "time order" may be made (a) when the creditor applies for an enforcement order, (b) on an application by the debtor, after service of a default notice, a notice of termination of the agreement or a notice of intention to demand early payment, or repossess goods or land or treat a right as terminated, restricted or deferred, and (c) when the creditor brings an action to enforce the agreement, or a security, or recover possession of any goods or land.

In any of these circumstances the court may make a "time order" providing for payment by instalments or for the remedying of any breach by the debtor within a specified time.[28] In any order made in relation to an agreement the court may make the operation of a term conditional on the doing of certain acts by any party or suspend the operation of any term.[29] The court may also include in the order such provision as it considers just for amending the agreement or security in consequence of a term of the order.[30] On the application of the creditor or owner, the court may make such order as it thinks just for the protection of his property or property subject to a security pending the determination of the proceedings.[31]

20. Negotiable Instruments

Except in the case of a non-commercial agreement, a negotiable instrument cannot be taken as a security for discharge of a sum due under a regulated agreement and a negotiable instrument other than a bank note or cheque cannot be taken from a debtor or surety in discharge of a sum payable.[32] The person taking the negotiable instrument is not a holder in due course and is not entitled to enforce it.[33] A cheque taken in discharge cannot be negotiated except to a banker[34] and negotiation to a non-banker is a defect in

---

27 s.127(5).
28 s.129.
29 s.135.
30 s.136.
31 s.131.
32 s.123.
33 s.125(1).
34 s.123(2).

the negotiator's title.[35] Contravention of these provisions makes the agreement or security enforceable on order of the court only.[36] The rights of a holder in due course of a negotiable instrument are not affected but where the debtor or surety becomes liable to a holder in due course as a result of a contravention of these provisions the creditor must indemnify him.[37]

21. Securities

Documents embodying regulated agreements have to embody any security provided in relation to the agreement by the debtor.[38] If the person by whom a security is provided (the "surety") is not the debtor, the security must be expressed in writing in the prescribed form, the document containing all the terms of the security other than implied terms must be signed by or on behalf of the surety and a copy of the document and the principal agreement given to him.[39] If these requirements are not satisfied, the security is enforceable against the surety only on an order of the court and if an application for such an order is dismissed (except on technical grounds) the security is treated as never having effect, property lodged with the creditor for purposes of the security must be returned, any entry relating to the security in any register must be cancelled and any amount received by the creditor on realisation of the security must be repaid to the surety;[40] there is a partial exemption for heritable securities. The creditor is obliged to give the surety on request a copy of the principal agreement and of the security instrument and information about the present state of the debtor's indebtedness.[41]

A copy of any default notice served on the debtor must be served on the surety.[42] The realisation of securities is subject to regulation.[43] A security cannot be enforced so as to benefit the creditor to an extent greater than would be the case if there were no security and the obligations of the debtor were carried out to the extent (if any) to which they would be enforced under the Act.[44] Accordingly,

---

[35] s.125(2).
[36] s.124.
[37] s.125(3), (4).
[38] s.105(9).
[39] s.105.
[40] s.106.
[41] ss.107-110.
[42] s.111.
[43] s.112.
[44] s.113(1).

if a regulated agreement is enforceable only on a court order or on an order of the Director the security is enforceable only where an order has been made[45] and, generally, if the agreement is cancelled or becomes unenforceable, the security becomes ineffective.[46]

---

45 s.113(2).
46 s.113(3).

CHAPTER 4

CREDIT TRANSACTIONS

1. Loan of Money

Mutuum is defined by Bell as "a real contract, by which one gives and transfers a fungible to another without hire, for use by consumption, on an engagement to restore as much of the same thing at the stipulated time."[1] Although interest is usually payable on a loan of money, such a loan can be treated as a species of *mutuum*. The borrower's obligation is to restore the sum lent. The lender has only a personal right to repayment.

It is possible for advances of money to be made on the footing that they will be repaid only if the receiver is able to do so.[2] Where a loan between mercantile men was "to be repaid by instalments as found most convenient to" the borrower, it was held that this referred to mercantile convenience—a time when the borrower had money sufficient in amount and free from the ordinary purposes of his business—and that the onus of proof as to this was on the lender.[3]

If a loan is made, the creditor is entitled to demand repayment at any time unless this is precluded by some conventional provision.[4]

If there is a stipulation that the loan will not be called up so long as interest is paid "punctually" on a specified day, a payment on a later date is not made "punctually".[5]

A penalty for failure in punctual payment is not enforceable.[6] There may be a provision that the rate of interest will be lower if the interest is paid punctually.[7]

A loan falls under the quinquennial prescription.[8] If the contract stipulates the date for repayment, that date is the *terminus a quo*; if there is no stipulation as to the date of repayment, the prescriptive

---

1 *Prin.*, § 200.

2 *Forbes* v. *Forbes* (1869) 8 M.85; *Mylne* v. *Balfour Melville* (1901) 8 S.L.T.454.

3 *Shaw* v. *Kay* (1904) 12 S.L.T.6, 262.

4 *Thomson* v. *Geekie* (1861) 23 D.693, *per* L.J.-C. Inglis at p.701.

5 *Gatty* v. *Maclaine*, 1921 S.C.(H.L.) 1; *Kennedy* v. *Begg Kennedy & Elder Ltd.*, 1954 S.L.T.(Sh.Ct.)103.

6 *Nasmyth* v. *Samson* (1785) 3 Pat.App.9; Debts Securities (Scotland) Act 1856, s.5.

7 *Gatty* v. *Maclaine, supra*.

8 Prescription and Limitation (Scotland) Act 1973, Sched. 1, para. 1.

period runs from the date where a written demand for repayment is made by or on behalf of the creditor to the debtor.[9]

2. Proof of Loan

As a general rule, a loan of money exceeding 100 pounds Scots (£8·33) can be proved only by writ or oath of the borrower.[10] The defender must state a plea to this effect and if he fails to do so and a proof *prout de jure* is allowed, the case will be decided on the whole evidence led.[11]

The rule does not apply to an advance which was to form the pursuer's contribution to the capital of a partnership, if it was formed.[12] It has also been held that the rule does not apply where the borrower stands in a special fiduciary relationship to the lender—for example, the relationship between director and company.[13]

A loan not exceeding 100 pounds Scots can be proved *prout de jure*,[14] but, where a loan of over that amount is averred, parole proof is not admitted by restricting the sum sued for to £8·33.[15] An advance of £16 to pay wages of three servants, each wage being less than £8·33, was held to be one loan.[16] Parole evidence is not allowed to prove a payment made on behalf of the debtor if the debtor holds a receipt for the payment.[16]

3. Series of Transactions

It seems that the general rule as to proof suffers an exception where there is alleged, not an isolated loan transaction, but a series of transactions. The limits of this exception are not at all clear. In one case it was held that indorsed cheques were sufficient to vouch advances constituting items in a current account between agent and client, there being other advances shown in the account and vouched by bills, IOUs or receipts.[17] In another case, where the

---

[9] Sched. 2, para. 2(2).

[10] Erskine, IV, 2, 20; Bell, *Prin.*, § 2257.

[11] *Dick's Exrx.* v. *Dick*, 1964 S.L.T.(Sh.Ct.)41; *Cuthbertson* v. *Paterson*, 1968 S.L.T.(Sh.Ct.)21.

[12] *Hendry* v. *Cowie & Son & Co.* (1904) 12 S.L.T.31, 261.

[13] *John S. Boyle Ltd.* v. *Boyle's Trs.*, 1949 S.L.T.(Notes)45.

[14] *Annand's Trs.* v. *Annand* (1869) 7 M.526. See also *Muir* v. *Steven* (1896) 12 Sh.Ct.Rep.368.

[15] *Whyte* v. *Smith* (1886) 2 Sh.Ct.Rep.257.

[16] *Annand's Trs.* v. *Annand*, *supra*.

[17] *Robb* v. *Robb's Trs.* (1884) 11 R.881.

defender admitted that heritage held in his name was truly the property of his father but claimed that it was so held by him in security of advances made by him to his father over a period, it was held that in "a going series of transactions" proof was not necessarily restricted to writ or oath, the series must be taken as a whole and the question was "what would be the natural way of preserving evidence of what was done among ordinary business men."[18] The basis of the decision was, however, that the question was not whether a loan was constituted but upon what terms was property to be reconveyed. This distinction has been emphasised subsequently in a case in which it was said that, in any event, the exception could not extend to a loan made in instalments.[19] Where a father made a series of advances to a forisfamiliated son and took no document of debt therefor but made entries in his books, it was held that these facts did not amount to "natural proof" of loan.[20] Three separate loans made at intervals of several months are not sufficient to form a series of transactions for purposes of the exception.[21]

4. Pleading

Any admission made by the defender in his pleadings must be taken with any qualification adjected to it. The distinction between intrinsic and extrinsic qualifications has no application to judicial admissions.[22] So if it is admitted that there was a loan which has been repaid or abandoned, the pursuer must still rebut the qualification by writ or oath.[23] Similarly, if the receipt of money is admitted but it is averred that the sum was paid for services rendered, the loan must still be established by writ or oath.[24] On the other hand, when the defender avers that the money was received as a gift, it seems that the onus is on him to prove this unless the alleged donor was under a natural obligation to provide for the recipient.[25]

---

18 *Smith's Tr.* v. *Smith*, 1911 S.C.653. See *Grant's Exrx.* v. *Grant*, 1922 S.L.T.156; *Boyd* v. *Millar*, 1934 S.N.7. See also *Inglis* v. *Inglis's Tr.*, 1925 S.L.T.686.

19 *McKie* v. *Wilson*, 1951 S.C.15.

20 *Grant's Exrx.* v. *Grant*, *supra*.

21 *Ainslie* v. *McGowan*, 1974 S.L.T.(Sh.Ct.)19.

22 *Gray* v. *Munro* (1829) 8 S.221; *Milne* v. *Donaldson* (1852) 14 D.849; *Picken* v. *Arundale & Co.* (1872) 10 M.987.

23 *Walker* v. *Garlick*, 1940 S.L.T.208; *Kerr's Trs.* v. *Ker* (1883) 11 R.108.

24 *Gow's Exrs.* v. *Sim* (1866) 4 M.578; *McKie* v. *Wilson*, 1951 S.C.15.

25 *Malcolm* v. *Campbell* (1889) 17 R.255; *Penman* v. *White*, 1957 S.C.338; *McVea* v. *Reid*, 1958 S.L.T.(Sh.Ct.)60; Walker & Walker, *Evidence*, p.66, n.2. *Cf. Paul* v. *Craw* (1956) 72 Sh.Ct.Rep.60.

5. Writ

The writ need not be holograph or tested.[26] It need not be granted contemporaneously with the making of the loan but an acknowledgment granted by the borrower after his sequestration cannot be used.[27] A writ of the borrower's agent may be constructively the borrower's writ.[28] Parole evidence is admissible to prove the borrower's handwriting and signature, the borrower's instructions to his agent and the fact of delivery.[29] Parole evidence may also be admitted to prove that a document was signed by the grantor as a partner and authorised agent of a firm,[30] or by the grantors as directors and agents of a company.[31]

It would appear that the writ must be a *chirographum*—a document which was given by the recipient to the payer of the money as a record of the transaction and which is retained in the possession of the payer.[32] It is therefore doubtful whether an entry in the debtor's books *per se* can establish loan although it has been said that "no better proof can be found" of *payment* of money.[33] It may be that it is a question of the regularity and authenticity of the books.[34] Entries made in a pass-book by the creditor on the debtor's instructions, the pass-book being retained by the debtor, are sufficient.[35] Where an unqualified acknowledgment of the receipt of money is produced, there is a presumption of loan which the defender may rebut.[36] If, however, the acknowledgment is qualified by an explanation that the money was received on some footing other than that of loan, the debt is not established.[37] Similarly where the qualification is that the debt was repaid, this must be taken with the admission and resting-owing must be proved by the defender's writ

---

26 *Paterson* v. *Paterson* (1897) 25 R.144.

27 *Carmichael's Tr.* v. *Carmichael*, 1929 S.C.265.

28 *Bryan* v. *Butters Bros. & Co.* (1892) 19 R.490; *Clark's Exrx.* v. *Brown*, 1935 S.C.110(banker); *Dryburgh* v. *Macpherson*, 1944 S.L.T.116.

29 *Per* L.P. Inglis, *Haldane* v. *Speirs* (1872) 10 M.537 at 541; *per* Lord Kinnear, *Dunn's Tr.* v. *Hardy* (1896) 23 R.621 at 633.

30 *King, Sons & Paterson* v. *Ferrie* (1942) 58 Sh.Ct.Rep.124(creditor's averment); *McKenzie* v. *Jones* (1926) 42 Sh.Ct.Rep.289(debtor's averment).

31 *Field* v. *R.H. Thomson & Co.* (1902) 10 S.L.T.261.

32 *Per* L.P. Inglis, *Haldane* v. *Speirs*, *supra*, at p.541; *per* Lord Neaves, *Duncan's Trs.* v. *Shand* (1873) 11 M.254 at 259.

33 *Per* Lord Neaves, *ibid*.

34 *Wink* v. *Speirs* (1868) 6 M.657; *Waddel* v. *Waddel* (1790) 3 Pat.App.188; *Hope* v. *Derwent Rolling Mills Co. Ltd.* (1905) 7 F.837.

35 *Bruce* v. *Calder* (1904) 20 Sh.Ct.Rep.288.

36 *Thomson* v. *Geekie* (1861) 23 D.693; *Christie's Trs.* v. *Muirhead* (1870) 8 M.461.

37 *Duncan's Trs.* v. *Shand*, *supra*; *Morison's Trs.* v. *Mitchell*, 1925 S.L.T.231.

or oath.[38] The acknowledgment must be so expressed as to imply existing indebtedness.[39] A cheque in favour of the defender and indorsed by him establishes payment of money but not loan.[40] A post-dated cheque may, however, establish a loan.[41] Similarly, a deposit-receipt in the pursuer's name and indorsed by the defender on the back does not prove loan.[42] But if payment of money is proved by a cheque, other writs may be used to show *quo animo* the money passed;[43] and if the cheque has a receipt by the defender on its face, that is sufficient.[44] Letters which do not specify the nature or amount of the loan are not sufficient.[45] Non-repudiation does not amount to an admission.[46] If there is a clear admission of liability, a creditor's letter may be looked at to identify the debt.[46]

An income tax return has been held to be sufficient acknowledgment.[47]

Where the creditor holds a receipt in which a third party acknowledges a payment by the debtor, the creditor may prove *prout de jure* that the creditor made the payment from his own funds on the debtor's behalf;[48] *a fortiori* such proof is competent where the receipt bore that the payment was "per" the creditor.[49] Receipts for interest granted by the creditor have been held to be constructively the writ of the debtor.[50]

6. Reference to Oath

If the pursuer wishes to resort to proof by the oath of the defender, he must lodge a minute of reference.[51] It is important that the

38 *Burns* v. *Burns*, 1964 S.L.T.(Sh.Ct.)21.

39 *Patrick* v. *Patrick's Trs.* (1904) 6 F.836.

40 *Haldane* v. *Speirs* (1872) 10 M.537; *Dunn's Tr.* v. *Hardy* (1896) 23 R.621; *Scotland* v. *Scotland*, 1909 S.C.505; *Skiffington* v. *Dickson*, 1970 S.L.T.(Sh.Ct.)24. An unindorsed cheque which appears to have been paid by the banker on whom it is drawn is evidence of the receipt by the payee of the sum payable by the cheque: Cheques Act 1957, s.3. Payments in a current account may be vouched by indorsed cheques: *Robb* v. *Robb's Trs.* (1884) 11 R.881.

41 *A.* v. *B.C. & Co.* (1956) 72 Sh.Ct.Rep.29.

42 *Nimmo* v. *Nimmo* (1873) 11 M.446.

43 *Hope* v. *Derwent Rolling Mills Co. Ltd.* (1905) 7 F.837.

44 *Gill* v. *Gill*, 1907 S.C.532.

45 *Rutherford's Exrs.* v. *Marshall* (1861) 23 D.1276; *Morison's Trs.* v. *Mitchell*, 1925 S.L.T.231; *Inverfleet Ltd.* v. *Woelfell*, 1976 S.L.T.(Sh.Ct.)62.

46 *MacBain* v. *MacBain*, 1930 S.C.(H.L.)72 (a prescription case).

47 *Clarkson* v. *Johnston* (1934) 50 Sh.Ct.Rep.318.

48 *Fairbairn* v. *Fairbairn* (1868) 6 M.640.

49 *Brand* v. *Allan* (1913) 29 Sh.Ct.Rep.76.

50 *Wood* v. *Howden* (1843) 5 D.507; *Wilson* v. *Wilson* (1901) 17 Sh.Ct.Rep.44.

51 See Walker & Walker, *Evidence*, pp.339-341; *Muir* v. *Steven* (1896) 12 Sh.Ct.Rep.368.

minute should make clear what is referred. The effect of an oath does not, as a rule, depend on credibility. The only question for the court is *quid juratum est*.[52] The principal difficulty arises where an admission in the oath is in some way qualified. The effect of the qualification depends upon whether it is intrinsic or extrinsic. If it is intrinsic it is given effect; if it is extrinsic it is ignored. So the oath is negative if the defender admits the receipt of a sum of money from the pursuer but says that it was received as a gift,[53] or in payment of services previously rendered,[54] or in payment of a debt due for lodgings,[55] or in payment of a debt due to the defender by a third party.[56] If the defender admits the constitution of the loan but says that it was subsequently repaid or extinguished by some other method agreed upon by the parties at the time the loan was made, the oath is negative because these are treated as intrinsic qualifications.[57] On the other hand, if the constitution of the loan is admitted but the defender says that the debt was subsequently extinguished by compensation this is an extrinsic qualification and the oath is affirmative unless, it seems, the compensation was effected by an express agreement. A qualification that the debt was subsequently remitted by the creditor is intrinsic.[58]

In certain circumstances reference may be made to the oath of someone other than the alleged debtor:

(a) *Agents*—As a general rule reference cannot be made to the oath of the debtor's agent. This has been held with regard to the debtor's solicitor[59] and to a son contracting as his father's agent.[60] But it has been suggested that where the debtor has entrusted the whole conduct of his business to a general manager, reference can be made to the manager's oath.[61] Reference can be made to the wife's oath to prove the constitu-

---

[52] *Per* Lord Deas, *Cowbrough* v. *Robertson* (1879) 6 R.1301 at 1306; see, however, Walker & Walker, *op.cit.*, at p.346.

[53] *Penney* v. *Aitken*, 1927 S.C.673.

[54] *Gow's Exrs.* v. *Sim* (1866) 4 M.578.

[55] *Thomson* v. *Duncan* (1855) 17 D.1081.

[56] *Minty* v. *Donald* (1824) 3 S.394.

[57] *Newlands* v. *McKinlay* (1885) 13 R.353; *Adam's Trs.* v. *Burns* (1939) 55 Sh.Ct.Rep.196.

[58] *Galbraith* v. *Cuthbertson* (1866) 4 M.295; *Cowbrough* v. *Robertson* (1879) 6 R.1301.

[59] *Sawers* v. *Clark* (1892) 19 R.1090.

[60] *Kirkwood* v. *Wilson* (1823) 2 S.425.

[61] *Encyclopaedia of the Laws of Scotland*, Vol. X., p.400.

tion of a debt in respect of household supplies and to the husband's oath to establish resting-owing.[62]

(b) *Incapaces*—Where the debt is allegedly due by a pupil reference may be made to the oath of the tutor or factor *loco tutoris*[63] but not in relation to transactions prior to his appointment[64] or after he is *functus*.[65] But a debt allegedly due by a minor cannot be referred to the curator's oath.[66]

(c) *Executors and Trustees*—A debt incurred by the deceased cannot be proved by the oaths of his executors or trustees unless they are also the beneficiaries.[67] Debts incurred in the administration of a testamentary or public trust can, however, be referred to the oaths of the trustees.[68]

(d) *Bankrupt*—It is not competent to refer a debt to the oath of a bankrupt who is undischarged or discharged on payment of a composition.[69]

(e) *Firms and Corporate Bodies*—A debt due by a firm can be referred to the oath of a managing partner[70] but where all the partners are acting,[71] or where the firm has been dissolved,[72] the debt cannot be referred to the oath of one. It seems that reference is competent to the oath of the managing director, manager or officer of a limited company who "in some real sense represents the corporation."[73] Reference was made to the oath of the magistrates of a burgh.[74]

(f) *Co-obligants*—The oath of one co-obligant[75] or co-owner[76] binds himself alone.

(g) *Assignations*—The oath of the cedent binds the assignee before

---

62 *Mitchell* v. *Moultry* (1882) 10 R.378, *per* Lord Young at p.381.
63 Erskine, IV. 2, 10; *Hepburn* v. *Hamilton* (1661) Mor.12480.
64 *Stewart* v. *Syme*, 12 Dec. 1815, F.C.
65 *Waddel* v. *Wadderstoun* (1707) Mor.12484.
66 *Forbes* v. *Pitsligo* (1628) Mor.12479.
67 *Monteith* v. *Smith* (1624) Mor.12477; Erskine, IV, 2, 10.
68 *Murray* v. *Laurie's Trs.* (1827) 5 S.515; *Moore* v. *Young* (1843) 5 D.494.
69 *Mein* v. *Towers* (1829) 7 S.902; *Dyce* v. *Paterson* (1846) 9 D.310.
70 *Gow* v. *McDonald* (1827) 5 S.472.
71 *McNab* v. *Lockhart* (1843) 5 D.1014.
72 *Nisbet's Trs.* v. *Morrison's Trs.* (1829) 7 S.307.
73 *H. D. Rodgers & Co. Ltd.* v. *The Paradise Restaurant* (1955) 71 Sh.Ct.Rep.128; *A. Wilson (Aberdeen) Ltd.* v. *Stewart & Co. Ltd.* (1957) 73 Sh.Ct.Rep.217.
74 *Johnston* v. *Dean of Guild of Aberdeen* (1676) Mor.12480.
75 *Allan* v. *Ormiston* (1817) Hume 477.
76 *Dickson* v. *Blair* (1871) 10 M.41.

intimation but not thereafter[77] unless the debt was litigious before intimation[78] or the assignation was gratuitous.[79]

7. Consumer Credit Act

If payment of the amount of the loan is made to the borrower and the agreement is not made by the creditor under pre-existing arrangements between himself and a supplier in the knowledge that the loan is to be used to finance a transaction between the debtor and the supplier, the agreement is a debtor-creditor agreement.[80]

The rate of the total charge for credit may be such that it is an exempt agreement falling under category (14) or (16).[81]

8. Connected Lender Liability

In a debtor-creditor-supplier agreement made after 1 July 1977 in which there are "arrangements" between the creditor and the supplier (*e.g.* a credit card) if the debtor has, in relation to a transaction financed by the agreement, any claim against the supplier in respect of a misrepresentation or breach of contract, he has a like claim against the creditor who is jointly and severally liable with the supplier but has a right to be indemnified by the supplier.[82] The liability is not affected by the fact that the debtor exceeded the credit limit or otherwise contravened a term of the agreement. The provision does not apply to a non-commercial agreement nor where the claim relates to any single item to which the supplier has attached a cash price not exceeding £30 or more than £10,000. In the case cited[83] rescission of the supply contract was treated as a "claim" which affected the credit agreement; the better view is that the rescission of the supply contract gives rise to a claim for repetition and damages which can be set off against the debt due under the credit agreement.

---

[77] *Lord Pitfoddels* v. *Glenkindy* (1662) Mor.12454; *Boyd* v. *Storie* (1674) Mor.12456.

[78] *Sommerville* (1673) Mor.8325.

[79] *Steel* v. *Orbiston* (1679) Mor.8467.

[80] See Chap. 3, para. 3.

[81] See Chap. 3, para. 4.

[82] Consumer Credit Act 1974, s.75; A.S.(Sheriff Court Procedure, Consumer Credit) 1977 (S.I.1977/1180). It is possible for the section to apply to buildings: see Adams (1975) 39 *Conveyancer* 94.

[83] *United Dominions Trust* v. *Taylor,* 1980 S.L.T.(Sh.Ct.)28. See Gane [1980] J.B.L.277; Davidson (1980) 96 L.Q.R.343.

The creditor may, of course, be liable to the debtor in respect of misrepresentations made by the supplier as his deemed agent.[84]

9. Credit-Sale Agreement

A credit-sale agreement is an agreement for the sale of goods under which the price or part of it is payable by instalments but which is not a conditional sale agreement.[85] If the purchaser is not a body corporate, and the amount payable by instalments does not exceed £5,000, the agreement is a debtor-creditor-supplier agreement.[86] It may be an exempt agreement if the number of payments to be made by the debtor does not exceed four.[87]

10. Hire-Purchase and Conditional Sale

A hire-purchase agreement is an agreement, other than a conditional sale agreement, under which (a) goods are hired in return for periodical payments by the person to whom they are hired, and (b) the property in the goods will pass to that person if the terms of the agreement are complied with and one of the following occurs: (i) the exercise of an option to purchase by that person, (ii) the doing of any other specified act by any party to the agreement, (iii) the happening of any other specified event.[88]

The agreement is treated as providing fixed-sum credit to finance the transaction of an amount equal to the total price of the goods less the aggregate of the deposit (if any) and the total charge for credit.[89] A hire-purchase agreement is a debtor-creditor-supplier agreement.[90] It does not qualify as an exempt agreement.

A conditional sale agreement is a sale agreement under which the price or part of it is payable by instalments and the property in the goods is to remain in the seller (notwithstanding that the buyer is to be in possession of them) until such conditions as to the payment of instalments or otherwise as may be specified in the agreement are fulfilled.[91] If the purchaser is not a body corporate and the amount payable by instalments does not exceed £5,000 the agreement is a

---

[84] See Chap. 3, para. 14, *supra*; Fairest & Rudkin (1978) 128 N.L.J.243.
[85] See next paragraph.
[86] See Chap. 3, para. 3.
[87] See Chap. 3, para. 4 (category 9).
[88] Consumer Credit Act 1974, s.189(1).
[89] s.9(3).
[90] See Chap. 3, para. 3.
[91] s.189(1).

debtor-creditor-supplier agreement.[92] It does not qualify as an exempt agreement.

The buyer under a conditional sale agreement which is a consumer credit agreement is not to be taken as a person who has bought or agreed to buy goods for purposes of s.25(1) of the Sale of Goods Act 1979, and he thus cannot give a good title to a sub-purchaser.[93] In consequence, the differences between a hire-purchase and conditional sale under the 1974 Act are slight and most of the special regulatory provisions apply to both transactions. The "total price" under a hire-purchase or conditional sale agreement is the total sum payable thereunder, including any sum payable on the exercise of an option to purchase but excluding any sum payable as a penalty or as compensation or damages for a breach of the agreement.

The following provisions apply to both hire-purchase and conditional sale agreements:

(1) if the debtor is in breach of the agreement after he has paid one-third or more of the total price of the goods and while the goods are still the creditor's property, the creditor cannot recover possession of the goods (which in this context are "protected goods") except on an order of the court;[94] if he does take the goods without a court order, the agreement terminates, the debtor is released from all liability thereunder and is entitled to recover all sums already paid from the creditor. Where there is an installation charge specified in the agreement the one-third figure is the sum of the installation charge and one-third of the remainder of the total price. The protection does not apply if the debtor has terminated the agreement. On the debtor's death the protection continues until confirmation is expede. In certain circumstances there may be protection although one-third of the price has not been paid if there had been such payment under a prior agreement relating to the same goods or some of them.

(2) If, without a court order, the creditor enters premises to take possession of the goods, the entry is actionable as a breach of statutory duty.[95]

---

[92] See Chap. 3, para. 3.

[93] Sale of Goods Act 1979, s.25(2) (not yet in force but see Hire-Purchase (Scotland) Act 1965, s.50).

[94] Consumer Credit Act 1974, s.90.

[95] s.92.

(3) At any time before the final payment, the debtor is entitled to terminate the agreement by giving notice.[96] On termination, the debtor is liable, unless the agreement provides for a smaller payment or for no payment, to pay to the creditor the amount by which one-half of the total price exceeds the aggregate of the sums paid and the sums due in respect of the total price immediately before termination.[97] The liability may be reduced by the court to an amount representing the loss sustained by the creditor in consequence of the termination. The debtor is also liable to recompense the creditor if he has failed to take reasonable care of the goods. If the debtor wrongfully retains possession of the goods, the court may order delivery of the goods to the creditor without giving the debtor an option to pay the value of the goods. If, under a conditional sale agreement, the property in the goods has passed to the debtor and has then been transferred to a third party who did not become the debtor under the agreement, the debtor cannot terminate the agreement.[98] If the property has passed to the debtor but there has been no further transfer to a third party the debtor can terminate the agreement and the property will vest in the person who owned the goods before they became the property of the debtor.[99]

(4) The goods, if they have not become the debtor's property, are not subject to the landlord's hypothec in the period between service of a default notice and the date of its expiry or compliance with it; nor are they so subject in the period between the commencement and the termination of an action by the creditor to enforce an agreement which is enforceable on the order of a court only.[1]

(5) A time order[2] providing for instalment payments may deal with sums which, although not payable at the time of the order, would if the agreement continued become payable subsequently.[3]

(6) After the making of a time order the debtor is treated as

---

96 s.99. See *Wadham Stringer Finance Ltd.* v. *Meaney* [1980] 3 All E.R.789.

97 s.100.

98 s.99(4).

99 s.99(5).

1 s.104.

2 See Chap. 3, para. 19.

3 s.130(2).

custodier of the goods notwithstanding that the agreement has terminated.[4]

(7) In an action for an enforcement order or for a time order or for recovery of the goods, the court may make a "return order" or a "transfer order".[5] A return order is for return of the goods to the creditor. A transfer order is for the transfer to the debtor of the creditor's title to such part of the goods as seems just and the return of the remainder of the goods to the creditor. Such an order can be made only when the "paid-up sum" exceeds the part of the total price referable to the transferred goods by an amount equal to at least one-third of the unpaid balance of the total price. The "paid-up sum" is the part of the total price which has been paid with any adjustments made by the court in its discretion. Where a return order or transfer order has been made, the debtor has the option to pay the balance of the total price and on fulfilment of any other necessary conditions retain all the goods. If the debtor fails to return the goods as ordered, the court may revoke the order and order the debtor to pay the unpaid portion of so much of the total price as is referable to those goods.

(8) If, under a time, return or transfer order, the total price is paid and any other necessary conditions are fulfilled, the creditor's title to the goods vests in the debtor.[6] There is a curious provision about "adverse detention"[7] which seems to have no relevance in Scotland.

11. Consumer Hire Agreements

The hirer can terminate the agreement by giving notice but the notice cannot expire earlier than 18 months after the making of the agreement.[8] A minimum period of notice is prescribed. There is no statutory right to terminate if (a) the total annual payments exceed £300, or, (b) the goods are hired for purposes of a business carried on by the hirer or the hirer holds himself out as requiring the goods for those purposes and the goods are selected by the hirer and acquired by the owner at the hirer's request from any person other than the owner's associate, or (c) the hirer requires, or holds himself

---

[4] s.130(4).
[5] s.133.
[6] s.133(5).
[7] s.134.
[8] s.101.

out as requiring, the goods for the purpose of hiring them to other persons in the course of his business. The Director may give a dispensation from this termination provision to a person carrying on a consumer hire business.

The debtor is treated as custodier of the goods if he is in possession of them notwithstanding that the agreement has been terminated following the making of a time order.[9]

If the owner recovers possession of the goods otherwise than by action, the hirer may ask the court to order that any sums paid by the hirer in respect of the goods shall be repaid and the obligation to pay the whole or part of any sum owed by the hirer to the owner shall cease. A like provision may be made in an order for delivery of the goods.[10]

In making a suspension order, the court shall not use its powers so as to extend the period for which, under the agreement, the hirer is entitled to possession of the goods.[11]

12. Conditional Sale of land

On breach of a regulated conditional sale agreement relating to land, the creditor can recover possession of the land on an order of the court only.[12] Such an agreement cannot be terminated by the debtor after the title has passed to him.[13]

13. Credit-Tokens

A credit-token agreement is a regulated agreement for the provision of credit in connection with the use of a credit-token.[14] A credit-token is a card, check, voucher, coupon, stamp, form, booklet or other document or thing given to an individual by a person carrying on a consumer credit business, who undertakes: (a) that on production of it (whether or not some other action is also required) he will supply cash, goods and services (or any of them) on credit, or (b) that, where, on the production of it to a third party (whether or not any other action is also required) the third party supplies cash,

---

[9] s.130(4).

[10] s.132.

[11] s.135(3).

[12] s.92. As to the court's discretion when the agreement is for purchase of a dwelling-house by three or more instalments, see Tenants' Rights (Scotland) Act 1980, s.74.

[13] s.99(3).

[14] s.14(2).

goods and services (or any of them) he will pay the third party for these (whether or not deducting any discount or commission), in return for payment to him by the individual.[15] The credit is provided when the third party supplies the cash, goods or services.[16]

The debtor is liable for loss to the creditor from the use of the token by a person who possessed it with the debtor's consent.[17] The debtor is also liable to a maximum of £30 for loss to the creditor from the use of the token by persons not authorised by the debtor. Neither liability can arise from use of the token after notice of the loss or theft of the token has been given orally (in which case written confirmation may be required), or in writing, to the creditor at an address stated in the agreement. If the debtor avers that any use was unauthorised, the onus is on the creditor to prove that the use was authorised or that the use occurred before notice had been given to the creditor.[18] Except in the case of a small agreement, on the renewal of a token, the creditor must give the debtor a copy of the executed agreement and of any document referred to in it; the agreement cannot be enforced during default.[19]

---

[15] s.14(1); *Elliott* v. *Director General of Fair Trading* [1980] 1 W.L.R.977; *R.* v. *Lambie* [1981] 3 W.L.R.88.

[16] s.14(3).

[17] s.84.

[18] s.171(4)(*b*).

[19] s.85.

CHAPTER 5

BONDS AND BILLS

1. Bond

"A bond in Scots law, is—broadly—neither more nor less than a written obligation to pay or perform."[1] The essential part of a bond for money is "an engagement, absolutely or conditionally, at a day certain or in a specified event, to pay a definite sum of money."[2] A clause of registration for execution is not a requisite.[3] The document must be attested or holograph.[4]

The most important characteristic of a bond is that the holder "need not concern himself with the debt for which it was granted, so long as the instrument retains its virtue—for he sues on it, and not on the debt, while the holder of a mere acknowledgment of debt must sue on the debt with the acknowledgment as evidence, which may be sufficient or not, according to circumstances, whether *per se* or aided by other evidence."[5]

2. Negotiable Instruments

The characteristics of a negotiable instrument are (a) "when transferred it passes in its own *corpus* the thing it represents without intimation"[6], (b) a good title is acquired by a party who takes it bona fide for value, notwithstanding any defect of title in the party from whom it is so taken.[7] It can be contrasted with other documents of debt in that assignation followed by intimation is not required to transfer it and the maxim *assignatus utitur jure auctoris* does not apply. A document may be transferable by indorsation and yet not negotiable[6]—a deposit receipt, for example.[8] A bill of lading can be transferred by delivery but it does not always give the transferee a

---

[1] *North of Scotland Bank* v. *Inland Revenue*, 1931 S.C.149, *per* L.P. Clyde at p.154.

[2] Bell, *Comm.*, I, 352.

[3] *Purdie* v. *Hamilton* (1900) 8 S.L.T.83.

[4] Bell, *Comm.*, I, 352.

[5] *Neilson's Trs.* v. *Neilson's Trs.* (1883) 11 R.119, *per* Lord Young at p.123.

[6] *Per* Lord Neaves, *Connal & Co.* v. *Loder* (1868) 6 M.1095 at 1102.

[7] *Crouch* v. *Credit Foncier of England Ltd.* (1873) 8 Q.D.B.374.

[8] *Wood* v. *Clydesdale Bank Ltd.*, 1914 S.C.397.

better title than that of the transferor.[9] Debenture bonds payable to bearer are negotiable instruments.[10]

A document acquires the privilege of negotiability only by statute or by mercantile usage and the parties themselves cannot make a document negotiable.[11]

3. Definition of a Bill

Bills of exchange, "the simplest of all obligations in form, and the least trammelled with solemnities, are, in respect of performance, the most strict, and in execution the most rapid, of all the obligations known in law."[12] A bill of exchange[13] is an unconditional order in writing, addressed by one person to another, signed by the person giving it,[14] requiring the person to whom it is addressed to pay on demand, or at a fixed or determinable future time, a sum certain in money to or to the order of a specified person, or to bearer. A bill is payable to bearer which is expressed to be so payable or on which the only or last indorsement is an indorsement in blank.[15] No stamp is required now.[16] The person who gives the order is the *drawer;* the person to whom the order is addressed is the *drawee;* and the specified person to whom the money is to be paid is the *payee*.

Polite expressions such as "please" do not mean that the document is not an order.[17] A document which orders an act to be done in addition to the payment of money is not a bill.[18] An order to pay out of a particular fund is not unconditional but an unqualified order to pay, coupled with (a) an indication of a particular fund out of which the drawee is to reimburse himself, or a particular account to be debited with the amount, or (b) a statement of the transaction which gives rise to the bill, is unconditional.[19]

The drawee must be named or indicated with reasonable certainty.[20] There may be two or more drawees but not in the

---

[9] *Simmons* v. *London Joint Stock Bank* [1891] 1 Ch.270.

[10] *Bechuanaland Exploration Co.* v. *London Trading Bank Ltd.* [1898] 2 Q.B.658; *Edelstein* v. *Schuler & Co.* [1902] 2 K.B.144.

[11] *Dixon* v. *Bovill* (1856) 3 Macq. 1.

[12] Bell, *Comm.*, I, 411.

[13] Bills of Exchange Act 1882, s.3(1).

[14] A mark attested by witnesses is sufficient but not effectual for summary diligence: *Adair* v. *Cunningham* (1887) 4 Sh.Ct.Rep.51.

[15] s.8(3). As to foreign bills, see ss.4, 51, 72.

[16] Finance Act 1970, Sched. 7, para. 2.

[17] *Provost of Airdrie* v. *French* (1915) 31 Sh.Ct.Rep.189.

[18] s.3(2).

[19] s.3(3).

[20] s.6(1).

alternative nor in succession.[21] If the drawer and the drawee are the same person or the drawee is fictitious or is *incapax*, the holder may treat the instrument, at his option, as a bill or as a promissory note.[22]

If the bill is not payable to bearer, the payee must be named or indicated with reasonable certainty.[23] There may be joint payees or the bill may be payable in the alternative to one of two, or one or some of several payees. A bill may be payable to the holder of an office for the time being.[24] If the payee is a fictitious or non-existing person the bill may be treated as payable to bearer.[25] An order "Pay Cash or Order" is not a bill.[26]

A sum "together with any interest that may accrue thereon" is not certain.[27] A sum is certain although it is to be paid with interest or by instalments, by instalments with a provision that on default the whole will become due, or at an indicated rate of exchange or rate to be ascertained as directed. Where there is a discrepancy between words and figures, the sum denoted by words is the amount payable.[28]

A bill is payable on demand if it is expressed to be payable on demand, or at sight or on presentation or in which no time of payment is expressed.[29] A bill is payable at a determinable future time if it is expressed to be payable at a fixed period after date or sight or on or at a fixed period after the occurrence of a specified event which is certain to happen, though the time of happening may be uncertain.[30] An instrument expressed to be payable on a contingency is not a bill.

The bill is due and payable in all cases on the last day of the time of payment as fixed by the bill or, if that is a non-business day, on the succeeding business day. There are now no days of grace.[31] Non-business days are Saturday, Sunday, Good Friday, Christmas

---

21 s.6(2). As to a referee in case of need, see s.15.

22 s.5(2).

23 s.7(1). The bill may be payable to, or to the order of, the drawer or drawee: s.5(1).

24 s.7(2).

25 s.7(3), See Byles, pp.24-27.

26 *Orbit Mining & Trading Co. Ltd.* v. *Westminster Bank Ltd.* [1963] 1 Q.B.794.

27 *Lamberton* v. *Aiken* (1899) 2 F.189. But see Chalmers, p.29; *cf.* Byles, p.18.

28 s.9. Bills and notes (other than cheques) for sums less than £1 are prohibited in Scotland: Bank Notes (Scotland) Act 1845, ss.16, 20.

29 s.10(1).

30 s.11. The fixed period is calculated by excluding the day from which it runs and including the day of payment: s.14(2).

31 s.14(1) as substituted by Banking and Financial Dealings Act 1971, s.3(2).

Day, a bank holiday and a day appointed as a public fast or thanksgiving day.[32]

A bill is not invalid by reason that it is not dated, that it does not specify the value given or that any value has been given therefor or that it does not specify the place where it is payable.[33] The usual procedure is that the drawer delivers the bill to the payee who may present it to the drawee for acceptance. The drawee, if he is prepared to obey the order, normally accepts the bill by writing "accepted" across its face and signing his name beneath; but a mere signature is sufficient.[34] The drawee, who becomes by his acceptance the *acceptor,* returns the bill to the payee. On the day the bill falls due the payee presents the bill to the acceptor for payment and receives the sum due.

If the bill is payable at sight or on demand, presentment for acceptance is obviously unnecessary; if the bill is payable at a fixed period after sight, or if the bill expressly stipulates that it shall be presented for acceptance, or if it is payable elsewhere than at the residence or place of business of the drawee, presentment for acceptance is necessary;[35] in other cases, presentment for acceptance is optional but it is advantageous in that it obtains the drawee's liability on the bill.

4. Negotiation

The payee may *negotiate* the bill if (a) it is expressed to be payable to order, (b) it is payable to a particular person and does not contain words prohibiting transfer or indicating an intention that it should not be transferable, (c) it is expressed to be payable to bearer.[36] In cases (a) and (b) the bill is negotiated by the payee's indorsing it, *i.e.,* placing his signature on the bill and delivering it to the *indorsee.*[37] The indorsement may be *special, i.e.,* it may specify the person to whom or to whose order the bill is to be payable; or it may

---

32 s.92.

33 s.3(4). The holder may insert a date: s.12.

34 s.17.

35 s.39.

36 s.8. An intention that the bill should not be transferable is evinced by the words "Pay X only" or, in the case of a bill other than a cheque, "Not Negotiable": *Hibernian Bank Ltd.* v. *Gysin and Hanson* [1939] 1 K.B. 483, but see Byles, p.74, as to that decision.

37 ss.31, 32. See, as to indorsement on the back of the document, *K. H. R. Financings Ltd.* v. *Jackson,* 1977 S.L.T.(Sh.Ct.)6. As to restrictive and conditional indorsements, see ss.31(5), 33 and 35.

be *in blank, i.e.* specify no indorsee, in which case it becomes payable to bearer.[38] A bill expressed to be payable to bearer is negotiated by delivery.[39] The payee or indorsee of a bill who is in possession of it or the person in possession of a bill which is payable to bearer is a holder.[40] The holder is in right of the bill and can present it for acceptance, if that has not been done already, and present it for payment; he can also, of course, negotiate the bill further.

5. Dishonour

If the bill is dishonoured by non-acceptance, *i.e.*, if the drawee refuses to accept it, an immediate right of recourse against the drawer and indorsers accrues to the holder and he need not present the bill for payment.[41] A similar right accrues to the holder where a bill is dishonoured by non-payment, *i.e.* when payment is refused or cannot be obtained;[42] here, of course, the holder may have a right against the acceptor as well. In all cases of dishonour by non-acceptance or non-payment, the holder, to preserve his right of recourse, must give notice of dishonour to the drawer and to each indorser; a drawer or indorser to whom notice is not given is discharged.[43] Further, if the bill is to be enforced by summary diligence against any of the parties liable thereon it must be protested for non-acceptance or non-payment, as the case may be.[44] An indorser who has been compelled to pay the bill may in his turn seek payment from the drawer or any prior indorsers, provided that he has given notice of dishonour to them.[45] A drawer who has been compelled to pay the bill can enforce payment of it against the acceptor.[46]

6. Liability

It will therefore be seen that no one is liable on a bill unless his

---

[38] s.34.
[39] s.31(2).
[40] s.2.
[41] s.43. The drawee may be liable to the holder by virtue of the assignation effected under s.53(2)—See Chap. 6, paras. 6, 8.
[42] s.47. As to acceptance and payment for honour, see ss.65-68.
[43] s.48.
[44] See Chap. 17, para. 6.
[45] s.55. See also s.49(14).
[46] s.59(2) (unless it is an accommodation bill: s.59(3)).

signature appears thereon as acceptor, drawer or indorser.[47] A *transferor by delivery, i.e.* a holder of a bill payable to bearer who has negotiated it by delivery without indorsing it, is not liable on the bill.[48] The acceptor is the party primarily liable and the drawer and indorsers have a secondary liability in the event of dishonour.

A document in the form of a bill which bears the signature of the acceptor, but not that of the drawer, is not a valid bill but it is evidence of the acceptor's indebtedness to the person to whom he had delivered it.[49]

7. Accommodation Bills

For the purpose of lending his name to some other person, a person may sign a bill as drawer, acceptor, or indorser without receiving value therefor. For example, the drawee may accept a bill although he in fact does not owe money to the drawer. Such a person is known as an "accommodation party".[50] An accommodation party is liable on the bill to a holder for value even if the holder for value, when he took the bill, knew that he was an accommodation party.[51] The accommodation party is not, however, liable in a question with the accommodated party and the true relationship of the parties *inter se* can be proved by parole evidence.[52]

8. Enforcement by Action; Lost Bills

The holder,[53] or a transferee for value,[54] can sue on the bill in his own name. Where a bill has been lost before it is overdue, the person who was the holder of it may apply to the drawer to give him another bill of the same tenor, giving security to the drawer if required to indemnify him against all persons whatever in case the bill alleged to have been lost shall be found again.[55] If the drawer on request refuses to give such a duplicate bill, he may be compelled to

---

47 s.23; a person who signs a bill otherwise than as drawer or acceptor thereby incurs the liabilities of an indorser to a holder in due course (s.56); such a signature is called an "aval".

48 s.58.

49 *Lawson's Exrs.* v. *Watson*, 1907 S.C.1353.

50 s.28(1); *McLelland* v. *Mackay* (1908) 24 Sh.Ct.Rep.157.

51 s.28(2); he is also liable to a transferee for value: *Hood* v. *Stewart* (1890) 17 R.749; the accommodation is not a defect: *Downie* v. *Saunders' Trs.* (1898) 6 S.L.T.134.

52 *Nicol's Trs.* v. *Sutherland*, 1951 S.C.(H.L.) 21, *pèr* Lord Simonds at p.27.

53 s.38(1).

54 s.31(4); *Hood* v. *Stewart* (1890) 17 R.749.

55 s.69.

do so. In any action or proceeding upon a bill, the court may order that the loss of the instrument shall not be set up, provided an indemnity be given to the satisfaction of the court against the claims of any other person upon the instrument in question.[56]

9. Holder in Due Course

A holder in due course is a holder who has taken a bill, complete and regular on the face of it,[57] under the following conditions:

(a) that he became the holder of it before it was overdue, and without notice that it had been previously dishonoured, if such was the fact;

(b) that he took the bill in good faith and for value, and that at the time the bill was negotiated to him he had no notice of any defect in the title of the person who negotiated it.[58] The title of the person who negotiated the bill is defective if he obtained the bill, or the acceptance thereof, by fraud, duress, or force and fear, or other unlawful means, or for an illegal consideration or if he negotiated it in breach of faith or under such circumstances as amount to a fraud.[59]

Value may be constituted by "any consideration sufficient to support a simple contract", or by an antecedent debt or liability.[60] If the holder has a lien on the bill, by contract or implication of law, he is deemed to be a holder for value to the extent of the sum for which he has a lien.[61] Once value has been given for a bill the holder is deemed to be a holder for value as regards the acceptor and all parties to the bill who became parties prior to such time.[62] Every party whose signature appears on a bill is prima facie deemed to have become a party thereto for value.[63]

A holder in due course holds the bill free from any defect of title of prior parties as well as from mere personal defences available to prior parties among themselves, and may enforce payment against all parties liable on the bill.[64]

---

56 s.70; see *Enever* v. *Craig*, 1913 2 S.L.T.30.

57 "Looking at the bill, front and back, without the aid of outside evidence, it must be complete and regular in itself", *per* Denning L.J., *Arab Bank Ltd.* v. *Ross* [1952] 2 Q.B.216 at 226.

58 s.29(1). As to a bill drawn in a set, see s.71.

59 s.29(2); the list of defects is perhaps not exhaustive: Chalmers, p.98.

60 s.27(1).

61 s.27(3).

62 s.27(2).

63 s.30(1).

64 s.38(2).

Every holder of a bill is prima facie deemed to be a holder in due course, but if in an action on the bill it is admitted or proved that the acceptance, issue, or subsequent negotiation of the bill is affected with fraud, duress, or force and fear, or illegality, the burden of proof is shifted, unless and until the holder proves that, subsequent to the alleged fraud or illegality, value has in good faith been given for the bill.[65] Except where an indorsement bears a date after the maturity of the bill, every negotiation is prima facie deemed to have been effected before the bill was overdue.[66]

A holder (whether for value or not) who derives his title through a holder in due course, and who is not himself a party to any fraud or illegality affecting it, has all the rights of that holder in due course as regards the acceptor, and all parties to the bill prior to that holder.[67] So, if the bill is negotiated by a holder in due course back to the drawer, the latter has the rights of a holder in due course.[68] The same would apply to a payee, to whom the bill had been negotiated by a holder in due course.

The payee as such, although he is a holder,[69] is not a holder in due course because the bill has not been "negotiated" to him as required by s.29(1)[70] and he is not affected by the provisions of s.30(2) of the Act.[71] As regards the drawer, the payee is merely in the position of the holder of a writ *in re mercatoria* which bears the grantor's signature and which *ex facie* records an obligation of the grantor to the holder.[72]

A person to whom an overdue bill is negotiated acquires it subject to any defect of title affecting it at its maturity and cannot acquire or give a better title than that which the person from whom he took it has.[73] A demand bill is overdue for this purpose when it appears on the face of it to have been in circulation for an unreasonable length of time.

Where a bill which is not overdue has been dishonoured, any person who takes it with notice of dishonour takes it subject to any defect of title attaching to it at the time of dishonour.[74]

---

65 s.30(2).
66 s.36(4).
67 s.29(3).
68 *Jade International* v. *Robert Nicholas Ltd.* [1978] Q.B.917.
69 s.2.
70 *R.E. Jones Ltd.* v. *Waring and Gillow Ltd.* [1926] A.C.670.
71 *Talbot* v. *Von Boris* [1911] 1 K.B.854.
72 *Thompson* v. *J. Barke and Company (Caterers) Ltd.*, 1975 S.L.T.67.
73 s.36(2).
74 s.36(5).

10. Forgery

The person against whom the bill is being enforced may deny that he signed it. The onus of proving that a signature is genuine is on the person founding on the bill.[75] However, a person may bar himself by his conduct from relying on the forgery, as where he has said that the signature was his or has failed to notify interested parties once the forgery has come to his knowledge.[76]

11. Ultra Vires

A cheque drawn on the account of a company by two directors in order to repay a personal debt of one of them was held to be not enforceable by the payee against the company because the circumstances of its issue were such as to put him on his inquiry.[77]

12. Unauthorised Signature

Even if the defender did not himself write his name on the bill, he may have to meet an allegation that the name was written by his agent acting within the scope of his authority.

13. Agency

Liability on a bill may be incurred through an agent. The principal's name must be written on the bill before he can be liable and, although it is provided that no one can be liable on a bill unless he has signed it,[78] there is a further provision that the signature may be written by another person by authority of the first.[79] Accordingly, the agent may write his principal's name on the bill and, if this is within his actual or ostensible authority, the principal will be liable. Alternatively, there may be a *per procurationem* signature, *i.e.* the agent signs "pp. Jones & Co., James Smith" or uses expressions such as "on behalf of" or "for".[80] Such a signature operates as notice that the agent has but a limited authority to sign and the principal is only bound if the agent was acting within the actual

---

[75] *McIntyre* v. *National Bank of Scotland,* 1910 S.C.150.

[76] s.24; *Brook* v. *Hook* (1871) L.R.6 Ex.89; *Greenwood* v. *Martins' Bank Ltd.* [1933] A.C.51; see also *McKenzie* v. *British Linen Co.* (1881) 8 R.(H.L.)8; *British Linen Co.* v. *Cowan* (1906) 8 F.704.

[77] *Thompson* v. *J. Barke and Company (Caterers) Ltd., supra.*

[78] s.23; but a person who signs a trade or assumed name is liable as if he had signed his own name.

[79] s.91(1).

[80] Byles (p.59) suggests that a "signature by procuration" under s.25 of the Act requires a formal procuration or power of attorney.

limits of his authority.[81] If the agent merely signs his own name followed by words indicating that he is an agent but not disclosing the principal's name, the principal is not liable even if the party transacting with the agent knew his identity.[82]

There is one exceptional situation in which the principal may be liable even although his name is not written on the bill. Where the bill is drawn on the principal, and the agent, acting within his authority, accepts it in his own name, with representative words added, it seems that the principal is liable.[83]

The agent's authority can be proved by parole evidence.[84] If the signature is unauthorised it is wholly inoperative and no right to retain the bill or to give a discharge therefor or to enforce payment thereof against any party thereto can be acquired through or under the signature,[85] but (a) the signature may be ratified if it does not amount to a forgery, (b) the party against whom it is sought to retain or enforce payment may be precluded from setting up the lack of authority, (c) the acceptor cannot deny to a holder in due course the drawer's authority to draw,[86] (d) an indorser cannot deny to a holder in due course the regularity in all respects of the drawer's signature and of all previous indorsements.[87]

The signature of a firm name is equivalent to the signatures of all the persons liable as partners.[88] A bill or promissory note is deemed to have been signed on behalf of a company if it is signed in the name of, or by or on behalf or on account of, the company by any person acting under its authority.[89] If the company's articles provide that one director may be authorised by the board to sign bills on behalf of the company, a party transacting with the company is not bound to inquire whether the power was in fact granted.[90] The secretary of a company may be presumed to have authority to sign bills on its behalf.[91]

[81] s.25; as to *per procurationem* signatures generally, see *L.C.C.* v. *Agricultural Food Products Ltd.* [1955] 2 Q.B.218; *Morison* v. *London County and Westminster Bank Ltd.* [1914] 3 K.B.356.

[82] Chalmers, p.68.

[83] Bowstead, *Agency* (14th ed., 1976) p.268; Powell, *Law of Agency* (2nd ed., 1961), p.183.

[84] Thorburn, p.27.

[85] s.24.

[86] s.54(2).

[87] s.55(2).

[88] s.23(2).

[89] Companies Act 1948, s.33.

[90] *Dresdner Bank* v. *Wolfson & Sons Ltd.* (1928) 44 Sh.Ct.Rep.262.

[91] *Commercial Bank* v. *Fraser Ross & Co. Ltd.* (1906) 22 Sh.Ct.Rep.169.

14. Personal Liability of Agent

In certain circumstances a person who has intended to sign a bill as an agent is personally liable thereon. He is not liable if his name is not written on the bill. As a general rule, he is not liable if he has added words to his signature indicating that he signs for and on behalf of a principal, or in a representative character.[92] But the mere addition to the signature of words describing him as an agent, or as filling a representative character—"a description for the purpose merely of showing who he is and how he came to sign"[93]—does not exempt him from personal liability. So the addition of "director" followed by the company name is not sufficient to elide liability;[94] It is necessary to use an expression such as "on behalf of"[95] or "for and on behalf of Jones as agent."[96] The construction most favourable to the validity of the instrument is adopted.[97]

There is a doubt about the effect of words which clearly indicate that the signature is as an agent but which do not disclose the principal's name.[98]

Where the bill is drawn on the agent and the agent accepts it by writing the principal's name thereon, it seems that neither is liable because only the drawee can accept;[99] if such a bill is accepted by the agent's signing his own name, the principal is obviously not liable and the agent obviously is;[1] if such a bill is accepted by the agent's signing his own name followed by words indicating that the acceptance is on behalf of the principal, it seems that the principal is not liable and the question of the agent's liability is in doubt.[2]

Where the bill is drawn on the principal and the agent accepts by signing his own name without qualification, it seems that the agent is not liable.[3]

---

92 1882 Act, s.26(1).

93 *per* Scrutton L.J., *Elliott* v. *Bax-Ironside* [1925] 2 K.B.301 at 307.

94 *Brebner* v. *Henderson,* 1925 S.C.643; see also *Brown* v. *Sutherland* (1875) 2 R.615; *McMeekin* v. *Easton* (1889) 16 R.363; *Landes* v. *Marcus* (1909) 25 T.L.R.478; *Kettle* v. *Dunster* (1928) 138 L.T.158.

95 *per* Lord Sands, *Brebner* v. *Henderson, supra,* at p.648. See also *Rolfe Lubell & Co.* v. *Keith* [1979] 1 All E.R.860.

96 *per* Scrutton L.J., *Elliott* v. *Bax-Ironside, supra,* at p.307.

97 s.26(2).

98 Powell, *op.cit.*, p.251.

99 Bowstead, *op.cit.*, p.364; Chalmers, *op.cit.*, p.42.

1 ss.23, 26.

2 Bowstead, *op.cit.*, p.364; Powell, *op.cit.*, p.251; *cf. Encyclopaedia of the Laws of Scotland,* Vol. II., p.245.

3 Bowstead, *op.cit.*, p.364.

An agent who signs as agent a bill outwith his authority is not personally liable on the bill.[4]

If an officer of a company or any person on its behalf signs or authorises to be signed on behalf of the company any bill, promissory note, endorsement or cheque wherein the company's name is not correctly stated in legible characters, he is personally liable to the holder of the bill, note or cheque for the amount thereof unless it is duly paid by the company;[5] liability may be elided if the incorrect wording was written by the person enforcing the bill.[6]

15. Delivery

If the bill is in the hands of a holder in due course a valid delivery of the bill by all parties prior to him so as to make them liable to him is conclusively presumed.[7]

If the bill is in the hands of an immediate party or a remote party who is not a holder in due course, it is a defence that delivery was not made by or under the authority of the party drawing, accepting, or indorsing as the case may be.[8] Where, however, the bill is no longer in the possession of a party who has signed it as drawer, acceptor or indorser, a valid and unconditional delivery by him is presumed until the contrary is proved.[9] It is also a defence to show that the delivery was conditional or for a special purpose only and not for the purpose of transferring the property in the bill.[10] Such a condition can be proved by parole evidence.[11]

Although the general rule is that every contract on a bill—the drawer's, the acceptor's, or an indorser's—is incomplete and revocable until delivery to give effect thereto, if an acceptance is written on a bill and the drawee gives notice to or according to the directions of the person entitled to the bill that he has accepted it, the acceptance then becomes complete and irrevocable.[12]

---

4 Bowstead, *op.cit.*, p.364.

5 Companies Act 1948, s.108(4); *Scottish and Newcastle Breweries Ltd.* v. *Blair*, 1967 S.L.T.72; *British Airways* v. *Parish* [1979] 2 Lloyd's Rep.361.

6 *Durham Fancy Goods Ltd.* v. *Michael Jackson (Fancy Goods) Ltd.* [1968] 2 Q.B.839.

7 1882 Act, s.21(2); but see *Encyclopaedia of the Laws of Scotland*, Vol. II., p.212.

8 s.21(2).

9 s.21(3).

10 s.21(2).

11 *Semple* v. *Kyle* (1902) 4 F.421; s.100.

12 s.21(1).

16. Fraud or Force and Fear

These are not defences against a holder in due course,[13] but if it is proved that the acceptance, issue or subsequent negotiation of a bill was affected with fraud, or force and fear, the burden of proof is shifted unless and until the holder proves that, subsequently, value was in good faith given for the bill.[14]

They are defences against an immediate party or a remote party who is not a holder in due course.[15]

17. Incapacity

Intoxication is not a defence unless it amounts to loss of reason.[16]

18. Absence of Consideration

Non-onerosity is not *per se* a defence.[17] A bill granted as a gift is valid.[18] Failure of the consideration may constitute a defence in a question with an immediate party but not against a holder in due course. So, where a bill had been accepted for the price of goods, and the goods were subsequently rejected, the seller's agent could not enforce payment.[19] Where a bill had been granted in terms of an agreement to form a partnership, and the contract was subsequently resiled from, it was held that the consideration could be impeached by parole evidence.[20]

19. Agreements Qualifying Obligation

Agreements qualifying the obligation on the bill are ineffectual unless they can be proved by writ or oath. This rule is not affected by the terms of s.100 which provides that any fact relating to a bill which is relevant to any question of liability thereon may be proved by parole evidence. So where the holder sued the drawer it was held incompetent for the defender to prove by parole evidence an

---

[13] s.38(2); by the former law of Scotland force and fear was a defence even in a question with a holder in due course and the extent of the change made by the Act has been questioned: Thorburn, p.83; *Encyclopaedia of the Laws of Scotland,* Vol. II., p.210; as to fraud, see *Clydesdale & North of Scotland Bank Ltd.* v. *Diamond* (1963) 79 Sh.Ct.Rep.145.

[14] s.30(2); *Nelson* v. *Easdale Slate Quarries Co. Ltd.*, 1910 1 S.L.T.21.

[15] *Ayres* v. *Moore* [1940] 1 K.B.278 (fraud).

[16] *Laing* v. *Taylor,* 1978 S.L.T.(Sh.Ct.)59.

[17] *Law* v. *Humphrey* (1876) 3 R.1192.

[18] Thorburn, p.76.

[19] *Wallace & Brown* v. *Robinson Fleming & Co.* (1885) 22 S.L.R.830.

[20] *Pert* v. *Bruce,* 1937 S.L.T.475.

arrangement that the acceptor alone would be liable on the bill;[21] where bills had been granted for the price of goods in terms of a written agreement it was held incompetent to prove parole a verbal agreement that the bills were to be renewed at maturity if the goods had not been delivered by then;[22] and, in an action by the holder against the acceptor, the averment of an agreement that the bill was not to be demandable until the indorser had raised "sufficient working capital" was held to be irrelevant.[23] It seems that a customer can prove by parole evidence that a bill was indorsed to his bank only for purposes of collection and not with the intention of transferring the property in the bill.[24]

20. Illegality

In a question with an immediate party or a remote party other than a holder in due course it is a valid defence that the bill was granted for an illegal consideration. It is not a defence against a holder in due course,[25] but if it is admitted or proved that the acceptance, issue or negotiation of the bill is affected with illegality, the burden of proof is shifted unless and until the holder proves that, subsequently, value was in good faith given for the bill.[26]

21. Forgery of Another Party's Signature

The person against whom the bill is being enforced may claim that the signature of some other party is not genuine. For example, the acceptor may claim that an indorsement has been forged. If a signature is forged, it is wholly inoperative and no right to retain the bill or to give a discharge therefor or to enforce payment against any party thereto can be acquired through or under that signature.[27] If payment has been made, it can be recovered.[28] It is doubtful if a

---

21 *National Bank of Australasia* v. *Turnbull & Co.* (1891) 18 R.629. Acceptors cannot prove that they are merely cautioners: *Exchange Loan Co.* v. *McAweeny* (1907) 24 Sh.Ct.Rep.217.

22 *Stagg & Robson Ltd.* v. *Stirling*, 1908 S.C.675; see also *Gibson's Trs.* v. *Galloway* (1896) 23 R.414. *Drybrough & Co. Ltd.* v. *Roy* (1903) 5 F.665, was disapproved in *Nicol's Trs.* v. *Sutherland*, 1951 S.C.(H.L.)21.

23 *Manchester & Liverpool District Banking Co.* v. *Ferguson & Co.* (1905) 7 F.865.

24 *Clydesdale Bank* v. *Liqrs. of James Allan Senior & Son*, 1926 S.C.235.

25 s.38(2); Gloag, p.589.

26 s.30(2); for a case where the burden of proof was not discharged, see *Tyler* v. *Maxwell* (1892) 30 S.L.R.583.

27 s.24.

28 *London & River Plate Bank Ltd.* v. *Bank of Liverpool* [1896] 1 Q.B.7. See also *Alexander Beith Ltd.* v. *Allan*, 1861 S.L.T.(Notes)80.

forged signature can be ratified.[29] There are, however, certain circumstances in which a person against whom the bill is being enforced may be precluded from setting up a forgery; (a) the acceptor cannot deny the genuineness of the drawer's signature to a holder in due course; but if the bill is payable to the drawer's order, he can dispute the genuineness of the drawer's indorsement; and if the bill is payable to the order of a third party he can dispute the genuineness of the indorsement;[30] (b) an indorser cannot deny to a holder in due course the genuineness of the drawer's signature and of all previous indorsements;[31] (c) if the person has barred himself by his conduct from relying on the forgery as where he has failed to notify interested parties once the forgery has come to his knowledge.[32] A further possible exception to the general rule arises where the payee is a fictitious or non-existing person. The bill may then be treated as payable to bearer and the authenticity of the indorsement is consequently of no account.[33]

22. Payment

The bill is discharged if the drawee or acceptor, or someone on his behalf, makes payment in due course, *i.e.* payment at or after the maturity of the bill to the holder thereof in good faith and without notice that his title to the bill is defective.[34] So if a bank pays a cheque drawn on it when the grantor has no funds at credit, it cannot sue the grantor on the cheque as a document of debt.[35] Payment by a drawer or indorser, however, does not discharge the bill. If a bill payable to, or to the order of, a third party is paid by the drawer, he may enforce the bill against the acceptor but cannot re-issue the bill.[36] If a bill is paid by the indorser, or if a bill payable to the drawer's order is paid by the drawer, the party paying it is remitted to his former rights as regards the acceptor or antecedent

---

[29] Chalmers, p.74; *cf. McKenzie* v. *British Linen Co.* (1881) 8 R.(H.L.)8.

[30] s.54(2).

[31] s.55(2).

[32] s.24; *Brook* v. *Hook*, (1871) L.R.6 Ex.89; *Greenwood* v. *Martins' Bank Ltd.* [1933] A.C.51; see also *McKenzie* v. *British Linen Co.* (1881) 8 R.(H.L.)8; *British Linen Co.* v. *Cowan* (1906) 8 F.704.

[33] s.7(3). See Byles, pp.24-27.

[34] s.59(1). As to discharge by waiver, cancellation and material alteration, see ss.62-64.

[35] *Coats* v. *Union Bank of Scotland*, 1929 S.C.(H.L.)114.

[36] s.59(2)(*a*).

parties and he may, if he thinks fit, strike out his own and subsequent indorsements and again negotiate the bill.[37] Where an accommodation bill is paid in due course by the party accommodated the bill is discharged.[38]

Notwithstanding the terms of s.100,[39] it is not competent to prove payment by parole evidence; proof *scripto vel juramento* is required.[40] The debtor's possession of the bill raises a presumption of payment.[41]

23. Prescription

A bill of exchange is subject to the quinquennial and vicennial prescriptions but in neither case is the running of the prescriptive period subject to interruption by an acknowledgment of the subsistence of the obligation.[42] The *terminus a quo* is the date when the obligation became enforceable. Under the prior law the *terminus a quo* was the date when the bill was "exigible" and it would seem that the former rules still apply; if the bill is payable on demand the *terminus* is the date of the bill, if the bill is payable at a specified period after sight, it is the date of demand for payment; if the bill is payable at a fixed future date, it is the date when the bill is due; if acceptance is refused it runs from the date of refusal.[43]

24. Not Presented for Acceptance

If a bill payable after sight is negotiated, the holder must either present it for acceptance or negotiate it within a reasonable time. If he does not do so, the drawer and all indorsers prior to that holder are discharged.[44] The presentment must be made by or on behalf of the holder to the drawee or to some person authorised to accept or refuse acceptance on his behalf at a reasonable hour on a business day and before the bill is overdue. If there are two or more drawees,

---

37 s.59(2)(*b*).

38 s.59(3).

39 The section allows "any fact relating to a bill of exchange . . . which is relevant to any question of liability thereon" to be proved by parole evidence.

40 *Nicol's Trs.* v. *Sutherland*, 1951 S.C.(H.L.)21.

41 Erskine, III, 4, 5.

42 Prescription and Limitation (Scotland) Act 1973, ss.6(1), 7(1). Sched. 1, para. 1(*e*).

43 *ibid*, s.6(3); *Broddelius* v. *Grischotti* (1887) 14 R.536; *Stephenson* v. *Stephenson's Trs.* (1807) Mor. "Bill of Exchange" Appx. No. 20; *Ferguson* v. *Douglas* (1796) 3 Pat.App.503; Thomson, p.462.

44 1882 Act, s.40.

who are not partners, presentment must be made to them all, unless one has authority to accept for all, in which case presentment may be made to him only. If the drawee is dead, presentment may be made to his personal representative; where the drawee is bankrupt, presentment may be made to him or to his trustee. A presentment through the post office is sufficient where authorised by agreement or usage.[45]

Where the holder of a bill, drawn payable elsewhere than at the place of business or residence of the drawee, has not time, with the exercise of reasonable diligence, to present the bill for acceptance before presenting it for payment on the day that it falls due, the delay caused by presenting the bill for acceptance before presenting it for payment is excused and does not discharge the drawer and indorsers.[46] Presentment is excused where (a) the drawee is dead or bankrupt or is a fictitious person or a person not having capacity to contract by bill, (b) after the exercise of reasonable diligence presentment cannot be effected, (c) although the presentment has been irregular, acceptance has been refused on some other ground.[47] The fact that the holder has reason to believe that the bill, on presentment, will be dishonoured does not excuse presentment.[48]

25. Not Presented for Payment

If a bill is not duly presented for payment the drawer and indorsers are discharged.[49] Presentment must be made on the day the bill falls due; if the bill is payable on demand presentment must be made a reasonable time after its issue to render the drawer liable and within a reasonable time after its indorsement to render the indorser liable.[50] Presentment must be made by the holder or some person authorised on his behalf at a reasonable hour on a business day at the proper place either to the person designated by the bill as payer or to some person authorised to pay or refuse payment on his behalf if with the exercise of reasonable diligence such person can there be found.[51] If the bill is drawn upon or accepted by two or more persons

---

45 s.41(1).
46 s.39(4).
47 s.41(2).
48 s.41(3).
49 s.45.
50 s.45(1), (2); see as to the due date s.14 and, as to a reasonable time, s.45(2).
51 s.45(3); as to the proper place, see s.45(4); the bill must be exhibited to the person from whom payment is demanded: s.52(4).

who are not partners and no place of payment is specified, presentment must be made to them all.[52] If the drawee or acceptor is dead and no place of payment is specified presentment must be made to a personal representative, if such there be, and with the exercise of reasonable diligence he can be found.[53] Presentment through the post office is sufficient where authorised by agreement or usage.[54]

Where a bill is presented at the proper place, and after the exercise of reasonable diligence no person authorised to pay or refuse payment can be found there, no further presentment to the drawee or acceptor is required.[55] Delay in presentment is excused if it is caused by circumstances beyond the holder's control and not imputable to his default, misconduct or negligence; presentment must be made with reasonable diligence when the cause of delay ceases to operate.[56] Presentment is dispensed with where (a) it cannot be effected after the exercise of reasonable diligence (the fact that the holder has reason to believe that the bill will, on presentment, be dishonoured does not dispense with the necessity for presentment); (b) the drawee is a fictitious person, (c) as regards the drawer, where the drawee or acceptor is not bound as between himself and the drawer to accept or pay the bill and the drawer has no reason to believe that the bill would be paid if presented[57]; (d) as regards an indorser, where the bill was accepted or made for the accommodation of that indorser, and he has no reason to expect that the bill would be paid if presented; (e) by waiver of presentment, express or implied.[58]

If the bill is accepted generally, presentment for payment is not necessary to render the acceptor liable.[59] If a qualified acceptance requires presentment, the acceptor is not discharged by failure to present for payment at maturity unless there is an express stipulation to that effect. Summary diligence may proceed against the acceptor although the bill was not presented for payment on the day it fell due but within six months thereafter.[60]

---

[52] s.45(6).
[53] s.45(7).
[54] s.45(8).
[55] s.45(5).
[56] s.46(1).
[57] See *Bank of Scotland* v. *Lamont & Co.* (1889) 16 R.769.
[58] s.46(2); see, as to waiver made in error, *Mactavish's J. F.* v. *Michael's Trs.*, 1912 S.C.425.
[59] s.52.
[60] *McNeill & Son* v. *Innes, Chambers & Co.*, 1917 S.C.540.

26. No Notice of Dishonour

Notice of dishonour is not necessary to render the acceptor liable.[61]

Any drawer or indorser to whom notice of dishonour by non-acceptance or non-payment is not given is discharged, but (a) if a bill is dishonoured by non-acceptance and notice of dishonour is not given, the rights of a holder in due course subsequent to the omission are not prejudiced by the omission, (b) if a bill is dishonoured by non-acceptance and due notice of dishonour is given, it shall not be necessary to give notice of a subsequent dishonour by non-payment unless the bill has in the meantime been accepted.[62]

Notice must be given by or on behalf of the holder or an indorser who, at the time of giving it, is himself liable on the bill; it may be given by an agent in his own name or in the name of any party entitled to give notice, whether that party be his principal or not.[63] A notice given by or on behalf of a holder enures for the benefit of all subsequent holders and all prior indorsers who have a right of recourse against the party to whom it is given; a notice given by or on behalf of an indorser entitled to give notice enures for the benefit of the holder and all indorsers subsequent to the party to whom notice is given.

The notice may be in writing or by personal communication and may be given in any terms which sufficiently identify the bill and intimate that the bill has been dishonoured. The return of the bill is sufficient. A written notice need not be signed and, if insufficient, may be supplemented and validated by verbal communication. A misdescription of the bill does not vitiate the notice unless the party to whom the notice is given is in fact misled thereby.

The notice may be given to the party or his agent. If the drawer or indorser is dead, notice must be given to a personal representative if such there be, and with the exercise of reasonable diligence he can be found. If the drawer or indorser is bankrupt, notice is given to the party himself or to the trustee. Where there are two or more drawers or indorsers who are not partners, notice must be given to each of them, unless one of them has authority to receive such notice for the others.

A notice of dishonour can be posted before the due date for

---

61 s.52(3).

62 s.48.

63 s.49.

payment of the bill but it is bad if it is received before the bill itself was dishonoured; where on the evidence it is not clear whether the receipt of the notice preceded dishonour of the bill, the maxim *ut res magis valeat quam pereat* applies.[64]

Notice must be given within a reasonable time of dishonour which means that, in the absence of special circumstances, where the two parties reside in the same place, notice must be given in time to reach the recipient on the day after dishonour; and where the parties reside in different places, notice must be sent off on the day after dishonour if there is a post at a convenient hour, and if there be no such post, then by the next post thereafter.[65] If the bill is dishonoured in the hands of an agent he may give notice to the party liable or to his principal in which event he must do so within the same time as if he were the holder, and the principal upon receipt of such notice has himself the same time for giving notice as if the agent had been an independent holder.[66] Where a party receives due notice of dishonour, he has the same time after receipt for giving notice to antecedent parties that the holder has after dishonour.[67]

Where a notice of dishonour is duly addressed and posted, the sender is deemed to have given due notice of dishonour, notwithstanding any miscarriage by the post office.[68]

Delay in giving notice is excused if it is caused by circumstances beyond the control of the giver and not imputable to his default, misconduct, or negligence; where the cause of delay ceases to operate the notice must be given with reasonable diligence.[69]

Notice of dishonour is dispensed with: (a) when after the exercise of reasonable diligence, notice cannot be given to or does not reach the drawer or indorser concerned, (b) by waiver, express or implied, occurring before or after the omission,[70] (c) as regards the drawer, (i) where drawer and drawee are the same person, (ii) where the drawee is a fictitious person, or a person not having capacity to contract, (iii) where the drawer is the person to whom the bill is presented for payment, (iv) where the drawee or acceptor

---

64 *Eaglehill Ltd.* v. *J. Needham Ltd.* [1973] A.C.992.

65 s.49(12); *Lombard Banking Ltd.* v. *Central Garage and Engineering Co. Ltd.* [1963] 1 Q.B.220.

66 s.49(13).

67 s.49(14).

68 s.49(15).

69 s.50(1).

70 *Aberdeen Town and County Bank* v. *Davidson* (1885) 1 Sh.Ct.Rep.212; *McLelland* v. *Mackay* (1908) 24 Sh.Ct.Rep.157.

is as between himself and the drawer under no obligation to accept or pay the bill, (v) where the drawer has countermanded payment, (d) as regards the indorser, (i) where the drawee is a fictitious person or a person not having capacity to contract and the indorser was aware of the fact at the time he indorsed the bill, (ii) where the indorser is the person to whom the bill is presented for payment, (iii) where the bill was accepted or made for his accommodation.[71]

27. Promissory Notes

A promissory note is an unconditional promise in writing made by one person to another signed by the maker, engaging to pay, on demand or at a fixed or determinable future time, a sum certain in money, to, or to the order of, a specified person or to bearer.[72] A note payable to the maker's order is not a promissory note until it has been indorsed by the maker.[73] A note may contain a pledge of collateral security with authority to sell or dispose thereof,[74] but apart from that it must be a promise to pay money and nothing more.[75] The consideration may be stated and provisions relating to the "giving of time" are acceptable.[76]

For purposes of stamp duty a promissory note was defined as including any document or writing (except a banknote) containing a promise to pay any sum of money. This definition included a document which was a promissory note within the meaning of s.83 of the 1882 Act[77] but its terms were obviously much wider. The definition was, however, restricted by judicial interpretation. The sum of money had to be definite.[78] There had to be in substance a promise to pay although the use of the word "promise" was not necessary.[79]

---

[71] s.50(2); *McLelland* v. *Mackay, supra.*

[72] s.83(1); a promise to repay "on or before" a specified date is not a promissory note because the time is not determinable: *Williamson* v. *Rider* [1963] 1 Q.B.89; *cf. Creative Press* v. *Harman* [1973] I.R.313.

[73] s.83(2).

[74] s.83(3).

[75] *Nawab Major Sir Mohammad Akbar Khan* v. *Attar Singh* [1936] 2 All E.R.545; *Mortgage Insurance Corporation* v. *C.I.R.* (1888) 21 Q.B.D.352; *Dickie* v. *Singh*, 1974 S.L.T.129.

[76] *Kirkwood* v. *Carroll* [1903] 1 K.B.531.

[77] Alpe, *Law of Stamp Duties* (23rd ed.), p.93; *McTaggart* v. *MacEachern's J.F.*, 1949 S.C.503. No stamp is required now.

[78] *Tennent* v. *Crawford* (1878) 5 R.433; *Henderson* v. *Dawson* (1895) 22 R.895, *per* Lord McLaren at p.901; *Lamberton* v. *Aiken* (1899) 2 F.189.

[79] *Macfarlane* v. *Johnston* (1864) 2 M.1210; *Vallance* v. *Forbes* (1879) 6 R.1099; *Watson* v. *Duncan* (1896) 4 S.L.T.75; *Bell* v. *Bell* (1897) 4 S.L.T.214; *Thomson* v. *Bell* (1894) 22 R.16; *Cairney* v. *Macgregor's Trs.*, 1916 1 S.L.T.357.

To be a promissory note the document had to be unilateral in the sense that it became effectual on delivery and required nothing done on the other side to make it operative.[80] It was not necessary that the time of payment or the payee should have been stated.[81] A record of an obligation constituted against the grantor with no direct expression of a promise to pay was not a promissory note.[82]

A promissory note may be made by two or more makers who are liable thereon jointly, or jointly and severally, according to its tenor. A note which runs "I promise to pay" and is signed by two or more persons is deemed to be their joint and several note.[83]

A note is inchoate and incomplete until it is delivered to the payee or bearer.[84] The maker engages that he will pay the note according to its tenor and is precluded from denying to a holder in due course the existence of the payee and his then capacity to indorse.[85]

Presentment for payment is not necessary to make the maker liable unless the note is in the body of it made payable at a particular place.[86]

Presentment on the date of payment is not necessary to render the maker liable.[87] To make the indorser liable, however, presentment for payment is necessary and where the note is in the body of it made payable at a particular place, presentment at that place is necessary; where the place is indicated by way of memorandum only, presentment to the maker elsewhere will suffice.[88]

If a note payable on demand has been indorsed and has not been presented for payment within a reasonable time of the indorsement, the indorser is discharged.[89] What is a reasonable time depends on the nature of the instrument, the usage of trade and the facts of the case.[90] Where a note payable on demand is negotiated, it is not deemed to be overdue, for the purpose of affecting the holder with defects of title which he had no notice, by reason that it appears that

---

80 *Thomson* v. *Bell, supra, per* Lord McLaren at p.18.

81 *McTaggart* v. *MacEachern's J.F., supra.*

82 *Semple's Executrices* v. *Semple,* 1912 1 S.L.T.382; see also *Dick* v. *Dick,* 1950 S.L.T.(Notes)44.

83 s.85.

84 s.84.

85 s.88.

86 s.87(1).

87 *Gordon* v. *Kerr* (1898) 25 R.570.

88 s.87(2), (3).

89 s.86(1).

90 s.86(2).

a reasonable time for presenting it for payment has elapsed since its issue.[91]

In general the provisions of the 1882 Act relating to bills apply to promissory notes, the maker being deemed to correspond with the acceptor of a bill and the first indorser of the note being deemed to correspond with the drawer of an accepted bill payable to drawer's order.[92] The provisions of the Act relating to acceptance, presentment for acceptance, acceptance *supra* protest and bills in a set do not apply to notes.[93] Protest of a dishonoured foreign note is unnecessary.[94]

A promissory note is subject to the quinquennial and vicennial prescriptions but in neither case is the running of the prescriptive period interrupted by an acknowledgment of the subsistence of the obligation.[95]

---

91 s.86(3).
92 s.89(1), (2).
93 s.89(3).
94 s.89(4).
95 Prescription and Limitation (Scotland) Act 1973, Sched. 1, para. 1(*e*); ss.6(1), 7(1). A banknote is exempt from the quinquennial prescription: Sched. 1, para. 2 (*b*).

CHAPTER 6

CHEQUES

1. Cheque

A cheque is a bill of exchange drawn on a banker payable on demand.[1] The banker on whom the cheque is drawn is known as "the *paying banker*". The banker who collects the amount of the cheque on behalf of the payee or indorsee is "the *collecting banker*". Broadly, the law as to bills of exchange applies to cheques but the following special features must be noticed:

(a) it is at least doubtful whether a cheque can be accepted;[2] certification of a cheque is not acceptance;
(b) special duties arise from the relationship of banker and customer;
(c) the duty and authority of the bank to pay a cheque drawn by a customer are determined by countermand of payment and also by notice of the customer's death;[3]
(d) summary diligence on a cheque is incompetent;[4]
(e) there are relaxations of the rules relating to indorsement;
(f) certain precautions can be taken against theft and forgery of cheques;
(g) special protection is given to the paying banker and to the collecting banker.

Before the 1882 Act value was not presumed in the case of a cheque. Now, it is clear that value is presumed in a question between remote parties.[5] So far as a cheque held by the payee is concerned it is sometimes said that value is not presumed[6] but it is doubtful whether this view gives sufficient weight to the fact that the 1882 Act makes a cheque a species of bill.[7]

2. Banker and Customer

A banker who opens an account-current with a customer under-

[1] Bills of Exchange Act 1882, s.73.
[2] See *Bank of Baroda* v. *Punjab National Bank* [1944] A.C.176.
[3] s.75.
[4] *Glickman* v. *Linda*, 1950 S.C.18.
[5] s.30.
[6] *Thompson* v. *J. Barke & Co. (Caterers) Ltd.*, 1975 S.L.T.67, *per* Lord Dunpark at p.69.
[7] Thorburn, p.174.

takes to honour his cheques as presented to the extent to which there are funds at the credit of the customer in the account; if he fails to do so he is liable in damages for the injury to the customer's credit arising out of his breach of contract.[8] The principle does not apply to a deposit account.[9] If the banker has been in the habit of honouring cheques to the extent of the customer's credit upon an account-current, he is not entitled without notice at any moment to refuse to honour a cheque on the ground that if the account-current was massed together with the customer's loan and cash accounts, there would be a debit balance.[10] The fact that the banker holds a security against a debit balance does not mean that there are funds available for payment of cheques,[10] but if the customer has been allowed to overdraw against a security the banker cannot without giving notice, refuse to honour further cheques.[11] Where money has been paid in for credit of the customer's account, it cannot be drawn upon until a reasonable time for the necessary book-keeping operations has elapsed.[12] Where cheques have been lodged for credit of the customer, they are not available until they have been cleared unless the bank has expressly or implicitly agreed to allow the customer to draw against uncleared effects.[13] The banker can, of course, at any time terminate his relationship with his customer by intimating that he will refuse to honour cheques in future but, if he does this, he must nevertheless honour any cheques drawn prior to the date of intimation.[14] Two sentences printed on the cover of a new cheque-book may not be sufficient notice of a proposed alteration in the contractual relationship.[15]

The bank has no authority to pay a post-dated cheque before the date which it bears and, if it does pay, it takes the risk of a countermand arriving before business hours of the date on which the cheque bears to be drawn.[16]

Where a cheque card has been given to the customer, the bank

---

[8] *King* v. *British Linen Co.* (1899) 1 F.928; see also *Joachimson* v. *Swiss Bank Corporation* [1921] 3 K.B.110; *Royal Bank* v. *Skinner*, 1931 S.L.T.382.

[9] *Gibb* v. *Lombank Scotland Ltd.*, 1962 S.L.T.288.

[10] *Kirkwood & Sons* v. *Clydesdale Bank*, 1908 S.C.20.

[11] Wallace & McNeil, p.20.

[12] Paget, p.304.

[13] See *Westminster Bank Ltd.* v. *Zang* [1966] A.C.182.

[14] *King* v. *British Linen Co., supra.*

[15] *Burnett* v. *Westminster Bank* [1966] 1 Q.B.742.

[16] *Commercial Bank* v. *Henderson* (1897) 13 Sh.Ct.Rep.136.

undertakes to pay cheques of the amount stipulated on presentation, if the conditions of issue of the card have been complied with.[17]

3. Stale Cheques

Where a cheque is not presented for payment within a reasonable time of its issue, and the drawer or the person on whose account it is drawn had the right at the time of such presentment as between him and the banker to have the cheque paid and suffers actual damage through the delay, he is discharged to the extent of such damage, that is to say, to the extent to which such drawer or person is a creditor of such banker to a larger amount than he would have been had such cheque been paid. If the drawer or person is discharged in this way, the holder of the cheque becomes a creditor, in lieu of the drawer or person, of the banker to the extent of the discharge and is entitled to recover the amount from him.[18]

What is a reasonable time depends on the nature of the instrument, the usage of trade and of bankers, and the facts of the particular case. In practice cheques presented more than six months after date are not paid before confirmation has been obtained from the drawer.

4. The Necessity of Indorsement

Prior to 1957, the rules as to the indorsement of cheques did not differ from those applicable to the indorsement of other bills of exchange. The payee or indorsee of the cheque had to indorse it when he paid it into his bank (the collecting bank) for credit of his account. Moreover, the paying banker required the payee's indorsement even where the payee presented the cheque personally. In 1957 the Mocatta Committee[19] recommended that, in order to achieve "a substantial saving of unproductive work", indorsement should not be necessary on a cheque being collected by a bank on behalf of a customer who was the payee. Following upon this report, the Cheques Act 1957 provided that: (1) where the paying banker in good faith and in the ordinary course of business pays a cheque drawn on him, which is not indorsed or is irregularly indorsed, he does not, in doing so, incur any liability by reason only of the absence of, or irregularity in, indorsement, and he is deemed

[17] Byles, p.7. See *Regina* v. *Charles* [1977] A.C.177; Dobson [1977] J.B.L.126.
[18] s.74.
[19] Cmnd. 3 H.M.S.O. 1956.

to have paid it in due course,[20] (2) that the collecting banker is not to be treated for purposes of s.4 of the 1957 Act as having been negligent by reason only of his failure to concern himself with absence of, or irregularity in, indorsement of an instrument.[21]

Now, it would seem that these provisions apply, not only to cheques being collected by a bank on behalf of a customer who is the payee, but also to cheques collected by a bank on behalf of a customer who is not the payee but an indorsee. The banks, however, have not interpreted the Act so widely and in their view: "The intention of the Act is to relieve customers from the task of endorsing instruments which are to be collected for the payees' Accounts . . ."[22] In practice, therefore, the banks still require indorsement in the following cases: (i) cheques paid in for the credit of someone other than the ostensible payee, (ii) where the payee's name is mis-spelt or the payee is incorrectly designated and the surrounding circumstances are suspicious, (iii) cheques payable to joint payees which are tendered for credit of an account to which all are not parties, (iv) combined cheque and receipt forms marked "R" on the face, (v) bills of exchange other than cheques, (vi) promissory notes, (vii) drafts and other instruments drawn on the General Post Office or payable at a post office, (viii) Inland Revenue warrants, (ix) drafts drawn on H.M. Paymaster General or the Queen's and Lord Treasurer's Remembrancer, (x) drafts drawn on the Crown Agents, High Commissioners for Pakistan or India, and other paying agents, (xi) travellers' cheques, (xii) instruments payable by banks abroad. The paying banker requires the payee's signature on cheques cashed at the counter.

The result probably is that these requirements now form part of the "ordinary course of business" for purposes of s.1 of the 1957 Act.[23]

---

[20] s.1; the section applies to some documents other than cheques *viz.*: a document issued by the banker's customer which, though not a bill of exchange, is intended to enable a person to obtain payment from him of the sum mentioned in the document (*e.g.* an instrument in which the order is "Pay cash or order"—*Orbit Mining and Trading Co. Ltd.* v. *Westminster Bank Ltd.* [1963] 1 Q.B.794); and a draft payable on demand drawn by him upon himself, whether payable at the head office or some other office of his bank; in these cases, payment in good faith and in the ordinary course of business discharges the instrument.

[21] s.4(3); see also para. 13, *infra*.

[22] Circular dated 23 September 1957 issued by the Committee of London Clearing Bankers; see also J. Milnes Holden, *The Bankers' Magazine* (1957) Vol. CLXXXIV, page 101; F. R. Ryder, *The Bankers' Magazine* (1962) Vol. CXCIII, p.266; Antonio, *The Scottish Bankers' Magazine* (1957) Vol. XLIX, p.139.

[23] Paget, p.342.

Indorsement is, of course, still necessary when the payee negotiates the cheque to a third party.

Another important section of the 1957 Act is designed to put a collecting banker who has given value for a cheque in the position of a holder even although it is not indorsed. It is provided that a banker who gives value for, or has a lien on, a cheque payable to order which the holder delivers to him for collection without indorsing it, has such (if any) rights as he would have had if, on delivery, the holder had indorsed it in blank.[24] The section applies where the holder delivers the cheque to the bank for collection for the credit of an account other than his own.[25] Where the managing director and controlling shareholder of a company delivered to the bank an unindorsed cheque in favour of himself for collection for credit of the company's account, it was held that he did so as a "holder".[25] The bank gives value for the cheque (i) if it cashes it, (ii) if it in fact allows the customer to draw against the uncleared cheque[26], (iii) if there is an express or implied agreement that the customer is to be entitled to draw against uncleared effects,[27] (iv) if the bank has a lien on the cheque,[28] (v) if the bank accepts the cheque as a conditional payment in reduction of an overdraft.[29]

5. Method of Indorsement

The indorsement is written on the cheque and is signed by the indorser. A simple signature without additional words is sufficient.[30] If the payee or indorsee is wrongly designated or if his name is mis-spelt, he should indorse as he is described and add his correct signature.[31] The payee's initials or Christian names are an essential part of the indorsement but titles are not. If the cheque is payable to "Mrs. A.B." the indorsement should be the payee's normal signature followed by "wife of A.B." If there are two or more payees, all must indorse unless either the one indorsing has the authority to indorse for the others or the payees are partners in which case one partner may sign the firm name or sign in his own

24 s.2; see *Midland Bank Ltd.* v. *R. V. Harris Ltd.* [1963] 2 All E.R.685.

25 *Westminster Bank* v. *Zang* [1966] A.C.182.

26 *Westminster Bank* v. *Zang, supra.*

27 *A. L. Underwood Ltd.* v. *Bank of Liverpool* [1924] 1 K.B.775.

28 *Barclays Bank* v. *Astley Industrial Trust Ltd.* [1970] 2 Q.B.527.

29 *McLean* v. *Clydesdale Bank* (1883) 11 R.(H.L.)1; *Midland Bank* v. *Reckitt* [1933] A.C.1; *Barclays Bank Ltd.* v. *Astley Industrial Trust Ltd., supra.*

30 1882 Act, s.32(1).

31 s.32(4); Chalmers, p.115.

name expressly on behalf of the firm. In the case of joint stock companies the indorsement should be by a duly authorised officer, normally a director, secretary or manager.[32] If there are only two trustees or executors, both must indorse, but if there are more than two a majority will suffice. Where the cheque is payable to the holder of an office, the official's signature with his designation appended is necessary.[33]

6. Transfer

Obviously, when the paying banker honours a cheque a transfer of funds is effected. It is, however, important to notice that by s.53(2) *presentation* of a bill operates as an assignation of the sum for which it is drawn in favour of the holder if the bank has in its hands funds available for payment thereof.[34] Any doubt as to whether this subsection applies to cheques as fully as it does to other bills is, it is submitted, unfounded; the reservations expressed by Lord President Inglis in *British Linen Co. Bank* v. *Carruthers and Fergusson*[35] were the product of a state of the law prior to the 1882 Act in which it was not clear that a cheque was a species of bill. It seems that the subsection applies even if the cheque is post-dated or not properly indorsed.[36]

7. Insufficient Funds

If the funds at credit of the customer are less than the amount of the cheque, the cheque is returned marked "insufficient funds" and the amount at credit is transferred to a separate account bearing reference to the cheque as the presentation of the cheque has operated as an assignation.[37] Payment of the sum in that account can be made to the holder of the cheque if he delivers up the cheque.

8. Countermand

The banker's duty and authority to pay a cheque are determined if

---

32 *Phillips* v. *Italian Bank Ltd.*, 1934 S.L.T.78.

33 For a fuller treatment of this subject see Wallace & McNeil, pp.199-202; Chorley, *Law of Banking*, 6th ed., pp.83-88.

34 The assignation is in favour of a *holder* as defined in the 1882 Act: *Dickson* v. *Clydesdale Bank Ltd.*, 1937 S.L.T.585.

35 (1883) 10 R.923. See Mr D. J. Cusine's illuminating article at 1977 J.R.98.

36 Finlayson, pp.55-56.

37 *British Linen Co. Bank* v. *Carruthers and Fergusson* (1883) 10 R.923; Wallace & McNeil, p.13.

there is a countermand of payment by the customer.[38] The notice of countermand must be given to the branch on which the cheque is drawn.[39] To be effectual, the countermand must, of course, be communicated to the bank before payment has been made. It seems that payment is made when the necessary entries are made in the bank's cash book. If the accounts of the drawer and payee are at the same branch, it is thought that payment is made when the payment has been entered in the payee's pass book even although the drawer's ledger account has not been debited and the payee's ledger account has not been credited.[40]

Where countermand is made before presentation of the cheque for payment or after presentation but before payment has been made, the banker cannot in safety make payment.[41] Presentation, however, by virtue of s.53(2) of the 1882 Act, operates as an assignation to the holder of any funds in the banker's hands available for payment and accordingly the bank must transfer to a suspense account an amount sufficient to meet the cheque or, if the funds available are insufficient, the whole credit balance.[42] If the drawer and the holder of the cheque do not subsequently agree as to the disposal of the funds the question is settled by a multiplepoinding. It has been stated that the holder has no direct right of action against the bank[43] but the case cited[44] was decided prior to the 1882 Act when a cheque was not regarded as being a bill of exchange and presentation of it did not *per se* effect an assignation; it is difficult to see why in principle the assignee should not have a right of action against the debtor.

Where the countermand is effectual in this way, the holder can sue the drawer and any indorsers on the cheque.[45] The onus is on the drawer to justify the countermand.[46] He will not usually succeed if the holder is a holder in due course.

[38] s.75. The terms of the agreement between bank and customer on the issue of a cheque card will provide that the customer cannot countermand cheques accepted on production of the card.

[39] Wallace & McNeil, p.214.

[40] Finlayson, p.59.

[41] See *Waterston* v. *City of Glasgow Bank* (1874) 1 R.470 (pre-Act).

[42] Wallace & McNeil, p.215. See *Andrews* v. *Andrews*, 1967 S.L.T.(Sh.Ct.)14.

[43] Wallace & McNeil, p.214.

[44] *Waterston* v. *City of Glasgow Bank* (1874) 1 R.470. See also *Sutherland* v. *Commercial Bank* (1882) 20 S.L.R.139.

[45] *McLean* v. *Clydesdale Bank* (1883) 11 R.(H.L.)1.

[46] *Webster & Co. Ltd.* v. *Hutchin* (1922) 39 Sh.Ct.Rep.231; *cf. Williams* v. *Williams*, 1980 S.L.T.(Sh.Ct.)25. The onus probably depends on what is admitted as to the circumstances in which the cheque was delivered.

9. Customer's Death

Notice of his customer's death determines the duty and authority of the banker to pay cheques drawn on him by the customer.[47] However, presentment of the cheque after notice of death has been received still operates as an assignation of any funds available for payment of the amount of the cheque.[48] Whether there are funds available for payment must be determined on a true state of all the accounts between the customer and the bank and not merely on the state of the current account.[49]

10. Customer's Sequestration

If the customer is sequestrated, the sum at credit of the account (or the balance where there are several accounts[50]) vests in the trustee as at the date of sequestration.[51] If, however, a cheque has been presented before the date of sequestration, and payment has been refused because of insufficient funds, the credit balance is nevertheless transferred to the holder of the cheque,[52] at least to the extent that the cheque was in payment of a debt which was due by the bankrupt at the date of presentation.[53] The principle is the same where payment was refused before the date of sequestration because of a countermand; if, in the end of the day, it appears that the holder of the cheque was entitled to payment from the customer, the funds in the bank's hands are transferred to him to the extent of the amount of the cheque.

11. Precautions against Theft and Forgery

A cheque is crossed generally by putting on its face two parallel transverse lines with or without the words "and company" or any abbreviation thereof between the lines; a cheque is crossed specially to a banker by putting across its face the name of the banker.[54] A cheque may be crossed by the drawer or holder and a holder may cross specially a cheque crossed generally. The banker to whom a cheque is crossed specially may cross it specially to another banker

---

47 s.75; an undated cheque cannot be given testamentary effect: *Stewart's Trs.*, 1953 S.L.T.(Notes)25.

48 s.53(2); *Bank of Scotland* v. *Reid* (1886) 2 Sh.Ct.Rep.376.

49 *Kirkwood & Sons* v. *Clydesdale Bank*, 1908 S.C.20.

50 *Kirkwood & Sons* v. *Clydesdale Bank*, 1908 S.C.20.

51 Bankruptcy (Scotland) Act 1913, s.97(1).

52 s.53(2): *British Linen Co. Bank* v. *Carruthers and Fergusson* (1883) 10 R.923.

53 *Commercial Bank* v. *Lyon* (1909) 25 Sh.Ct.Rep.312.

54 s.76.

for collection. A collecting banker may cross specially to himself an uncrossed cheque or a cheque crossed generally.[55] The crossing is a material part of the cheque and it is unlawful to obliterate it or, except as authorised by the Act, to add to or alter it.[56]

The crossing is a direction to the paying banker that, if it is crossed generally, he must pay only to a banker, or, if it is crossed specially, he must pay only to the banker to whom it is crossed or his agent for collection being a banker. If the paying banker disregards this direction he is liable to the true owner of the cheque for any loss he may sustain owing to the cheque having been paid otherwise than as directed.[57] If, however, the crossing has been obliterated or altered so that at payment it does not appear to be crossed or to have had a crossing obliterated or altered, and the paying banker pays it in good faith and without negligence to someone other than a banker, he does not incur liability. The paying banker is protected by s.80 if he pays in accordance with the crossing.[58]

Crossing is only a partial safeguard because, of course, the person who has misappropriated the cheque may manage to obtain payment through a banker or he may transfer the cheque to someone else who obtains payment in good faith through a banker. If the indorsement of the payee has been forged the person taking the cheque from the thief cannot be a holder in due course; but if the cheque has been validly indorsed in blank before the theft the person to whom the cheque is negotiated by the thief can be a holder in due course. To avoid this result, it is possible to write on the face of a crossed cheque the words "not negotiable".[59] The effect of this is that the cheque can still be transferred but a person taking such a cheque does not have and cannot give a better title to the cheque than that which the person from whom he took it had.[60] In other words, no one can be a holder in due course of such a cheque.

The addition of the words "Account Payee" to a cheque has no statutory basis but it is not an unlawful addition to the crossing.[61] It

[55] s.77.

[56] s.78.

[57] s.79; see *Phillips* v. *Italian Bank*, 1934 S.L.T.78.

[58] See para. 12, *infra*.

[59] s.76; the cheque must be crossed: Paget, p.252; Byles, p.242; *Union Bank* v. *National Bank* (1924) 40 Sh.Ct.Rep.111; *cf.* Wallace & McNeil, p.223; Chorley, *Law of Banking*, 6th ed., p.57; the section does not apply to bills of exchange other than cheques: *Hibernian Bank Ltd.* v. *Gysin and Hanson* [1939] 1 K.B.483.

[60] s.81; *Great Western Railway Co.* v. *London & County Banking Co. Ltd.* [1901] A.C.414.

[61] *Akrokerri (Atlantic) Mines Ltd.* v. *Economic Bank* [1904] 2 K.B.465.

does not affect the negotiability of the cheque.[62] It is a direction to the collecting banker that payment of the proceeds should be made for credit of the payee's account.[63] If the collecting banker accepts such a cheque for credit of another account without a satisfactory explanation he is probably negligent and loses the protection of s.4 of the Cheques Act 1957.[64] A question has been raised as to whether the paying banker might lose the protection of ss.60 and 80 of the 1882 Act if he acts upon such a cheque which bears indorsements subsequent to that of the payee and which, therefore, is presumably being collected for someone else.[65] It is thought that "Account Payee Only" has the same significance as "Account Payee".[66]

12. The Paying Banker

The paying banker is not protected if he honours as a cheque a document on which the signature of his customer, the drawer, has been forged.[67] He cannot debit his customer with the amount paid unless the customer is in some way barred from relying on the forgery.[68] Nor can he debit his customer if the amount on the cheque has been fraudulently increased unless the customer has negligently drawn the cheque in such a way as to facilitate fraud or forgery.[69]

The paying banker is, however, protected where an indorsement has been forged or made without authority. If he pays a cheque in good faith and in the ordinary course of business he is deemed to have paid it in due course even although the indorsement was forged or made without authority[70] and he can debit his customer. Payment across the counter of a cheque indorsed in blank can be protected but there may be circumstances in which such payment is not in the ordinary course of business.[71]

Secondly, where a banker pays a crossed cheque in accordance with the crossing, and in good faith and without negligence, he is

---

62 *National Bank* v. *Silke* [1891] 1 Q.B.435.

63 *Morison* v. *London County and Westminster Bank Ltd.* [1914] 3 K.B.356, *per* Lord Reading C. J. at p.373.

64 *Importers Company* v. *Westminster Bank Ltd.* [1927] 2 K.B.297.

65 Paget, p.258.

66 Paget, p.259.

67 *Orr and Barber* v. *Union Bank of Scotland* (1854) 1 Macq.513.

68 See Chap. 5, para. 10.

69 *London Joint Stock Bank Ltd.* v. *Macmillan* [1918] A.C.777.

70 s.60.

71 *Bank of England* v. *Vagliano Brothers* [1891] A.C.107, *per* Lord Halsbury L.C. at p.117; *Auchteroni & Co.* v. *Midland Bank Ltd.* [1928] 2 K.B.294; *Phillips* v. *Italian Bank Ltd.*, 1934 S.L.T.78.

entitled to the same rights and is placed in the same position as if payment had been made to the true owner of the cheque even although he has in fact paid to a banker collecting for a thief or finder.[72] This section, of course, does not give protection where the drawer's signature is forged.

The third protection of the paying banker is that, under s.1 of the Cheques Act 1957, where he pays in good faith and in the ordinary course of business a cheque[73] which is not indorsed or is irregularly indorsed, he does not, in doing so, incur any liability by reason only of the absence of, or irregularity in, indorsement, and he is deemed to have paid in due course. The object of this section is not altogether clear. It may be that it was merely intended to maintain the protection of ss.60 and 80 of the 1882 Act once indorsements were made unnecessary by the 1957 Act.[74]

13. Liability of Collecting Banker

In collecting a cheque, a bank may be acting merely as an agent for its customer or it may be collecting for itself. Where the bank acts as an agent: "The customer says to his banker—'Act as my agent and collect this bill.' The bill is delivered for a special and limited purpose. There is no transfer of the property. The only right the banker has to the bill is to carry out the instructions of his customer regarding it."[75] On the other hand, the bank may have given value to its customer for the cheque and be collecting the proceeds for itself. The determination of the capacity in which the bank is acting is a question of fact.[76] The mere fact that the bank in its books enters the value of the cheque on the credit side of the account does not without more constitute the bank a holder for value.[77] It seems that even if the bank is acting as an agent for collection it may be a "holder" or "holder for value" of the cheque.[78]

---

72 s.80.

73 s.1(2) gives similar protection in respect of drafts (which are also affected by Stamp Act 1853, s.19) and certain other documents.

74 See Paget, p.341.

75 *Clydesdale Bank* v. *Liqrs. of James Allan Senior & Son*, 1926 S.C.235; *per* L.J.-C. Alness at p.241.

76 *McLean* v. *Clydesdale Bank* (1883) 11 R.(H.L.)1.

77 *Whatmough's Tr.* v. *British Linen Bank*, 1934 S.C.(H.L.)51, *per* Lord Thankerton at p.60. This was supported by reference to the opinion of Atkin L.J. in *A. L. Underwood Ltd.* v. *Barclays Bank* [1924] 1 K.B.775, which is criticised by Paget (p.433) as ignoring *Sutters* v. *Briggs* [1922] 1 A.C.1. *Whatmough's Tr.* is not cited in Paget or Byles.

78 *Sutters* v. *Briggs, supra; Barclays Bank* v. *Astley Industrial Trust* [1970] 2 Q.B.527.

If the bank was acting merely as an agent and was in good faith it is not liable if it has collected a cheque on which the signatures of the drawer and the indorser were forged.[79] If the bank has constituted itself a holder in due course of a cheque it does not, of course, incur any liability in respect of the proceeds. When, however, the bank has collected for itself a cheque to which it had no title because the customer from whom the cheque was acquired had a defective title, the bank may be liable to pay the proceeds to the true owner of the cheque even if, because it had given value for the cheque, it has not been enriched by the transaction.[80] There is also a general principle that a person cannot retain a benefit obtained by the fraud of another, even though himself innocent of fraud, unless a valuable consideration has been given.[81] It seems that all these forms of liability are based on repetition or other principles of unjust enrichment.

Section 4(1) of the Cheques Act 1957[82] is primarily intended to give protection against the English tort of conversion but it may serve to protect Scottish banks against some of the foregoing liabilities.

"Where a banker in good faith and without negligence (a) receives payment for a customer of [a cheque]; or, (b) having credited a customer's account with the amount of [a cheque], receives payment thereof for himself; and the customer has no title, or a defective title, to [the cheque] the banker does not incur any liability to the true owner of [the cheque] by reason only of having received payment thereof."[83] A banker is not to be treated as having been negligent by reason only of his failure to concern himself with the absence of, or irregularity in, indorsement of the cheque.[84]

The wording of paragraph (*b*) of s.4(1) is rather odd in that it

---

79 *Clydesdale Bank* v. *Royal Bank* (1876) 3 R.586.

80 *Alexander Beith Ltd.* v. *Allan*, 1961 S.L.T.(Notes) 80.

81 *Clydesdale Bank* v. *Paul* (1877) 4 R.626. See also *Traill* v. *Smith's Trs.* (1876) 3 R.770; *New Mining and Exploring Syndicate Ltd.* v. *Chalmers & Hunter*, 1912 S.C.126.

82 This section replaces section 82 of the 1882 Act which, however, applied only to crossed cheques; s.4 of the 1957 Act applies to all cheques, crossed and uncrossed, and also to the other instruments defined in subs. (2). See Cusine, 1978 J.R.233. See also Banking Act 1979, s.47.

83 s.4(1).

84 s.4(3); as to negligence see *Orbit Mining & Trading Co. Ltd.* v. *Westminster Bank Ltd.* [1963] 1 Q.B.794, and the cases cited therein.

seems to be based on the view that crediting the customer's account does put the bank in the position of receiving payment for itself.[85]

14. IOU

An IOU is a document consisting of the expression "I owe you" or "IOU" and indicating a sum of money. It must be holograph of the granter and signed by him.[86] It need not be dated or addressed to a creditor.[87] It does not require a stamp.[88]

An IOU is an acknowledgment of debt due by the grantor to the grantee and it implies an obligation to repay on demand.[89] "If nothing more is known about an IOU except what can be gathered from the terms of the document, it is thus *per se* a good warrant for a claim on the part of the creditor named in the document to whom it has been delivered to sue for repayment."[90] This would indicate that the IOU is a document of debt and not merely an adminicle of evidence[91] and the pursuer is under no obligation to explain to the court how the indebtedness arose.[92] The genuineness of the handwriting has, of course, to be proved.[93] In the absence of express stipulation, interest does not begin to run on the principal sum *ex lege* until repayment is demanded.[94]

Payment can be proved only by the writ or oath of the creditor.[95] It is not a relevant defence to prove that no money passed at the granting of the document;[95] or that there was no antecedent debt;[96] or that the document is a sham.[97] The following defences can be proved parole: (a) a collateral agreement as to the date at which

---

85 See Paget, pp.388, 429; Byles, pp.265, 268.

86 *per* Lord Deas, *Bowe and Christie* v. *Hutchison* (1868) 6 M.642 at 646; *per* L.P. Inglis, *Haldane* v. *Speirs* (1872) 10 M.537 at 541.

87 *Brunton* v. *Bone* (1858) 1 Scot.Law Journal, 58; *Fereneze Spinning Co.* v. *Wallace* (1858) 1 Scot.Law Journal, 93.

88 *per* Lord Trayner, *Thiem's Trs.* v. *Collie* (1899) 1 F.764 at 777.

89 *per* L.P. Normand, *Black* v. *Gibb*, 1940 S.C.24 at 26.

90 *per* Lord Moncrieff, *Black* v. *Gibb*, *supra*, at p.28.

91 It has been suggested that this is a distinction without a difference (*per* Lord Johnston, *Bishop* v. *Bryce*, 1910 S.C.426 at 435; see also *Thiem's Trs.* v. *Collie*, *supra*, *per* Lord Trayner at p.774) but it does affect the form of the action—see *Encyclopaedia of Scottish Legal Styles*, Vol. VI, p.19; Dobie, *Sheriff Court Styles*, p.257, n.7.

92 But see *Bertram* v. *McIntyre* (1934) 50 Sh.Ct.Rep.194.

93 *per* L.P. Inglis, *Haldane* v. *Speirs*, *supra*, at p.541.

94 *Winestone* v. *Wolifson*, 1954 S.C.77.

95 *Thiem's Trs.* v. *Collie* (1899) 1 F.764.

96 *Black* v. *Gibb*, *supra*. *Cf. Paterson* v. *Wilson* (1883) 21 S.L.R.272.

97 *McCreadie's Trs.* v. *McCreadie* (1897) 5 S.L.T.153; *Gray* v. *Bain* (1954) 70 Sh.Ct.Rep.65.

payment is to be made;[98] (b) that "facts and circumstances have arisen which really show that the party putting forward the IOU has no proper right to have the document of debt with him";[99] (c) that there exists a state of facts which is inconsistent with the continued subsistence of the debt;[1] (d) where the granting of the IOU is admitted, that it was destroyed by the instructions of the creditor who intended that the money advanced should be a gift to the defender.[2] Moreover, if both parties agree that the IOU is not a true record of the transaction between them and that in fact no debt was outstanding which the debtor *ex facie* of the document undertook to repay, the document is ignored and the pursuer must prove his debt by other means.[3] As to prescription, see Chapter 14, para. 4 *et seq*.

An IOU is not a negotiable instrument and can be transferred only by intimated assignation.[4]

15. Deposit Receipt

A deposit receipt is a contract whereby a bank promises to pay upon a certain order but it does not give any indication as to the person to whom the money belongs after it has been paid.[5] There are two distinct questions: (a) what is the obligation to pay which the bank has undertaken? and (b) who is the true owner of the fund which is the subject of the deposit?[6] The terms of the receipt are not conclusive evidence as to the ownership of the fund and *per se* do not instruct an *inter vivos* donation[7], a *mortis causa* donation[8], or a testamentary bequest;[9] with other evidence, however, some of these effects may be established.[10] In general, the ownership of the fund has to be determined on the evidence.[11]

---

98 *Black* v. *Gibb, supra*.

99 *per* L.P. Dunedin, *Bishop* v. *Bryce* 1910 S.C.426 at 430; Gloag, p.716, interprets this decision thus: "that the document of debt was granted for a particular purpose, that this purpose has been carried into effect, and that the document ought to have been given up."

1 *McKenzie's Exrx.* v. *Morrison's Trs.*, 1930 S.C.830.

2 *Anderson's Trs.* v. *Webster* (1883) 11 R.35.

3 *Black* v. *Gibb, supra*.

4 Gloag & Irvine, p.575.

5 *Dickson* v. *National Bank*, 1917 S.C.(H.L.)50, *per* Lord Dunedin at p.53.

6 *Anderson* v. *North of Scotland Bank* (1901) 4 F.49, *per* Lord McLaren at p.54.

7 *Barstow* v. *Inglis* (1857) 20 D.230; *Lord Advocate* v. *Galloway* (1884) 11 R.541.

8 *Jamieson* v. *McLeod* (1880) 7 R.1131.

9 *Crosbie's Trs.* v. *Wright* (1880) 7 R.823.

10 *Grant's Trs.* v. *McDonald*, 1939 S.C.448 (*inter vivos* donation); *Macpherson's Exrx.* v. *Mackay*, 1932 S.C.505; *Graham's Trs.* v. *Gillies*, 1956 S.C.437 (donation *mortis causa*).

11 *Bank of Scotland* v. *Robertson* (1870) 8 M.391.

Questions of retention[12] and the effect of arrestment[13] in the hands of the bank are treated elsewhere.

The deposit receipt is not a negotiable document and right to the fund is not transferred by indorsation; it can be assigned.[14] If the receipt is lost, the bank may refuse payment unless caution is given or there is a judicial order for payment.[15]

---

12 See Chap. 13, para. 4.
13 See Chap. 16, para. 3.
14 See *Wood* v. *Clydesdale Bank Ltd.*, 1914 S.C.397.
15 *Pirrie* v. *Mags. of Hawick* (1901) 17 Sh.Ct.Rep.294.

CHAPTER 7

SECURITIES: CORPOREAL MOVEABLES

1. Securities

A right in security is "any right which a creditor may hold for ensuring the payment or satisfaction of his debt, distinct from, and in addition to, his right of action and execution against the debtor under the latter's personal obligation."[1] The right may be a *jus in personam,* a right against persons other than the debtor, or a *jus in re,* a right over specific property. It has been held that the granting of a voucher for an existing debt—an IOU or a promissory note, for example—is not the constitution of a security unless its effect is to give the creditor a preference as regards diligence.[2] However, the word "security" is used in more than one way: "The word 'security' has two meanings. It may refer to some property deposited or made over or some obligation entered into by or on behalf of a person in order to secure his fulfilment of an obligation he has undertaken. Or it may refer to a document held by a creditor as evidence or a guarantee of his right to repayment."[3] A promissory note was held to be a "security" for purposes of the Money-lenders Acts[4] and bonds, bills and notes are within the definition of "security" in the Consumer Credit Act 1974.[5]

A mere pecuniary obligation is not a security even if it designates a fund of the debtor out of which it is to be paid.[6]

In the Consumer Credit Act 1974, a "security" means a "mortgage" (including a heritable security), charge, pledge, bond, debenture, indemnity, guarantee, bill, note or other right provided by the debtor or at his request to secure the carrying out of his obligations.[7]

2. Consumer Credit Act 1974

Documents embodying regulated agreements have to embody any

1 Gloag & Irvine, p.1.

2 *Matthew's Tr.* v. *Matthew* (1867) 5 M.957.

3 *per* Lord Migdale, *Cleveleys Investment Trust Co.* v. *Inland Revenue,* 1971 S.C.233 at 243.

4 *George Shaw Ltd.* v. *Duffy,* 1943 S.C.350.

5 s.189.

6 *Graham & Co.* v. *Raeburn & Verel* (1895) 23 R.84.

7 Consumer Credit Act 1974, s.189.

security provided in relation to the agreement by the debtor.[8] If the person by whom a security is provided (the "surety") is not the debtor, the security must be expressed in writing in the prescribed form, the document containing all the terms of the security other than implied terms must be signed by or on behalf of the surety and a copy of the document and the principal agreement given to him.[9] If these requirements are not satisfied, the security is enforceable against the surety only on an order of the court and if an application for such an order is dismissed (except on technical grounds) the security is treated as never having effect, property lodged with the creditor for purposes of the security must be returned, any entry relating to the security in any register must be cancelled and any amount received by the creditor on realisation of the security must be repaid to the surety;[10] there is a partial exemption for heritable securities. The creditor is obliged to give the surety on request a copy of the principal agreement and of the security instrument and information about the present state of the debtor's indebtedness.[11]

A copy of any default notice served on the debtor must be served on the surety.[12] The realisation of securities is subject to regulation.[13] A security cannot be enforced so as to benefit the creditor to an extent greater than would be the case if there were no security and the obligations of the debtor were carried out to the extent (if any) to which they would be enforced under the Act.[14] Accordingly, if a regulated agreement is enforceable only on a court order or an order of the Director the security is enforceable only where an order has been made[15] and, generally, if the agreement is cancelled or becomes unenforceable, the security becomes ineffective.[16]

3. Corporeal Moveables

The general principle is that a security cannot be created over corporeal moveables unless they are delivered to the creditor.[17]

---

[8] s.105(9).
[9] s.105.
[10] s.106.
[11] ss.107-110.
[12] s.111.
[13] s.112.
[14] s.113(1).
[15] s.113(2).
[16] s.113(3).
[17] Bell, *Comm.*, II, 21; *Clark* v. *West Calder Oil Co.* (1882) 9 R.1017; *cf. Rhind's Tr.* v. *Robertson & Baxter* (1891) 18 R.623; *Pattison's Tr.* v. *Liston* (1893) 20 R.806.

There may be some relaxation of the rule where delivery is impossible[18] and there are the following exceptions:
(i) floating charges;[19]
(ii) agricultural charges in favour of banks;[20]
(iii) Inland Revenue charges for unpaid capital transfer tax;[21]
(iv) maritime liens;
(v) mortgages of ships and aircraft.[22]
A solicitor's "charge" for expenses on property recovered or preserved in an action may prevail in a sequestration or liquidation although it yields to a bona fide purchaser or lender.[23]

There have been attempts to evade the principle. It is not possible to constitute a security over corporeal moveables *retenta possessione* by means of a fictitious sale. The provisions of the Sale of Goods Act 1979 do not apply to a transaction in the form of a contract of sale which is intended to operate by way of mortgage, pledge, charge or other security.[24] In particular, a sale followed by a letting or hire-purchase back to the seller will not be effectual if there has been no delivery.[25] A genuine *pactum de retrovendendo* is not struck at.[26]

It has been suggested that the recent affirmation[27] that an individual can declare a trust of his own property with himself as sole trustee opens a further way of evasion but the difficulty may be that a trust for creditors is superseded by sequestration.[28]

Pledge is the form of security appropriate to corporeal moveables. It is defined as "a real contract, by which one places in the hands of his creditor a moveable subject, to remain with him in security of a debt or engagement, to be re-delivered on payment or

---

18 *Darling* v. *Wilson's Tr.* (1887) 15 R.180.
19 See Chap. 9, para. 2.
20 Agricultural Credits (Scotland) Act 1929, Pt.II.
21 Finance Act 1975, Sched. 4, para. 20.
22 See *infra,* paras. 5 and 6.
23 Solicitors (Scotland) Act 1980, s.62.
24 1979 Act, s.62(4). See *Robertson* v. *Hall's Tr.* (1896) 24 R.120; *Jones & Co.'s Tr.* v. *Allan* (1901) 4 F.374; *Hepburn* v. *Law,* 1914 S.C.918. Evasion by use of a lease and the landlord's hypothec is ineffectual: *Heritable Securities Investment Association Ltd.* v. *Wingate & Co.'s Tr.* (1880) 7 R.1094.
25 *Rennet* v. *Mathieson* (1903) 5 F.591; *Newbigging* v. *Ritchie's Tr.,* 1930 S.C.273; *Scottish Transit Trust* v. *Scottish Land Cultivators Ltd.,* 1955 S.C.254; *G. & C. Finance Corporation Ltd.* v. *Brown,* 1961 S.L.T.408.
26 *Gavin's Tr.* v. *Fraser,* 1920 S.C.674; but see Gloag's view of this decision—*Encyclopaedia of the Laws of Scotland,* Vol. *XIII.,* p.311.
27 *Allan's Trs.* v. *Lord Advocate,* 1971 S.C.(H.L.)45.
28 *Salaman* v. *Rosslyn's Trs.* (1900) 3 F.298.

satisfaction; and with an implied mandate, on failure to fulfil the engagement at the stipulated time or on demand, to have the pledge sold by judicial authority."[29] Actual delivery may be effected either by physical transfer or by placing the goods in a separate part of the debtor's premises, the key of which is given to the creditor.[30] Mere labelling or setting apart of the goods is not sufficient.[31]

The creditor, being owner of the premises on which the goods are situated, may have possession of them although the debtor, as contractor or lessee, has the use of them.[32] In the case of a bill of lading there may be symbolic delivery, the bill being regarded as equivalent to the goods it represents.[33] Possession is not lost if the bill is returned to the debtor so that he may, as the creditor's agent, sell the goods.[34] When the goods are in the hands of an independent third party[35] such as a storekeeper, there may be constructive delivery.[36] This is effected by an intimation to the custodier in the form of a delivery order that the goods are to be held for the transferee. The goods must be specific in the sense that they are either a total undivided quantity stored in a particular place or a specified quantity forming part of an identified whole.[37]

On the debtor's default, the creditor can sell the subject of pledge if he is expressly authorised by the contract to do so. Otherwise, he must apply to the sheriff for a warrant for sale.[38] It seems that the subject cannot be retained for payment of debts other than the one for which it was pledged.[39] The security may be destroyed if the creditor by donation loses legal possession of the article.[40]

Where the security is in the form of an *ex facie* absolute transfer of

---

29 Bell, *Prin.*, § 203.

30 *Liqr. of West Lothian Oil Co. Ltd.* v. *Mair* (1892) 20 R.64.

31 *Gibson* v. *Forbes* (1833) 11 S.916; *Boak* v. *Megget* (1844) 6 D.662; *Orr's Tr.* v. *Tullis* (1870) 8 M.936.

32 *Moore* v. *Gledden* (1869) 7 M.1016; *Orr's Tr.* v. *Tullis* (1870) 8 M.936.

33 Bell, *Prin.*, § 417; *Hayman & Son* v. *McLintock*, 1907 S.C.936.

34 *North-Western Bank Ltd.* v. *Poynter, Son and Macdonalds* (1894) 22 R.(H.L.)1.

35 *Anderson* v. *McCall* (1866) 4 M.765; *Dobell, Beckett & Co.* v. *Neilson* (1904) 7 F.281.

36 *Pochin & Co.* v. *Robinows & Marjoribanks* (1869) 7 M.622, *per* L.P. Inglis at p.628; *Inglis* v. *Robertson & Baxter* (1898) 25 R.(H.L.)70; *Hayman & Co.* v. *McLintock, supra; Price & Pierce Ltd.* v. *Bank of Scotland,* 1910 S.C.1095; 1912 S.C.(H.L.)19. See, as to the technical nature of the transaction, Rodger, 1971 J.R.193.

37 *Pochin & Co.* v. *Robinows & Marjoribanks, supra, per* L.P. Inglis at p.629.

38 Bell, *Prin.*, § 207.

39 *Hamilton* v. *Western Bank of Scotland* (1856) 19 D.152.

40 *Wolifson* v. *Harrison,* 1978 S.L.T.95.

the property in the subjects, the creditor can sell on default at his own hand and can retain the security against any debt due to him by the debtor.[39]

4. Pledges: Consumer Credit Act

The provisions of the Consumer Credit Act as to pledges do not apply to pledges of documents of title or bearer bonds or to non-commercial agreements. It is an offence to take an article in pawn from a minor.[41] It is also an offence for the "pawnee" to fail to give the "pawner" a copy of the agreement, notice of his cancellation rights and a pawn-receipt.[42] The period during which the pawn is redeemable (the "redemption period") is six months after it was taken or the period fixed for the duration of the credit, if longer, or such longer period as the parties may agree; the pawn remains redeemable after the expiry of the redemption period until it is realised or the property in it passes to the pawnee.[43] No special charges or higher charges for safe keeping of the pawn can be made on redemption after the expiry of the redemption period.

The pawnee must deliver the pawn on surrender of the receipt and payment of the amount owing unless he knows or suspects that the bearer of the receipt is not the owner of the pawn.[44] If the owner claiming the pawn does not have the receipt he may make a statutory declaration (or, where the loan is not over £15, a written statement in prescribed form) which is treated as the receipt.[45] It is an offence to fail without reasonable cause to allow redemption of a pawn.[46] Where a pawn is an article which has been stolen or obtained by fraud the court which has convicted a person of the offence may order delivery of the pawn to the owner subject to such conditions as to payment of the debt as it thinks fit.[47]

If the credit does not exceed £15, and the pawn has not been redeemed at the end of the redemption period of six months, the property in the pawn passes to the pawnee.[48] In other cases, the pawn becomes realisable if it has not been redeemed at the end of

---

39 *Hamilton* v. *Western Bank of Scotland* (1856) 19 D.152.
41 Consumer Credit Act 1974, s.114(2).
42 s.115.
43 s.116.
44 s.117.
45 s.118.
46 s.119.
47 s.122.
48 s.120.

the redemption period. The pawner must be given notice of the pawnee's intention to sell and, after the sale, information as to the sale, its proceeds and expenses. If the net proceeds are not less than the debt, the debt is discharged and any surplus is payable to the pawner; otherwise the debt is reduced *pro tanto*. On challenge, it is for the pawnee to prove that he used reasonable care to ensure that the true market value was obtained and that the expenses of sale were reasonable.[49]

5. Ships

A mortgage over a registered ship or a share therein may be registered by the registrar of the ship's port of registry.[50] The mortgagee has power to sell the ship but not without the concurrence of any prior mortgagee unless a court order is obtained.[51] He may also enter into possession of the ship. There are provisions as to the discharge and transfer of mortgages.[52] Mortgages rank according to the date of registration.[53] They are postponed to bottomry bonds,[54] and maritime liens[55] but a mortgagee in possession is preferred to an arrester.[56]

There is an odd provision that a registered mortgage is not to be affected by a subsequent "act of bankruptcy" by the mortgagor.[57] The intended effect of the section in Scotland is obscure but it is settled that it does not prevent the reduction of the mortgage under the Bankruptcy Act 1696.[58]

6. Aircraft

A security can be created over an aircraft together with its spare parts[59] by executing a mortgage[60] which is entered in the Register of Aircraft Mortgages kept by the Civil Aviation Authority. Delivery

---

49 s.121.

50 Merchant Shipping Act 1894, s.31.

51 s.35, See *Robertson Durham* v. *Constant* (1907) 15 S.L.T.131.

52 ss.32, 37, 38.

53 s.33.

54 *The St. George* [1926] P.217.

55 *The Athena* (1921) 8 LL.L.R.482.

56 *Clydesdale Bank* v. *Walker & Bain,* 1926 S.C.72.

57 s.36.

58 *Anderson* v. *Western Bank* (1859) 21 D.230.

59 Mortgaging of Aircraft Order 1972 (S.I. 1972/1268), arts. 3, 4; Mortgaging of Aircraft (Amendment) Order 1981 (S.I.1981/611).

60 Sched. 2, Pt. II.

of the aircraft to the mortgagee is not necessary.[61] A priority notice, that is, a notice of intention to make an application to enter a contemplated mortgage in the register, may be entered in the register.[62] On the mortgagor's default the mortgagee can either apply to the Court of Session for warrant to take possession of the aircraft[63] or sell the aircraft by a prescribed procedure;[64] the proceeds of the sale are held by the mortgagee in trust for payment in the following priority:[65] (i) the expenses of sale; (ii) amounts due under prior mortgages; (iii) amounts due under his mortgage and any mortgage ranking *pari passu;* (iv) amounts due under postponed mortgages; (v) amounts due under unregistered mortgages. Any residue is paid to the owner.

A registered mortgage has priority over an unregistered one.[66] Registered mortgages rank according to the time of entry in the register except that where a priority notice has been entered and the contemplated mortgage has been entered within 14 days thereafter that mortgage has priority from the time of registration of the priority notice.[67] A registered mortgage is postponed to any possessory lien in respect of work done on the aircraft and to any right to detain the aircraft under any Act of Parliament.[68]

There is a provision[69] that the mortgage is not affected by the mortgagor's "act of bankruptcy" after the date of registration of the mortgage.

7. Liens in General

A lien is a right to retain possession of goods or documents belonging to another until a debt has been paid.[70] The owner of the property must have been in a position to give a good title of possession.[71] Possession must have been obtained with the owner's consent, not by mistake.[72] The articles must have come into the

61 Sched. 2, para. 3.
62 Art. 5.
63 Sched. 2, para. 11.
64 Sched. 2, para. 9.
65 Sched. 2, para. 10.
66 Art. 14(1).
67 Art. 14(2). There is a special priority for mortgages made before 1 October 1972 and registered before 31 December 1972.
68 Art. 14(5). See *Channel Airways* v. *Manchester Corporation* [1974] 1 Lloyd's Rep. 456.
69 Art. 15. See preceding paragraph.
70 Bell, *Prin.*, § 1410.
71 *National Bank of Scotland* v. *Thomas White and Park,* 1909 S.C. 1308.
72 *Louson* v. *Craik* (1842) 4 D. 1452.

creditor's possession in the course of the legal relationship which gives rise to the lien.[71] The lien must be consistent with the terms of the contract under which possession is given so if articles are appropriated to a particular purpose there cannot be a lien over them.[73] Whether the creditor has possession is a question of fact.[74] The possession must be that of someone more than a mere servant of the debtor.[75] Civil possession may be retained by the creditor if the articles are given to a broker or borrower.[76] The lien falls with loss of possession and does not revive upon subsequent recovery of possession.[77] Relinquishing possession of part of the goods or documents does not affect the lien over the remainder for the full amount of the debt.[78] A lien held in one relationship cannot be used in respect of a debt arising from another relationship.[79] Taking a bill for the debt may be a resignation of the lien.[80]

8. Special Liens

A right of retention or special lien arises wherever property comes into the possession of someone other than the proprietor under a contract which creates rights *hinc inde*. The right "is part of the law of mutual contract, entitling one to withhold performance, or retain possession of that which forms the subject of the contract, till the counter obligation be performed."[81]

So a person who has carried out work on goods under contract is entitled to retain the goods in his possession until he is paid for the work done on the goods[82] or until he is paid damages for breach of contract.[83] This right arises from an implied condition of the

---

71 *National Bank of Scotland* v. *Thomas White and Park*, 1909 S.C.1308.

73 *Borthwick* v. *Bremner* (1833) 12 S.121.

74 *Barr & Shearer* v. *Cooper* (1875) 2 R.(H.L.)14; *Ross & Duncan* v. *Baxter & Co.* (1885) 13 R.185.

75 *Dickson* v. *Nicholson* (1885) 17 D.1011; *Callum* v. *Ferrier* (1825) 1 W. & S.399; *Gladstone* v. *McCallum* (1896) 23 R.783; *Barnton Hotel Co.* v. *Cook* (1899) 1 F.1190.

76 *Renny* v. *Rutherford* (1840) 2 D.676; *Wilmot* v. *Wilson* (1841) 3 D.815; *Gairdner* v. *Milne and Co.* (1858) 20 D.565; *Ure & Macrae* v. *Davies* (1917) 33 Sh.Ct.Rep.109.

77 *Morrison* v. *Fulwell's Tr.* (1901) 9 S.L.T.34.

78 *Gray* v. *Graham* (1855) 2 Macq.435.

79 *Largue* v. *Urquhart* (1883) 10 R.1229.

80 *Palmer* v. *Lee* (1880) 7 R.651.

81 Bell, *Prin.*, § 1419; *Moore's Carving Machine Co.* v. *Austin* (1896) 33 S.L.R.613; *Paton's Trs.* v. *Finlayson* 1923 S.C.872.

82 Bell, *Comm.*, II, 87.

83 *Moore's Carving Machine Co.* v. *Austin, supra.*

contract. It has been recognised in Scotland in the cases of an engine-builder,[84] a store-keeper,[85] and a carrier.[86]

In the case of a bleacher, the implied right is over each parcel of goods for his whole account for work done within the year.[87]

It has been held in the sheriff court that repairers exercising a lien over a car are not entitled to recover garage dues covering the period of the lien but it is not clear that this is justified by the authority cited.[88]

There is Scottish authority to the effect that a repairer cannot acquire a lien over an article on hire-purchase if the hire-purchase contract excludes the hirer's right to create a lien. The decision seems wrong.[89]

The owner is entitled to delivery of the goods on payment of the unpaid account and is not bound to find security for the expenses of the action for delivery.[90] The creditor's ultimate remedy is to petition the court to have the goods sold.[91]

9. Lien over Papers

The principle of lien has been extended to give an accountant the right to retain books and papers until he has been paid for the work done with them;[92] and a factor is in the same position.[93] The lien falls with loss of possession and does not revive upon recovery of possession.[94] On the sequestration or liquidation of the debtor, the books and papers must be delivered up to the trustee or liquidator under reservation of the lien;[95] the effect of the reservation is that if eventually a valid lien is found to have existed, the person who held the documents is entitled to a preference in the liquidation, presumably similar to that obtained by a solicitor's lien but is, of

---

84 *Ross & Duncan* v. *Baxter & Co.* (1885) 13 R.185.

85 *Laurie* v. *Denny's Tr.* (1853) 15 D.404.

86 *Stevenson* v. *Likly* (1824) 3 S.291; *Youle* v. *Cochrane* (1868) 6 M.427.

87 *Anderson's Tr.* v. *Fleming* (1871) 9 M.718.

88 *Carntyne Motors* v. *Curran,* 1958 S.L.T.(Sh.Ct.)6; *Stephen* v. *Swayne* (1861) 24 D.158.

89 *Lamonby* v. *Foulds Ltd.*, 1928 S.C.89; *Mitchell* v. *Heys & Sons* (1894) 21 R.600. See Gow, *Law of Hire-Purchase*, 2nd ed., p. 164.

90 *Garscadden* v. *Ardrossan Dry Dock Co. Ltd.*, 1910 S.C.178.

91 *Gibson and Stewart* v. *Brown & Co.* (1876) 3 R.328; *Parker* v. *Brown & Co.* (1878) 5 R.979.

92 *Meikle & Wilson* v. *Pollard* (1880) 8 R.69; *Findlay* v. *Waddell,* 1910 S.C.670; *J.Penman Ltd.* v. *Macdonald* (1953) 69 Sh.Ct.Rep.284.

93 *Robertson* v. *Ross* (1887) 15 R.67.

94 *Morrison* v. *Fulwell's Tr.* (1901) 9 S.L.T.34.

95 *Train & McIntyre* v. *Forbes,* 1925 S.L.T.286.

course, in the case of an accountant limited to the amount of the account for the work done on the papers held.

10. General Lien

A general lien is a right of retention until payment of any balance due on trade operations. If the relationship between the debtor and creditor is not one of those giving rise to a general lien, goods cannot be retained for all debts which may be due.[96] A general lien rests on express or implied contract[97] or usage of trade[98] or, in the case of a factor, on the nature of the contract.[99] The following have a general lien: a banker,[1] a stockbroker,[99] a solicitor,[2] an auctioneer,[3] and a hotel proprietor.[4]

A factor has a general lien if he is required to make payments or undertake liabilities for his principal and goods of his principal come into his possession in the ordinary course of his employment;[99] it is suggested that this lien is confined to cases of mercantile agency.[5]

A bank has a general lien over negotiable instruments belonging to a customer and in its possession.[6] The lien does not apply to securities deposited for safe custody.[7] The lien does not apply when the documents have been delivered for a special purpose.[6]

11. Solicitor's Lien

A solicitor has a general lien over his client's titles, securities, documents of debt and other papers for payment of his professional account and ordinary disbursements.[8] It does not cover advances to the client.[9]

---

96 *Harper* v. *Faulds* (1791) Mor.2666.
97 *Miller* v. *Hutcheson & Dixon* (1881) 8 R.489.
98 *Strong* v. *Philips & Co.* (1878) 5 R.770.
99 *Glendinning* v. *Hope & Co.*, 1911 S.C.(H.L.)73.
1 Bell, *Comm.*, II, 113.
2 See *infra*, para. 11.
3 *Crockart's Tr.* v. *Hay & Co. Ltd.*, 1913 S.C.509; *Mackenzie* v. *Cormack*, 1950 S.C.183. Only one judge in *Miller* v. *Hutcheson & Dixon, supra,* which is cited in these decisions, opined that an auctioneer has a general lien but an auctioneer is in any event a factor or mercantile agent.
4 Bell, *Prin.*, § 1428; Hotel Proprietors Act 1956, ss.1, 2.
5 *Macrae* v. *Leith,* 1913 S.C.901.
6 *Robertson's Tr.* v. *Royal Bank* (1890) 18 R.12.
7 *Brandao* v. *Barnett* (1846) 12 Cl. & F. 787.
8 Bell, *Prin.*, § 1438.
9 *Wylie's Exrx.* v. *McJannet* (1901) 4 F.195.

It does not cover accounts incurred on behalf of the client which the solicitor has not in fact paid and for which he is not personally liable.[10] It does not, in the case of a country solicitor, cover his Edinburgh agent's account.[11] There cannot be a lien over a company register.[12] The client must have been in a position to give a good title of possession.[13] The lien terminates with loss of possession.[14] There is no lien over titles which did not come into the solicitor's possession until after the relationship of solicitor and client had terminated.[15] If the solicitor has acted for lender and borrower he cannot exercise his lien against the borrower to the prejudice of the lender.[16] The solicitor for a proprietor or postponed heritable creditor cannot acquire a lien over writs against a heritable creditor after the date of recording of that creditor's security.[17] The solicitor for the heritable creditor cannot retain titles against the proprietor for payment of amounts due by his client.[18] Relinquishing possession of some papers does not prevent the exercise of the lien over the rest for the full account.[19] The papers cannot be sold for payment of the debt.[20]

On sequestration or liquidation of the client, the solicitor must deliver up the documents to the trustee or liquidator under reservation of his lien; he will retain his preference if he can show that if there had been no order for delivery he would have had an effectual lien.[21] An express reservation may not be necessary in a sequestration as the lien may be preserved by ss.76 and 97 of the Bankruptcy (Scotland) Act 1913.[22]

The effect of the lien is to give the solicitor a preferential right to payment of the sum due to him from the general assets of the estate;[23] he is not restricted to the assets to which the papers relate.

---

10 *Liqr. of Grand Empire Theatres* v. *Snodgrass*, 1932 S.C.(H.L.)73.
11 *Largue* v. *Urquhart* (1883) 10 R.1229.
12 *Liqr. of the Garpel Haematite Co.* v. *Andrew* (1866) 4 M.617.
13 *National Bank* v. *Thomas White and Park*, 1909 S.C.1308.
14 *Tawse* v. *Rigg* (1904) 6 F.544.
15 *Renny and Webster* v. *Myles & Murray* (1847) 9 D.619.
16 *Drummond* v. *Muirhead & Guthrie Smith* (1900) 2 F.585.
17 Conveyancing (Scotland) Act 1924, s.27.
18 *Boyd* v. *Turnbull & Findlay*, 1911 S.C.1006.
19 *Gray* v. *Graham* (1855) 2 Macq.435.
20 *Ferguson and Stuart* v. *Grant* (1856) 18 D.536.
21 *Renny and Webster* v. *Myles & Murray, supra; Rorie* v. *Stevenson*, 1908 S.C.559.
22 *Garden Haig Scott & Wallace* v. *Stevenson's Tr.*, 1962 S.C.51. In a liquidation there is Companies Act 1948, ss.243, 258.
23 *Skinner* v. *Henderson* (1865) 3 M.867.

But if the trustee or liquidator does not demand the titles and abandons the property to which they relate, there is no preference.[24] The preference is postponed to the expenses of administration of the sequestration or liquidation.[25] It is not clear how it ranks in relation to other preferential debts but there is some authority for the view that it ranks before other preferential debts.[26] The court has an equitable power to control the solicitor's lien.[27] The trustee in the solicitor's sequestration can have no higher right in respect of the lien than the solicitor himself.[28]

12. Hypothec

The landlord has a right of security over the *invecta et illata* on the subjects let for the current year's rent and the arrears of the past year's rent if sequestration proceeds within three months of the term of payment.[29] Broadly, the hypothec now exists only in urban subjects and agricultural subjects where the land does not exceed two acres in extent.[30]

The hypothec does apply to goods or a single article on hire or hire-purchase,[31] to goods on sale or return,[32] to goods in the gratuitous possession of the tenant after expiry of the hiring agreement,[33] and containers temporarily on the premises,[34] but it does not apply to a single article belonging to a third party, and hired to someone living with the tenant where the remainder of the furniture does not fall under the hypothec and the rent is payable in advance;[35] a hired article which is the only article on the premises not belonging to the landlord;[36] possibly, articles on hire for a very

---

24 *Ure & Macrae* v. *Davies* (1917) 33 Sh.Ct.Rep.109.

25 *Miln's J.F.* v. *Spence's Trs.*, 1927 S.L.T.425.

26 Bell, *Comm.*, II, 108; Gloag & Henderson, p.245.

27 *Ferguson and Stuart* v. *Grant, supra*.

28 *Inglis* v. *Moncreiff* (1851) 13 D.622.

29 Bell, *Prin.*, § 1277.

30 Hypothec Abolition (Scotland) Act 1880, s.1.

31 *Penson and Robertson*, 6 June 1820, F.C.; *Nelmes & Co.* v. *Ewing* (1883) 11 R.193; *Dundee Corporation* v. *Marr*, 1971 S.C.96; *Smith* v. *Po and Capaldi*, 1931 S.L.T.(Sh.Ct.)31. See also *McIntosh* v. *Potts* (1905) 7 F.765.

32 *Lawsons Ltd.* v. *Avon Indiarubber Co. Ltd.*, 1915 2 S.L.T.327.

33 *Smith Premier Typewriter Co.* v. *Cotton* (1907) 14 S.L.T.764.

34 *Scottish & Newcastle Breweries Ltd.* v. *Edinburgh District Council*, 1979 S.L.T. (Notes)11.

35 *Bell* v. *Andrews* (1885) 12 R.961.

36 *Edinburgh Albert Buildings Co.* v. *General Guarantee Corporation*, 1917 S.C.239.

short period;[37] possibly, a hired article where the hiring arrangement excludes the hypothec and this has been intimated to the landlord;[38] articles already sold under diligence but remaining on the premises;[39] articles which the tenant is wrongfully withholding from the true owner;[40] articles under a hire-purchase or conditional sale agreement subject to the Consumer Credit Act 1974 in the period between the service of a default notice and the date on which the notice expires or is complied with, or, if the agreement is enforceable on the order of the court only, during the period between the commencement and the termination of the creditor's action to enforce the agreement;[41] articles stored in the premises in respect of which the tenant is receiving a rent;[42] articles sent to the tenant as samples.[43] The hypothec is not affected by the Bankruptcy Act[44] but the landlord's right is postponed to the superior's hypothec for feuduty, all privileged debts, rates and taxes and certain wages.[45]

The superior has a hypothec over the crop and stock or *invecta et illata* for the last or current feuduty, similar but preferable to the landlord's hypothec.[46]

---

37 *Adam* v. *Sutherland* (1863) 2 M.6, *per* Lord Deas at p.8.
38 *Jaffray* v. *Carrick* (1836) 15 S.43; *Orr* v. *Jay & Co.* (1911) 27 Sh.Ct.Rep.158.
39 *Adam* v. *Sutherland, supra.*
40 *Jaffray* v. *Carrick, supra.*
41 Consumer Credit Act 1974, s.104.
42 Bell, *Comm.*, II, 31.
43 *Pulsometer Engineering Co. Ltd.* v. *Gracie* (1887) 14 R.316.
44 Bankruptcy (Scotland) Act 1913, s.115.
45 Bell, *Prin.*, § 1241; Taxes Management Act 1970, s.64; Local Government (Scotland) Act 1947, s.248; Graham Stewart, p.489.
46 Bell, *Prin.*, § 698.

CHAPTER 8

SECURITIES: OTHER PROPERTY

1. Incorporeal Moveables

A security over incorporeal moveables is effected by assignation followed by intimation.[1] Mere delivery of the document of title has no effect, nor has a mere contractual obligation to create a security.[2] If the assignation is *ex facie* absolute, it is a security for any debt due by the debtor to the creditor notwithstanding that a back letter mentions a specific debt; if the assignation specifies the debt for which it is to constitute a security, the creditor must grant a retrocession on payment of that debt.[3]

In the case of shares in a company the only fully satisfactory method of creating a security is to obtain and register a duly executed transfer. A deposit of the share certificates has no effect.[4] There is a practice of delivery to the creditor of the share certificates together with a duly executed transfer to be held by him so that he can register it at any time. Completion within six months of notour bankruptcy is not a fraudulent preference.[5] He can complete his security by registration even after the debtor's sequestration if the trustee has not completed his title[6] but on the other hand his right is liable to be defeated by an arrestment or a fraudulent subsequent transfer executed by the debtor. The identical shares should be retransferred on repayment of the loan.[7] The creditor may be liable to the debtor if he fails to subscribe for a "rights issue"[8] or if he sells more shares than are required to pay the debt.[9]

A security can be granted over a patent.[10]

---

1 See Chap. 24.

2 *Christie* v. *Ruxton* (1862) 24 D.1182; *Robertson* v. *British Linen Bank* (1891) 18 R.1225; *Wylie's Exx.* v. *McJannet* (1901) 4 F.195; *Bank of Scotland* v. *Liqrs. of Hutchison Main & Co. Ltd.*, 1914 S.C.(H.L.)1.

3 *National Bank* v. *Forbes* (1858) 21 D.79; *Robertson's Tr.* v. *Riddell,* 1911 S.C.14. It may be different if the back letter specifically limits the future advances to be secured: *Anderson's Tr.* v. *Somerville & Co.* (1899) 36 S.L.R.833.

4 *Gourlay* v. *Mackie* (1887) 14 R.403.

5 *Guild* v. *Hannan* (1884) 22 S.L.R.520.

6 See Chap. 19, para. 13.

7 *Crerar* v. *Bank of Scotland,* 1921 S.C.736; 1922 S.C.(H.L.)137.

8 *Waddell* v. *Hutton,* 1911 S.C.575.

9 *Nelson* v. *National Bank,* 1936 S.C.570.

10 Patents Act 1977, s.31.

2. Heritage

A security cannot be created over heritage by mere deposit of the titles.[11] In general, the only method by which a security can be created over heritage is by the granting of a standard security.[12] Where a deed which is not in the form of a standard security, for the purpose of securing a debt, contains a disposition or assignation of an interest in land, it is to that extent void and unenforceable and the creditor may be required to grant a deed to clear the register.[13] The granter of a standard security need not have a recorded or registered title and can deduce his title.[14] The security is in a specified form.[15] Unless specially qualified the import of the clause imposing a personal obligation is:[16]

(a) where the security is for a fixed amount advanced or payable at, or prior to, the delivery of the deed, the clause undertaking to make payment to the creditor imports an acknowledgment of receipt by the debtor of the principal sum advanced or an acknowledgment by the debtor of liability to pay that sum and a personal obligation undertaken by the debtor to repay or pay to the creditor on demand in writing at any time after the date of delivery of the standard security the said sum, with interest at the rate stated payable on the dates specified, together with all expenses for which the debtor is liable;

(b) where the security is for a fluctuating amount, whether subject to a maximum amount or not and whether advanced or due partly before and partly after delivery of the deed or whether to be advanced or to become due wholly after such delivery, the clause undertaking to make payment to the creditor imports a personal obligation by the debtor to repay or pay to the

---

11 *Christie* v. *Ruxton* (1862) 24 D.1182.

12 Conveyancing and Feudal Reform (Scotland) Act 1970, s.9(3). A security could be created by bond and disposition in security under the Small Dwellings Acquisition (Scotland) Acts 1899-1923: 1970 Act, s.9(7); but s.9(7) is repealed by Tenants' Rights, Etc. (Scotland) Act 1980, s.84, Sched. 5. Securities over entailed estates can be created by bond and disposition in security.

13 1970 Act, s.9(4). This no doubt may give rise to problems similar to those created by what is now s.62(4) of the Sale of Goods Act 1979; see Chap. 7, para. 3.

14 s.12. Under registration of title, a deduction of title will not be necessary if the midcouples or links are produced to the Keeper: Land Registration (Scotland) Act 1979, s.15(3).

15 Sched. 2, Forms A or B.

16 s.10(1). Under standard condition 12, the debtor is personally liable for the expenses of creating, varying, restricting, discharging, calling-up the security and of realising the security subjects.

creditor on demand in writing the amount, not being greater than the maximum amount, if any, specified in the deed, advanced or due and outstanding at the time of demand, with interest on each advance from the date when it was made until repayment thereof, or on each sum payable from the date on which it became due until payment thereof, and at the rate stated payable on the dates specified, together with all expenses for which the debtor is liable.

The sum secured need not be specified.[17] The clause of consent to registration in the specified form imports a consent to registration in the Books of Council and Session, or in the books of the appropriate sheriff court, for execution.[18] The security is regulated by the "standard conditions" set out in Schedule 3 of the Act unless these have been varied.[19] A third party has no notice of a variation of the conditions which has not entered the Sasine Register but a reference in the standard security to the possibility of variation by a document not on the register is sufficient to put the third party on inquiry.[20] When the security is recorded or registered it vests the interest over which it is granted in the grantee as a security for the performance of the contract to which the security relates.[21]

Ranking of a standard security, in the absence of express provision, is by date of recording in the Sasine Register. Under registration of title, registered interests rank according to date of registration. A registered interest and an interest recorded in the Sasine Register rank according to the respective dates of registration and recording.[22]

The ranking of the security may be regulated by the parties but, apart from that, where the creditor receives notice of the creation of a subsequent recorded security over the same subjects or of a subsequent recorded conveyance of the subjects themselves, his

---

[17] s.9(6). Under registration of title there is no indemnity by the Keeper of the Registers in respect of a claim relating to the amount due under a heritable security: Land Registration (Scotland) Act 1979, s.12(3)(*o*).

[18] s.10(3).

[19] s.11(2).

[20] *Trade Development Bank* v. *Warriner & Mason (Scotland) Ltd.*, 1980 S.L.T.223.

[21] s.11(1). Under registration of title, a security is registered by amending the title sheet of the relevant interest in land. The creditor will be given a charge certificate containing details of his security and disclosing any prior or *pari passu* security: Land Registration (Scotland) Act 1979, s.5.

[22] Land Registration (Scotland) Act 1979, s.7.

preference is restricted to security for his advances up to that time and any future advances which he may be required to make under the contract to which the security relates and interest present or future thereon (including any such interest which has accrued or may accrue) and for any expenses or outlays (including interest thereon) which may be, or may have been, reasonably incurred in the exercise of any power conferred on any creditor by the deed expressing the existing security.[23] The recording of a deed is not, but a conveyance of the security subjects by operation of law is, sufficient notice to the creditor.

The security may be transferred in whole or in part by assignation in the statutory form,[24] recording or registration of which vests the security in the assignee as if it had been granted in his favour. The assignation also has the effect of vesting in the assignee the full benefit of all corroborative or substitutional obligations for the debt, or any part thereof, whether these obligations are contained in any deed or arise by operation of law or otherwise.[25]

There is provision for restriction, variation and discharge of the security.[26] The debtor has a right to redeem the security on giving two months' notice but this is subject to any agreement to the contrary.[27]

If the creditor intends to require discharge of the debt secured, he must serve a calling-up notice on the proprietor and on any other person against whom he wishes to preserve any right of recourse in respect of the debt. The debtor is in default if he does not comply with the notice and the creditor can proceed to sell the security subjects and exercise his other remedies under the Act.[28] The debtor is also in default if he has failed to comply with any other requirement arising out of the security; the creditor may serve a "notice of default" requiring fulfilment of the obligation; if that is not complied with, the creditor can exercise his remedies under the Act other than entering into possession.[29] Alternatively, he can,

---

23 1970 Act, s.13. As to the effect of a security to a third creditor, see Gretton (1980) 25 J.L.S.275; Halliday (1981) 26 J.L.S.26.

24 s.14(1); Sched. 4, Forms A or B.

25 s.14(2).

26 ss.15-17.

27 s.18(1A) added by Redemption of Standard Securities (Scotland) Act 1971, s.1.

28 ss.19, 20(1), (2); Sched. 3, standard condition 9(1)(*a*). Remedies other than those provided by the 1970 Act (*i.e.* (1), (2), (6) and (7) *infra*) can be exercised without complying with the statutory conditions.

29 Sched. 3, standard condition 9(1)(*b*); ss.21, 23(2).

instead of serving a notice, apply to the court for warrant to exercise any of his remedies under the Act. The third type of default arises where the debtor is insolvent;[30] the creditor can apply to the court for warrant to exercise his remedies.[31]

The creditor's remedies[32] are:

(1) to raise an action on the personal obligation. The obligation transmits against a person taking by succession, gift or bequest, *quanto lucratus,* but it transmits against a person taking by onerous conveyance only where there is an agreement to that effect *in gremio* of the conveyance and the conveyance is signed by him.[33]

(2) to execute summary diligence under the personal obligation. This can, of course, be done only where the deed contained a clause of consent. Where the personal obligation is created by succession, gift or bequest, summary diligence is competent thereon only if the obligant has executed an agreement to the transmission of the obligation.[34]

(3) to enter into possession of the security subjects and receive the rents.[35]

(4) to sell the security subjects in accordance with the statutory procedure.[36] The money received is held by the creditor in trust for payment in the following priority:[37] (i) his expenses of sale, (ii) the whole amount due under any prior security to which the sale is not made subject, (iii) the whole amount due under his security and any security ranking *pari passu* with his, (iv) the amounts due under any postponed securities. The residue is payable to the person entitled to the security subjects at the time of sale or any person authorised to give receipts for the proceeds of sale. The recording or registration of the disposition to the purchaser, bearing to be in implement of the sale,

---

30 Sched. 3, standard conditions 9(1)(*c*), 9(2). See *United Dominions Trust Ltd.* v. *Site Preparations Ltd. (No. 1),* 1978 S.L.T.(Sh.Ct.)14. *Cf. United Dominions Trust Ltd.* v. *Site Preparations Ltd. (No. 2),* 1978 S.L.T.(Sh.Ct.)21.

31 s.24(1).

32 He has the choice of remedy: *McWhirter* v. *McCulloch's Trs.* (1887) 14 R.918.

33 Conveyancing (Scotland) Act 1874, s.47; Conveyancing (Scotland) Act 1924, s.15(1).

34 1924 Act, s.15(2).

35 1970 Act, Sched. 3, standard condition 10(3)-(6).

36 1970 Act, ss.20-25.

37 s.27.

disburdens the subjects of the security and of *pari passu* and postponed securities.[38]

(5) to apply to the court for decree of foreclosure after a failure to sell the subjects at a price not exceeding the amount due under the security and any *pari passu* or prior securities.[39] The court may order another sale at a price fixed by the court at which the creditor can bid and purchase or it may grant a decree of foreclosure declaring the creditor's right to the subjects at the price at which they were last exposed. The result of decree of foreclosure on its being recorded or registered is to extinguish any right of redemption, to vest the subjects in the creditor as if he had received an irredeemable disposition thereof duly recorded from the proprietor, to disburden the subjects of the security and all postponed securities and diligences and to give the creditor the same right as the debtor to redeem prior or *pari passu* securities.[40] The debtor's personal obligation remains in force so far as not extinguished by the price at which the subjects have been acquired.[41]

(6) to attach the moveables belonging to the proprietor or the subjects by a poinding of the ground.[42] The procedure is by raising an action in the sheriff court or Court of Session. Service creates a nexus over the moveables on the subjects at that time. A warrant to poind is granted and when the moveables have been inventoried a warrant for sale can be obtained.

(7) to raise an action of adjudication.[42] Adjudications on *debita fundi* are preferable to adjudications on personal debts and rank *inter se* according to priority of infeftment.

3. Heritable Securities: Sequestration

Heritable estate which is subject to a security may be sold in any of the following ways:

(a) the heritable creditor may sell in terms of his security notwithstanding the sequestration. The trustee may concur to fortify the title but this is not necessary. The trustee or any posterior

---

38 s.26. A prior security is not affected but the selling creditor can redeem it: s.26(2).

39 s.28.

40 s.28(6).

41 s.28(7).

42 This remedy is not mentioned in the 1970 Act but it is thought to be available: Halliday, *The Conveyancing and Feudal Reform (Scotland) Act 1970*, 2nd ed., p.205.

heritable creditor may by petition to the court compel the selling creditor and the purchaser to account for any reversion of the price.[43]

(b) the heritable creditor may concur with the trustee in selling the estate and the price is paid to the parties entitled thereto.[44]

(c) the general creditors may resolve that the trustee shall dispose of the heritage by public or judicial sale. A heritable creditor cannot interfere with this if he has not commenced proceedings for sale before the resolution or if he has commenced such proceedings before the resolution and has thereafter unduly delayed them. The estate must not be sold for less than an upset price which is sufficient to pay the debt, principal, interest and expenses of the heritable creditor.[45]

(d) the trustee with the concurrence of a majority of creditors in number and value, and of the heritable creditors and the Accountant of Court may sell the estate by private bargain on such terms as the trustee with the consent of the parties fixes.[46]

Where the estate has been sold by the trustee, he must make up a scheme of ranking and division of the claims of the heritable creditors and other creditors on the price. The scheme is reported to the court and judgment thereon is a warrant for payment out of the price against the purchaser of the heritage.[47]

4. Heritable Securities: Consumer Credit Act

In the language of the Act, a "land mortgage" is any security "charged" on land, "land" being defined to include heritable subjects of whatever description.[48]

The general provisions as to the cancellation of regulated agreements[49] do not apply to agreements secured on land but before sending to the debtor for signature an unexecuted agreement where the prospective regulated agreement is to be secured on land, the

---

43 Bankruptcy (Scotland) Act 1913, s.108. As to liquidation, see Companies Act 1948, s.327(1)(*c*).

44 s.109.

45 s.110.

46 s.111.

47 s.112.

48 Consumer Credit Act 1974, s.189. Many heritable securities will relate to exempt agreements: see Chap. 3, para. 4. For the requirements of the Act which apply to all securities, see Chap. 3, para. 21.

49 Chap. 3, para. 13.

creditor must give the debtor a copy of the unexecuted agreement containing a notice indicating the debtor's right to withdraw from the prospective agreement and how and when the right is exercisable.[50] This does not apply to a restricted-use agreement to finance the purchase of the land or to an agreement for a bridging loan in connection with the purchase of the security subjects or other land. The regulated agreement is not properly executed unless (a) the copy agreement and notice of the withdrawal right is sent to the debtor, (b) the unexecuted agreement is sent by post to the debtor for his signature not less than seven days after the copy was given to him, (c) in the period between the giving of that copy and the expiry of seven days after the sending of the unexecuted agreement for his signature (or its return signed if earlier) the creditor refrained from approaching the debtor, in person, by telephone or letter or otherwise except in response to a specific request made by the debtor, (d) no notice of withdrawal by the debtor was received by the creditor before the sending of the unexecuted agreement.[51]

A "land mortgage" securing a regulated agreement is enforceable (so far as provided in relation to the agreement) on an order of the court only; retaking of the land is an enforcement.[52] There would appear to be no sanction for breach of this provision. The debtor could no doubt obtain an interdict. The provision does not prevent enforcement with the consent of the debtor given at that time.[53]

There is a general saving provision that nothing in the Act is to affect the rights of a heritable creditor, other than one carrying on the business of debt-collecting, who became the creditor for value and without notice of any defect in title arising by virtue of the other provisions of the Act or who derived title from such a creditor.[54]

5. Leases

A security can be granted over a lease which is not registrable by assignation followed by possession; if the lease is registrable, a standard security must be used.

---

50 s.58.

51 s.61. As to the enforcement of improperly executed agreements, see Chap. 3, para. 18. As to the effects of withdrawal, see s.57.

52 ss.126, 65(2).

53 s.173(3).

54 s.177.

A lease is registrable if it is probative, it is for a period exceeding 20 years and it contains a description of the subjects.[55] An assignee who has taken possession before recording of the standard security prevails.[56]

Under registration of title, however, a lessee under a long lease (*i.e.* a probative lease for a period which exceeds, or at the option of the grantee, could exceed 20 years) attains a real right only by registration and registration is the only means of making rights or obligations relating to the lease real rights or obligations or of affecting such real rights or obligations.[57] But two kinds of interest under leases are "overriding interests" which can prevail over registered interests. The first is the interest of a lessee under a lease which is not a long lease; the second is the interest of a lessee under a long lease who, prior to the commencement of the Land Registration (Scotland) Act 1979, has acquired a real right to the subjects of the lease by possession.[58] The second of these, but not the first, may be noted in the Land Register.[59]

6. Catholic and Secondary Securities

A catholic creditor is one whose security extends over two or more subjects; a secondary creditor is one whose security is over one of these subjects and is postponed to that of the catholic creditor. Where there is one secondary creditor, the catholic creditor is not entitled to proceed so as to injure the secondary creditor while not obtaining any benefit for himself. So if his security extends over subjects B and C, and the postponed security of the secondary creditor is over B, the catholic creditor must either take payment so far as possible from C or if he takes payment from B, assign his security right to the secondary creditor.[60] This equitable right of the secondary creditor can however be defeated by the sale of C, by the debtor creating a postponed security over C, or by the creditor renouncing his security over C.[61] The principle does not apply where the catholic creditor has a postponed security over C for

---

55 Registration of Leases (Scotland) Act 1857 as amended by Long Leases (Scotland) Act 1954, s.27, and Land Tenure Reform (Scotland) Act 1974, Sched. 6, paras. 1, 5.

56 *Rodger* v. *Crawfords* (1867) 6 M.24, *per* Lord Neaves at p.31.

57 Land Registration (Scotland) Act 1979, s.3(3).

58 1979 Act, s.28.

59 1979 Act, ss.6(4), 9(4).

60 *Littlejohn* v. *Black* (1855) 18 D.207; *Nicol's Tr.* v. *Hill* (1889) 16 R.416.

61 *Morton* (1871) 10 M.292.

a separate debt.[62] Where there is a secondary security over each subject the catholic creditor must not unfairly benefit one secondary creditor to the prejudice of the other. The debt must be paid proportionally out of the two subjects.[63]

The foregoing principles apply whether the property is heritable or moveable and whether the question arises on operation of the security or in a sequestration.[64]

---

62 Gloag & Irvine, p.63.

63 *Littlejohn* v. *Black, supra, per* L.P. McNeill at p.213; *Earl of Moray* v. *Mansfield* (1836) 14 S.886.

64 *Littlejohn* v. *Black, supra.*

CHAPTER 9

SECURITIES GRANTED BY A COMPANY

1. Registration

Certain charges created by a company registered in Scotland are void against the liquidator and creditors unless prescribed particulars are lodged with the registrar of companies within 21 days after the date of creation of the charge[1] (*i.e.* the date of execution by the company in the case of a floating charge and in the case of other charges the date on which the creditor's right was constituted as a real right). Registrable charges are:

(a) a charge on land wherever situated, or any interest therein, not including a charge for any rent, ground annual or other periodical sum payable in respect of the land, but including a charge created by a heritable security;
(b) a security over the company's uncalled share capital;
(c) a security over incorporeal moveable property of any of the following categories:
  (i) the book debts of the company;
  (ii) calls made but not paid;
  (iii) goodwill;
  (iv) a patent or licence thereunder;
  (v) a trademark;
  (vi) a copyright or licence thereunder;
(d) a security over a ship or aircraft[2] or any share in a ship;
(e) a floating charge. There are special provisions relating to debentures.

A book debt is a debt arising in the course of a business which would or could in the ordinary course of business be entered in well-kept books relating to that business whether it is in fact entered in the books of the business or not.[3] Sums due under hire-purchase agreements were held to be book debts[3] but rights under an Export Credits Guarantee policy were held not to be.[4] Evidence of accountancy practice is relevant. Where a negotiable instrument has been

---

[1] Companies Act 1948, s.106A.
[2] Mortgaging of Aircraft Order 1972 (S.I.1972/1268), art.16.
[3] *Independent Automatic Sales Ltd.* v. *Knowles & Foster* [1962] 1 W.L.R.974.
[4] *Paul & Frank Ltd.* v. *Discount Bank (Overseas) Ltd.* [1967] Ch.348.

given to secure the payments of any book debts of the company, the deposit of the instrument for the purpose of securing an advance to the company is not a charge on those book debts.[5]

The list of registrable charges does not include fixed securities over corporeal moveables nor does it include fixed securities over incorporeal moveables not falling within the specified categories; in particular, a fixed security over shares is not registrable.[6]

Where the company acquires property subject to a registrable charge the prescribed particulars must be registered.[7]

The court may allow late registration.[8] If a charge becomes void by a failure to deliver particulars, the money secured thereby immediately becomes payable. It is failure to deliver particulars and not failure in registration which makes the charge void.[9]

A company registered in Scotland which has an established place of business in England must register in England charges it creates on property in England and charges on property in England which it acquires. It must, therefore, register in both Scotland and England a charge on English land, and for that matter any other property of the prescribed types situated in England.[10]

A company registered in England must register in England broadly the same types[11] of charge but it need not register with the registrar of companies in Scotland charges affecting property in Scotland.[12]

A company incorporated outside Great Britain which has a place of business in Scotland must register in Scotland charges it creates on property in Scotland and charges on property in Scotland which it acquires.[13] The obligation does not depend upon the registration of the company under Part X of the Companies Act 1948.[14]

---

5 Companies Act 1948, s.106A(5).

6 *Scottish Homes Investment Co.*, 1968 S.C.244.

7 s.106C.

8 s.106G; *M. Milne Ltd.* (1963) 79 Sh.Ct.Rep.105; *Archibald Campbell, Hope & King Ltd., Petrs.*, 1967 S.L.T.83.

9 *National Provincial and Union Bank of England* v. *Charnley* [1924] 1 K.B.431.

10 Companies Act 1948, s.106; *Amalgamated Securities Ltd.*, 1967 S.C.56.

11 The additions are a charge securing debentures and a charge created or evidenced by an instrument which, if executed by an individual, would require registration as a bill of sale, *i.e.* certain securities over what in Scotland would be corporeal moveables.

12 s.95.

13 s.106K.

14 *N.V. Slavenburg's Bank* v. *Intercontinental Ltd.* [1980] 1 W.L.R.1076.

2. Floating Charge: Creation

A company may create a floating charge over all or any part of the property (including uncalled capital) which may from time to time be comprised in its property and undertaking.[15] The charge may secure any debt or other obligation (including a cautionary obligation) incurred or to be incurred by, or binding upon, the company or any other person. The floating charge is created by the execution under the seal of the company, or by an attorney on its behalf, of an instrument or bond or other written acknowledgment of debt or obligation which purports to create such a charge.[16]

Prescribed particulars of the charge together with a certified copy of the instrument creating or evidencing it must be delivered to or received by the registrar of companies within 21 days after the date of its creation.[17] If there is no such registration, the charge is void against the liquidator and any creditor but this is without prejudice to any contract or obligation for repayment of the money thereby secured and, on the charge becoming void, the money secured thereby immediately becomes payable. The court may grant relief in respect of a failure to register timeously.[18]

3. Operation

The creditor may apply to the court for winding up of the company if his security is in jeopardy, that is, that events have occurred or are about to occur which render it unreasonable in the interests of the creditor that the company should retain power to dispose of the property which is subject to the floating charge.[19] On winding up, the floating charge attaches to the property then comprised in the company's property and undertaking (or part thereof) and has effect as if the charge were a fixed security over the property to which it has attached in respect of the principal of the debt or obligation to which it relates and any interest due or to become due thereon.[20] Interest accrues until payment of the sum due under the charge.[21] A fixed security is a security, other than a floating charge

[15] Companies (Floating Charges and Receivers) (Scotland) Act 1972, s.1(1).
[16] s.2(1).
[17] Companies Act 1948, s.106A. Recording in the Sasine Register is not necessary: 1972 Act, s.3. Under registration of title a floating charge is an "overriding interest": Land Registration (Scotland) Act 1979, s.28.
[18] s.106G.
[19] 1972 Act, s.4.
[20] s.1(2). As to attachment, see *infra*, para. 8.
[21] s.1(4).

or a charge having the nature of a floating charge, which on winding up in Scotland would be treated as an effective security; a heritable security is a fixed security.[22]

The attaching of the charge is, however, subject to:

(1) the rights of any person who has "effectually executed diligence" on the property or any part of it.[23]

(2) the rights of the holder of a fixed security arising by operation of law,[24] *e.g.* a lien, the landlord's hypothec.

(3) the rights of the holder of a fixed security or another floating charge over the property ranking in priority to the floating charge.[25] The instrument creating the floating charge or an instrument of alteration may contain provisions prohibiting or restricting the creation of a fixed security or other floating charge having priority over or ranking *pari passu* with the floating charge or regulating the order in which it will rank with any other subsisting or future floating charges or fixed securities. If there are no such provisions, a fixed security has priority over a floating charge if it has been constituted as a real right before the floating charge has attached; floating charges rank with one another according to the time of registration; floating charges received by the registrar by the same postal delivery rank with one another equally.[26] Where, however, the holder of a floating charge receives intimation in writing of the registration of another floating charge over the same property or part thereof, his preference is restricted to his present advances, future advances he is required to make under the instrument creating his charge or any instrument of alteration or any document executed before registration of the charge; interest due or to become due on all such advances and any expenses or outlays reasonably incurred by him.[27]

(4) payment of the preferential payments specified in Chapter 23, para. 8, in so far as the assets of the company available for payment of general creditors are insufficient to meet them.[28] The priority is created over "the claims of holders of debentures

---

[22] s.31(1).
[23] s.1(2). See Chap. 16, para. 14.
[24] s.5(2).
[25] s.1(2).
[26] s.5(4).
[27] s.5(5).
[28] Companies Act 1948, s.319(5).

under any floating charge" so there may be a technical argument that it does not exist where there are no debentures but the wide and vague meaning of "debenture" is a counter-argument.[29] The liquidator acting in the name of the company is the appropriate pursuer to recover a contribution from the floating charge assets to the preferential debts once the assets available for payment of general creditors have been exhausted.[30]

4. Fraudulent Preferences

A floating charge is not voidable as an alienation or fraudulent preference under the general insolvency law[31] but if it is created within 12 months of the commencement of liquidation it is invalid unless the company was "solvent" at the date of creation except to the amount of any cash paid to the company "at the time of or subsequently to the creation of, and in consideration for, the charge," together with interest thereon at five per cent.[32] A company is not solvent if it cannot pay its debts as they become due.[33]

An arrangement that the cash paid to the company will be applied in payment of specified debts does not necessarily invalidate the charge[34] but if the object and effect of the transaction under which the cash was paid was to benefit certain creditors and not to benefit the company the charge is invalid.[35] An arrangement that, in exchange for a cheque for the amount of the advance, the creditor would be given a cheque for a lesser amount representing the prior indebtedness was held to invalidate the debenture to the extent of the lesser amount.[36]

Whether a payment is "at the time" of creation of the charge is a question of fact; it may be slightly before the execution of the instrument creating the charge;[37] a delay, however, requires explanation and the acquiescence of the lender in the delay may be fatal.

---

29 1948 Act, s.455; *Knightsbridge Estates Trust Ltd.* v. *Byrne* [1940] A.C.613.

30 *Westminster Corporation* v. *Chapman* [1916] 1 Ch.161.

31 1948 Act, s.322(3), added by 1972 Act, s.8.

32 1948 Act, s.322.

33 *Re Patrick and Lyon* [1933] Ch.786.

34 *Re Matthew Ellis Ltd.* [1933] Ch.458.

35 *Re Destone Fabrics Ltd.* [1941] Ch.319; *Re Orleans Motor Co. Ltd.* [1911] 2 Ch.41. See also *Re Ambassadors (Bournemouth)* (1961) 105 S.J.969; *Libertas-Kommerz GmbH,* 1978 S.L.T.222.

36 *Revere Trust* v. *Wellington Handkerchief Works* [1931] N.I.55.

37 *Re Columbian Fireproofing Co. Ltd.* [1910] 2 Ch.120; *Re Olderfleet Shipbuilding Co.* [1922] 1 I.R.26.

Advances may be "in consideration for" the charge if they are made in reliance on the existence of the charge and it is not necessary that they should be made in implement of a binding obligation made at the time the charge was created.[38] Where the company had an overdrawn account at the granting of the charge to the bank, it was held that each advance after the creation of the charge was cash paid to the company in consideration of the charge and that the bank was entitled under the rule in Clayton's case to apply subsequent payments in by the company to the pre-charge indebtedness.[39]

5. Receivers

The alternative remedy of the holder of the floating charge is to have a receiver appointed.

The holder may appoint a receiver himself on the occurrence of an event specified in the instrument creating the charge as entitling him so to do and, unless the instrument otherwise provides, on the occurrence of:

(a) the expiry of 21 days after a demand for payment of the whole or part of the principal sum secured, without payment having been made;
(b) the expiry of two months during the whole of which interest due and payable under the charge has been in arrears;
(c) the making of an order or the passing of a resolution to wind up the company;
(d) the appointment of a receiver by virtue of another floating charge created by the company.[40]

A receiver may be appointed by the court in any of these circumstances (including the events specified in the instrument) except (d) and also where the court, on the application of the holder of the charge, pronounces itself satisfied that the position of the holder is likely to be prejudiced if no appointment is made.[41]

The holder appoints the receiver by an instrument of appointment, a certified copy of which must be sent to the registrar of companies so that the particulars can be entered in the register of charges. The date of the instrument is the date of appointment and

---

38 *Re F. & E. Stanton Ltd.* [1929] 1 Ch.180.
39 *Re Yeovil Glove Co.* [1965] Ch.148.
40 1972 Act, s.12(1).
41 s.12(2).

the charge then attaches to the property subject to it as if it were a fixed security.[42] Where the appointment is made by the court, a certified copy of the interlocutor must be sent to the registrar; the charge attaches at the date of appointment.[43]

6. Receiver: Powers

The receiver has power to take possession of, collect and get in the property subject to the charge from the company but his powers are subject to the rights of creditors who have effectually executed diligence and of those who hold securities ranking prior to or *pari passu* with the floating charge by virtue of which he was appointed.[44] He must pay out of the assets coming into his hands in priority to any claim for principal or interest by the holder of the floating charge the preferential debts specified in Chapter 23, para. 8, insofar as these have become known to him within six months after advertisement by him for claims.[45] The periods of time used for computing these debts are reckoned from the date of the receiver's appointment. He will be liable to the preferential creditors if he disposes of the assets without paying them.[46] He may recoup the payments he makes as far as may be out of the assets of the company available for payment of ordinary creditors. If the floating charge affects only part of the company's assets, the receiver is not required to pay preferential debts incurred by the company between the date of his appointment and the commencement of a subsequent liquidation because the priority given by s.319(5)(*b*) of the Companies Act 1948 arises only where a charge is still floating at the commencement of liquidation.[47] Where the same creditor holds a floating charge and a fixed security over the same assets, the fixed security prevails and has priority over the preferential debts.[48]

The receiver has wide powers including power to sell the property and power to carry on the business of the company so far as he thinks it desirable to do so.[49] He is deemed to be the agent of the company in relation to the property subject to the charge.[50]

---

42 ss.13(6), (7). As to attachment, see *infra,* para. 8.
43 ss.14(6), (7).
44 s.15.
45 s.19. See s.19(3) as to accrued holiday remuneration.
46 *I.R.C.* v. *Goldblatt* [1972] Ch.498.
47 *Re Griffin Hotel Co. Ltd.* [1941] Ch.129.
48 *Re Lewis Merthyr Consolidated Collieries* [1929] 1 Ch.498.
49 s.15(1)(*b*), (*o*).
50 s.17(1).

The receiver is personally liable on any contract entered into by him in the performance of his functions except in so far as the contract otherwise provides.[51] Where he is so personally liable he is entitled to be indemnified out of the property subject to the charge.[52] Prior contracts entered into by the company continue in force notwithstanding the receiver's appointment, subject to their terms, but the receiver does not by virtue only of his appointment incur any personal liability on such contracts.[53]

Where property subject to the floating charge is subject to a security (prior, *pari passu* or postponed) or is affected or attached by effectual diligence, and the receiver cannot obtain the consent of the creditor to a sale, he can apply to the court to authorise the sale of the property free of the security or diligence on such terms and conditions as the court thinks fit.[54] Authorisation will not be given where a fixed security ranking prior to the floating charge has not been met or provided for in full. The disencumbering of the property has effect from the date of delivery of the document of transfer or conveyance of the property, or from the date of recording, intimation or registration thereof where one of these is required.

7. Distribution of Funds

Monies received by the receiver are paid to the holder of the floating charge in or towards satisfaction of the debt secured but subject to the rights of holders of prior or *pari passu* fixed securities, persons who have effectually executed diligence, creditors in respect of debts incurred by the receiver, the receiver in respect of his liabilities, expenses and remuneration, and preferential creditors.[55] Any balance is paid in accordance with their respective rights and interests, as the case may require, to (a) any other receiver, (b) the holder of a fixed security over property subject to the floating charge, (c) the company or its liquidator.

It has been held in England that the receiver is not a debtor to the company for the balance which may ultimately be due to it and there is therefore, during the course of the receivership and before the final accounting, no debt which can be attached by a creditor.[56]

---

[51] s.17(2).
[52] s.17(3).
[53] s.17(4).
[54] s.21.
[55] s.20. There is no mention here of other floating charges.
[56] *Seabrook Estate Co. Ltd.* v. *Ford* [1949] 2 All E.R.94.

8. Attachment

On liquidation the floating charge attaches to the property subject to the charge and the provisions of the Companies Act relating to winding up except s.327(1)(*c*) (which applies provisions of the Bankruptcy Act) shall have effect "as if the charge were a fixed security over the property to which it has attached".[57] On the appointment of a receiver the floating charge attaches to the property subject to it and the attachment has effect "as if the charge were a fixed security over the property to which it has attached."[58] The operation of this statutory hypothesis has received little examination.

Corporeal moveables subject to the floating charge are treated as if they were the subject of a pledge even although they are not in the possession of a creditor. Goods which have been sold but were still in the company's ownership and possession at the date of attachment are subject to the security of the holder of the floating charge even if the price has been paid.

Goods which are on conditional sale or hire-purchase and which were still in the company's property but which are in the possession of the acquirer are not, it is thought, affected by the crystallisation of the charge. The floating charge creditor should not be in this respect in a better position than a liquidator; the acquirer has a right of retention over the goods which, being a security arising by operation of law, prevails over the floating charge.

On the sale in the ordinary course of business of corporeal moveables which were the property of the company at crystallisation, the resultant debt is clearly still subject to the charge—the sale is by a pledgee.[59]

Incorporeal moveable property will be subject to the crystallised security which will prevail over assignees who have not intimated or registered their transfer at the date of crystallisation. There would seem to be no ground for importing here the rule of the "race to register" which obtains in sequestration and liquidation.[60]

The appointment of a receiver is one of the events on which the company's rights under a third party liability insurance policy are transferred to the third party.[61]

---

57 s.1(2).
58 ss.13(7), 14(7).
59 *N. W. Robbie & Co. Ltd.* v. *Witney Warehouse Co. Ltd.* [1963] 1 W.L.R.1324.
60 See Chap. 19, para. 13.
61 Third Parties (Rights against Insurers) Act 1930, s.1(1)(*b*).

In England it has been held that a debt due by Y acquired by X by assignment after crystallisation of a charge over Y's assets cannot be set off against amounts which were due by X to Y before crystallisation; the pre-crystallisation debts had been assigned to the floating charge holder at a time when there was no debt due by Y to X which could be set off.[62] A debt arising because of the rescission of a contract by the receiver cannot be set off against a debt due to the company before crystallisation.[63] A debt due by the company before crystallisation can, however, be set off against a debt arising from the receiver's performance after crystallisation of a contract made before crystallisation.[64]

The floating charge affects heritage in the form of a hypothetical standard security. It will be a burden on the right of a purchaser who had not recorded or registered his title at the date of crystallisation.

A sum recovered by the liquidator as a fraudulent preference is not attached by the floating charge as it was not part of the company's property when the charge attached.[65] Sums recovered in misfeasance proceedings do, however, go to the floating charge creditor.[66]

9. Several Charges

Where two or more equally ranking floating charges affect the same property and a receiver has been appointed under each, the receivers act jointly.[67] The two charges may not be in precisely the same position if the dates of appointment of the receivers are different and a fixed security has been constituted as a real right between these dates.

Where the two or more floating charges do not rank equally the receiver appointed under the one having priority exercises the powers of a receiver to the exclusion of any other receiver.[68] In consequence, a receiver may be superseded by a receiver appointed under a prior charge; his powers are suspended but revive when the prior charge ceases to attach to the property then the subject to the charge.

---

62 *N. W. Robbie & Co. Ltd.* v. *Witney Warehouse Co. Ltd.* [1963] 1 W.L.R.1324.

63 *Business Computers Ltd.* v. *Anglo-African Leasing Ltd.* [1977] 1 W.L.R.578. This seems to be wrong.

64 *Rother Iron Works Ltd.* v. *Canterbury Precision Engineers Ltd.* [1974] Q.B.1.

65 *Re Yagerphone Ltd.* [1935] Ch.392.

66 *Re Anglo-Austrian Printing and Publishing Union* [1895] 2 Ch.891.

67 s.16(2).

68 s.16(1).

If the company is not in liquidation before the appointment of any of the receivers, and the receivers are not appointed at the same time, the charges will have different dates of attachment.

10. Appointment after Liquidation

Where the company is in liquidation prior to the receiver's appointment, he recovers the property subject to the floating charge from the liquidator. The charge has attached to the property at the commencement of winding up.[69] It would appear that the liquidator can withhold assets from the receiver insofar as they are required to satisfy the preferential debts.[70]

---

[69] s.1(2), (3).
[70] s.20.

CHAPTER 10

CAUTIONARY OBLIGATIONS

1. Cautionary Obligations

A cautionary obligation is "an accessory obligation or engagement, as surety for another, that the principal obligant shall pay the debt or perform the act for which he has engaged, otherwise the cautioner shall pay the debt or fulfil the obligation."[1] It has to be distinguished from an independent obligation,[2] delegation,[3] a representation as to credit,[4] an indemnity[5] and insurance.[6] An indemnity is an obligation to relieve the other contracting party of any loss incurred by him by entering into a certain transaction; it is bilateral while cautionry is trilateral. Insurance is an obligation to pay a sum on the occurrence of an event. If C pays only a dividend on his liability to D, he can recover the full amount of the liability from B under a contract of insurance but if it is a contract of indemnity he can only recover from B what he has paid.[7]

A cautionary obligation must be in writing;[8] it is not clear whether the writing must be either attested or holograph but in many cases the question has been avoided by invoking either the doctrine of *rei interventus,* or the privilege of documents *in re mercatoria.*[9]

Cautionry is proper when the fact that the parties are principal debtor and cautioner appears on the face of the deed; it is improper where they are bound as co-obligants although in fact they are principal and cautioner.[10] The significance of the distinction is that in proper caution the creditor has certain duties to the cautioner; in improper caution he can treat the cautioner as a co-obligant although the rules of cautionry apply between the cautioner and the

---

1 Bell, *Prin.,* § 245.

2 *Morrison* v. *Harkness* (1870) 9 M.35; *Stevenson's Tr.* v. *Campbell & Sons* (1896) 23 R.711; *Aitken & Co.* v. *Pyper* (1900) 38 S.L.R.74.

3 See Chap. 14, para. 2.

4 *Fortune* v. *Young,* 1918 S.C.1.

5 *Milne* v. *Kidd* (1869) 8 M.250; *Simpson* v. *Jack,* 1948 S.L.T.(Notes) 45.

6 *Laird* v. *Securities Insurance Co. Ltd.* (1895) 22 R.452.

7 *Nelson* v. *Empress Assurance Corporation* [1905] 2 K.B.281; *Liverpool Mortgage Insurance Co.'s Case* [1914] 2 Ch.617; *Law Guarantee Trust and Accident Society Ltd.* v. *Munich Reinsurance Co.* [1915] 31 T.L.R.572.

8 Mercantile Law Amendment Act (Scotland) 1856, s.6.

9 *National Bank* v. *Campbell* (1892) 19 R.885; *B.O.C.M. Silcock Ltd.* v. *Hunter,* 1976 S.L.T.217; Walker & Walker, *Evidence,* p.109.

10 Bell, *Prin.,* § 247.

principal debtor. Even if the debtor and cautioner are co-obligants *ex facie* of the deed, if the creditor knows at the time of entry to the obligation that they are in fact principal and cautioner he must treat them as such.[11]

Cautionry is an accessory obligation and the cautioner's liability cannot exceed that of the principal debtor.[12] Where the obligation is partial, the extent of the cautioner's liability and his right to rank on the estate of the principal debtor depend on the construction of the deed.[13] There may also be a question of construction as to whether the obligation covers interest as well as the sum stated.[14]

Unless there is a stipulation to the contrary, the creditor need not proceed against the debtor before proceeding against the cautioner.[15] It is, however, necessary that the debtor should be in default and whether there is a default is a question of fact.[16] The creditor need not await the result of a sequestration or liquidation to ascertain the amount of his loss.[17] He is not required to constitute the debt by an action against the debtor; he can constitute it in an action against the cautioner.[18] In general, the creditor is not obliged to give intimation to the cautioner that the debtor is in default.[19] It should be noticed that if the creditor does commence diligence against the debtor he cannot cease to prosecute it without good reason because this in effect is to give up a security.[20]

On payment of the debt, the cautioner is entitled to relief from the principal debtor unless, possibly, there was an agreement that the debtor would repay only when his circumstances allowed.[21] On full payment (not merely a dividend) he is entitled to an assignation from the creditor of the debt, any securities held and any diligence done.[22] He has no right to securities granted by third parties.[23]

---

11 *Mackenzie* v. *Macartney* (1831) 5 W. & S.504; Gloag & Irvine, p.674.

12 *Jackson* v. *McIver* (1875) 2 R.882.

13 *Harvie's Trs.* v. *Bank of Scotland* (1885) 12 R.1141; *Veitch* v. *National Bank,* 1907 S.C.554; *Mackinnon's Tr.* v. *Bank of Scotland,* 1915 S.C.411.

14 *National Commercial Bank* v. *Stuart,* 1969 S.L.T.(Notes) 52.

15 Mercantile Law Amendment Act (Scotland) 1856, s.8.

16 Gloag & Irvine, p.789.

17 *Willison* v. *Ferguson* (1901) 9 S.L.T.169.

18 *Morrison* v. *Harkness* (1870) 9 M.35; *Sheldon & Ackhoff* v. *Milligan* (1907) 14 S.L.T.703. See also *Clydesdale Bank* v. *D. & H. Cohen,* 1943 S.C.244.

19 *Brittania Steamship Insurance Association Ltd.* v. *Duff,* 1909 S.C.1261.

20 Gloag & Irvine, p.789.

21 *McMurray* v. *McFarlane* (1894) 31 S.L.R.531; *Williamson* v. *Foulds,* 1927 S.N.164.

22 *Ewart* v. *Latta* (1865) 3 M.(H.L.)36.

23 *Thow's Trustee* v. *Young,* 1910 S.C.588.

In proper caution, where there is more than one cautioner for the same debt, unless they are bound jointly and severally, they have the *beneficium divisionis* and each is liable only for his *pro rata* share unless the others are insolvent.[24] A cautioner who has paid more than his share has a right of relief against his co-cautioners.[25] He cannot obtain a joint and several decree against them because each solvent cautioner is only liable for his *pro rata* share.[26] The right of relief does not emerge until the amount of the whole debt has been ascertained.[27] A cautioner in the absence of agreement to the contrary,[28] is entitled to share the benefit of any security held by his co-cautioners[29] unless it was given by a third party and not the debtor.[30]

2. Cautionry: Prescription

A proper cautionary obligation is subject to the quinquennial prescription even although it is constituted or evidenced by a probative writ.[31] An improper cautionary obligation created by probative writ is also subject to the quinquennial prescription unless the original creditor was not aware at the time when the writ was delivered to him that the obligant was not truly a principal debtor.[32]

There is some doubt as to the *terminus a quo* of the prescriptive period. For most types of obligation, the *terminus* is the date when the obligation becomes enforceable. It has been suggested that a cautionary obligation falls under para. 2 of Sched. 2 to the Prescription and Limitation (Scotland) Act 1973 as being an "obligation to repay the whole, or any part of, a sum of money lent to . . . the debtor under a contract of loan . . ." and that the *terminus a quo* is accordingly the date stipulated for repayment or, if there is no stipulation, the date when a written demand for repayment is made.[33] It is thought, however, that a cautionary obligation does not fall under that paragraph because the natural referent of

---

24 Bell, *Prin.*, § 267.
25 Bell, *Prin.*, § 270.
26 *Buchanan* v. *Main* (1900) 3 F.215; *Anderson* v. *Dayton* (1884) 21 S.L.R.787.
27 *Beaton* v. *Wilkie* (1927) 43 Sh.Ct.Rep.193.
28 *Hamilton & Co.* v. *Freeth* (1889) 16 R.1022.
29 Bell, *Prin.*, § 270.
30 *Scott* v. *Young*, 1909 1 S.L.T.47.
31 Prescription and Limitation (Scotland) Act 1973, s.6, Sched. 1, paras. 1(*g*), 2(*c*).
32 Sched. 1, para. 3.
33 See Antonio, 1977 S.L.T.(News) 41; Halliday, *The Conveyancing and Feudal Reform (Scotland) Act 1970*, 2nd ed., p.128.

"the debtor" is the debtor in the "obligation to repay" and "the debtor" is the person to whom the money was lent.

A cautionary obligation is, of course, also subject to the vicennial prescription.

3. Discharge

The cautionary obligation is discharged by:

(1) direct discharge of the cautioner.

(2) extinction of the principal obligation. This may be by discharge,[34] but not by the creditor's assent to the debtor's discharge in his sequestration.[35] If the creditor merely agrees not to sue the principal debtor but reserves his rights against the cautioner, the cautioner is not discharged.[36]

(3) giving time. "In the language of the law, to give time does not consist in refraining from suing, but in the creditor putting himself under a disability to sue by agreeing to postpone payment of his debt."[37] The cautioner is discharged because he is deprived of his chance of considering whether he will have recourse to his remedy against the principal debtor or not and because it is then out of his power to operate the same remedy against him as he would have had under the original contract.[38] Postponing the date of repayment of a loan is giving time.[39] The taking of bills at a currency is giving time[38] unless the period of credit given is not unreasonable in the trade.[40] Prejudice resulting to the cautioner need not be shown.[38] The cautioner is not discharged if the creditor in giving time to the debtor reserved his rights against the cautioner,[41] nor if the cautionary agreement allows the creditor to give time.[42]

(4) alteration of the contract. If the creditor and debtor make a material alteration in the principal obligation the cautioner is discharged.[43]

---

[34] *Aitken's Trs.* v. *Bank of Scotland,* 1944 S.C.270.

[35] Bankruptcy (Scotland) Act 1913, s.52.

[36] *Muir* v. *Crawford* (1875) 2 R.(H.L.)148.

[37] *per* Lord Rutherford Clark, *Hay & Kyd* v. *Powrie* (1886) 13 R.777, at 782. See *Hamilton's Exor.* v. *Bank of Scotland,* 1913 S.C.743.

[38] *C. & A. Johnstone* v. *Duthie* (1892) 19 R.624.

[39] *Scottish Provident Institution* v. *Ferrier's Trs.* (1871) 8 S.L.R.390.

[40] *Calder & Co.* v. *Cruikshank's Tr.* (1889) 17 R.74. A bill at sight is different: *Nicolsons* v. *Burt* (1882) 10 R.121.

[41] *Muir* v. *Crawford* (1875) 2 R.(H.L.)148.

[42] *Hamilton's Exr.* v. *Bank of Scotland,* 1913 S.C.743.

[43] Bell, *Prin.,* § 259; *Allan Buckley Allan & Milne* v. *Pattison* (1893) 21 R.195; *N. G. Napier Ltd.* v. *Crosbie,* 1964 S.C.129.

(5) discharge of a co-cautioner without the consent of the other cautioners discharges all the cautioners.[44] It has been held that this applies only where the cautioners are bound jointly and severally.[45] If there are two separate debts the rule does not apply.[45] If the cautioners are bound in respect of the same debt, but not jointly and severally, it has been suggested that the discharge of one does not discharge the others because the others retain their right of relief against the one.[46]

The following terminate the obligation in the sense it does not apply to future advances:

(1) recall by the cautioner in terms of the agreement.[47] If the creditor bank then closes the account the cautioner has no right to require future lodgements by the debtor to be applied to redeem the indebtedness.[48]
(2) the death of the principal debtor.[49]
(3) a change in the constitution of a firm which is the creditor or principal debtor in the absence of agreement to the contrary.[50]

4. Pro Tanto Discharge

The giving up of a security by the creditor[51] or the creditor's failure to make a security effectual,[52] liberates the cautioner to the extent of the security.

---

44 Mercantile Law Amendment Act (Scotland) 1856, s.9. In the proviso to the section that "nothing herein contained shall be deemed to extend to the case of a cautioner consenting to the discharge of a co-cautioner who may have become bankrupt," "cautioner" should be "creditor", probably: Bell, *Prin.*, § 261A, n.(a).

45 *Morgan* v. *Smart* (1872) 10 M.610. But see Bell, *Prin.* (10th ed.) § 261A.

46 *Union Bank of Scotland* v. *Taylor,* 1925 S.C.835, *per* L.P. Clyde at p.841.

47 *Doig* v. *Lawrie* (1903) 5 F.295.

48 *Buchanan* v. *Main* (1900) 3 F.215.

49 *Woodfield Finance Trust (Glasgow) Ltd.* v. *Morgan,* 1958 S.L.T.(Sh.Ct.) 14. The cautioner's death does not terminate the obligation: *British Linen Co.* v. *Monteith* (1858) 20 D.557.

50 Partnership Act 1890, s.18.

51 *Sligo* v. *Menzies* (1840) 2 D.1478.

52 *Fleming* v. *Thomson* (1826) 2 W. & S. 277, but see Bell, *Comm.*, I, 379, n.4.

CHAPTER 11

RECOVERY OF DEBTS

1. Demand for Payment

Whatever the position may be in England,[1] there is no requirement in Scotland that the creditor must preface his action by a demand for payment. "The worst that can happen to any Scottish pursuer who raises a petitory action without prefacing it by a demand is that he may be found liable in the expenses of an *ex hypothesi* premature and unnecessary action."[2] "I am clearly of the opinion that when a debt of money is demanded, and the defender is not first told how much is asked of him, and when it is to be paid, but a summons is raised at once, and the pursuers then ask expenses, the defender is entitled to expenses, and not the pursuer."[3] On the same principle, where the pursuer in an action of reparation had failed without reasonable cause to intimate a claim before service of the summons and had accepted a tender lodged with the defences, the defenders were awarded expenses.[4] The debtor cannot avoid liability for expenses by consigning the amount of the debt in the hands of the court before the creditor has raised an action.[5]

2. Partial Payment

When a debtor sends his creditor a cheque for a sum less than the amount claimed and states that it is sent "in full and final settlement", a question arises as to whether the creditor, if he cashes the cheque, can thereafter sue for the balance. Two cases have been distinguished.[6] Where the cheque is sent for the purpose of compromising a dispute, it is a question of fact to be ascertained from the circumstances whether the creditor has accepted the compromise. Thus, when the creditor replied to the debtor that he was not accepting the cheque in full settlement and, on receiving no answer, cashed the cheque, it was held that the creditor could

---

1 *Joachimson* v. *Swiss Bank Corporation* [1921] 3 K.B.110.

2 *Per* L.J.-C. Cooper, *Macdonald* v. *North of Scotland Bank,* 1942 S.C.369.

3 *Per* Lord Shand, *Magistrates of Leith* v. *Lennon* (1881) 18 S.L.R.313 at 315.

4 *Crombie* v. *British Transport Commission,* 1961 S.L.T.115.

5 *Alexander* v. *Campbell's Trustees* (1903) 5 F.634; *A.B. & Co.* v. *C.D.* (1909) 25 Sh.Ct.Rep.106.

6 *McNicoll* v. *Kwasnica* (1952) 68 Sh.Ct.Rep.295.

recover the balance.[7] The onus of proving acceptance of the compromise rests on the debtor. In the second type of case the sending of the cheque in purported settlement of a larger amount admittedly due is merely an attempt to escape from a contractual obligation. Here, it seems, the retention and cashing of the cheque have no effect on the creditor's claim for the full sum due;[8] if the debtor had been sued, his admission would have resulted in interim decree for the lower amount being granted.[9] In either case, it is important that the creditor, on retaining the cheque, should immediately inform the debtor that he is still demanding the balance.

3. Action of Payment

A debt is normally recovered by an action for payment which is a type of petitory action, *i.e.* an action in which "some demand is made upon the defender, in consequence either of a right of property or credit in the pursuer."[10] The terms of the conclusion or crave are for payment to the pursuer by the defender of a certain sum, with interest thereon to a certain date, and of the expenses of the action.

4. Accounting

An action of accounting, more properly called an action of count, reckoning and payment, is appropriate "wherever there is a right to demand and liability to render an account."[11] It may be brought, for example, by a beneficiary against a trustee, by a principal against his agent, and by a ward against his guardian. It is not a suitable form of action for the determination of conflicting claims on a trust estate which involves questions of vesting.[12] Nor should it be a vehicle for general criticisms of trust administration but the question of the liability of trustees for a higher rate of interest than was in fact

---

[7] *Smith & Archibald* v. *Ryness,* Second Division, 18 July 1929, reported at 1937 S.L.T.(News) 81; *Day* v. *McLea* (1889) 22 Q.B.D.610; *Neuchatel Asphalte Co. Ltd.* v. *Barnett* [1957] 1 W.L.R.356; *Gilbey Vintners Scotland Ltd.* v. *Perry,* 1978 S.L.T.(Sh.Ct.) 48. Most of the extensive prior case law on this topic is set forth in *Lord Doune* v. *John Dye & Son Ltd.,* 1972 S.L.T.(Sh.Ct.)30 in which Sheriff Kydd pointed out that a dictum of Lord McLaren in *Pollock* v. *Goodwin's Trs.* (1898) 25 R.1051, which has been frequently cited in prior cases on this subject, relates to an entirely different situation. See also *Duthie & Co.* v. *Merson & Gerry,* 1947 S.C.43.

[8] *McNicoll* v. *Kwasnica, supra; Tyrie* v. *Goldie* (1942) 58 Sh.Ct.Rep.24.

[9] *Priestley & Son* v. *Arthur & Co.* (1882) 3 Sh.Ct.Rep.450.

[10] Erskine, IV, 1, 47.

[11] Mackay, *Manual of Practice in the Court of Session,* p.372.

[12] *Davidson* v. *Davidson's Trs.,* 1952 S.L.T.(Notes)3.

realised can be entertained.[13] An employer cannot bring such an action against his manager because the latter is not an independent person keeping his own books.[14] The action is competent even although accounts have admittedly been lodged.[15]

The conclusion of the summons is for a count and reckoning and payment of the balance due or, alternatively, for payment of a specified sum. Decree may be granted for any sum found due although it exceeds the sum specified in the alternative.[16] The date to which the accounting is sought should be specified if it is later than the date of citation.[17]

If there is no appearance, decree in absence is given for the specified sum. If the action is defended, the first question to be determined is the existence of the liability to account.[18] If there is such a liability, the defender is ordered to lodge accounts. The pursuer may then frame objections to items of the account. The purpose of the objections is to show that the balance brought out should be larger either because the defender has credited an item which he is not entitled to credit or because he has failed to debit an item he should have debited. Each objection should deal with a particular item and must be supported by relevant averments.[19] The defender answers the objections, a record is made up and the action proceeds to debate or proof. There may be a remit to an accountant for a report.

5. Multiplepoinding

Multiplepoinding is the form of action most appropriate where two or more parties have competing claims to the same fund or property. It may be raised by the holder of the fund, who in this event is the pursuer and real raiser, or by a claimant, in which event the holder is the pursuer and nominal raiser and the claimant is the defender and real raiser. It is difficult to delimit the circumstances in which this form of action is competent. There must be double distress—a "double claim to one fund or property on separate and hostile grounds."[20] In the strict sense double distress is competition

---

13 *Melville* v. *Noble's Trs.*, (1896) 24 R.243.

14 *Govan Old Victualling Society Ltd.* v. *Wagstaff* (1907) 44 S.L.R.295.

15 *Cunningham-Jardine* v. *Cunningham-Jardine's Trs.*, 1979 S.L.T.298.

16 *Spottiswoode* v. *Hopkirk* (1853) 16 D.59.

17 *Wallace* v. *Henderson* (1875) 2 R.999.

18 See "Procedure in Actions of Accounting" (1950) 66 S.L.R.276. See also *Smith* v. *Barclay*, 1962 S.C.1.

19 *Guthrie* v. *McKimmie's Tr.*, 1952 S.L.T.(Sh.Ct.)49.

20 *Russel* v. *Johnston* (1859) 21 D.886, *per* Lord Kinloch at p.887.

created by rival diligence but practice has extended the meaning of the term.

Circumstances in which a multiplepoinding has been held competent are:

(a) where property is claimed by an arrester and another party;[21]
(b) where the proceeds of an insurance policy are claimed by the policy holder and by an arrester;[22]
(c) where a share of an executry estate was claimed by a beneficiary and by the assignees of the beneficiary;[23]
(d) where trustees are unable to obtain a discharge from the beneficiaries.[24]

In outline, the procedure is:

(1) The summons calls all known claimants as defenders. If the action is raised by the holder a condescendence of the fund *in medio* is annexed to the summons.
(2) A claimant need only enter appearance at this stage if he wishes to challenge the competency of the action. This objection is then disposed of.
(3) If no defences are lodged, claimants can then object to the condescendence of the fund *in medio* and these objections are then disposed of.
(4) When the fund is settled, an order is made for claims to be lodged. Claims are then lodged, a record is made up and the action proceeds in the ordinary way.

The creditor of a claimant whose debt is liquid and constituted can lodge a riding claim in the multiplepoinding and may be ranked on any portion of the fund *in medio* to which the debtor is found entitled *primo loco*.

A multiplepoinding does not stop diligence by creditors who are not claimants but the holder of the fund can use the dependence of the multiplepoinding as a ground for suspension of diligence used against him.[25]

6. Partial Claim

The general law is that if a pursuer sues and obtains decree for only a part of a debt due to him, he is held to have abandoned all claim to

---

21 *North British Railway Co.* v. *White* (1881) 9 R.97.
22 *Colonial Mutual Life Assurance Society Ltd.* v. *Brown,* 1911 1 S.L.T.158.
23 *Fraser's Executrix* v. *Wallace's Trs.* (1893) 20 R.374.
24 *Mackenzie's Trs.* v. *Sutherland* (1895) 22 R.233.
25 *Ferguson* v. *Bothwell* (1882) 9 R.687.

the balance. He can, however, expressly reserve any further claim arising out of the same grounds of action and he is not then precluded from recovering the balance in another action.[26]

7. Interest

The general rule[27] is that interest does not run on a debt until there has been either a judicial demand for payment[28] or intimation by the creditor that if payment is not made by a specified date interest will begin to run.[29] Rendering of an account is not sufficient to make interest run.[30] So it has been held that interest *ex lege* does not run on a solicitor's fees,[31] arrears of feuduty,[32] or rent,[33] demurrage,[34] or sums due under an obligation of relief from public burdens.[35] But it is competent to stipulate that interest will run after a specified period of credit.[36] This may be done by a statement on an invoice, for example.[37] Again, interest may be due by virtue of a custom of trade.[38] Then there is "a very limited class of debts"[39] on which interest does run *ex lege, viz:* (a) loans:[40] an obligation to pay interest is implied in the contract of loan although there may be circumstances which show that this was not the lender's intention;[41] a law agent, therefore, can recover interest on advances to a client;[42] (b) where money has been paid under protest on the footing that it

---

26 *Findlay's Trs.* v. *Shanks,* 1930 S.L.T.(Sh.Ct.)32.

27 *Blair's Trs.* v. *Payne* (1884) 12 R.104.

28 See *supra,* para. 3.

29 *Liquidators of Linlithgow Oil Co.* v. *N.B. Railway Co.* (1904) 12 S.L.T.421.

30 *Cardno & Darling* v. *Steuart* (1869) 7 M.1026; *Blair's Trs.* v. *Payne, supra.*

31 *Blair's Trs.* v. *Payne, supra; Bunten* v. *Hart* (1902) 9 S.L.T.476; *Somervell's Tr.* v. *Edinburgh Life Assurance Co.,* 1911 S.C.1069; but as to advances by a law agent see *infra.*

32 *Marquis of Tweeddale's Trs.* v. *Earl of Haddington* (1880) 7 R.620.

33 *Moncreiff* v. *Lord Dundas* (1835) 14 S.61.

34 *Per* L.P. Dunedin, *Pollich* v. *Heatley,* 1910 S.C.469 at 478.

35 *Durie's Trs.* v. *Ayton* (1894) 22 R.34.

36 *Per* Lord Westbury, *Carmichael* v. *Caledonian Rlwy. Co.* (1870) 8 M.(H.L.)119 at 131; *Liquidators of Linlithgow Oil Co.* v. *N.B. Rlwy. Co., supra.*

37 *Per* Lord Fraser, *Blair's Trs.* v. *Payne, supra,* at p.112.

38 *Findlay Bannatyne & Co.'s Assignee* v. *Donaldson* (1864) 2 M.(H.L.)86.

39 *Per* Lord Dunedin, *Pollich* v. *Heatley, supra,* at p.478.

40 *Thomson* v. *Geekie* (1861) 23 D.693, L.J.-C. Inglis at p.701; *Cuninghame* v. *Boswell* (1868) 6 M.890.

41 *Forbes* v. *Forbes* (1869) 8 M.85; *Christie* v. *Matheson* (1871) 10 M.9; *Smellie's Exrx.* v. *Smellie,* 1933 S.C.725; *Williamson* v. *Williamson's Tr.,* 1948 S.L.T.(Notes) 72.

42 *Blair's Trs.* v. *Payne, supra.*

will be repaid in a certain event;[43] (c) where the purchaser of heritage obtains entry to the subjects interest runs on the unpaid price until settlement or consignation;[44] (d) interest is due on bills of exchange and promissory notes;[45] (e) interest is due on the accounts of mercantile agents;[46] (f) where a cautioner has paid on behalf of the principal debtor, interest runs;[47] (g) partners are entitled to interest at 5% on advances made to the firm.[48]

In the foregoing cases, the summons should conclude for interest from the appropriate date. In actions for an ascertained sum, such as the price of goods, it is usual to conclude for interest from the date of citation. The basis of this is that payment has been "wrongfully, or unjustifiably and improperly, withheld".[49] This applies also to a *quantum meruit* claim.[50]

The court has no common law power to award interest on statutory compensation from a date prior to the date on which the amounts are agreed or determined.[51]

In actions of damages, the common law rule was that unless there was unreasonable delay, interest ran only from the date of the final decree because it is only then that the illiquid claim is quantified and made liquid.[52] There are some cases in which interest was awarded because the pursuer had been deprived of an interest-bearing security or a profit-producing chattel.[53]

However, by statute,[54] the interlocutor awarding damages may include interest at a specified rate on the whole or part of the sum awarded for the whole or any part of the period between the date when the right of action arose and the date of the interlocutor.

---

[43] *Glasgow Gas Light Co.* v. *Barony Parish of Glasgow* (1868) 6 M.406; *Haddon's Exrx.* v. *Scottish Milk Marketing Board,* 1938 S.C.168.

[44] *Grandison's Trs.* v. *Jardine* (1895) 22 R.925; *Greenock Harbour Trs.* v. *Glasgow & South Western Rlwy. Co.,* 1909 S.C.(H.L.)49; *Prestwick Cinema Co.* v. *Gardiner,* 1951 S.C.98.

[45] Bills of Exchange Act 1882, s.57.

[46] *Findlay Bannatyne & Co.'s Assignee* v. *Donaldson, supra.*

[47] Erskine, III, 3, 78; Bell, *Prin.,* §32.

[48] Partnership Act 1890, s.24, r.3.

[49] *F.W. Green & Co. Ltd.* v. *Brown & Gracie Ltd.,* 1960 S.L.T.(Notes) 43.

[50] *Keir Ltd.* v. *East of Scotland Water Board,* 1976 S.L.T.(Notes) 72.

[51] *British Railways Board* v. *Ross and Cromarty C.C.,* 1974 S.L.T.274.

[52] *Flensburg Steam Shipping Co.* v. *Seligmann* (1871) 9 M.1011; *Clancey* v. *Dixon's Ironworks Ltd.,* 1955 S.L.T.36.

[53] *Kolbin & Sons* v. *Kinnear & Co.,* 1931 S.C.(H.L.) 128, *per* Lord Atkin at p.137; *Dunn & Co.* v. *Anderston Foundry Co. Ltd.* (1894) 21 R.880; *Vitruvia S.S. Co.* v. *Ropner Shipping Co.,* 1923 S.C.574.

[54] Interest on Damages (Scotland) Act 1958, s.1, as substituted by Interest on Damages (Scotland) Act 1971, s.1.

Where the sum includes damages or solatium in respect of personal injuries, the court must award interest on such part of each of the damages and solatium as it considers appropriate unless it is satisfied "that there are reasons special to the case why no interest should be given."[55] Interest can be awarded on parts only where the award of damages has identifiable elements.[55] Pre-decree interest should not be awarded on damages representing future loss.[56] The rate of pre-decree interest should be the average of the rates obtaining for post-decree interest during the period in question.[57] Although s.1(2)(*a*) provides that nothing in the Act authorises the granting of interest on interest, the pre-decree interest should be included in the sum on which interest is awarded from the date of decree.[58] A tender is to be taken to be in full satisfaction of any claim to interest.[59]

In cases other than those of personal injury, it has been said that interest should be awarded only where there is some special circumstance such as undue delay and that the fact that the damages are substantial is not such a circumstance.[60] It has also been said that interest from a date prior to decree should be awarded only on quantified loss.[61]

In actions of damages for breach of contract it seems that, apart from the 1958 Act, interest can be awarded from the date of citation only if the sum can be quantified at that date.[62] It has been suggested that interest can be awarded under the statute more readily in breach of contract cases.[63]

It has been held that post-decree interest cannot be at a rate higher than the prevailing legal rate even if the action is undefended;[64] the opposing and preferable view is that a rate agreed in the contract can be used.[65]

---

55 *Ross* v. *British Railways Board,* 1972 S.C.154; *Orr* v. *Metcalfe,* 1973 S.C.57.

56 *Macrae* v. *Reed and Mallik Ltd.,* 1961 S.C.68; *McCuaig* v. *Redpath Dorman Long Ltd.,* 1972 S.L.T.(Notes)42.

57 *Smith* v. *Middleton,* 1972 S.C.30.

58 *Smith* v. *Middleton, supra; Mouland* v. *Ferguson,* 1979 S.L.T.(Notes)85.

59 s.1(1B).

60 *R. & J. Dempster Ltd.* v. *Motherwell Bridge and Engineering Co. Ltd.,* 1964 S.L.T.353; *Buchanan* v. *Cameron,* 1973 S.C.285.

61 *Fraser* v. *J. Morton Wilson Ltd.,* 1965 S.L.T.(Notes)85; *Bell's Sports Centre (Perth) Ltd.* v. *William Briggs & Sons Ltd.,* 1971 S.L.T.(Notes)48.

62 *F.W. Green & Co. Ltd.* v. *Brown & Gracie Ltd., supra.*

63 *Macrae* v. *Reed & Mallik Ltd., supra, per* Lord Mackintosh at p.81.

64 *Bank of Scotland* v. *Bruce,* 1968 S.L.T.(Sh.Ct.)58; *Avco Financial Services Ltd.* v. *McQuire,* 1976 S.L.T.(Sh.Ct.)33; *National Commercial Bank* v. *Stuart,* 1969 S.L.T.(Notes)52.

65 *Bank of Scotland* v. *Forsyth,* 1969 S.L.T.(Sh.Ct.)15.

Where a decree includes interest, it is deemed to be at 11 per cent. per annum, unless otherwise stated.[66] Interest should be asked for before the decree for damages is given.[67]

8. Arrestment Ad Fundandam Jurisdictionem

A person who is not otherwise subject to the jurisdiction of the Scottish courts may be rendered subject to the jurisdiction if funds or property held for him in Scotland are arrested to found jurisdiction. The procedure is by inserting a warrant for arrestment to found jurisdiction in the summons in the Court of Session or by applying for letters of arrestment in the sheriff court.[68] The arrestment should be executed before or at the same time as the service of the summons.[69] Arrestment to found jurisdiction does not place a nexus on the subjects of arrestment and a separate arrestment on the dependence is necessary to obtain this result.[70] The schedule of arrestment must bear that the arrestment is to found jurisdiction.[71]

9. Subjects Arrestable

The subjects which can be arrested to found jurisdiction are the same as those which can be arrested in execution.[72] Corporeal moveables, to be arrestable, must have a commercial value[73] but the value may be quite small[74] as long as it is not elusory.[75] The arrestee must be under an obligation to the common debtor at the date of arrestment[76] but jurisdiction can be established even if the obliga-

---

66 R.C.66; A.S. (Interest in Sheriff Court Decrees or Extracts) 1975 (S.I. 1975/948).

67 *Handren* v. *Scottish Construction Co. Ltd.*, 1967 S.L.T.(Notes) 21.

68 R.C.74; Dobie, *Sheriff Court Styles*, p.44.

69 *Walls' Trs.* v. *Drynan* (1888) 15 R.359; *North* v. *Stewart* (1890) 17 R.(H.L.)60.

70 *Fraser-Johnston Engineering Co.* v. *Jeffs*, 1920 S.C.222; *Alexander Ward & Co. Ltd.* v. *Samyang Navigation Co. Ltd.*, 1975 S.C.(H.L.)26.

71 *Sutherlands of Peterhead (Road Hauliers) Ltd.* v. *Allard Hewson & Co. Ltd.*, 1972 S.L.T.(Notes) 83.

72 *Trowsdale's Tr.* v. *Forcett Rlwy. Co.* (1870) 9 M.88; *Leggat Bros.* v. *Gray*, 1908 S.C.67; see Chap. 16, paras. 3, 4.

73 *Trowsdale's Tr.* v. *Forcett Rlwy. Co.*, *supra*.

74 *Shaw* v. *Dow and Dobie* (1869) 7 M.449 (£1:8:6d); *Ross* v. *Ross* (1878) 5 R.1013 (9/3d.); *Dalrymple's Trs.* v. *Lancashire Trust Corporation* (1894) 2 S.L.T.79 (brass door plate).

75 *Lindsay* v. *London & North Western Rlwy. Co.* (1855) 18 D.62, aff.(1858) 3 Macq.99; *Millar & Lang* v. *Polak* (1907) 14 S.L.T.788; *Millar & Lang* v. *Poole* (1907) 15 S.L.T.76; *Shankland & Co.* v. *McGildowny*, 1912 S.C.857.

76 *Young* v. *Aktiebolaget Ofverums Bruk* (1890) 18 R.163; *North* v. *Stewart* (1890) 17 R.(H.L.)60.

tion is contingent[77] or defeasible.[78] The obligation need not rest on an express contract.[79] An obligation to account is sufficient even if in the event nothing is due to the common debtor.[80] If it appears that *prima facie* an obligation to account exists, the court will not generally allow an investigation of the accounts between the arrestee and the common debtor.[81] If, however, the court in its discretion does allow a preliminary proof which establishes that nothing is due by the arrestee, the arrestment is ineffectual to found jurisdiction.[82] If the arrestee denies the existence of any obligation to account, there is no jurisdiction.[83] It has been held that where the defender deposited funds with a building society at its London office jurisdiction can be established in Scotland by arresting in the hands of the building society at its Scottish branch;[84] but if under the terms of an insurance policy payments can only be made at the insurer's London office, the debt is localised in London and there is nothing to arrest in Scotland.[85] It is not possible to create jurisdiction in Scotland against a foreign debtor by assigning the debt to a third party who then arrests in the hands of the cedent a smaller counter claim due to the debtor.[86] A creditor cannot arrest in his own hands.[87]

10. Arrestment on the Dependence

The object of this type of arrestment, which is a matter of right to anyone who raises an action, is to keep fixed some asset of the defender so that the asset may be made good to satisfy the decree which the pursuer assumes he is going to obtain. Arrestment on the dependence is competent wherever there is a conclusion or crave

---

77 *MacLaren & Co.* v. *Preston* (1893) 1 S.L.T.75.

78 *North* v. *Stewart, supra; Baird* v. *Baird,* 1910 1 S.L.T.95; similarly it did not matter that the arrestee might have been able to plead the triennial prescription: *Shaw* v. *Dow and Dobie, supra.*

79 *Moore & Weinberg* v. *Ernsthausen Ltd.,* 1917 S.C.(H.L.)25.

80 *Baines and Tait* v. *Compagnie Generale des Mines d'Asphalte,* (1879) 6 R.846; *MacLaren & Co.* v. *Preston* (1893) 1 S.L.T.75.

81 *Douglas* v. *Jones* (1831) 9 S.856.

82 *Wyper* v. *Carr & Co.* (1877) 4 R.444; *Napier Shanks & Bell* v. *Halvorsen* (1892) 19 R.412; *Mitchell & Muil Ltd.* v. *Ferniscliffe Products Co. Ltd.,* 1920 1 S.L.T.199.

83 *Smith* v. *Rosenbloom,* 1915 2 S.L.T.18.

84 *McNairn* v. *McNairn,* 1959 S.L.T.(Notes)35.

85 *J. Verrico & Co. Ltd.* v. *Australian Mutual Provident Society,* 1972 S.L.T.(Sh.Ct.)57.

86 *O'Hare* v. *Reaich,* 1956 S.L.T.(Sh.Ct.)78.

87 *Grant Melrose & Tennent Ltd.* v. *W. & G. DuCros Ltd.* (1927) 43 Sh.Ct.Rep.347.

for a pecuniary claim other than expenses.[88] The claim may be alternative or subsidiary. It is not warranted to arrest on the dependence of an action to enforce a future debt unless the defender is *vergens ad inopiam* or *in meditatione fugae*.[89] There may be arrestment on the dependence of a counter claim.[90]

A warrant for arrestment can be inserted in a Court of Session summons and can be craved for in a sheriff court initial writ.[91] If this is not done, a warrant can be obtained by motion in the Court of Session action and in the sheriff court a precept of arrestment can be obtained from the sheriff clerk on production of a writ containing pecuniary conclusions upon which a warrant of citation has been granted.[92]

The arrestment can be executed before service of the action on the defender but in the Court of Session the action must be served within 20 days and the summons called within 20 days of the diet of compearance. In the ordinary sheriff court the arrestment must be forthwith reported to the sheriff clerk and the action must be served within 20 days of the execution and tabled within 20 days of the first court day after the expiry of the *induciae;* if it is undefended decree in absence must be taken within 20 days of the expiry of the *induciae*.[93] In the summary cause procedure, the arrestment must be reported forthwith to the sheriff clerk and the arrestment falls unless the summons is served within 42 days from the execution of the arrestment.[94] Arrestment on the dependence is competent at any time up to the issue of the extract of the final decree.

The subjects which can be arrested on the dependence are broadly those which can be arrested in execution except that it is not competent to arrest on the dependence any wages or salary (including fees, bonuses, commission, overtime pay or other emoluments) or pension (including any annuity in respect of past services, any periodical payments in compensation for loss of employment, and any disability pension).[95]

---

88 Debtors (Scotland) Act, 1838, s.16; *Stafford* v. *McLaurin* (1875) 3 R.148.

89 *Symington* v. *Symington* (1875) 3 R.205; *Burns* v. *Burns,* (1879) 7 R.355; *Brash* v. *Brash,* 1966 S.L.T.157; *cf. Wilson* v. *Wilson,* 1981 S.L.T.101.

90 R.C.84(*c*); it is competent under proposed rule 65.

91 R.C.74.

92 R.C.74(*d*); S.C.R.18 (proposed rule 47).

93 Debtors (Scotland) Act 1838, s.17; S.C.R.127 (proposed rule 116). See *Brash* v. *Brash,* 1966 S.L.T.157.

94 A.S.(Summary Cause Rules, Sheriff Court) 1976 (S.I. 1976/476), rule 47.

95 Law Reform (Miscellaneous Provisions) (Scotland) Act 1966, s.1.

The arrestee must be subject to the jurisdiction of the Scottish courts. The effect of the arrestment is to interpel the arrestee from paying over the arrested funds. If the schedule of arrestment states a sum followed by the words "more or less" the sum attached by the arrestment is not necessarily restricted to the sum stated.[96] As a matter of practice, the Scottish banks refuse to disclose whether anything has in fact been attached by an arrestment on the dependence. The effect of the arrestment continues even after a final decree of *absolvitor* if the pursuer appeals.[97] The three-year period for the prescription of arrestment runs, in the case of an arrestment on the dependence, from the date of the final decree in the cause.[98]

Once the pursuer has obtained decree he may raise an action of furthcoming on the arrestment on the dependence, a further arrestment in execution not being necessary.[99] The arrestment covers the principal debt, the interest thereon and the expenses of the action constituting it but not the expenses of the arrestment itself.[1] In the sheriff court the expenses of the furthcoming are covered.[2]

Interdict may be obtained against the threatened use of arrestment on the dependence if malice and oppression can be instantly verified[3] or if caution is found[4]. Once an arrestment has been used, the defender can apply to have it loosed on finding caution or to have it recalled, or restricted.[5] The grounds of recall may be that the debt is future or contingent or that the arrestment is nimious or oppressive, *e.g.* that the pursuer's claim is for a random figure,[6] that the pursuer has delayed in proceeding with the action.[7]

As a rule, the validity of the arrestment must be determined in the furthcoming and not in a petition for recall[8] but in special circumstances the question of whether a fund is arrestable can be decided in the petition for recall.[9]

---

96 *Ritchie* v. *McLachlan* (1870) 8 M.815.

97 *Countess of Haddington* v. *Richardson* (1822) 1 S.362.

98 Debtors (Scotland) Act 1838, s.22; *Paterson* v. *Cowan* (1826) 4 S.477; Graham Stewart, p.223.

99 Graham Stewart, p.231.

1 *ibid.*, p.133.

2 S.C.R.129.

3 *Beattie & Son* v. *Pratt* (1880) 7 R.1171.

4 *Duff* v. *Wood* (1858) 20 D.1231.

5 *Tweedie* v. *Tweedie,* 1966 S.L.T.(Notes)89.

6 *Cullen* v. *Buchanan* (1862) 24 D.1280; *Levy* v. *Gardiner,* 1964 S.L.T.(Notes)68.

7 *Telford's Exor.* v. *Blackwood* (1866) 4 M.369; *Mowat* v. *Kerr,* 1977 S.L.T.(Sh.Ct.)62.

8 *Vincent* v. *Chalmers & Co.'s Tr.* (1877) 5 R.43.

9 *Lord Ruthven* v. *Drummond,* 1908 S.C.1154.

The application may be made either to the Court of Session or to the sheriff from whose books the warrant of arrestment has been issued.[10] In the Court of Session the application is generally made by way of motion before the Lord Ordinary before whom the action depends or, if the arrestment is used before the calling of the action, by letter to the Deputy Principal Clerk.[11]

The arrestee cannot petition for recall if the subject of the arrestment is a debt or a corporeal moveable which is admittedly the property of the common debtor but he can seek recall if the subject arrested is a corporeal moveable which, in his contention, is not the property of the common debtor. In such a case the arrestment will be recalled unless the arrester can establish a *prima facie* case that the subject arrested is the property of the common debtor.[12] A person who is neither the arrestee nor the common debtor cannot petition for recall on the ground that the subjects arrested truly belong to him.[13]

11. Inhibition on the Dependence

It is possible to inhibit on the dependence of an action for payment of money other than expenses. If the action is for a future debt, inhibition on the dependence is appropriate only if the debtor is *vergens ad inopiam* or *in meditatione fugae.* In a Court of Session action a warrant for inhibition on the dependence can be inserted in the will of the summons and, when the summons has been signeted, the messenger can serve an inhibition. Alternatively a warrant can be obtained at any later stage by motion to the Lord Ordinary. In a sheriff court action, it is necessary to present the initial writ and warrant, or a certified copy thereof, together with a Bill for Letters of Inhibition to the Petition Department of the Court of Session. A *fiat* is obtained and the Letters of Inhibition can then be signeted. Partial recall of an inhibition on the dependence is competent.[14]

12. Diligence in Security

Where the debt is liquid but future or contingent—a bond or bill which is not yet due, for example— it is possible to arrest and inhibit

10 Debtors (Scotland) Act 1838, ss.20, 21; *Drummond & Dobie* v. *Boyd* (1834) 12 S.454; as to the summary cause, see A.S.(Summary Cause Rules, Sheriff Court) 1976 (S.I. 1976/476) r.48.

11 *Stuart* v. *Stuart,* 1926 S.L.T.31; R.C.74.

12 *Barclay Curle & Co. Ltd.* v. *Sir James Laing & Sons Ltd.*, 1908 S.C.82.

13 *Brand* v. *Kent* (1892) 20 R.29; *"Nordsoen"* v. *Mackie, Koth & Co.*, 1911 S.C.172.

14 *McInally* v. *Kildonan Homes Ltd.*, 1979 S.L.T.(Notes)89.

in security on the document of debt without the necessity of a summons if the debtor is *vergens ad inopiam* or *in meditatione fugae*.[15] In the Court of Session the procedure is by bill. In the sheriff court, a precept of arrestment can be obtained.[16]

13. Partial Admissions

There are three cases here:

(a) where it is conceded that a distinct part of the sum sued for, definite in amount, is due to the pursuer, *e.g.* where the action is for the sum of the prices of two articles and it is admitted that the price of one of them is due, or where the only defence is compensation and there is a balance of the sum sued for after deduction of the amount set off;

(b) where it is conceded that something is due to the pursuer in respect of his whole claim but the parties are not agreed as to the *quantum* of the claim, *e.g.* in an action of reparation for personal injuries where liability is admitted;

(c) where the defender disputes that any amount is due but is willing to make some payment to the pursuer "for the sake of peace."[17]

In (a) the defender should make the appropriate admission in the defences. The pursuer can then move for *interim* decree; the court may in its discretion grant such a decree prior to the closing of the record.[18] The decree is extractable in the ordinary way.

In (b) and (c) the appropriate course is to make, by formal minute, a judicial tender including an offer of expenses down to its date. Such a tender should not be referred to on record, and should not be mentioned in evidence or in any other way brought to the notice of the judge or jury.[19] If the pursuer has not intimated a claim to the defender prior to the raising of the action, a tender lodged with the defences need not include an offer of expenses and, even if

[15] Graham Stewart, pp.15, 528.

[16] S.C.R.18.

[17] *per* L.J.-C. Inglis, *Ramsay's Trs.* v. *Souter* (1864) 2 M.891, at p.892.

[18] *McKinlay* v. *McKinlay* (1849) 11 D.1022; *Conacher* v. *Conacher* (1857) 20 D.252; Maclaren, *Court of Session Practice*, p.1090; *George Hotel (Glasgow) Ltd.* v. *Prestwick Hotels Ltd.*, 1961 S.L.T.(Sh.Ct.)61.

[19] *Smeaton* v. *Dundee Corporation*, 1941 S.C.600; *Avery* v. *Cantilever Shoe Co. Ltd.*, 1942 S.C.469; *Key* v. *Scottish Chemist Supply Co. Ltd.*, 1956 S.L.T.(Notes)43; in the sheriff court where a tender has been lodged the sheriff should be asked to reserve consideration of expenses until the merits have been dealt with—*Jack* v. *Jack* (1953) 69 Sh.Ct.Rep.34; *Associated Portland Cement Manufacturers Ltd.* v. *McInally*, 1970 S.L.T.(Sh.Ct.)9.

the tender is accepted immediately, the defender may be awarded expenses against the pursuer.[20] If an extrajudicial offer has been made by the defender prior to the raising of the action, it may be repeated on record but should not be brought to the notice of the jury or referred to in evidence or debate.[21] If such a tender has been so repeated and the pursuer accepts it, the defender may be entitled to full expenses against the pursuer; it is a question of circumstances.[22] If an extrajudicial offer is not repeated on record and the pursuer after the raising of the action accepts the amount offered, no expenses are due to or by either party.[23] If he is awarded less than the offer the whole expenses may be awarded to the defender.[24] An extrajudicial tender during the course of the action may be taken into consideration.[25]

A tender by the defender is appropriate where a liquid claim is met by an illiquid counterclaim.[26]

14. Tenders

A tender is an offer by the defender to pay part of the sum sued for. It must, as a rule, include the expenses of process to its date.[27] It must be unconditional although it is competent and usual to state that liability is not admitted and to reserve all rights and pleas. If there is more than one pursuer a lump sum cannot be offered to them without apportionment.[28]

A tender has an important effect on expenses. If the pursuer eventually recovers more than the amount tendered, he is awarded full expenses.[29] If he is awarded the amount tendered or less, he is entitled to his expenses down to the date of the tender and the defender is entitled to his expenses incurred in the natural progress of the cause against the pursuer from that date.[30] If the tender

20 *Crombie* v. *British Transport Commission,* 1961 S.L.T.115.

21 *Avery* v. *Cantilever Shoe Co. Ltd., supra.*

22 *Gunn* v. *Hunter* (1886) 13 R.573.

23 *Ramsay's Trs.* v. *Souter, supra; Critchley* v. *Campbell,* (1884) 11 R.475; but see the doubts expressed in *Miller* v. *McPhun* (1895) 22 R.600.

24 *O'Donnell* v. *A.M. & G. Robertson,* 1965 S.L.T.155.

25 *Pearce & Co.* v. *Owners of S.S. "Hans Maersk",* 1935 S.C.703.

26 *Sidlaw Industries Ltd.* v. *Cable Belt Ltd.,* 1979 S.L.T.(Notes)40.

27 *Little* v. *Burns* (1881) 9 R.118; *Graham* v. *Graham,* 1955 S.L.T.(Notes)15.

28 *Flanagan* v. *Dempster Moore & Co.,* 1928 S.C.308; *McNeil* v. *National Coal Board,* 1966 S.L.T.237.

29 *Heriot* v. *Thomson* (1833) 12 S.145.

30 *Jacobs* v. *Provincial Motor Cab Co. Ltd.,* 1910 S.C.756; *McLean* v. *Galbraith Stores Ltd.,* 1935 S.C.165.

is accepted within a reasonable time, the pursuer is entitled to expenses down to the date of acceptance. If the tender is accepted more than a reasonable time after its date the pursuer is entitled to expenses down to the date at which it was reasonable to expect the tender to be accepted or refused and the defender is entitled to his expenses against the pursuer from that date.[31] The determination of the date should normally be left to the Auditor.[32]

A tender, until it is withdrawn, can be accepted at any time unless there has been an important change of circumstances, *e.g.* the death of the original pursuer,[33] the pronouncement of judgment by the Lord Ordinary,[34] the lodging of a report by a judicial referee.[35]

The acceptance of a tender made by one defender does not preclude the pursuer from continuing to proceed against another defender.[36] Where one defender tenders "expenses to date" this includes the expenses for which the pursuer is liable to another defender who is to be assoilzied.[37] Where each of two defenders who were sued jointly and severally lodged a tender, and the award to the pursuer against both jointly and severally was more than either tender but less than the total sum of the two tenders, the defenders were awarded expenses against the pursuer from the date of the second tender.[38]

Where, in an action for damages against two defenders, the first defender lodged a "tender" whereby, subject to the concurrence of the second defender, he offered to admit liability jointly and severally with the second defender on the basis that the defenders would be liable *inter se* to contribute to damages and expenses in the proportion of three-quarters to the first defender and one-quarter to the second defender, and the jury awarded two-thirds of the damages against the first defender and one-third against the second defender, it was held that all the pursuer's expenses to the date of the tender and his subsequent expenses so far as applicable to the quantification of damages should be paid in the proportion of two-thirds by the first defender and one-third by the second

---

31 *Jack* v. *Black,* 1911 S.C.691.

32 *Smeaton* v. *Dundee Corporation,* 1941 S.C.600; *Wood* v. *Miller,* 1960 S.C.86.

33 *Sommerville* v. *N.C.B.,* 1963 S.L.T.334.

34 *Bright* v. *Low,* 1940 S.C.280.

35 *Macrae* v. *Edinburgh Street Tramways Co.* (1885) 13 R.265.

36 *McNair* v. *Dunfermline Corporation,* 1953 S.C.183. See Chap. 25, para. 5.

37 *Macdonald* v. *Scottish Motor Traction Co.,* 1948 S.C.529.

38 *Jackson* v. *Clyde Navigation Trust,* 1961 S.L.T.(Sh.Ct.)35—the court has a discretion because one defender might be a man of straw.

defender, each defender bearing his own expenses; and that the expenses of the pursuer and first defender incurred subsequent to the date of the tender and attributable to the determination and apportionment of liability should be paid by the second defender.[39]

15. Summary Cause

The sheriff court summary cause includes actions for payment of money not exceeding £1,000 in amount, exclusive of interest and expenses, and actions of multiplepoinding, furthcoming and sequestration for rent where the sum involved does not exceed £1,000.[40] It is commenced by a summons in the statutory form, the *induciae* being 14 days if the defender's residence or place of business is within the British Islands or Irish Republic, 28 days if it is in Europe and 42 days if it is outwith Europe.[41] If the defender lodges neither a notice of intention to appear nor a notice of offer to pay by instalments on or before the "return day" specified in the summons (which must be after the expiry of the *induciae*) the pursuer can, by entering a minute in the Book of Summary Causes, obtain decree in absence on the day specified in the summons as the "first calling day" (which is seven days after the "return day").[42] The defender may within 14 days after execution of a charge or an arrestment, whichever first occurs, following on the decree, apply for recall of the decree.[43] If the defender appears there is power to award an instalment decree.[44]

There is an appeal to the sheriff principal on a question of law.[45] An extract may be issued 14 days after the granting of the decree.[46]

16. Ordinary Court Action

An ordinary action in the sheriff court is appropriate if the sum sued for exceeds £1,000. It is commenced by an initial writ, the *induciae*

---

39 *Williamson* v. *McPherson,* 1951 S.C.438. As to delay in accepting such a tender, see *Morton* v. *O'Donnell,* 1979 S.L.T.(Notes)26. As to the effect of acceptance of such a tender after refusal of a previous tender, see *Houston* v. *British Road Services Ltd.*, 1967 S.L.T.329.

40 Sheriff Courts (Scotland) Act 1971, s.35; A.S.(Summary Cause Rules, Sheriff Court) 1976 (S.I.1976/476).

41 Rule 4.

42 Rule 55.

43 Rule 19.

44 1971 Act, s.36.

45 1971 Act, s.38.

46 Rule 89.

being 14 days unless the defender is outside Europe when it is three weeks if citation is personal and six weeks if it is postal.[47] Decree in absence may be granted at any time after the expiry of the *induciae*.[48] An extract may be issued after the expiry of seven days from the date of the decree.[49] The defender may be reponed at any time before implement of the decree.[50] The decree is entitled to the privilege of a decree *in foro* after 20 years or in six months from its date or the date of a charge on it if the service of the writ or charge was personal.[51]

On decree being granted in a defended action, extract may be issued after the lapse of 14 clear days from the date of the interlocutor.[52] An appeal may be taken within three months of the decree if it has not sooner been extracted or implemented.[53] The appeal may be to the Court of Session or the sheriff principal.

17. Court of Session Action

An action for debt in the Court of Session must be for a sum exceeding £500 in amount exclusive of interest and expenses.[54] The action is commenced by a summons, the *induciae* being 14 days.[55]

The summons cannot be called before the day on which the *induciae* expires.[56] If the defender wishes to defend he must enter appearance within three days of the calling.[57] If he fails to do so, the pursuer can enrol a motion for decree in absence and the cause appears on the Roll of Undefended Causes on the first available day.[58] The defender may have the decree in absence recalled within

---

47 Sheriff Courts (Scotland) Act 1907; 1st Sched., r.5. Under the proposed rules the *induciae* is the same as in the summary cause—see *supra*, para. 15.

48 R.23.

49 R.24 (14 days under proposed rule 26).

50 Rr.27-32 (proposed rule 29) see *McKelvie* v. *Scottish Steel Scaffolding Co.*, 1938 S.C.278.

51 R.25 (proposed rule 27).

52 R.85 (14 days after the interlocutor disposing of expenses—proposed rule 91).

53 R.92 (14 days—proposed rule 92).

54 1907 Act, s.7; Sheriff Courts (Scotland) Act 1971 (Privative Jurisdiction) Order 1976 (S.I.1976/900).

55 R.C.72.

56 R.C.78.

57 R.C.81.

58 R.C.89(*a*). The special provisions of this rule as to defenders furth of Scotland should be noted.

10 days.[59] Extract is obtainable after 11 days on a decree in absence; after eight days in other causes.

A reclaiming motion may be taken within 21 days of the date of the interlocutor.[60]

---

[59] R.C.89(*f*).
[60] R.C.264.

CHAPTER 12

PAYMENT

1. Mode of Payment

A creditor is entitled to require payment in legal tender.[1] The validity of methods of payment depends on the instructions of the creditor and the normal way of doing business. Unless there is a request to remit a cheque by post, the cheque is sent at the risk of the sender.[2] It is not normal business practice to send large sums of notes by post and the loss falls on the sender.[3] If the creditor has accepted payment in one form he cannot require payment in another form in strict compliance with the contract without giving fair notice to the debtor.[4] If the ordinary way of paying is by post an account will be held to have been paid by a remittance duly posted although the remittance does not reach the creditor.[5]

2. Payment by Cheque

Payment by cheque is equivalent to payment in cash. It was held that an amount had been "paid and received" on the day on which the cheque was received although it could not be presented until the following day;[6] and when a cheque sent in payment of a debt has been received by the creditor there is no debt in existence which can be arrested in the hands of the sender of the cheque.[7] On the other hand, a creditor is not bound to accept payment by cheque or otherwise than by legal tender.[8] He is entitled to reject the cheque by returning it to the debtor although it has been doubted whether in the absence of some reasonable doubt as to the debtor's solvency, he is entitled to proceed with diligence forthwith.[9] If he retains the cheque, however, he must countermand any diligence which has

---

[1] *Glasgow Pavilion Ltd.* v. *Motherwell* (1903) 6 F.116, *per* Lord Young at p.119. See Chap. 1, para. 2.

[2] *Baker* v. *Lipton* (1899) 15 T.L.R.435; *Robb* v. *Gow Bros. & Gemmell* (1905) 8 F.90; *Coats* v. *Glasgow Corporation* (1912) 28 Sh.Ct.Rep.38.

[3] *Mitchell-Henry* v. *Norwich Union Life Insurance Society Ltd.* [1918] 2 K.B.67.

[4] *Tankexpress A/S* v. *Compagnie Financière Belge des Petroles S.A.* [1949] A.C.76.

[5] *Thorey* v. *Wylie & Lochhead* (1890) 6 Sh.Ct.Rep.201.

[6] *Glasgow Pavilion Ltd.* v. *Motherwell* (1903) 6 F.116.

[7] *Leggat Brothers* v. *Gray*, 1908 S.C.67.

[8] *per* Lord Young, *Glasgow Pavilion Ltd.* v. *Motherwell, supra,* at p.119.

[9] Gloag, p.709.

been commenced,[10] although it would seem that he can still take decree in absence against the debtor.[11] Again, once the cheque has been accepted and paid into the creditor's bank, he cannot reject it;[12] and if he has rejected the cheque on some other ground which is later shown to be invalid, he cannot then rely on the point that the cheque was not legal tender.[13] If, of course, the cheque is dishonoured there is no payment and the debt revives.[14]

3. Place of Payment

In general, the debtor should tender payment at the creditor's residence or place of business.[15] It has been held that payment by the debtor in good faith into the creditor's bank account, with intimation to the creditor, but without his authority, is ineffectual discharge of the debt but it is doubtful if this is correct.[16]

4. Ascription of Payments

Where the same person is debtor in more than one debt to the same creditor a question may arise as to the debt to which a payment by the debtor is to be ascribed. The rule is that the debtor may appropriate the payment to a particular debt.[17] He may not, however, appropriate a payment to principal rather than interest.[18] If the debtor does not appropriate, the creditor may do so, either in his receipt or at a later point. It has been said that he can appropriate "up to the last moment"[19] but not after issue has been joined.[20] The creditor's ascription cannot preclude challenge of the validity of the debt.[21] If the creditor does not appropriate expressly, his implied or presumed intention governs.[22] The intention may be inferred from the form and statement of the account but the entry in

---

10 *Macdougall* v. *McNab* (1893) 21 R.144.

11 *Pollock* v. *Goodwin's Trs.* (1898) 25 R.1051.

12 *Mintons* v. *Hawley & Co.* (1882) 20 S.L.R.126.

13 *Holt* v. *National Bank of Scotland,* 1927 S.L.T.484.

14 *Walker & Watson* v. *Sturrock* (1897) 35 S.L.R.26; *Leggat Brothers* v. *Gray,* 1908 S.C.67; *McLaren's Tr.* v. *Argylls Ltd.,* 1915 2 S.L.T.241.

15 *Haughhead Coal Co.* v. *Gallocher* (1903) 11 S.L.T.156.

16 *Wood* v. *Bruce* (1908) 24 Sh.Ct.Rep.24.

17 *Allan* v. *Allan & Co.* (1831) 9 S.519; *Mitchell* v. *Cullen* (1852) 1 Macq.190.

18 *Gourlay* v. *Clydesdale Bank Ltd.* (1900) 7 S.L.T.473.

19 *Cory Brothers & Co. Ltd.* v. *Owners of the "Mecca",* L.R. [1897] A.C.286, *per* Lord Macnaghten at p.294.

20 *Jackson* v. *Nicoll* (1870) 8 M.408—"before action and while the debtor is solvent": Gloag & Irvine, p.852.

21 *Dougall* v. *Lornie* (1899) 1 F.1187.

22 *Cory Brothers & Co. Ltd.* v. *Owners of the "Mecca", supra.*

the creditor's own books is not conclusive.[23] In the case of an account-current, there is a presumption by virtue of the rule in *Devaynes* v. *Noble*[24] that the earliest credit is applied to extinguish the earliest debit. The presumption is redargued however if the course of dealing between the parties shows a different intention[25] or if the form and statement of the account or other evidence shows that the creditor's intention was different.[26] Between banker and customer the presumption is rebutted by the existence of two accounts or the closing of one account and the opening of another.[27] An account-current is normally between banker and customer[28] but it may be between agent and client,[29] mercantile houses,[30] or dealers.[31] The rule does not apply to a tradesman's account; there, payments go against general indebtedness.[32] Where the debtor owes both principal and interest a payment will be first appropriated to interest even although the interest is not payable at fixed terms.[33]

Where a debtor is liable to make to the same person payments in respect of two or more regulated agreements under the Consumer Credit Act 1974 he may appropriate any sum paid by him towards the sum due under any one of the agreements or towards the sum due under two or more agreements in such proportions as he thinks fit. If he fails to make an appropriation where one of the agreements is a hire-purchase agreement, a conditional sale agreement, a consumer hire agreement or an agreement in relation to which any security is provided the payment is appropriated towards the satis-

---

[23] *Cory Brothers & Co. Ltd.* v. *Owners of the "Mecca", supra; Jackson* v. *Nicoll, supra;* but see *National Commercial Bank of Scotland* v. *Millar's Tr.*, 1964 S.L.T.(Notes) 57.

[24] (1816) 1 Mer.572 (known in England as Clayton's Case). This was accepted as the law of Scotland in *Houston* v. *Speirs* (1829) 3 W. & S. 392, and *Royal Bank* v. *Christie* (1841) 2 Robinson 118.

[25] *Hay* v. *Torbet*, 1908 S.C.781; *Macdonald Fraser & Co. Ltd.* v. *Cairns's Exrx.*, 1932 S.C.699. See also *Deeley* v. *Lloyds Bank Ltd.* [1912] A.C.756.

[26] *Cory Brothers & Co. Ltd.* v. *Owners of the "Mecca", supra.*

[27] *Re Sherry* (1884) 25 Ch.D.692; *Buchanan* v. *Main* (1900) 3 F.215; *Bradford Old Bank Ltd.* v. *Sutcliffe* [1918] 2 K.B.833; *Commercial Bank* v. *Turner* (1944) 60 Sh.Ct.Rep.95.

[28] As in *Cuthill* v. *Strachan* (1894) 21 R.549. The rule can apply to bank accounts other than current accounts—*Re Yeovil Glove Co. Ltd.* [1963] Ch.528.

[29] *Lang* v. *Brown* (1859) 22 D.113.

[30] *Houston* v. *Speirs, supra.*

[31] *McKinlay* v. *Wilson* (1885) 13 R.210.

[32] *Dougall* v. *Lornie* (1899) 1 F.1187; *Hay* v. *Torbet, supra.*

[33] *Watt* v. *Burnett's Trs.* (1839) 2 D.132.

faction of the sums due under the several agreements respectively in the proportions which these sums bear to one another.[34]

A payment by a debtor to his creditor is presumed to be on account of the debt[35].

5. Payment to Third Parties

Payment of the amount of a debt to the creditor's agent who has, or appears to have, authority to receive it, is valid.[36] Notice on the invoice that payment is to be made direct to the principal is sufficient to negative the agent's authority.[37] The onus is on the debtor to prove the actual or ostensible authority.[38] A solicitor has ostensible authority to receive a sum sued for[39] and to receive the price of shares which have been sold through him.[40] An agent who has acted for both parties in a loan transaction has no implied authority to receive repayment.[41] Payment by a litigant to his country agent may not be payment to his Edinburgh agent.[42] A factor authorised to uplift interest has no power to give a discharge for the principal sum even although the document of debt is in his possession.[43] The partner of a firm who made a contract is entitled to discharge payments under it.[44] Payment to the *curator bonis* of a minor who had not extracted or found caution was not valid.[45]

6. Deduction of Tax

Tax at the basic rate may be deducted from the following when made out of chargeable profits or gains[46]:

(1) annuities and other annual payments except (a) interest, (b) small maintenance payments[47] (*i.e.* those less than £33 a week or £143 a month).

---

34 Consumer Credit Act 1974, s.81.

35 *Spence* v. *Paterson's Trs.* (1873) 1 R.46, *per* Lord Deas at p.60.

36 *International Sponge Importers Ltd.* v. *Watt & Sons,* 1911 S.C.(H.L.)57.

37 *Ell Bros.* v. *Sneddon* (1929) 45 Sh.Ct.Rep.351.

38 *Encyclopaedia of the Laws of Scotland,* Vol. XI., p.168; *British Bata Shoe Co. Ltd.* v. *Double M. Shah Ltd.*, 1981 S.L.T.(Notes)14.

39 *Smith* v. *North British Rlwy.* (1850) 12 D.795.

40 *Pearson* v. *Scott* (1878) 9 Ch.D.198.

41 *Falconer* v. *Dalrymple* (1870) 9 M.212.

42 *Clark & Macdonald* v. *Schulze* (1902) 4 F.448.

43 *Duncan* v. *River Clyde Trs.* (1851) 13 D.518; aff.(1853) 25 Sc.Jur.331.

44 *Nicoll* v. *Reid* (1878) 6 R.216.

45 *Donaldson* v. *Kennedy* (1833) 11 S.740.

46 Income and Corporation Taxes Act 1970, s.52. As to life insurance premiums, see Finance Act 1976, Sched. 4.

47 1970 Act, s.65; Income Tax (Small Maintenance Payments) Order 1980 (S.I. 1980/951).

(2) a royalty or other sum in respect of the user of a patent.
(3) rents and royalties in respect of mines, quarries and similar concerns.
(4) rents for electric line wayleaves exceeding £2·50.

The accumulation or capitalisation of interest does not constitute a "payment" so as to entitle the debtor to recover the tax.[48] "Payment" does, however, include payment by cheque or bill, by transfer of marketable securities, by making of credit entries in books of account, by the discharge of an obligation expressed in foreign currency or, in general, by any method which is in a commercial sense a payment.[49] The deduction is at the basic rate for the year in which the payment becomes due. The payee must allow the deduction on receipt of the residue,[50] and the payer is acquitted and discharged of the sum represented by the deduction. Where the amount paid is to be set off against a debt due by the payee to the payer, only the net amount can be set off.[51] The question of whether tax is deductible from a payment can be determined in an action to which the Revenue is not a party.[52] The payer, if requested by the payee, must furnish a certificate of deduction of tax. It has been said that in the case of royalties, at least, a payer who has failed to deduct may recover the tax from the payee by a *condictio indebiti.*[53] In the case cited,[54] it was held that a debtor who, for a long number of years, failed to deduct bond interest at the time of payment could not claim the deduction in a subsequent settlement with the creditor. Trustees who have misconstrued the trust deed cannot recover from the beneficiary the tax which they failed to deduct.[55]

A person making a termly payment is entitled to deduct only in respect of a sum that he is currently paying, and not in respect of the full termly payment, the balance of which alone is currently being paid.[56]

Deduction must be made from certain payments not made wholly out of profits or gains already taxed.[57] The relevant payments are

---

48 *Paton* v. *I.R.C.* [1938] A.C.341.
49 *Rhokana Corporation Ltd.* v. *I.R.C.* [1937] 1 K.B.788.
50 Finance Act 1971, s.36.
51 *Butler* v. *Butler* [1961] P.33.
52 *David Allen & Sons Billposting Ltd.* v. *Bruce,* 1933 S.C.253.
53 *Agnew* v. *Ferguson* (1903) 5 F.879.
54 *Galashiels Provident Building Society* v. *Newlands* (1893) 20 R.821.
55 *Rowan's Trs.* v. *Rowan,* 1940 S.C.30.
56 *Fletcher* v. *Young,* 1936 S.L.T.572.
57 1970 Act, ss.53, 54.

those mentioned in the previous paragraph and: yearly interest paid (a) by a company or local authority, otherwise than in a fiduciary or representative capacity, (b) by a partnership of which a company is a member, (c) by any person to another person whose usual place of abode is outside the U.K. but excepting from (a), (b) and (c), (i) interest payable in the U.K. on an advance from a bank carrying on a bona fide banking business in the U.K., (ii) interest paid by such a bank in the ordinary course of that business. Deduction is made at the basic rate in force at the time of the payment.[50] A certificate of deduction of tax must be provided on request. It is implied that the payee must allow the deduction and treat the payer as acquitted of liability in respect of the amount deducted.[58] The payer must account for the tax to the Revenue.

Any provision, written or oral, for the payment of interest "less tax" or using words to that effect, is to be construed, in relation to interest payable without deduction of tax, as if the words were not included.[59]

It is a question of construction whether a deed directs payment of a sum without deduction of tax. A reference to "all deductions" may not suffice.[60] It is also a question of construction whether the direction covers higher rates of income tax.[61]

If the clause is effectual, and the payment is one from which the payer is obliged by law to deduct tax, the result is to increase the sum payable and the amount of tax deducted.

Every agreement for payment of interest, rent or other annual payment in full without allowing for the authorised deduction is void.[62] A promissory note is an "agreement"[63] but the provision clearly does not apply to payments made under a will or an order of court.[64] The provision does not avoid an agreement to pay a sum "free of tax"; such an agreement is construed as an obligation to pay, in addition to the stated sum, any tax becoming due by reason of the payments being made.[65] It does not affect an agreement between a trust beneficiary and another party whereby the trustees

---

58 *Allchin* v. *South Shields Corporation* [1943] 25 T.C.445, *per* Viscount Simon at p.461.

59 Income and Corporation Taxes Act 1970, s.425.

60 *Belk* v. *Best* [1942] 1 Ch.77.

61 See, *e.g.* *Prentice's Trs.* v. *Prentice*, 1935 S.C.211.

62 Taxes Management Act 1970, s.106(2).

63 *C.I.R.* v. *Hartley* (1956) 36 T.C.348.

64 *Spilsbury* v. *Spofforth* (1937) 21 T.C.247.

65 *Inland Revenue* v. *Ferguson*, 1969 S.C.(H.L.) 103.

are directed to pay to the other party a fraction of the income due to the beneficiary after deduction of tax coupled with a stipulation that the sum paid shall not fall below a certain amount.[66] An obligation to make such an annual payment that, after deduction of tax, a certain sum of money will be available is not void.[67] An obligation by A to pay B's tax on the whole or a portion of his income is not struck at.[68]

Special statutory provisions alter the effect of deeds, wills, orders of court and other instruments made before 3 September 1939 which provided for payments free of income tax.[69]

Where there is an effectual clause in the normal form the payer is entitled to deduct the gross amount from his total income. The payee has the gross amount added to his total income and may have to pay higher rate tax thereon. On the other hand if he is entitled to reliefs he may be able to recover tax which he can retain. However, in some cases the language of the clause may be susceptible of the interpretation that the sum of £X has to be arrived at not merely by taking into account the basic rate of income tax but also any reliefs which the payee may be able to claim. Under the rule in *Re Pettit,*[70] the payee must claim the relief due from the Revenue and repay it to the payer. It seems that this rule applies in Scotland.[71]

7. Onus of Proof

As a general rule, once the creditor has proved the constitution of the debt, the onus of proving payment is on the debtor.[72] There are, however, certain circumstances in which there is a presumption of payment.

First of all, certain types of debt are presumed to have been paid. There is a conclusive presumption that counsel's fees have been paid except where there is some special promise or contract.[73] Tavern and hotel bills are presumed to have been paid if the guest

---

66 *Brooke* v. *Price* [1917] A.C.115.

67 *Booth* v. *Booth* [1922] 1 K.B.66; *Noel* v. *Trust and Agency Co. of Australasia Ltd.* [1937] 1 Ch.438.

68 *Hutchison* v. *C.I.R.,* 1930 S.C.293.

69 Income and Corporation Taxes Act 1970, s.422.

70 [1922] 2 Ch.765.

71 *Hunter's Trs.* v. *Mitchell,* 1930 S.C.978; *Milne's Trs.,* 1936 S.C.706. *Cf. Richmond's Trs.* v. *Richmond,* 1935 S.C.585; *Rowan's Trs.* v. *Rowan,* 1940 S.C.30. In *Turner's Trs.* v. *Turner,* 1943 S.C.389, the point was conceded. See also *Inland Revenue* v. *Cook,* 1945 S.C.(H.L.)52.

72 Gloag, p.744.

73 Bell, *Prin.,* §568.

has left as this is "a presumption of practical life". The creditor may rebut the presumption *prout de jure.*[74] There was, at one time, a presumption that physician's fees had been paid but this is now of doubtful validity.[75]

Where wages were distributed in envelopes the onus of proving correct payment is on the employer.[76]

8. Possession of Voucher

Chirographum apud debitorem repertum praesumitur solutum. If the written voucher which constitutes the obligation is found in the hands of the debtor (or cautioner[77]), it is presumed that the debt has been paid.[78] This applies to heritable bonds[79] as well as other obligations but not to bilateral deeds.[80] The creditor can prove *prout de jure* that the voucher reached the debtor's possession otherwise than by payment, *e.g.* by force or fraud or without the creditor's consent.[81] An averment that the document was returned to the debtor for a special purpose without abandonment of the creditor's right, must be proved by writ or oath.[82]

9. Apocha Trium Annorum

If three consecutive discharges of periodical payments—rent, interest, feuduties or salaries, for example—are produced, payment of all preceding is presumed.[83] The presumption can be rebutted by parole evidence.[84] The presumption does not apply where there have been three consecutive payments but no discharge in writing;[85] nor where one discharge has been granted for three consecutive payments;[86] nor where arrears have been constituted by

---

74 *Barnett* v. *Colvill* (1840) 2 D.337.

75 *Russell* v. *Dunbar* (1717) Mor. 11,419; *Sanders* v. *Hewat* (1822) 1 S.333; Medical Act 1886, s.6; Gloag, p.718.

76 *Robertson* v. *Bent Colliery Co. Ltd.* (1919) 35 Sh.Ct.Rep.290.

77 *Gordon* v. *Johnston's Heirs* (1703) Mor.11,408.

78 Erskine, III, 4, 5.

79 *Rollo* v. *Simpson* (1710) Mor.11,411.

80 *Stewart* v. *Riddoch* (1677) Mor.11,406.

81 *Edward* v. *Fyfe* (1823) 2 S.431; *Knox* v. *Crawford* (1862) 24 D.1088; *per* L.P. Inglis, *Henry* v. *Miller* (1884) 11 R.713 at 717.

82 Dickson, *Evidence,* § 933.

83 Stair, I, 18, 2; Erskine, III, 4, 10.

84 *per* Lord Kincairney (Ordinary), *Cameron* v. *Panton's Trs.* (1891) 18 R.728 at 729; *Stenhouse* v. *Stenhouse's Trs.* (1899) 6 S.L.T.368.

85 *Moriston* v. *Tenants of Eastnisbet* (1631) Mor.11,394.

86 Erskine, III, 4, 10; Dickson, *Evidence,* §177.

bill or bond even although there are three consecutive discharges for subsequent terms;[87] nor where two discharges have been granted unknown to the heir, by an ancestor, and a third by the heir;[88] nor where the receipts are for hire and the claim is for overtime charges.[89] The position where the discharges have been granted by a factor is doubtful.[90]

10. Mode of Proof

Parole proof of payment is competent in a ready-money transaction—"where payment of the price is the counterpart and the immediate counterpart of the delivery at the same time of the subject sold".[91] A short time may elapse between delivery and payment but they must be *unico contextu*. But even where the transaction on credit is verbal, and even where the sum involved is under 100 pounds Scots, a payment made under an antecedent obligation is in general provable only by the writ or oath of the creditor.[92]

There are, however, certain exceptional cases where payment under an antecedent obligation can be proved by parole evidence. There must be "a state of facts, capable of being proved by parole evidence, which is inconsistent with the continued subsistence of the debt."[93] It has also been said that there must be proof of "some transaction or settlement between the creditor and the debtor subsequent to the contraction of the debt which necessarily leads to the conclusion that the debt was discharged,"[94] but in a later case[95] it was held that a transaction was not indispensable. Mere lapse of time,[96] or the absence of correspondence about the debt,[97] is not *per se* sufficient.

---

87 *Patrick* v. *Watt* (1859) 21 D.637.

88 *Gray* v. *Reid* (1699) Mor.11,399.

89 *Star Motor Express Co.* v. *Booth Ltd.* (1930) 46 Sh.Ct.Rep.239.

90 Dickson, *Evidence*, §180; *Preston* v. *Scot* (1667) Mor.11,397; *Earl of Marshall* v. *Fraser* (1682) Mor.11,399; *Grant* v. *Maclean* (1757) Mor.11,402.

91 *Shaw* v. *Wright* (1877) 5 R.245, *per* Lord Gifford at p.247.

92 *Burt* v. *Laing*, 1925 S.C.181; *Hope Brothers* v. *Morrison*, 1960 S.L.T.80. As to reference to a manager's oath, see *Craig & Rose Ltd.* v. *Lamarra*, 1975 S.C.316.

93 *per* Lord McLaren, *Chrystal* v. *Chrystal* (1900) 2 F.373 at 379; see also *Mackie* v. *Watson* (1837) 16 S.73; *Ryrie* v. *Ryrie* (1840) 2 D.1210; *Mitchell* v. *Berwick* (1845) 7 D.382; *Spence* v. *Paterson's Trs.* (1873) 1 R.46; *Neilson's Trs.* v. *Neilson's Trs.* (1883) 11 R.119; *British Bata Shoe Co. Ltd.* v. *Double M. Shah Ltd.*, 1981 S.L.T.(Notes)5.

94 *per* Lord Moncreiff, *Thiem's Trs.* v. *Collie* (1899) 1 F.764 at 780.

95 *McKenzie's Exx.* v. *Morrison's Trs.*, 1930 S.C.830.

96 *Thiem's Trs.* v. *Collie*, *supra*.

97 *Patrick* v. *Watt* (1859) 21 D.637.

Part payment can be inferred from an account rendered by the creditor to the debtor.[98]

11. Receipts—Execution

A debt constituted by a probative document requires a probative receipt to discharge it.[99] Otherwise, the general rule is that a receipt need not be probative.[1] In particular, a receipt for rent,[2] a receipt *in re mercatoria*,[2] a receipt for a legacy,[3] and a discharge of a claim for damages[4] need not be probative. The onus of proof of authenticity is, of course, in such cases on the person founding on the document.[4]

A receipt does not now require a stamp.[5]

12. Construction of Discharge

Where the discharge bears to be in respect of specified debts it will not cover by implication other debts due to the grantor which are not specified.[6] Where a bond and disposition in security had been granted in favour of a building society and was subsequently discharged, the discharge did not affect a liability under the society's rules to pay interest on arrears of interest due under the bond.[7] Where specified debts are followed by a general discharge the latter covers only debts of the same kind as those specified.[8] A general discharge covers all debts due at its date even although the term of payment has not arrived[9] but it does not cover debts of an uncommon kind which were not in the contemplation of the parties,[10] *e.g.* a cautioner's right of relief against the principal debtor where no payment has been made by the cautioner at the date of the

---

98 *Stewart & Taylor* v. *Grimson* (1904) 20 Sh.Ct.Rep.166.

99 *per* L.J.-C. Aitchison, *Davies* v. *Hunter*, 1934 S.C.10 at 15.

1 Bell, *Prin.*, §565; *Encyclopaedia of the Laws of Scotland*, Vol. V., p.587.

2 Bell, *Prin.*, §565.

3 *McLaren* v. *Howie* (1869) 8 M.106.

4 *Davies* v. *Hunter, supra*.

5 Finance Act 1970, Sched. 7, para. 2.

6 *Marquis of Tweeddale* v. *Hume* (1848) 10 D.1053.

7 *Galashiels Provident Building Society* v. *Newlands* (1893) 20 R.821.

8 Stair, IV, 40, 34; Erskine, III, 4, 9; Bell, *Prin.*, §583; *Talbot* v. *Guydet* (1705) Mor.5027.

9 *Adam* v. *Macdougall* (1831) 9 S.570; *British Linen Co.* v. *Esplin* (1849) 11 D.1104.

10 Stair, I, 18, 2; Erskine, III, 4, 9; Bell, *Prin.*, §584; *Wood* v. *Gordon* (1695) Mor.5035.

discharge.[11] Similarly, if the grantor of the discharge was unaware of the existence of a debt it is not affected.[12] A general discharge does not include a debt which has been assigned by the grantor before the date of the discharge but has not yet been intimated to the debtor.[13]

Although it has been said that in construing a discharge the court must look only at the instrument and not at extrinsic evidence,[14] it seems that parole evidence is admissible to show what was in the contemplation of the parties at the time the instrument was granted.[15]

A compromise made by the creditor as a result of an *error calculi* when he had the means of knowing the true facts cannot be rectified.[16]

A discharge on composition with an expressed understanding that the debtor would pay the balance when he was able to do so has been held to discharge the debt completely, the qualification being merely an obligation of honour.[17]

An agreement between an insolvent debtor and some of his creditors by which they bind themselves not to sue for their debts if they receive payment by instalments may be reducible at the instance of another creditor as a fraudulent preference but it is not a *pactum illicitum* and is binding on the creditors who are parties to it.[18]

13. Eliding Receipt

If a receipt is in possession of the debtor, proof that the debt was not in fact paid is competent only by the debtor's writ or oath.[19] It is, however, competent to prove by parole evidence that the receipt got into the debtor's hands by fraud, error, or accident or was given

[11] *Campbell* v. *Napier* (1678) Mor.5035; *Oliphant* v. *Newton* (1682) Mor.5035; *McTaggart* v. *Jeffrey* (1828) 6 S.641; revd. (1830) 4 W. & S.361; see also *Dickson's Trs.* v. *Dickson's Trs.*, 1930 S.L.T.226—discharge by legatee did not cover later claim arising as heir *in mobilibus*.

[12] *Greenock Banking Co.* v. *Smith* (1844) 6 D.1340; *Dickson* v. *Halbert* (1854) 16 D.586; *Purdon* v. *Rowat's Trs.* (1856) 19 D.206.

[13] *Lady Logan* v. *Affleck* (1736) Mor.5041.

[14] *per* Lord Wynford, *McTaggart* v. *Jeffrey, supra,* at p.367.

[15] *McAdam* v. *Scott* (1912) 50 S.L.R.264 (here the discharge was ambiguous).

[16] *Belhaven Engineering & Motors Ltd.* v. *Reid* (1910) 26 Sh.Ct.Rep.234.

[17] *Ritchie* v. *Cowan & Kinghorn* (1901) 3 F.1071; *Rankin* v. *Milne* (1916) 32 Sh.Ct.Rep.109.

[18] *Munro* v. *Rothfield,* 1920 S.C.118.

[19] *Macfarlane* v. *Watt* (1828) 6 S.556; *Gordon* v. *Trotter* (1833) 11 S.696; *Anderson* v. *Forth Marine Insurance Co.* (1845) 7 D.268; *cf. Crawford* v. *Bennet* (1827) 2 W. & S. 608.

to the debtor for some special purpose.[20] A bank may prove parole that an entry in a customer's pass-book was made in error.[21]

Where an account was discharged with the words "paid by cheque" with a date, the creditor could prove only by writ or oath that the cheque was for less than the amount of the account and that there was a balance resting owing; it was suggested that the object of the words was to prevent the discharge being founded on as conclusive if the cheque should be dishonoured.[22]

Between banker and customer, a pay-in slip[23] is prima facie evidence of payment and, similarly, a bank passbook[24] which passes between banker and customer is prima facie evidence against the banker. On the other hand, if the customer has in writing acknowledged that the balance at credit of his account is correct he is barred from subsequently impugning it because the account has become a fitted or settled account which is probative.[25]

It may be, however, that the rigour of that rule is confined to the banker-customer relationship and whether the admission results in more than a shift in the onus of proof depends on the degree of formality with which approval is given.

Generally where parties have agreed by signing or docquetting an account as to the position between them the account is known as a fitted or settled account to be distinguished from an open account.[26] Such an account raises a presumption that there has been a final settlement between the parties; it is still possible to dispute the accuracy of the account but there is a heavy onus on the challenger.[27]

14. Lost Receipt

It seems possible to prove payment by parole evidence to the effect that the receipt has been lost. This was allowed where a passbook

---

20 *Smith* v. *Kerr* (1869) 7 M.863; *Henry* v. *Miller* (1884) 11 R.713.

21 *Commercial Bank of Scotland* v. *Rhind* (1860) 3 Macq.643.

22 *Kelly & Co.* v. *Rae* (1909) 25 Sh.Ct.Rep.3.

23 *Docherty* v. *Royal Bank,* 1962 S.L.T.(Notes) 102.

24 *Commercial Bank* v. *Rhind* (1860) 3 Macq.643; *Couper's Trs.* v. *National Bank* (1889) 16 R.412.

25 *Connochie* v. *British Linen Bank* (1943) 59 Sh.Ct.Rep.44, in which the opinion of Lord Carmont in *Dickson* v. *Clydesdale Bank,* 18 December 1936, unreported, is quoted and followed. See also *British Linen Co.* v. *Thomson* (1853) 15 D.314.

26 *Commercial Bank* v. *Rhind* (1860) 3 Macq.643, *per* Lord Campbell L.C. at p.650.

27 *Laing* v. *Laing* (1862) 24 D.1362; *Struthers* v. *Smith,* 1913 S.C.1116.

vouching receipt had been lost by the creditor;[28] where a receipt had been lost by the debtor;[29] and where a letter acknowledging repayment of a loan had been lost.[30]

15. Cheques

Prior to 1957, it was established that a cheque indorsed by the payee was evidence of receipt by him of the amount of the cheque.[31] Section 1 of the Cheques Act 1957 rendered indorsement by the payee unnecessary and, in consequence, section 3 of the Act provided that: "An unindorsed cheque which appears to have been paid by the banker on whom it is drawn is evidence of the receipt by the payee of the sum payable by the cheque." This section sets up only a prima facie presumption and it has been said that the unindorsed cheque does not appear to be as cogent evidence as a cheque indorsed by the payee.[32]

---

28 *Young* v. *Thomson,* 1909 S.C.529.

29 *James Scott & Co. (Electrical Engineers) Ltd.* v. *McIntosh* (1960) 76 Sh.Ct.Rep.26 (this goes further than *Young* in that there was no course of dealing between the parties).

30 *Simpson's Trs.* v. *Simpson,* 1933 S.N.22.

31 *Haldane* v. *Speirs* (1872) 10 M.537.

32 *Westminster Bank Ltd.* v. *Zang* [1966] A.C.182.

CHAPTER 13

COMPENSATION AND RETENTION

1. "Set-off"[1]

The question now to be considered is, in general terms, whether a debt due by the pursuer to the defender can be set off against the pursuer's claim for a debt due to him by the defender. The preliminary question is whether there are in fact two separate debts or whether there are merely two items in a running account in which case the question of set-off disappears and the balance on the account is the only debt due. A running account or account-current is one in which the intention of the parties was that the transactions should be set down on different sides of the account against each other and a balance struck at the end with periodical settlements.[2]

If there are two separate debts there arise two distinct questions which are often confused. The first is: in an action for debt is it a relevant defence to plead that a debt is due by the pursuer to the defender? The second is: in an action for debt, what types of debt can form the basis of a counter claim by the defender? The answers to these questions are not necessarily the same because a debt due by the pursuer to the defender may be the basis of a counter claim even although it is not a relevant defence; the pursuer will be granted decree for the full amount of his claim but the counter claim may be allowed to continue as a substantive action.

The answer to the first question is that the debt is a relevant defence only in circumstances where the doctrines of compensation, balancing of accounts in bankruptcy or retention operate.

Compensation under the Act 1592, c.143 operates where both debts are liquid and certain other conditions are fulfilled; retention operates where both debts, liquid or illiquid, arise out of the same contract; balancing of accounts in bankruptcy operates where the creditor or debtor in the liquid claim is bankrupt. If one of these doctrines is applicable the pursuer's claim is extinguished or reduced *pro tanto*. If none of these doctrines is applicable the existence of the defender's claim is no defence and is no bar to

---

[1] "Set-off" is used as a convenient neutral term. It is not a term of art in Scots law: *Laing* v. *Lord Advocate,* 1973 S.L.T.(Notes)81.

[2] *McKinlay* v. *Wilson* (1885) 13 R.210.

the pursuer's obtaining decree for his claim because it is clearly established that in general an illiquid claim is not an answer to a liquid claim.[3] As has already been indicated, however, this does not necessarily mean that the debt due to the defender cannot form the basis of a counter claim.

2. Competent Counter Claims

It is hardly necessary to say that a counter claim will lie only where an independent action could be brought—"a counter claim is a sword, whereas compensation is only a shield, and the right to defend one's self with the latter does not imply the right to wield the former."[4]

In the Court of Session, in terms of rule 84, the defender may counter-claim in respect of "any matter forming part of, or arising out of the grounds of, the pursuer's action, or the decision of which is necessary for the determination of the question in controversy between the parties or which, if the pursuer had been a person not otherwise subject to the jurisdiction of the Court, might competently have formed the subject of an action against such pursuer in which jurisdiction would have arisen *ex reconventione;* provided that, in any case, the counter claim is such as might have formed matter of a separate action, and that, if such separate action had been raised, it would not have been necessary to call as defender thereto any person other than the pursuer." It has been held that where the counter claim is for damages and arises out of the same course of dealing as the pursuer's claim, but not out of the same contract, and thus cannot be set off against the pursuer's claim, the pursuer can be granted interim decree *de plano* for the amount of his claim and the defenders can then be allowed to proceed with the counter claim as if it was an independent claim.[5]

In the sheriff court, rule 55 provides: "Where a defender pleads a counter claim it shall suffice that he state the same in his defences, and the sheriff may thereafter deal with it as if it had been stated in a substantive action, and may grant decree for it in whole or in part, or for the difference between it and the claim sued on." At first a

---

[3] *per* Lord Cranworth L.C., *National Exchange Co.* v. *Drew* (1855) 2 Macq.103 at p.122; *Scottish N.E. Rlwy. Co.* v. *Napier* (1859) 21 D.700; *Burt* v. *Bell* (1861) 24 D.13; *Mackie* v. *Riddell* (1874) 2 R.115; *Armour & Melvin* v. *Mitchell,* 1934 S.C.94.

[4] *J. E. Binstock Miller & Co.* v. *E. Coia & Co. Ltd.* (1957) 73 Sh.Ct.Rep.178.

[5] *Scott* v. *Aitken,* 1950 S.L.T.(Notes)34; *Fulton Clyde Ltd.* v. *J. F. McCallum & Co. Ltd.,* 1960 S.C.78.

restrictive view was taken of this rule and it was thought that only items which could be set off against the pursuer's claim could found a counter claim.[6] It is now established that a claim which cannot be set off can form a counter claim.[7] If the pursuer's claim is admitted, the pursuer is given interim decree for its amount together with expenses[8] and the counter claim may proceed as an independent substantive action. The court, however, probably has a discretionary power to prevent a counter claim quite unconnected with the pursuer's claim proceeding.[9]

If the pursuer's claim has to go to proof, the counter claim falls to be dismissed.[9] If the pursuer's action is abandoned or dismissed as irrelevant the counter claim can proceed.[10] It has been suggested that in some circumstances the defender could obtain decree before judgment is issued on the pursuer's claim.[11]

3. Compensation

The Compensation Act 1592, provides: "that any debt *de liquido in liquidum,* instantly verified by writ, or oath of party, before the giving of decree, be admitted by all judges within this realm by way of exception, but not after the giving thereof in the suspension, or in reduction of the same decree." The conditions for the operation of compensation are: (1) the debts must be of the same kind, (2) the debts must both be due and liquid, (3) there must be *concursus debiti et crediti,* (4) it must be pleaded before decree.[12]

4. Concursus Debiti et Crediti

Each party must be debtor and creditor in the same capacity. A sum due to the defender as an executor cannot be compensated against a sum due by him personally,[13] unless, perhaps, where he is also the sole beneficiary of the executry estate.[14] Although a tutor who is sued on a bond granted by himself *qua* tutor can set off a debt due to

---

[6] *Christie* v. *Birrells,* 1910 S.C.986; *Fingland & Mitchell* v. *Howie,* 1926 S.C.319.

[7] *Armour & Melvin* v. *Mitchell,* 1934 S.C.94. Proposed rule 62 is in slightly different terms.

[8] *Grant* v. *McAlister* (1948) 64 Sh.Ct.Rep.261.

[9] *Croall & Croall* v. *Sharp* (1954) 70 Sh.Ct.Rep.129.

[10] *Feld British Agencies Ltd.* v. *Jas. Pringle Ltd.,* 1961 S.L.T.123.

[11] *per* Lord Skerrington, *British Motor Body Co. Ltd.* v. *Thomas Shaw (Dundee) Ltd.,* 1914 S.C.922 at 930.

[12] Bell, *Prin.,* § 575.

[13] *Stuart* v. *Stuart* (1869) 7 M.366.

[14] *per* L.P. Inglis, *Stuart* v. *Stuart, supra,* at 367; Bell, *Comm.,* II, 125.

the pupil,[15] he cannot set off a debt due to the pupil against a debt due by him personally.[16]

Where A, acting as agent for C, contracts with B, the agency being disclosed, then A cannot set off a sum due under the contract by B to C against a debt due by him as an individual to B.[17] Similarly, B cannot set off a debt due to him by A against the amount due to C under the contract.[18] It seems, however, that B can set off a sum due to him and collected by A as agent for C against his debt to C.[19] C can obviously set off an amount due by B to A as agent against a debt due by him to B and this holds even in *del credere* agency.[20]

Where the existence of the agency is revealed but the principal's name is undisclosed, B nevertheless cannot set off sums due to him by A against sums due by him to C under the contract.[21] Where the agency is not disclosed, however, B is entitled to set off A's debt to him against the amount due to C.[22]

An executor is *eadem persona cum defuncto* and a creditor of the deceased may plead compensation against a debt due by him to the estate which resulted from a transaction with the executor after the death.[23] An heir who was sued for his ancestor's debt could plead compensation on a debt due by the creditor to the deceased even although the debt was moveable and would fall to the executor.[24] A beneficiary cannot set off a debt due to the trustees against a debt due by her personally.[25]

In bankruptcy, the *concursus* must have existed prior to the date of sequestration. A debtor of the bankrupt cannot plead compensation against the trustee on a debt due by the bankrupt which was acquired by assignation after the date of sequestration.[26] A creditor of the bankrupt cannot plead compensation against a debt due to

---

15 *Earl of Northesk* v. *Gairn's Tutor* (1670) Mor.2569.

16 *Elliot* v. *Elliots* (1711) Mor.2658.

17 *Ferguson* v. *Muir* (1711) Mor.2659.

18 *Liddell Brownlie & Co.* v. *Andrew Young & Son* (1852) 14 D.647.

19 *Macgregor's Tr.* v. *Cox* (1883) 10 R.1028.

20 *Ferrier* v. *British Linen Co.*, 20 Nov. 1807, F.C.

21 *Lavaggi* v. *Pirie & Sons* (1872) 10 M.312; *Matthews* v. *Auld & Guild* (1874) 1 R.1224; *National Bank of Scotland* v. *Dickie's Tr.* (1895) 22 R.740.

22 *Gall* v. *Murdoch* (1821) 1 S.77.

23 *Mitchell* v. *Mackersy* (1905) 8 F.198 (overruling *Gray's Trs.* v. *Royal Bank of Scotland* (1895) 23 R.199).

24 *Hay* v. *Crawford* (1712) Mor.2571; *Middleton* v. *Earl of Strathmore* (1743) Mor.2573.

25 *Johnston* v. *Johnston* (1875) 2 R.986.

26 *Cauvin* v. *Robertson* (1783) Mor.2581.

the trustee which arose after sequestration.[27] A person who is both creditor of, and debtor to, the bankrupt prior to sequestration can interdict the trustee from endorsing to a third party the bill due by him.[28] The same principles apply where a trust deed for creditors has been executed and also in liquidations.[29] It is not permissible to set off a claim in respect of breach of contract by the company against a sum payable in respect of a contract carried out by the liquidator.[30] However, when the liquidator has re-engaged employees of the company, any redundancy payments subsequently due to them in respect of periods of employment prior to liquidation can be set off by the Secretary of State against sums due by him to the liquidator.[31]

A sum due to one of several co-obligants by the creditor can be set off against the debt for which the co-obligants are liable.[32] But it is not possible to compensate a debt due by one of several co-creditors against the debt due to the co-creditors jointly and severally.[33] Where a deposit receipt was payable to either A or B or the survivor, it was held that the bank could not set off a debt due to it by A against a demand for payment by B.[34]

A bank can set off one account against another of the same customer but not if one is a fiduciary account.[35]

5. Liquidity

The debt used to compensate must be liquid in the sense that it is certain in amount, presently payable and not disputed. A claim cannot be used as a ground of compensation if it is future or contingent;[36] if it is an unquantified claim for damages;[37] if it requires investigation and proof;[38] or if it requires something in the

27 *Mill* v. *Paul* (1825) 4 S.219.

28 *Harvey Brand & Co.* v. *Buchanan Hamilton & Co.'s Tr.* (1886) 4 M.1128.

29 *Meldrum's Trs.* v. *Clark* (1826) 5 S.122; *Mill* v. *Paul, supra.*

30 *Asphaltic Limestone Co.* v. *Corporation of Glasgow,* 1907 S.C.463.

31 *Smith* v. *Lord Advocate,* 1978 S.C.259.

32 *Dobson* v. *Christie* (1835) 13 S.582. As to compensation in partnership, see Chap. 27, para. 11.

33 *Burrell* v. *Burrell's Trs.,* 1916 S.C.729.

34 *Anderson* v. *North of Scotland Bank Ltd.* (1901) 4 F.49.

35 *Kirkwood & Sons* v. *Clydesdale Bank Ltd.,* 1908 S.C.20; *United Rentals Ltd.* v. *Clydesdale and North of Scotland Bank* (1963) 79 Sh.Ct.Rep.118.

36 *Paul & Thain* v. *Royal Bank* (1869) 7 M.361.

37 *National Exchange Co.* v. *Drew* (1855) 2 Macq.103; *Scottish North Eastern Rlwy. Co.* v. *Napier* (1859) 21 D.700; *Mackie* v. *Riddell* (1874) 2 R.115.

38 *Logan* v. *Stephen* (1850) 13 D.262; *Drew* v. *Drew* (1855) 17 D.559; *Urie* v. *Lumsden* (1859) 22 D.38; *Kerr* v. *Fife & Kinross Rlwy. Co.* (1860) 22 D.564; *Munro* v. *Graham* (1857) 20 D.72; *Macgregor* v. *City of Glasgow Bank* (1865) 3 M.896.

nature of an accounting to expiscate it.[39] But the rule *de liquido in liquidum* is to be understood *cum aliquo temperamento* and, in accordance with the brocard *quod statim liquidari potest, pro jam liquido habetur,*[40] the court has a discretion to allow an illiquid counter claim to be admitted if it can be ascertained almost immediately,[41] or is in the fair course of being made liquid,[42] or if it can be instantly verified by reference to the pursuer's oath,[43] or if it is equitable to admit it in the circumstances.[44] It seems that an illiquid claim is also admitted where the pursuer is *vergens ad inopiam.*[45]

6. Operation

Compensation does not operate *ipso facto;* it must be pleaded and sustained.[46] The mere fact that the two debts existed at the same time does not extinguish them. Nor is the statement of the plea sufficient; it must be sustained.[47] Compensation is "the operation of the judge rather than of the law."[48] So, a debt which has been extinguished by prescription cannot be pleaded to compensate a debt which has not prescribed even although an action for its recovery during the prescriptive period would have been met by a plea of compensation founded on the other debt.[49] The same result followed in the case of the triennial[50] and quinquennial[51] prescriptions but there it was possible to refer the prescribed debt instantly to the debtor's oath.[52] Other consequences of the general principle are that the party pleading compensation may abandon the plea

39 *Lawson* v. *Drysdale* (1844) 7 D.153; *McIntyre* v. *Macdonald* (1854) 16 D.485; *Blair Iron Co.* v. *Alison* (1855) 18 D.(H.L.)49; 6 W. & S. 56.

40 Erskine, III, 4, 16; *Seton* (1683) Mor.2566; *Brown* v. *Elies* (1686) Mor.2566.

41 *Logan* v. *Stephen* (1850) 13 D.262, *per* Lord Cuninghame at p.267; *Henderson & Co. Ltd.* v. *Turnbull & Co.*, 1909 S.C.510.

42 *Munro* v. *Macdonald's Exrs.* (1866) 4 M.687.

43 *Stuart* v. *Stuart* (1869) 7 M.366; *Ross* v. *Magistrates of Tayne* (1711) Mor.2568.

44 *Ross* v. *Ross* (1895) 22 R.461.

45 *Sim* v. *Lundy & Blanshard* (1868) 41 J.136; *Paul & Thain* v. *Royal Bank* (1869) 7 M.361.

46 Erskine, III, 4, 12; Bell, *Comm.*, II, 124; Bell, *Prin.*, §575; *National Westminster Bank* v. *Halesowen Presswork* [1972] A.C.785, *per* Lord Kilbrandon at p.822.

47 *Cowan* v. *Gowans* (1878) 5 R.581 (this case is relevant to the principle of balancing accounts in bankruptcy rather than compensation; it creates an exception to that principle because of the special position of a shareholder in relation to calls).

48 Erskine, III, 4, 12.

49 *Carmichael* v. *Carmichael* (1719) Mor.2677.

50 *Galloway* v. *Galloway* (1799) Mor.11,122.

51 *Baillie* v. *McIntosh* (1753) Mor.2680.

52 *Miller* v. *Baird,* 1819 Hume 480; Bell, *Comm.*, II, 123; Bell, *Prin.*, §574.

before decree, substitute another defence and use his claim for some other purpose;[53] where the defender is creditor in several debts he may choose which he pleases as a ground for compensation;[54] and prescription on the debt founded on is not interrupted till the plea is sustained.[55]

What might appear to be an exception to the rule arises where a debt has been assigned. If *concursus* existed before intimation, the debtor can plead against the assignee compensation on a debt due to him by the cedent.[56]

It is, of course possible for debts to be extinguished by an express agreement to compensate. There must be a specific agreement and probably writing is required.[57]

Where the plea of compensation has been sustained, however, it operates *retro* so that the debts are extinguished from the start of the *concursus* and interest on them is also extinguished from that time.[58] Liquifaction is also drawn back to the date of *concursus* so that if one debt was illiquid at the time of concourse but was liquified before the action was raised both debts are extinguished from the date of concourse.[59]

7. Pleaded Before Decree

In terms of the Compensation Act 1592, compensation must be pleaded before decree; it cannot be used in a suspension.[60] So a debt due by the pursuer which is acquired by the defender after decree cannot be used as a ground of compensation.[61] The rule applies even where the decree is given in absence[62] but exceptions are allowed where the creditor is bankrupt,[63] where there were several debtors,[64] and where the decree is null.[65] An award of expenses is

---

53 *Lord Balmerino* v. *Dick's Crs.* (1664) Mor.2681.

54 *Maxwell* v. *McCulloch's Trs.* (1738) Mor.2550.

55 *Sloan* v. *Birtwhistle* (1827) 5 S.742.

56 *Shiells* v. *Ferguson, Davidson & Co.* (1876) 4 R.250; see the argument in *Carmichael* v. *Carmichael, supra,* and Hume, *Lectures,* III, pp.43-44.

57 *Cowan* v. *Shaw* (1878) 5 R.680.

58 *Cleland* v. *Stevenson* (1669) Mor.2682.

59 *Inch* v. *Lee* (1903) 11 S.L.T.374.

60 Erskine, III, 4, 19; *Paterson's Crs.* v. *McAulay* (1742) Mor.2646; *Naismith* v. *Bowman* (1710) Mor.2645.

61 *Anderson* v. *Schaw* (1739) Mor.2646.

62 *Cuninghame Stevenson & Co.* v. *Wilson,* 17 Jan. 1809, F.C.

63 *Barclay* v. *Clerk* (1683) Mor.2641.

64 *Corbet* v. *Hamilton* (1707) Mor.2642; *A.* v. *B.* (1747) Mor.2648.

65 *Wright* v. *Sheill* (1676) Mor.2640.

outwith the general rule because the plea cannot be taken against it prior to decree.[66] The principle does not apply where the plea has been proponed and wrongfully repelled.[67]

8. Exceptions

Compensation cannot be pleaded against certain debts:

(a) where money has been paid to someone to be used for a specific purpose and that purpose fails, compensation cannot be pleaded against a claim for repayment.[68]

(b) compensation is not pleadable against a demand for alimentary payments but arrears of an alimentary fund are not protected.[69]

(c) it is not competent to take a set-off or counter claim in any proceedings by the Crown without leave of the court if the subject-matter of the counter claim does not relate to the Government department on whose behalf the proceedings are brought. Similarly, the Crown in any proceedings against a Government department cannot without leave of the court take a set-off or counter claim if the subject-matter thereof does not relate to that department. A set-off or counter claim cannot be taken in any proceedings by the Crown for recovery of taxes, duties or penalties and a subject cannot found a set-off or counter claim on a claim for repayment of such sums.[70]

(d) compensation cannot be pleaded by a director or other officer of a company against a claim in respect of misfeasance and breach of trust under s.333 of the Companies Act 1948.[71]

(e) in a liquidation, a contributory cannot set-off amounts due by the company to him against calls unless all the creditors have been paid in full.[72]

---

[66] *Fowler* v. *Brown,* 1916 S.C.597. See also *Masco Cabinet Co. Ltd.* v. *Martin,* 1912 S.C.896; *Galloway* v. *MacKinnon* (1936) 52 Sh.Ct.Rep.135.

[67] Erskine, III, 4, 19.

[68] *Middlemas* v. *Gibson,* 1910 S.C.577.

[69] *Reid* v. *Bell* (1884) 12 R.178; *Drew* v. *Drew* (1870) 9 M.163.

[70] Crown Proceedings Act 1947, s.50; as to the granting of leave see *Atlantic Engine Co. (1920) Ltd.* v. *Lord Advocate,* 1955 S.L.T.17; *Smith* v. *Lord Advocate (No. 2),* 1981 S.L.T.19. The rules apply to balancing of accounts in bankruptcy: *Laing* v. *Lord Advocate,* 1973 S.L.T(Notes)81.

[71] *Re Anglo-French Co-operative Society, Ex p. Pelly* (1882) 21 Ch.D.492, C.A.

[72] *Re Whitehouse & Co.* (1878) 9 Ch.D.595; Companies Act 1948, s.259(3). Section 20 of the 1948 Act does not prevent set-off if the company is not in liquidation: *Scottish Fishermen's Organisation Ltd.* v. *McLean,* 1980 S.L.T. (Sh.Ct.)76.

(f) a bank at which a solicitor keeps a special account for client's money cannot, in respect of any liability of the solicitor to the bank (not being a liability in connection with that account) have or obtain any recourse or right, "whether by way of set-off, counter claim, charge or otherwise, against money standing to the credit of that account".[73]

(g) where the debt is due under a contract the terms of which exclude set-off against the debt.[74]

9. Retention

The principle of retention is that "in cases of mutual contract a party in defence is entitled to plead and maintain claims in reduction or extinction of a sum due under his obligation where such claims arise from the failure of the pursuer to fulfil his part of the contract."[75] This is an aspect of the wider principle that "one party to a mutual contract, in which there are mutual stipulations, cannot insist on having his claim under the contract satisfied, unless he is prepared to satisfy the corresponding and contemporaneous claims of the other party to the contract."[76] Thus, a claim for freight can be met with a claim for damages for defective carriage;[77] and the rule has been applied to contracts of sale,[78] storage,[79] and service[80] and to building contracts.[81] The contract may be implied as where a store-keeper enforces his lien.[82] The principle has some application between landlord and tenant but there are complexities which cannot be treated here.[83]

It is not altogether clear whether the rule applies to a building contract where the price is payable by instalments.[84] In a contract where the price is payable by instalments, the employer cannot set a

[73] Solicitors (Scotland) Act 1980, s.61.

[74] *Robert Paterson & Sons Ltd.* v. *Household Supplies Co. Ltd.*, 1975 S.L.T.98.

[75] *per* Lord Shand, *Macbride* v. *Hamilton* (1875) 2 R.775 at 779n., approved by L.P. Strathclyde in *British Motor Body Co. Ltd.* v. *Thomas Shaw (Dundee) Ltd.*, 1914 S.C.922 at 928.

[76] *per* Lord Benholme, *Johnston* v. *Robertson* (1861) 23 D.646 at 652.

[77] *Taylor* v. *Forbes* (1830) 9 S.113; *cf. Henriksens A/S* v. *Rolimpex* [1974] Q.B.233.

[78] *British Motor Body Co. Ltd.* v. *Thomas Shaw (Dundee) Ltd., supra;* here, of course, there are also sections 11(5) and 53(1) of the Sale of Goods Act 1979.

[79] *Gibson and Stewart* v. *Brown & Co.* (1876) 3 R.328.

[80] *Sharp* v. *Rettie* (1884) 11 R.745.

[81] *Johnston* v. *Robertson, supra.*

[82] *Gibson and Stewart* v. *Brown & Co., supra.*

[83] See Gloag, pp.628-630.

[84] *Field & Allan* v. *Gordon* (1872) 11 M.132.

claim for damages against a claim for the earlier instalments due if the damages claim does not exceed the amount of the last instalment.[85]

The right to retain is, it seems, subject to the equitable control of the court and the defender may be prevented from taking advantage of a plea of retention for the purpose of delay or to try to establish a claim which probably could not be established in a cross action by the court refusing to give effect to the plea or by ordering consignation.[86]

It should be noted that a claim for damages in respect of fraudulent misrepresentations which induced the defender to enter the contract arises *ex delicto* and not from the contract, so such a claim cannot be pleaded against a sum due under the contract.[87] To allow retention, it is not enough that both claims arise from the same course of dealing between the parties; they must both arise from a contract which is one and indivisible; a person cannot transform a series of contracts into one by delaying payment of the accounts until several have been accumulated and re-rendered as one account.[88]

10. Balancing Accounts in Bankruptcy

Where one party is bankrupt or in liquidation, an illiquid claim can be set-off against a liquid claim.[89] So a future or contingent debt due by the bankrupt can be used to set-off a debt presently due to him.[90] Unquantified claims can similarly be utilised. It has been said that the debt used must be one which is capable of being ranked for.[91] It has been doubted, however, whether an illiquid claim for damages —one in respect of defamation, for example—can be set-off against a liquid claim.[92] This principle of balancing accounts in bankruptcy

---

85 *Dick & Stevenson* v. *Woodside Steel & Iron Co.* (1888) 16 R.242.

86 *per* Lord Ardwall, *Garscadden* v. *Ardrossan Dry Dock Co. Ltd.*, 1910 S.C.178 at 180; *per* Lord Skerrington, *British Motor Body Co. Ltd.* v. *Thomas Shaw (Dundee) Ltd., supra,* at p.929.

87 *Smart* v. *Wilkinson*, 1928 S.C.383.

88 *Grewar* v. *Cross* (1904) 12 S.L.T.84; *Scott* v. *Aitken*, 1950 S.L.T.(Notes)34; *Fulton Clyde Ltd.* v. *J. F. McCallum & Co. Ltd.*, 1960 S.L.T.253; *J. W. Chafer (Scotland) Ltd.* v. *Hope*, 1963 S.L.T.(Notes)11.

89 *Mill* v. *Paul* (1825) 4 S.219, *per* Lord Glenlee at p.220; *Scott's Trs.* v. *Scott* (1887) 14 R.1043, *per* L.P. Inglis at p.1051; *Ross* v. *Ross* (1895) 22 R.461, *per* Lord McLaren at p.465.

90 *Hannay & Sons' Tr.* v. *Armstrong & Co.* (1875) 2 R.399; (1877) 4 R.(H.L.)43; *Smith* v. *Lord Advocate (No. 2)*, 1981 S.L.T.19.

91 Goudy, p.553.

92 Gloag, p.626; Gloag & Irvine, p.315.

resembles compensation in that there must have been a *concursus debiti et crediti* prior to sequestration.[93] In other words, a debt contracted after notice of bankruptcy cannot be set-off against a debt due to the bankrupt estate which arose before bankruptcy; but this does not prevent a debt arising after sequestration or liquidation being set-off against one which also arose after that time.[94] It is doubtful whether a claim acquired within six months of bankruptcy can be used.[95] As in compensation some types of debt cannot be used to set-off.[96]

There is one major exception to the operation of the principle. Suppose A and B are jointly and severally liable to C but B is the primary debtor. A and B are both sequestrated and C ranks for the debt on both estates. A owes a debt of some other kind to B and B's trustee claims this in A's sequestration. A's trustee contends that he can set-off a claim for relief against B's estate in respect of the dividend paid to C. This cannot be done, however, because C has ranked for the same debt on B's estate and if A's trustee is allowed to set-off there would be a double ranking.[97] This applies only in sequestration and it does not extend to the case where C has got a composition from B.[98]

There is a further exception to the principle in the case of calls. After liquidation, a shareholder cannot set-off a debt due to him by the company against a call made before liquidation.[99]

Normally the bankrupt is creditor in the liquid claim and debtor in the illiquid claim but there is one case[1] in which an insurance company had a liquid claim against the bankrupt in respect of advances and was debtor to the bankrupt in respect of a future and contingent obligation under a policy. The company was relieved of its obligation under the policy on deducting the surrender value from its liquid claim.

---

93 *Mill* v. *Paul, supra; Cauvin* v. *Robertson* (1783) Mor.2581; *Taylor's Tr.* v. *Paul* (1888) 15 R.313.

94 *Liqrs. of Highland Engineering* v. *Thomson,* 1972 S.C.87.

95 Bell, *Comm.*, II, 124.

96 *Campbell* v. *Little* (1823) 2 S.484; *Reid* v. *Bell* (1884) 12 R.178.

97 *Anderson* v. *Mackinnon* (1876) 3 R.608; *cf. Christie* v. *Keith* (1838) 16 S.1224.

98 *Gibb* v. *Brock,* 12 May 1838, F.C.; *Mackinnon* v. *Monkhouse* (1881) 9 R.393.

99 *Cowan* v. *Gowans* (1878) 5 R.581; see *supra,* para. 8.

1 *Borthwick* v. *Scottish Widows' Fund* (1864) 2 M.595. *Cf. Campbell* v. *Carphin,* 1925 S.L.T.(Sh.Ct.)30.

CHAPTER 14

OTHER DEFENCES

1. Novation

Novation is "the substitution of a new engagement or obligation by the same debtor to the same creditor, to the effect of extinguishing the original debt."[1] There is a presumption against novation.[2] So the taking of a bill or other document of debt for the amount of an account does not extinguish the original debt,[3] and the creditor does not lose any lien he may have in respect of the original debt unless the period for which the bill is granted is so long as to make it unreasonable to suppose that the parties intended the lien to remain in force.[4] The taking of a renewal bill does not extinguish the liability on the original bill if the latter is retained by the creditor;[5] and where a party liable on a bill granted a heritable bond in favour of the creditor it was held that in the absence of evidence of an intention that the bond was to be substituted for the bill, the liability on the bill remained.[6] It has been said that before the defence of novation can be sustained either the original document of debt must have been given up or there must be a letter or other evidence to show that it was departed from.[7] So the giving up of a bill when a new bill is taken forms novation;[8] and an express declaration by the creditor that the prior obligations are discharged[9] or a statement to that effect in the narrative of a new bond[10] precludes the creditor from relying on the original debt.

The effect of novation is to extinguish the debt with its accessories.[11]

---

1 Bell, *Prin.*, § 576.

2 Stair, I, 18, 8.

3 *Wilson and Corse* v. *Gardner,* 1807 Hume 247.

4 *Gairdner* v. *Milne & Co.* (1858) 20 D.565; *Palmer* v. *Lee* (1880) 7 R.651.

5 *Hay & Kyd* v. *Powrie* (1886) 13 R.777.

6 *Roy's Trs.* v. *Stalker* (1850) 12 D.722.

7 *per* L.J.-C. Hope, *Roy's Trs.* v. *Stalker, supra,* at p.723.

8 *Stevenson* v. *Duncan,* 1805 Hume 245; *Simpson* v. *Jack,* 1948 S.L.T.(Notes) 45. *Hope Johnstone* v. *Cornwall* (1895) 22 R.314, is a special case.

9 *Cox* v. *Tait* (1843) 5 D.1283.

10 *Jackson* v. *MacDiarmid* (1892) 19 R.528.

11 Bell, *Prin.*, § 579.

2. Delegation

Delegation is "the substitution of a new debtor for the old, with consent of the creditor."[12] It is sometimes treated as a species of novation.[13] Delegation is not to be presumed;[14] there must be clear evidence of the intention of the three parties concerned to effect delegation but such intention may be inferred from facts and circumstances.[15] It may rest upon a usage of trade.[16] As in the case of novation, the surrender of the original document of debt supports the inference of delegation.[17] Where one limited company has amalgamated with another, strict proof is required before it can be held that a creditor of the first company has agreed to accept the amalgamated company as his debtor in place of the first.[18] Questions of delegation in relation to partnership are dealt with elsewhere.[19]

3. Confusio[20]

Where the same person in the same capacity becomes both creditor and debtor in the same obligation, the debt is extinguished *confusione.*[21] *Confusio* takes place only when the full and absolute right of the creditor and the full and absolute right of the debtor merge in one and the same person.[22] The principle operates *ipso jure* and independently of intention.[23] It does not operate where the person has an interest to maintain the debt in existence.[24] Where the cautioner acquires the creditor's right, the cautionary obligation is extinguished but the principal obligation is not.[25] Where a bondholder purchases the security subjects and pays the proprietor only the balance of the price after deduction of the bond, the debt is

---

12 Bell, *Prin.*, § 577.

13 Erskine, III, 4, 22.

14 *McIntosh* v. *Ainslie* (1872) 10 M.304.

15 *Dudgeon* v. *Reid* (1829) 7 S.729; *Hunter* v. *Falconer* (1835) 13 S.252; *Fox* v. *Anderson* (1849) 11 D.1194.

16 *North* v. *Bassett* [1892] 1 Q.B.333.

17 *Stevenson* v. *Duncan,* 1805 Hume 245.

18 *Re Family Endowment Society* (1870) L.R. 5 Ch.118.

19 See Chap. 27, para. 7.

20 The English term is merger.

21 Bell, *Prin.*, § 580; *Motherwell* v. *Manwell* (1903) 5 F.619, *per* Lord Kinnear at p.631.

22 *per* Lord Ardwall, *King* v. *Johnston,* 1908 S.C.684 at 689.

23 *Healy & Young's Tr.* v. *Mair's Trs.,* 1914 S.C.893.

24 *Fleming* v. *Imrie* (1868) 6 M.363.

25 Erskine, III, 4, 24.

extinguished, even although the bond is not discharged.[26] The result is the same where the debtor pays off the bond and obtains an assignation thereof.[27] An *ex facie* absolute disposition to the bond-holder in further security does not extinguish the bond.[28] Ground annuals cannot be extinguished *confusione*.[29] Feuduties are extinguished *confusione* when the superior and vassal are one.[30]

4. Quinquennial Prescription

An obligation to which the prescription applies is extinguished if it has subsisted for a continuous period of five years without any relevant claim having been made in relation to it and without its subsistence having been relevantly acknowledged.[31] It is not possible to contract out of the prescription.[32]

The prescription applies[33]:

(a) to any obligation to pay a sum of money due in respect of a particular period by way of interest; an instalment of an annuity; feuduty or other periodical payment under a feu grant; ground annual or other periodical payment under a contract of ground annual; rent or other periodical payment under a lease; a periodical payment in respect of the occupancy or use of land; a periodical payment under a land obligation;

(b) to any obligation based on redress of unjustified enrichment, including without prejudice to that generality any obligation of restitution, repetition or recompense;

(c) to any obligation arising from *negotiorum gestio;*

(d) to any obligation arising from liability (whether arising from any enactment or from any rule of law) to make reparation;

(e) to any obligation under a bill of exchange or a promissory note;

(f) to any obligation of accounting, other than accounting for trust funds;

(g) to any obligation arising from, or by reason of any breach of, a contract or promise.

The prescription does not apply[34]:

---

26 *Hogg* v. *Brack* (1832) 11 S.198.

27 *Murray* v. *Parlane's Tr.* (1890) 18 R.287.

28 *King* v. *Johnston, supra*.

29 *Healy & Young's Tr.* v. *Mair's Trs., supra*.

30 *Motherwell* v. *Manwell, supra, per* Lord Adam at p.627.

31 Prescription and Limitation (Scotland) Act 1973, s.6. The qualification as to acknowledgment does not apply to bills of exchange or promissory notes.

32 s.13.

33 Sched. 1, para. 1.

34 Sched. 1, para. 2.

(i) to any obligation to recognise or obtemper a decree of court, an arbitration award or an order of a tribunal or authority exercising jurisdiction under any enactment;
(ii) to any obligation arising from the issue of a banknote;
(iii) to any obligation constituted or evidenced by a probative writ, not being a cautionary obligation nor being an obligation to make a periodical payment specified in (a), *supra*;
(iv) to any obligation under a contract of partnership or of agency, not being an obligation remaining, or becoming prestable on or after the termination of the relationship between the parties under the contract;
(v) to any obligation relating to land (including an obligation to recognise a servitude) except obligations to make periodical payments;
(vi) to any obligation to satisfy any claim to terce, courtesy, *legitim, jus relicti* or *jus relictae,* or to any prior right of a surviving spouse under s.8 or 9 of the Succession (Scotland) Act 1964;
(vii) to any obligation to make reparation in respect of personal injuries or in respect of the death of any person as a result of such injuries;
(viii) to any imprescriptible obligation.

Imprescriptible obligations are:[35]

(a) any real right of ownership in land;
(b) the right in land of the lessee under a recorded lease;
(c) any right exercisable as a *res merae facultatis;*
(d) any right to recover property *extra commercium;*
(e) any obligation of a trustee:
    (i) to produce accounts of the trustee's intromissions with any property of the trust;
    (ii) to make reparation or restitution in respect of any fraudulent breach of trust to which the trustee was a party or was privy;
    (iii) to make furthcoming to any person entitled thereto any trust property, or the proceeds of any such property, in the possession of the trustee, or to make good the value of any such property previously received by the trustee and appropriated to his own use;

[35] Sched. 3. A trustee includes anyone holding property in a fiduciary capacity for another: s.15(1).

(f) any obligation of a third party to make furthcoming to any person entitled thereto any trust property received by the third party otherwise than in good faith and in his possession;
(g) any right to recover stolen property from the person by whom it was stolen or from any person privy to the stealing thereof;
(h) any right to be served as heir to an ancestor or to take any steps necessary for making up or completing title to any interest in land.

5. Terminus a Quo

As a general rule, the prescription runs from the date when the obligation became enforceable[36] but there are special provisions for loans, deposits, obligations arising from partnership or agency, obligations to pay money or execute work by instalments and series of transactions for the supply of goods or services.

Where the obligation is to repay the whole, or any part, of a sum of money lent to, or deposited with, the debtor under a contract of loan or deposit, if the contract contains a stipulation which makes provision with respect to the date on or before which repayment of the sum or the part thereof is to be made, the appropriate date is the date on or before which, in terms of that stipulation, the sum or part thereof is to be repaid; if the contract contains no such stipulation, but a written demand for repayment of the sum, or the part thereof, is made by or on behalf of the creditor to the debtor the appropriate date is the date when such demand is made or first made.[37]

In the case of an obligation under a contract of partnership or of agency, being an obligation remaining, or becoming, prestable on or after the termination of the relationship between the parties under the contract, if the contract contains a stipulation which makes provision with respect to the date on or before which performance of obligation is to be due, the appropriate date is the date on or before which, in terms of that stipulation, the obligation is to be performed; in any other case the appropriate date is the date when the relationship terminated[38].

Where the obligation is to pay an instalment of a sum of money payable by instalments, or to execute any instalment of work due to

---

36 s.6(3).
37 Sched. 2, para. 2.
38 Sched. 2, para. 3.

be executed by instalments, the appropriate date is the date on which the last of the instalments is due to be paid or, as the case may be, to be executed.[39]

Where the obligation, not being part of a banking transaction, is to pay money in respect of:

(a) goods supplied on sale or hire (including credit sale, conditional sale and hire-purchase),

(b) services rendered (not including the keeping of the account)

in a series of transactions between the same parties (whether under a single contract or under several contracts) and charged on continuing account,[40] the appropriate date is the date on which payment for the goods last supplied, or, as the case may be, the services last rendered, became due.[41]

Where there is a series of transactions between a partnership and another party, the series is regarded as terminated (without prejudice to any other mode of termination) if the partnership or any partner therein becomes bankrupt; but, subject to that, if the partnership is dissolved and is replaced by a single new partnership having among its partners any person who was a partner in the old partnership, then, the new partnership is regarded as if it were identical with the old partnership.

The liability of a partner for a partnership debt is enforceable from the date of constitution of the debt against the firm.[42] A claim to legal rights becomes enforceable at the date of death or at the date estate first falls into intestacy.[43]

An obligation to make reparation for loss, injury or damage (whether arising from any enactment or rule of law or from, or by reason of any breach of, a contract or promise) becomes enforceable when the loss, injury or damage occurs.[44] The *terminus a quo* is the date when *injuria* concurs with *damnum* even although some items of loss arise after that date.[45] If the loss, injury or damage results from a continuing neglect, act or default, it is deemed to have occurred when the act, neglect or default ceased. If, at the time of

---

[39] Sched. 2, para. 4.

[40] See *Ross* v. *Cowie's Exrx.* (1888) 16 R.224; *Christison* v. *Knowles* (1901) 3 F.480.

[41] Sched. 2, para. 1.

[42] *Highland Engineering Ltd* v. *Anderson,* 1979 S.L.T.122.

[43] *Campbell's Trs.* v. *Campbell's Trs.,* 1950 S.C.48; *Mill's Trs.* v. *Mill's Trs.,* 1965 S.C.384.

[44] s.11.

[45] *Dunlop* v. *McGowans,* 1980 S.L.T.129. See also *George Porteous (Arts) Ltd.* v. *Dollar Rae Ltd., 1979 S.L.T.(Sh.Ct.)51.*

occurrence of the loss, injury or damage, the creditor was not aware, and could not with reasonable diligence have been aware, that loss, injury or damage had occurred, the *terminus a quo* is the date when the creditor first became, or could with reasonable diligence have become, so aware.

If the commencement of the period falls at a time other than the beginning of a day, the period is deemed to commence at the beginning of the next following day.[46]

6. The Period

Except where the Act provides otherwise regard is to be had to the prior law applicable to the computation of periods of prescription for the purpose of the Prescription Act 1617.[47] The running of the period is interrupted (but not terminated) by any period during which the original creditor, while he was the creditor, was under legal disability by reason of nonage or unsoundness of mind.[48] Other forms of disability do not interrupt.[49] It is also interrupted by any period in which the creditor is induced to refrain from making a claim in relation to the obligation because of the fraud of the debtor or his agent or error induced by words or conduct of the debtor or his agent but this does not include any time occurring after the creditor could with reasonable diligence have discovered the fraud or error.[48] If the last day of the period is a Saturday, Sunday or bank holiday, the period is extended to include the next day which is not one of these.[50] Time before the commencement of the relevant part of the Act (25 July 1976) is reckonable towards the period but such time cannot exceed the prescriptive period so at least one day must be after the commencement date.[51]

7. Relevant Claim

A relevant claim[52] is a claim for implement or part-implement of the obligation made:

---

46 s.14(1)*(c)*.
47 s.14(1)(*e*).
48 s.6(4).
49 s.14(1)(*b*).
50 s.14(1)(*d*).
51 s.14(1)(*a*); *Dunlop* v. *McGowans, supra*.
52 s.9(1). See as to the content of the summons or writ, *Bank of Scotland* v. *W. & G. Fergusson* (1898) 1 F.96; *British Railways Board* v. *Strathclyde Regional Council*, 1980 S.L.T.63.

(a) in a court of competent jurisdiction in Scotland or elsewhere except proceedings in the Court of Session initiated by a summons which is not subsequently called;
(b) in an arbitration in Scotland;
(c) in an arbitration elsewhere the award in which would be enforceable in Scotland;
(d) by presenting or concurring in a petition for sequestration or liquidation of the debtor or by lodging a claim in the sequestration or liquidation;
(e) by the execution of any form of diligence directed to the enforcement of the obligation.

Where the nature of the claim has been stated in the notice served by one party to an arbitration on the other requiring him to agree to an arbiter or to submit the dispute to a named or designated arbiter, the date of service of the notice is taken to be the date of making of the claim.[53]

8. Acknowledgment

The subsistence of the obligation is acknowledged if, and only if, either there has been such performance by or on behalf of the debtor towards implement of the obligation as clearly indicates that the obligation still subsists, or there has been made by or on behalf of the debtor to the creditor or his agent an unequivocal written admission clearly acknowledging that the obligation still subsists.[54] Payment of interest on a bond and disposition in security does not prevent prescription of a bond of corroboration.[55]

Where there are joint debtors so that each is liable for the whole debt, acknowledgment by part performance has effect as respects the liability of each debtor but acknowledgment by admission has effect only as respects the liability of the person who makes it.[56] Acknowledgment by one of several trustees has effect as respects the liability of the trust estate and any liability of each of the trustees.[57]

9. Vicennial Prescription

An obligation to which the prescription applies is extinguished if it has subsisted for a continuous period of 20 years without any

---

53 s.9(3).
54 s.10(1); See *Marr's Exrx.* v. *Marr's Trs.*, 1936 S.C.64.
55 *Yuill's Trs.* v. *Maclachlan's Trs.*, 1939 S.C.(H.L.)40.
56 s.10(2).
57 s.10(3).

relevant claim having been made in relation to it and without its subsistence having been relevantly acknowledged.[58] It is not possible to contract out of the prescription.[59] The prescription applies to obligations of any kind (including the obligations to which the quinquennial prescription applies), other than imprescriptible obligations.[60] The *terminus a quo* is the date when the obligation became enforceable except in the case of obligations to make reparation where the provisions for the five-year prescription for such obligations, with the exception of the rule as to the creditor's knowledge, apply, the obligations including, for this prescription, the obligation to make reparation in respect of death or personal injury.[61] There is no interruption of the period by disability, fraud or error. The rules as to the relevant claim, the relevant acknowledgment and the first and the last days of the period are as for the quinquennial prescription.

10. Transitional Provisions

Where by virtue of an enactment made before 25 July 1973 a claim to establish a right or enforce implement of an obligation may be made only within a specified period of limitation, and if by the operation of the quinquennial or vicennial prescription the right or obligation would be extinguished before the expiration of the period of limitation, the prescriptive period is extended so that it expires on the date when the limitation period expires or, if on that date any such claim made within the period has not finally been disposed of, on the date when the claim is so disposed of.[62]

---

58 s.7(1). The last requirement does not apply to bills of exchange or promissory notes.

59 s.13.

60 s.7(2).

61 s.11(4).

62 s.12(1).

CHAPTER 15

DILIGENCE: POINDING

DILIGENCE

1. General Features of Diligence

Diligence is the legal process by which a debtor's person, lands or effects are attached for recovery of the debt. The principal forms of diligence are arrestment and poinding in relation to moveable property and inhibition and adjudication in relation to heritable property. Some of the special forms of diligence appropriate to particular types of debt, such as poinding of the ground and actions of maills and duties, are not dealt with in this work. The foundation of much of the present law is the Debtors (Scotland) Act 1838 (sometimes known as the Personal Diligence Act 1838); in recent years, "Practice Notes" have been issued by the sheriff principal of each sheriffdom but the validity of these has to be examined in each case.[1]

In general, diligence on a Court of Session decree must be executed by a messenger-at-arms and diligence on an ordinary sheriff court decree by a messenger or sheriff officer but in the islands and in a county where there is no resident messenger a sheriff officer has the powers of a messenger; diligence on a summary cause decree must be by a sheriff officer.[2] For simplicity, reference is made hereafter only to sheriff officers. A creditor is not entitled to seize the debtor's goods at his own hand to satisfy the debt. If he does so he can be made to restore the goods or their value or, if the value is unknown, to pay the debts of other creditors.[3]

2. Prior Claims

There are three types of claim which have a priority as regards diligence:

(a) no moveable goods and effects belonging to a person at the time any tax became in arrears or was payable are liable to be

---

[1] See *City Bakeries Ltd.* v. *S. & S. Snack Bars & Restaurants Ltd.*, 1979 S.L.T. (Sh.Ct.)28.

[2] Execution of Diligence (Scotland) Act 1926, s.1; A.S. (Summary Cause Rules, Sheriff Court) 1976 (S.I.1976/476), r.6.

[3] *Crawford* v. *Black* (1829) 8 S.158; *Smart & Co.* v. *Stewart*, 1911 S.C.668.

taken by virtue of any poinding, sequestration for rent, or diligence whatever unless the person doing diligence pays the tax (or the tax for one whole year where tax for more than one year is claimed)[4]; If the creditor does not pay the tax, the taxpayer's goods may be poinded by summary warrant procedure notwithstanding the diligence;

(b) no moveable goods and effects belonging to any person at the time any rates came in arrears or were payable by him are liable to be taken by any poinding, sequestration[5] or diligence unless the person doing diligence pays the rates or at least the rates for one whole year. If he does not so make payment the rates can be recovered by a summary warrant procedure notwithstanding the diligence but the sum recovered from the person who has done diligence cannot exceed the amount recovered by him from the goods under deduction of the expenses of taking the goods and of their preservation and sale;[6]

(c) the landlord's hypothec[7] is preferred to the diligence of ordinary creditors. If poinding takes place before the term of payment of the rent, the landlord can interdict the procedure until security for the rent is given.[8] After the term of payment, a poinding creditor can proceed with diligence only if he leaves sufficient goods to pay the rent.

POINDING

3. Its Use

Poinding is the form of diligence appropriate to attach corporeal moveables belonging to the debtor which are in the custody or control of the debtor himself. It can also be used where corporeal moveables belonging to the debtor are in the possession of the creditor.[9] At one time it was used where the debtor's moveables were in the possession of a third party but in modern practice arrestment is used in this situation.[10]

---

[4] Taxes Management Act 1970, s.64.

[5] This means sequestration for rent: *Sinclair* v. *Edinburgh Parish Council*, 1909 S.C.1353.

[6] Local Government (Scotland) Act 1947, s.248; Valuation and Rating (Scotland) Act 1956, s.34.

[7] See Chap. 7, para. 12; Debtors (Scotland) Act 1838, s.31.

[8] Graham Stewart, pp.483-484.

[9] *Lochhead* v. *Graham* (1883) 11 R.201; Sale of Goods Act 1979, s.40.

[10] *Mackenzie & Co.* v. *Finlay* (1868) 7 M.27. But see *McLean* v. *Boyek* (1894) 10 Sh.Ct.Rep.10; *McNaught & Co.* v. *Lewis* (1935) 51 Sh.Ct.Rep.138.

The warrant for poinding and to open shut and lockfast places is contained in an extract of a Court of Session decree, a sheriff court decree or a decree proceeding upon a deed or protest registered in the Books of Council and Session or sheriff court books.[11] A person who has acquired right to an extract presents the extract, the evidence of his right thereto and a minute to the Petition Department of the Court of Session and a deliverance subscribed on the extract then provides a warrant.[12] If a person has acquired right to a decree before extract he must proceed by letters of horning and poinding.[13]

4. Subjects of Poinding

The subjects of poinding are corporeal moveables—"things corporeally valuable and capable of being sold by the Sheriff's warrant".[14] "The essence of poinding is that the goods poinded may be taken to the market-cross and sold".[15] So books, papers and evidents cannot be poinded.[16] Growing crops can be poinded if they are of sufficient maturity to be capable of valuation.[17] The following cannot, however, be poinded: the debtor's wearing apparel;[18] his working tools;[19] horses, oxen, agricultural implements and other goods pertaining to the plough during the ploughing season, if there are other moveables available;[20] ships and goods on board them[21] (the appropriate diligence is arrestment);[22] goods within the Palace of Holyroodhouse;[23] subjects which have become *ex contractu* not

---

[11] Debtors (Scotland) Act 1838, s. 9; Sheriff Courts (Scotland) Extracts Act 1892, s.7; See *Mitchell* v. *St. Mungo Lodge of Ancient Shepherds,* 1916 S.C.689.

[12] Debtors (Scotland) Act 1838, ss.7, 12; *Mitchell* v. *St. Mungo Lodge of Ancient Shepherds, supra.*

[13] Graham Stewart, p.26.

[14] Bell, *Prin.,* §2289.

[15] *per* Lord Neaves, *Trowsdale's Tr.* v. *Forcett Ry. Co.* (1870) 9 M.88 at 95.

[16] *Trowsdale's Tr.* v. *Forcett Ry. Co., supra.*

[17] Erskine, III, 6, 22; *Parker* v. *Douglas Heron & Co.* (1783) Mor.2868; *Elders* v. *Allen* (1833) 11 S.902.

[18] *Pringle* v. *Neilson* (1788) Mor.1393.

[19] Erskine, IV, 3, 27, n.; *Reid* v. *Donaldson* (1778) Mor.1392; for what is included see Graham Stewart p.346; *Macpherson* v. *Macpherson's Tr.* (1905) 8 F.191, and Chap. 19, para. 6.

[20] The Diligence Act 1503; Erskine, III, 6, 22.

[21] For a discussion of this anomaly see Dirleton's *Doubts,* 385; Bell, *Comm.,* II, 60; there are exceptions under the Merchant Shipping Act 1894, s.693, and the Prevention of Oil Pollution Act 1971, s.20(1).

[22] See Chap. 16, para. 16.

[23] *Earl of Strathmore* v. *Laing* (1823) 2 S.223, revd. 2 W. & S.1.

moveable.[24] There is some doubt as to whether banknotes can be poinded[25] but the Crown can poind banknotes, money, bonds, bills and implements of husbandry.[26]

The following cannot be poinded if they are at the time of poinding in a dwelling-house (including a caravan) in which the debtor is residing and are reasonably necessary to enable him and any person living in family with him in that dwelling-house to continue to reside there without undue hardship: beds or bedding material; chairs; tables; furniture or plenishings providing facilities for cooking, eating or storing food; furniture or plenishings providing facilities for heating.[27] The debtor may appeal to the sheriff within seven days of a poinding on the ground that an article is exempted.

The goods poinded must be the property of the debtor so the following cannot be poinded: goods in common or joint ownership;[28] the property of a partnership for a debt due by a partner;[29] goods liferented by the debtor;[30] goods held on trust by the debtor even if the trust is latent[31] (but goods held in security of a debt due to the debtor can be poinded *tantum et tale*); goods on sale or return;[32] goods on hire-purchase[33] (even if the creditor is a local authority for rates[34]); goods which have been poinded and bought back by, or given to, the debtor.[35]

5. Charge

Before a poinding can be instituted, a charge must be served on the debtor. This is a formal requisition to pay the debt. It is in the form of a schedule which is served by the sheriff officer on the debtor. There is a doubt about the appropriate form of charge on a summary cause decree.[36] Poinding can proceed after the expiry of the appropriate number of days of charge.

---

24 *Elders* v. *Allen* (1833) 11 S.902.

25 See *Alexander* v. *McLay* (1826) 4 S.439; *Encyclopaedia of the Laws of Scotland*, Vol. XI, p.356.

26 Exchequer Court (Scotland) Act 1856, s.32.

27 Law Reform (Diligence) (Scotland) Act 1973, s.1; the list of exceptions can be varied by statutory instrument.

28 *Fleming* v. *Twaddle* (1828) 7 S.92.

29 *Dawson* v. *Cullen* (1825) 4 S.39.

30 *Scott* v. *Price* (1837) 15 S.916.

31 Graham Stewart, pp.67-68.

32 *Macdonald* v. *Westren* (1888) 15 R.988 *per* Lord Young at p.990; *Bell, Rannie & Co.* v. *Smith* (1885) 22 S.L.R.597.

33 *George Hopkinson Ltd.* v. *N. G. Napier & Son,* 1953 S.C.139.

34 Local Government (Miscellaneous Provisions) (Scotland) Act 1981, s.12.

35 *Anderson* v. *Buchanan* (1848) 11 D.270.

36 See Gray, 1977 S.L.T. (News) 129.

The service of a charge on a summary cause decree may be by registered post or recorded delivery if the place of execution is in any of the islands of Scotland or is in a county where there is no sheriff officer or is more than 12 miles from the seat of the court granting the decree.[37]

If a summary cause decree is not enforced by poinding within a year from a charge thereon, the decree cannot be enforced without a new charge being given.[38]

6. Days of Charge

Decree	Debtor	Days
Court of Session decrees	(1) Within Scotland[39]	15
	(2) Furth of Scotland[40]	14
Sheriff court decrees	(1) Within Scotland[41]	7
	(2) Furth of Scotland[42]	14
Summary cause decrees[43]		14
Decrees in Exchequer causes in favour of the Crown	(1) Within Scotland[44]	6
	(2) Furth of Scotland[44]	6
Extracts of deeds containing consent to registration for execution	(1) Within Scotland[45]	6
	(2) Furth of Scotland[46]	14

37 Execution of Diligence (Scotland) Act 1926, s.2.
38 A.S. (Summary Cause Rules, Sheriff Court) 1976 (S.I. 1976/476), r.91(2).
39 C.A.S. 1913, VIII, Sched. A.
40 Court of Session Act 1868, s.14.
41 Sheriff Courts (Scotland) Extracts Act 1892, s.7, Sched. 1.
42 Sheriff Courts (Scotland) Extracts Act 1892, s.7(6); S.C.R.15.
43 A.S. (Summary Cause Rules, Sheriff Court) 1976 (S.I. 1976/476) r.91.
44 Exchequer Court (Scotland) Act 1856, s.28, Sched. G.
45 Titles to Land Consolidation (Scotland) Act 1868, s.138.
46 Court of Session Act 1868, s.14.

Decree	Debtor	Days
Extracts of deeds recorded in Register of Sasines with consent and warrant of registration	(1) Within Scotland[47]	6
	(2) Furth of Scotland[48]	14
Registered protests of bills of exchange	(1) Within Scotland[49]	6
	(2) Furth of Scotland[50]	14
Extract certificates registered under the Judgments Extension Act 1868	Within Scotland[51]	15
Extract certificates registered under Inferior Court Judgments Extension Act 1882	Within the sheriffdom[52]	15
Foreign judgments or awards under Administration of Justice Act 1920, Foreign Judgments (Reciprocal Enforcement) Act 1933 or Arbitration (International Investment Disputes) Act 1966	Within Scotland[53]	15 (or period fixed by court)
Land court decrees	Within Scotland[54]	7

47 Titles to Land Consolidation (Scotland) Act 1868, s.138; Land Registers (Scotland) Act 1868, s.12.
48 Court of Session Act 1868, s.14.
49 Bills of Exchange Act 1681; Inland Bills Act 1696.
50 Court of Session Act 1868, s.14.
51 C.A.S. 1913, B. VI. 5.
52 C.A.S. 1913, L. IX. 2.
53 R.C.248(*f*), 249(11), 249A(7) (3).
54 Crofting Reform (Scotland) Act 1976, s.17(1).

Decree	Debtor	Days
Order for recovery of criminal fine	Within or furth[55] of Scotland	10

7. Procedure[56]

In a summary cause, the poinding must be executed within a year from the charge;[57] there is no special limit in the case of other decrees.

The sheriff officer with two (in summary causes one[58]) valuators, who also act as witnesses[59] goes to the place where the goods are and, in daylight,[60] carries out the following procedure:

(i) he demands payment of the debt;[61]
(ii) he inquires as to the ownership of the goods, and, in particular, if they are subject to hire-purchase or otherwise property of a third party;[62]
(iii) an inventory of the goods showing the value of each article as determined by the valuators is prepared in a schedule;
(iv) the goods are offered back to the debtor or someone appearing for him at the appraised values;[63]
(v) the sheriff officer adjudges the goods to the creditor;
(vi) a copy of the schedule specifying the goods poinded, the values thereof and the creditor's name is delivered to the debtor together with a notice of his rights of appeal to the sheriff if the poinding is in a dwelling.[64]

The goods are left in the possession of the debtor.

The effect of poinding is to lay a nexus on the goods and create a security over them in favour of the creditor.[65]

Within eight days of the poinding, the sheriff officer must report the execution to the sheriff, specifying the diligence under which the

---

55 Criminal Procedure (Scotland) Act 1975, s.411.

56 See, as to this procedure generally, *Le Conte* v. *Douglas and Richardson* (1880) 8 R.175; *Scottish Gas Board* v. *Johnstone,* 1974 S.L.T.(Sh.Ct.)65; McCreadie (1975-76) SCOLAG Bul. 135.

57 A.S. (Summary Cause Rules, Sheriff Court) 1976 (S.I. 1976/476), r.91(2).

58 *Ibid.*, r.90.

59 See *Norman* v. *Dymock,* 1932 S.C.131 at 134.

60 Graham Stewart, p.338.

61 *McTaggart* v. *Dalry Co-operative Society,* 1980 S.L.T.(Sh.Ct.)142.

62 Practice Notes.

63 Graham Stewart, p.348; *J. Ratcliff & Co. Ltd.* v. *McKelvie,* 1977 S.L.T. (Sh.Ct.)64; *S.S.E.B.* v. *Brogan,* 1981 S.L.T.(Sh.Ct.)8.

64 Debtors (Scotland) Act 1838, s.24; A.S. (Appeals against Poinding) 1973 (S.I. 1973/1860).

65 *Stephenson* v. *Dobbins* (1852) 14 D.510.

poinding was executed, the amount of the debt, the names and designations of the debtor, creditor and valuators, the goods poinded, the value thereof, the person in whose hands they were left and the delivery of the schedule.[66] The sheriff may give orders for the security of the goods and for the immediate disposal of those of a perishable nature.

Following a poinding there must be no undue delay in applying for and executing the warrant of sale.[67] In recent times, Practice Notes have regulated the period within which application for a warrant of sale must be made in some sheriffdoms; a warrant of sale will be granted without special inquiry (into delay) only if the application is made within six months after the poinding,[68] but Practice Notes providing that poindings subsist for only six months have been held *ultra vires*.[69] To prevent evasion of the foregoing requirements against delay, there are restrictions against repeated poindings and repeated warrants of sale. Thus, a second poinding cannot be executed on the same premises under the same decree on the instructions of the same creditor unless the debtor has, since the first poinding, brought further poindable goods into the premises.[70] Further, where the arrangements for a warrant sale are cancelled, a second warrant of sale will not normally be granted.[71] It has been held that the sheriff has a discretion to refuse warrant of sale on equitable grounds.[72] The sale must take place more than eight days (excluding the day of publication and the day of sale[73]), and not more than 20 days, after public notice of the sale by public roup has been given.[74] A copy of the warrant must be served on the debtor and on the possessor of the goods (if a different person) at least six days before the sale except where the goods are perishable. At the sale, the goods are offered at upset prices not less than the appraised values. The poinder or any other creditor may offer.[75] If a sale is

---

66 1838 Act, s.25.

67 *Henderson* v. *Grant* (1896) 23 R.659; *New Day Furnishing Stores Ltd.* v. *Curran,* 1974 S.L.T.(Sh.Ct.)20; *City Bakeries Ltd.* v. *S. and S. Snack Bars and Restaurants Ltd.,* 1979 S.L.T.(Sh.Ct.)28.

68 See G. Maher (1980) 25 J.L.S.385 at 387-8; and 1980 S.L.T.(News)265.

69 *Post Office* v. *Gorhan* (22 March 1977, unreported) noted in 1979 S.L.T. (Sh.Ct.) at p.31; *United Dominions Trust Ltd.* v. *Stark* (Sheriffdom of Lothian and Borders at Edinburgh, 17 October 1980, unreported).

70 Practice Notes; *New Day Furnishing Stores Ltd.* v. *Curran, supra.*

71 *City Bakeries Ltd.* v. *S. and S. Snack Bars and Restaurants Ltd., supra.*

72 *South of Scotland Electricity Board* v. *Carlyle,* 1980 S.L.T.(Sh.Ct.)98.

73 *McNeill* v. *McMurchy* (1841) 3 D.554.

74 1838 Act, s.26.

75 1838 Act, s.29.

effected, a report thereof is made to the sheriff within eight days and an order is given for payment of the proceeds, after deduction of lawful charges, to the poinding creditor, provided that the amount does not exceed the amount of his debt, interest and expenses, including the expenses of poinding.[76] If a sale is not effected, the goods are delivered to the poinding creditor to the extent necessary to satisfy, according to the appraised values, his debt, interest and expenses; the goods then become the creditor's property. The appraised values must be deducted from the debt even where the creditor has not uplifted the goods from the debtor's premises.[77]

If the debtor during the proceedings tenders either the amount of the debt with interest and expenses or the appraised value of the goods, the officer cannot proceed with the poinding. Though the creditor may poind and sell sufficient goods to pay for the expenses of diligence as well as the sum due under the decree (principal sum, interest and judicial expenses), he cannot execute a poinding and sale to recover the expenses of diligence if his debtor tenders the outstanding balance of the sum due under the decree.[78] The officer has no implied authority to receive payment for the creditor and if he has no express mandate the correct course is for the debtor to consign the money in a bank in the creditor's name and deliver the deposit receipt to the officer.[79] The creditor is entitled to retain the extract decree until payment of the expenses of diligence.[80]

Any person who, after the execution of the poinding, unlawfully intromits with or carries off the poinded effects is liable to be imprisoned until he restores the effects or pays double the appraised value.[81] The statutory form of complaint must be made to obtain this remedy.[82] There is the alternative remedy of damages at common law.[83] A bona fide purchaser of the goods is not an unlawful intromitter but if he is made aware of the poinding prior to payment of the price he must hold the price subject to the claim of the poinding creditor.[84]

---

[76] s.28; *McNeill* v. *McMurchy, supra.*

[77] *Scottish Gas Board* v. *Johnstone,* 1974 S.L.T.(Sh.Ct.)65 and Practice Notes.

[78] *Inglis* v. *McIntyre* (1862) 24 D.541; *Harvie* v. *Luxram Electric Ltd.* (1952) 68 Sh.Ct.Rep.181; *cf. Holt* v. *National Bank of Scotland,* 1927 S.L.T.484.

[79] Graham Stewart, pp.350-1. See, as to payment by cheque, *Caithness Flagstone Co.* v. *Threipland* (1907) 15 S.L.T.357.

[80] *Inglis* v. *McIntyre, supra.*

[81] 1838 Act, s.30.

[82] *Angus Brothers Ltd.* v. *Crocket* (1909) 25 Sh.Ct.Rep.322.

[83] Graham Stewart, p.358.

[84] Graham Stewart, p.358.

A person may claim that the goods being poinded belong to him and are not the property of the debtor. The debtor's wife may do this. If the claim is made during the execution of the poinding, the officer should examine the claimant on oath and consider any written title which is produced. The position is not clear but it seems that the officer can either stop the poinding or proceed with it and leave the matter of title to be determined by the sheriff.[85] If the claim is made after the execution of the poinding but before a warrant for sale has been granted, the claimant should lodge a minute in the poinding process and the sheriff will determine the question.[86] If the claim is made after the warrant of sale has been granted, the claimant should interdict the sale.[87] Where, after a sale at which there were no bidders, the goods have been delivered to the poinding creditor at the appraised value, the claimant's remedy is an action of delivery against the creditor.[88] Where the goods have been sold at the judicial sale to a bona fide purchaser, they can probably be recovered.[89]

If, during the execution of the poinding (*i.e.* before delivery of the schedule[90]) another creditor exhibits and delivers to the officer a warrant to poind (*e.g.* an extract decree on which a charge has been given and has expired), the creditor must be conjoined and the proceeds of sale are divided *pro rata* among the poinding and conjoined creditors.[91]

8. Competitions[92]

Where two poindings have not been conjoined, preference depends upon priority of execution. In the case of a sale of goods, if the property has passed before the execution, the purchaser is obviously preferred; if the sale and delivery of the goods take place after execution of the poinding, the purchaser is preferred but on notice that he must retain the price for the benefit of the poinder; if

---

85 Graham Stewart, p.352.

86 *Lamb* v. *Wood* (1904) 6 F.1091; interdict is competent: *Konchater* v. *Jarvie* (1949) 65 Sh.Ct.Rep.98.

87 *Jack* v. *Waddell's Trs.*, 1918 S.C.73; at this stage compearance by minute is incompetent: *Philp* v. *Stuart*, 1959 S.L.T.(Sh.Ct.)21.

88 *George Hopkinson Ltd.* v. *Napier & Son*, 1953 S.C.139.

89 *Carlton* v. *Miller*, 1978 S.L.T.(Sh.Ct.)36.

90 Graham Stewart, p.356.

91 1838 Act, s.23.

92 As to the landlord's hypothec see *supra*, para. 2.

the price is paid but the goods have not been delivered it seems that the poinder is preferred.[93]

Poinding is, of course, preferred to a pledge, if the execution was prior to completion of the security by delivery.

A personal poinding is defeated by a poinding of the ground if the heritable creditor serves his action before the sale in the personal poinding is complete, unless the infeftment of the poinder of the ground was after the execution of the personal poinding in which event preference depends upon priority of execution.[94]

It is, apparently, competent for the *poinder's* creditor to arrest in the hands of the owner of the poinded goods.[95] Crown diligence prevails over a poinding if it is executed before the poinder has effected a sale.[96]

In a competition with an arrestment the poinding is preferred if the sale is completed before the date of the decree in the furthcoming.[97]

9. Effect of Sequestration

A poinding executed on or after the sixtieth day prior to sequestration is ineffectual and the goods poinded or the proceeds thereof must be handed over to the trustee.[98] The poinder thus deprived of his diligence has a preference out of the goods or proceeds for the expense bona fide incurred by him in procuring the warrant for and executing such diligence.[99] This clearly applies where the execution of the poinding has taken place within the 60-day period and no sale has taken place. Where the poinding was executed before the 60 days but no sale has taken place at the date of sequestration, it seems that the diligence is struck down, even where there has been no unreasonable delay in carrying out the sale.[1]

---

93 Graham Stewart, pp.365-366.

94 *Tullis* v. *Whyte,* 18 June 1817, F.C.; Graham Stewart, p.366.

95 *Ferguson* v. *Bothwell* (1882) 9 R.687.

96 Goudy, p.538.

97 Graham Stewart, p.159.

98 Bankruptcy (Scotland) Act 1913 (hereinafter cited as "B.A."), s.104.

99 This does not cover the expenses of the litigation but it does include the expenses of ordering and obtaining extract and of executing the diligence; there is doubt as to the expenses of obtaining a decree in absence: *Warren & Stuart* v. *Galbraith* (1927) 43 Sh.Ct.Rep.58; *N. V. Elementenfabriek* v. *Gellatly* (1932) 48 Sh.Ct.Rep.103. See Chap. 16, para. 12, n.82.

1 *Wm. S. Yuile Ltd.* v. *Gibson,* 1952 S.L.T.(Sh.Ct.)22; *cf.* Graham Stewart, p.364; *Bendy Brothers Ltd.* v. *McAlister* (1910) 26 Sh.Ct.Rep.152.

The reason for this is that the diligence is not completed and there is no transfer of the property in the goods to the creditor until the sale. It should follow from this that the diligence is ineffectual where the poinding is outwith and the sale within the 60 days[2] and where both poinding and sale are within the 60 days. However, the views expressed in *Johnston* v. *Cluny Trs.*, 1957 S.C.184, that s.104 affects only diligence which is operative at the date of sequestration or liquidation, would lead to the contrary conclusion.

If poinded property is sold, not under the poinding but by agreement between the creditor and debtor, the transaction may be reducible as a fraudulent preference.[3]

10. Equalisation of Diligence

Section 10 of the Bankruptcy (Scotland) Act 1913, provides that arrestments and poindings used within 60 days prior to notour bankruptcy or within four months thereafter rank *pari passu* as if they had all been used at the same date and any creditor judicially producing in a process relative to the subject of such an arrestment or poinding liquid grounds of debt or a decree for payment within that period is entitled to rank as if he had executed such an arrestment or poinding. If a poinding creditor has carried through a sale he is accountable for the sum recovered to those eventually found to be entitled to a *pari passu* ranking thereon and is liable to pay them proportionately after deducting his expenses.[4]

Sequestration is equivalent to an executed or completed poinding.[5] Accordingly if sequestration occurs within four months of notour bankruptcy any poinding within the prescribed period is cut down.[6] The first notour bankruptcy is not the only one relevant here and a creditor producing liquid grounds of debt more than four months after the first notour bankruptcy but within four months of a second notour bankruptcy constituted by a poinding is entitled to rank *pari passu*.[7]

It should be added that equalisation of diligence by virtue of s.10 can operate where there is no sequestration. Indeed, for ordinary

---

2 But see Wardhaugh, *Scottish Bankruptcy Manual*, 5th ed., p.87.

3 *Stewart* v. *Gardner* (1932) 48 Sh.Ct.Rep.226.

4 *Stewart* v. *Stewart's Trs.* (1916) 32 Sh.Ct.Rep.43.

5 B.A., s.104.

6 *Galbraith* v. *Campbell's Trs.* (1885) 22 S.L.R.602.

7 B.A., s.7, reversing *Wood* v. *Cranston & Elliott* (1891) 18 R.382; *Campbell* v. *McKellar*, 1926 S.L.T.(Sh.Ct.)82.

creditors there is a certain advantage in proceeding under s.10 rather than by sequestration as arrestments can be equalised without satisfying the claims of preferential creditors. A claim under s.10 can be made in the process of a poinding or sale, in a furthcoming or in a direct action.

11. Liquidation

A winding-up is at the date of its commencement equivalent to an executed or completed poinding and no poinding of the company's effects executed on or after the sixtieth day prior to that date is effectual and the effects (or their proceeds if sold) have to be made forthcoming to the liquidator. A poinder thus deprived of benefit of his diligence has a preference out of the effects poinded for the bona fide expenses of the poinding incurred by him.[8]

It has been held that the provision of the Bankruptcy Act relating to equalisation of diligence[9] applies to a company registered under the Companies Acts.[10]

12. Appointment of Receiver

If a receiver is appointed by virtue of a floating charge his powers over property are subject to the rights of any person who has effectually executed diligence thereon.[11] A poinding which has not been followed by a warrant of sale is not effectual diligence.[12] For the position of an English receiver, see Chap. 16, para. 14.

13. English Bankruptcy

It seems that a receiving order in England has no effect on prior diligence executed on assets in Scotland.[13]

14. Suspension of Poindings

Diligence may be stayed by an action of suspension which is competent, unless excluded by statute, where a decree or document exists on which a charge may follow.[14] If a charge has not yet been

---

[8] Companies Act 1948, s.327.

[9] See preceding paragraph.

[10] *Clark* v. *Hinde, Milne & Co.* (1884) 12 R.347.

[11] Companies (Floating Charges and Receivers) Act 1972, s.15(2)(*a*).

[12] *Lord Advocate* v. *Royal Bank of Scotland*, 1977 S.C.155.

[13] *Hunter* v. *Palmer* (1825) 3 S.586; Graham Stewart, p.187; *cf.* Anton, *Private International Law*, p.442.

[14] Mackay, *Manual of Practice in the Court of Session*, p.421.

given, or if a charge has been given and the days of charge have not expired, or if the expired charge has not been followed out by poinding, the appropriate procedure is by a simple suspension.[15] If a poinding has followed on an expired charge but an order for sale has not been obtained, the procedure is a suspension and interdict. If an order for sale has been obtained the correct remedy is a suspension and suspension and interdict.[16] A simple suspension is the appropriate process to stay diligence for recovery of imperial taxes[17] but a suspension and interdict is required in the case of diligence proceeding on a warrant for collection of rates.[18]

Where the objection is to the diligence itself or is founded on a defect in the extract decree the sheriff court of the domicile of the person charged has jurisdiction in suspensions of charges or threatened charges on decrees granted by the sheriff.[19] The same sheriff court also has jurisdiction where the objection is to a decree of registration proceeding upon bonds, bills or other documents registered in any sheriff court books or the Books of Council and Session where, for example, it is alleged that the decree proceeded upon a promissory note the signature to which had been obtained by fraud.[20] The sheriff court cannot suspend its own decrees *in foro* apart from these cases.[21] The Court of Session can review the merits of decrees of lower courts but it cannot suspend its own decrees *in foro* unless the extract is defective or the decree is one of registration.[22] An objection to a decree *in foro* must be pursued in an action of reduction.[23]

The grounds for suspension of diligence are, broadly, defects in the extract decree or the diligence procedure,[24] a charge for an

---

15 *Paul* v. *Henderson* (1867) 5 M.1120.

16 *Hobbin* v. *Burns* (1904) 11 S.L.T.681.

17 *Encyclopaedia of the Laws of Scotland,* Vol. XIV, p.332.

18 *Encyclopaedia of the Laws of Scotland,* Vol. VIII, p.342.

19 Sheriff Courts (Scotland) Act 1907, s.5(5), S.C.R.123. For the summary cause procedure see A.S.(Summary Cause Rules, Sheriff Court) 1976 (S.I. 1976/476), r.92.

20 1907 Act, s.5(5) (amended by Law Reform (Miscellaneous Provisions) (Scotland) Act 1980, s.15); *Maclachlan* v. *Glasgow,* 1925 S.L.T.(Sh.Ct.)77.

21 *Lamont* v. *Hall,* 1964 S.L.T.(Sh.Ct.)25.

22 *Lamb* v. *Thompson* (1901) 4 F.88.

23 *McCarroll* v. *McKinstery,* 1923 S.C.94; *Greenwood* v. *Mundle* 1957 S.L.T.(Notes)15.

24 *Encyclopaedia of the Laws of Scotland,* Vol. VIII, p.343.

excessive amount,[25] and partial or total extinction of the debt subsequent to decree.[26]

In the Court of Session the first interlocutor orders intimation and answers and includes an interim sist of execution which may or may not require caution or consignation.[27] This prevents poinding and imprisonment but not arrestment, inhibition or adjudication. In the sheriff court, on sufficient caution being found for the sum charged for interest and expenses and for the expenses of the suspension, the sheriff may sist diligence, order intimation and answers, and proceed to dispose of the cause in a summary manner.[28] This, when intimated, prevents poinding and imprisonment but not arrestment or inhibition.[29]

---

25 *Haughhead Coal Co.* v. *Gallocher* (1903) 11 S.L.T.156—the charge is suspended *quoad* the excess.

26 *Fowler* v. *Brown,* 1916 S.C.597; *Brown* v. *Brown,* 1971 S.L.T.44 (adherence and aliment); See also *McCarroll* v. *McKinstery,* 1923 S.C.94.

27 Maclaren, *Bill Chamber Practice,* pp.63-64.

28 S.C.R.124.

29 Graham Stewart, p.755.

CHAPTER 16

ARRESTMENT

1. Its use

Arrestment is the diligence appropriate to attach obligations to account to the debtor by a third party and corporeal moveables belonging to the debtor which are in the hands of a third party. In relation to the arrestment, the arresting creditor is known as "the arrester", the third party as "the arrestee" and the debtor as "the common debtor".[1] Arrestment to enforce payment of a decree is known as arrestment in execution; arrestment to found jurisdiction and arrestment on the dependence are treated elsewhere.[2]

2. The Arrestee

The arrestee must be subject to the jurisdiction of the Scottish courts.[3] The arrestment must be made in the hands of a third party who is indebted to, or is under an obligation to account to, or holds goods which are the property of, the common debtor. It cannot be made in the hands of the arrester himself.[4] It cannot be made in the hands of a debtor of the common debtor's debtor.[5] It cannot be made in the hands of the common debtor himself or of "persons who are in law identified with him"[6] such as his wife,[7] his servants,[8] his factor,[9] or steward.[10] It can be made in the hands of someone who is under an obligation to account to the common debtor such as a trustee,[11] a commissioner,[12] a factor *loco absentis,*[13] an agent,[14] his

---

1 See as to the ambiguity of this nomenclature, Bell, *Comm.*, II, 63, n.6.

2 Chap. 11, para. 8; Chap. 11, para. 10.

3 *Brash* v. *Brash,* 1966 S.C.56; as to the locality of the debt, see Chap. 11, para. 9.

4 *Anderson* v. *Scottish N. E. Ry. Co.* (1867) 3 S.L.R.270. But see *E. & A. Denholm Young & Co.* v. *MacElwee* (1918) 34 Sh.Ct.Rep.193; Sale of Goods Act 1979, s.40.

5 Bell, *Prin.*, §2276; *J. & C. Murray* v. *Wallace Marrs & Co.*, 1914 S.C.114; (a bank instructed by the common debtor's bank).

6 Bell, *Comm.*, II, 70.

7 More's *Notes to Stair,* p.287.

8 *Cuningham* v. *Home* (1760) Mor.747.

9 *Dunlop* v. *Weir* (1823) 2 S.167.

10 Bell, *Comm.*, II, 70.

11 *Johnston* v. *Dundas's Trs.* (1837) 15 S.904.

12 *Brown* v. *Duff's Tr.* (1850) 13 D.149.

13 *Mitchell* v. *Scott* (1881) 8 R.875.

14 *Home* v. *Pringle* (1706) Mor.734.

law agent who holds the proceeds of a bond due to him,[15] the purchaser of heritage from him,[16] and an auctioneer.[17] A creditor of the exposer cannot arrest in the hands of a purchaser at an auction if the purchaser's obligation is to the auctioneer alone.[18]

A question arises where the arrestee has given the common debtor a cheque or bill for the amount due prior to the date of arrestment and it has not been presented for payment prior to that date. If the cheque is not post-dated there is nothing to arrest.[19] If a post-dated cheque or a bill payable at a currency is given there is still a debt which can be attached prior to the date for payment of the instrument, at least where there has been no transfer to a bona fide indorsee for value.[20] In that situation the arrestee cannot require delivery of the bill as a condition of payment to the arrester.[21]

The fact that the common debtor has refused to accept the sum owed to him by the arrestee and has unsuccessfully sued for a larger sum is of no significance.[22]

3. Subjects Arrestable—Debts

Apart from corporeal moveables, it is not only debts which are arrestable: "It is the obligation to account which is the proper subject of attachment."[23] The following debts and obligations are arrestable:

(a) *Wages.* At common law wages are arrestable only as to what is over and above a necessary aliment.[24] Further, by statute,[25] the wages of labourers, farm servants, manufacturers, artificers and workpeople are arrestable only to the extent of one half of the surplus over four pounds per week.[26] The exemption does not apply

---

15 *Telford's Exr.* v. *Blackwood* (1866) 4 M.369; for a case where the agent acted both for the vendor and the building society in a sale of heritage, see *Turner* v. *Woolwich Equitable Building Society* (1956) 72 Sh.Ct.Rep.300.

16 *Benjedward's Crs.* (1753) Mor.743.

17 *Adam* v. *Anderson* (1837) 15 S.1225; *Mackenzie & Co.* v. *Finlay* (1868) 7 M.27.

18 *Sharp* v. *Macdonald & Fraser* (1884) 1 Sh.Ct.Rep.37.

19 *Leggat Bros.* v. *Gray*, 1908 S.C.67.

20 *Elmslie* v. *Hunter* (1936) 52 Sh.Ct.Rep.181.

21 *Evans* v. *Pinchere* (1907) 23 Sh.Ct.Rep.111.

22 *Lennie* v. *Mackie & Co.* (1907) 23 Sh.Ct.Rep.85.

23 Bell, *Comm.*, II, 71.

24 Bell, *Prin.* § 2276; *Shanks* v. *Thomson* (1838) 16 S.1353; *Thomson* v. *Cohen* (1915) 32 Sh.Ct.Rep.15.

25 The Wages Arrestment Limitation (Scotland) Act 1870, as amended by the Small Debt (Scotland) Act 1924, and the Wages Arrestment Limitation (Amendment) (Scotland) Act 1960. As to wages paid into a bank, see *infra*, n.87.

26 It would seem that the computation should be on the gross wage.

to debts in respect of alimentary allowances and payments[27] nor to rates and taxes but arrestments to recover such debts must set forth the nature of the debt. The statute applies to a gamekeeper[28] and a greenkeeper[29] but not to a railway clerk.[30] The relevant amount of wages is the weekly total and not the proportion thereof earned at the date of arrestment.[31] Where wages and commission are earned they are treated separately.[32] Wages paid in kind are taken into account.[33] The earnings of Crown servants other than members of the armed forces are now arrestable in the hands of the chief officer in Scotland of the relevant department.[34]

(b) *Salaries* are arrestable subject to the exclusion of a sum for suitable aliment. This has been held in relation to a professor;[35] a rector of an academy;[36] a minister;[37] a Court of Session extractor;[38] a municipal clerk;[39] a police constable;[40] a surveyor[41] and an engineer.[42] It is thought that pensions, other than state pensions,[43] are treated as salaries.

(c) *Contract Payments*. Payments under a contract of *locatio operis* are arrestable even although the payment is not yet due and even although the obligation to pay is conditional upon completion of the work to the employer's satisfaction.[44] If payment is to be by instalments, only the next instalment is caught by the arrestment.[45]

(d) *Rents* are arrestable (but see para. 7 *infra*).

(e) *Insurance Policies*. The proceeds of a life insurance policy can be arrested during the life of the insured.[46] In the furthcoming the

---

27 See *infra*, exception (a).

28 *Marjoribanks* v. *Watson* (1903) 19 Sh.Ct.Rep.279.

29 *Auchterlonie* v. *McKelvie* (1908) 24 Sh.Ct.Rep.130.

30 *Thomson* v. *Cohen, supra.*

31 *Shiel & Co.* v. *Skinner & Co.* (1934) 50 Sh.Ct.Rep.101.

32 *McAulay* v. *Smith* (1913) 30 Sh.Ct.Rep.162.

33 *Skinner & Co.* v. *Anderson* (1915) 31 Sh.Ct.Rep.256.

34 Crown Proceedings Act 1947, s.46; Law Reform (Miscellaneous Provisions) (Scotland) Act 1966, s.2.

35 *Laidlaw* v. *Wylde* (1801) Mor. App. "Arrestment" No. 4.

36 *Murray* v. *Bell* (1833) 11 S.599.

37 *Learmonth* v. *Paterson* (1858) 20 D.418.

38 *Miller* v. *Wilson* (1827) 5 S.926.

39 *McIntyre* v. *Mackenzie* (1833) 11 S.658.

40 *Young* v. *Turnbull*, 1928 S.N.46.

41 *Webster* v. *Douglas* (1933) 49 Sh.Ct.Rep.294.

42 *Cochran's Tr.* v. *Cochran* (1958) 74 Sh.Ct.Rep.75.

43 *See infra*, except in (d).

44 *Marshall* v. *Nimmo & Co.* (1847) 10 D.328; *Park Dobson & Co. Ltd.* v. *Wm. Taylor & Son*, 1929 S.C.571; *MacLaren & Co.* v. *Preston* (1893) 1 S.L.T.75.

45 *Park Dobson & Co. Ltd.* v. *Wm. Taylor & Son, supra.*

46 *Strachan* v. *McDougle* (1835) 13 S.954.

policy may be sold or surrendered.[47] It is thought that the arrestment is not affected by payment of subsequent premiums.[48] In the case of indemnity insurance, the insurer is under no liability to the insured until judgment is given against the insured and nothing can be arrested in the hands of the insurer till then.[49]

(f) *Cash on Deposit Receipt.* Where a deposit receipt acknowledges that money received from A and B is "payable to either or the survivor", and the fund is arrested by a creditor of B, the bank is entitled to refuse to make payment to A.[50] A deposit receipt in the name of the common debtor "in trust" is arrestable.[51]

(g) *Bonds.* Personal bonds and heritable bonds upon which infeftment has not followed can be arrested as to principal and interest.[52] Heritable bonds on which infeftment has followed can be arrested only as to interest due and current, the appropriate diligence to attach the principal being adjudication.[53]

(h) *Partnership Interest.* A share in a partnership is arrestable.[54] A debt due to an English partnership is not due to one of the partners.[55]

(i) *Shares* in a limited company registered in Scotland are arrestable.[56] A subsidiary company can arrest shares of its holding company in the hands of the latter although a subsidiary company cannot acquire the shares of its holding company.[57] In the case of other corporate bodies the position may be regulated by special statutory provisions.[58]

(j) *Calls* on shares may be arrested in the hands of the shareholders.[59] The amount unpaid on shares cannot be arrested before a call is made, however.[60]

---

47 *Clark* v. *Scottish Amicable Insurance Co.* (1922) 38 Sh.Ct.Rep.170.

48 *Bankhardt's Trs.* v. *Scottish Amicable Life Assurance Society* (1871) 9 M.443.

49 *Kerr* v. *R. & W. Ferguson,* 1931 S.C.736; *Boland* v. *White Cross Insurance Association,* 1926 S.C.1066.

50 *Allan's Exr.* v. *Union Bank of Scotland Ltd.,* 1909 S.C.206.

51 *Union Bank* v. *Mills* (1926) 42 Sh.Ct.Rep.141.

52 The Arrestments Act 1661.

53 *Stuart* v. *Stuart* (1705) Mor.140.

54 Bell, *Comm.,* II, 536; *Cassells* v. *Stewart* (1879) 6 R.936, *per* Lord Gifford at p. 956.

55 *Parnell* v. *Walter* (1889) 16 R.917.

56 *Sinclair* v. *Staples* (1860) 22 D. 600; *American Mortgage Co. of Scotland Ltd.,* v. *Sidway,* 1908 S.C.500.

57 *Stenhouse London Ltd.* v. *Allwright,* 1972 S.C.209.

58 *Royal Bank* v. *Fairholm* (1770) Mor. App. "Adjudication" No. 3. .

59 *Hill* v. *College of Glasgow* (1849) 12 D.46.

60 Graham Stewart, p. 46; *Lindsay* v. *La Martona Rubber Estates Ltd.,* 1911 2 S.L.T.468.

(k) *Liability to Account.* In general a liability to account is arrestable. Where a bank held shares in security of a customer's overdraft, it was held that an arrestment in the hands of the bank attached any balance due to the customer after realisation of the shares and extinction of the overdraft.[61]

(l) *Expenses.* An award of expenses is arrestable even if it has not been quantified.[62]

(m) *Legitim.* A right to legitim is arrestable from the date of the ancestor's death even if the descendant has to elect between legitim and a non-vested conventional provision.[63]

(n) *Trust Interest.* A vested right in a trust estate is arrestable if the beneficiary's interest is moveable in character.[64] This depends on the terms of the trust deed and not on the nature of the estate. The interest is moveable "so long as it is not a claim several or *pro indiviso* to heritage, but merely a right to payment out of the general estate".[65] It seems that an interest which has vested subject to defeasance is arrestable.[66]

The following debts are not arrestable:

(a) Alimentary payments are not arrestable[67] except (i) as to arrears,[68] (ii) *quoad excessum,*[69] (iii) for alimentary debts.[70] A bank retirement pension is an alimentary payment.[71] Alimentary debts are "all articles of annual expenditure required for the comfort, or suitable to the situation of the party; and in regard to articles in which ready-money dealing is unusual and inconvenient, and in which an absolute disability to contract debt would operate to his advantage, that disability has been departed from."[72] What is alimentary depends on the party's station in life.[73] The price of

---

61 *Commercial Bank of Scotland Ltd.* v. *Eagle Star Insurance Co. Ltd.*, 1950 S.L.T. (Notes) 30.

62 *Agnew* v. *Norwest Construction Co.*, 1935 S.C.771.

63 *Waddell* v. *Waddell's Trs.*, 1932 S.L.T.201.

64 *Smith's Trs.* v. *Grant* (1862) 24 D.1142.

65 Graham Stewart, p. 62.

66 *Chambers' Trs.* v. *Smith* (1878) 5 R.(H.L.)151.

67 Bell, *Comm.*, I, 125. See *Douglas Gardiner & Mill* v. *Mackintosh's Trs.*, 1916 S.C.125.

68 *Drew* v. *Drew* (1870) 9 M.163.

69 *Livingstone* v. *Livingstone* (1886) 14 R.43.

70 *Lord Ruthven* v. *Pulford & Sons,* 1909 S.C.951.

71 *Officers' Superannuation and Provident Fund* v. *Cooper,* 1976 S.L.T. (Sh.Ct.)2.

72 *Per* Lord Fullerton, *Greig* v. *Christie* (1837) 16 S.242 at 244.

73 *Earl of Buchan* v. *His Creditors* (1835) 13 S.1112.

liquor may be an alimentary debt.[74] The expenses of an alimentary decree are alimentary.[75] Law accounts are not alimentary unless they are incurred for the defence of the alimentary fund or for the defence of the party on a capital charge.[76] A creditor who has made an advance for alimentary purposes is an alimentary creditor.[77] Arrears of contractual aliment do not constitute an alimentary debt.[78]

(b) Sums appropriated for a special purpose.[79]

(c) Earnings payable to a member of the armed forces of the Crown.[80]

(d) Any money payable by the Crown the assignation, charging or taking in execution of which is prohibited or restricted by statute.[81]

(e) Any money payable by the Crown on account of a National Savings Bank deposit.[81]

(f) A *spes successionis*.[82]

(g) The position of a right to damages in respect of delict or breach of contract is not clear. Where the wrong is of a personal nature—breach of promise, seduction, slander or personal injury, for example—nothing is arrestable until an action is raised or possibly, until a claim is intimated.[83] There may be exceptions. Even if an action has been raised the arrestment may be nugatory if the arrestee's insurers make an extra-judicial settlement.[84]

(h) Wages payable to a seaman employed on a ship registered in the

---

74 *Turnbull & Son* v. *Scott* (1899) 15 Sh.Ct.Rep.268.

75 *Hunter* v. *Wilson* (1917) 33 Sh.Ct.Rep.209.

76 *Greig* v. *Christie, supra.*

77 *Waddell* v. *Waddell* (1836) 15 S.151.

78 *Officers' Superannuation and Provident Fund* v. *Cooper, supra.*

79 *Souper* v. *Smith* (1756) Mor.744. Few of the cases usually cited on this matter are satisfactory. In *Baillie* v. *Wilson* (1840) 2 D.495 the sum was due under an agreement made directly between the arrestee and the person to whom the appropriation was made. In *British Linen Co.* v. *Kansas Investment Co. Ltd.* (1895) 3 S.L.T. 138 and 202 the fund was provided by a third party, not the debtor. As to sums consigned in court, see *Shankland & Co.* v. *McGildowny,* 1912 S.C.857.

80 Law Reform (Miscellaneous Provisions) (Scotland) Act 1966, s.2.

81 Crown Proceedings Act 1947, s.46; *e.g.* Social Security Act 1975, s.87(1); Supplementary Benefits Act 1976, s.16; *Macfarlane* v. *Glasgow Corporation* (1934) 50 Sh.Ct.Rep.247. But see *Macdonald's Tr.* v. *Macdonald,* 1938 S.C.536. See *Sinton* v. *Sinton,* 1976 S.L.T. (Sh.Ct.) 95.

82 *Trappes* v. *Meredith* (1871) 10 M.38.

83 Lord Dunedin's dissenting opinion in *Riley* v. *Ellis,* 1910 S.C.934, was approved by the House of Lords in *Caldwell* v. *Hamilton,* 1919 S.C.(H.L.)100; *Wardrop* v. *Fairholm and Arbuthnot* (1744) Mor.4860 establishes that the claim is arrestable once the action has been raised.

84 *Mather & Son* v. *Wilson & Co. Ltd.* (1908) 15 S.L.T.946.

United Kingdom (other than a fishing boat) except where the arrestment is under a maintenance order.[85]

A contractual provision that a debt will not be arrestable has no effect.[86] Where a debt which is not arrestable is paid into the common debtor's bank account the sum may still be protected if it can be identified.[87]

4. Subjects Arrestable: Corporeal Moveables

The corporeal moveables arrested must be the property of the common debtor and the arrestee must be under an obligation to the common debtor with regard to the moveables although the obligation need not rest upon an express contract.[88] It is not sufficient that the moveables belong to the common debtor if the arrestee is under an obligation to someone else in respect of them.[89] Similarly, it is not sufficient that the arrestee is under an obligation to the common debtor in respect of them if the moveables are not the property of the common debtor.[90] Property owned jointly by the common debtor and another party cannot be arrested.[91]

Goods can, therefore, be arrested in the hands of a depositary,[92] a carrier,[93] a consignee,[94] and ship-owners[95] (unless the ship is on a time charter at the disposal of the owner of the goods.)[96] It is not competent to arrest the furniture of a landlord in the hands of his tenant.[97] Possession sufficient to create a lien is not necessarily sufficient to permit arrestment, so a guest's baggage cannot be

---

85 Merchant Shipping Act 1970, s.11; Merchant Shipping Act 1979, s.39(2).

86 *Fritz's Agency Ltd.* v. *Moss' Empires Ltd.* (1922) 38 Sh.Ct.Rep.124.

87 *Woods* v. *Royal Bank,* 1913 1 S.L.T.499.

88 *Sir James Laing & Sons Ltd.* v. *Barclay Curle & Co. Ltd.,* 1908 S.C.82; S.C. (H.L.)1; *Moore & Weinberg* v. *Ernsthausen Ltd.,* 1917 S.C.(H.L.)25.

89 *Young* v. *Aktiebolaget Ofverums Bruk* (1890)18 R.163; *Heron* v. *Winfields Ltd.* (1894) 22 R.182.

90 *Millar & Lang* v. *Polak* (1907) 14 S.L.T.788.

91 *Byng* v. *Campbell* (1893) 1 S.L.T.371; *Lucas's Trs.* v. *Campbell & Scott* (1894) 21 R.1096.

92 *Bridges* v. *Ewing* (1836) 15 S.8.

93 *Matthew* v. *Fawns* (1842) 4 D. 1242; *Frederic Braby & Co. Ltd.* v. *Edwin Danks & Co. (Oldbury) Ltd.* (1907) 15 S.L.T. 161 (goods despatched by arresters).

94 *Stalker* v. *Aiton* (1759) Mor.745.

95 *Mitchell* v. *Burn* (1874) 1 R.900.

96 Graham Stewart, p. 108.

97 *Hunter* v. *Lees* (1733) Mor.736; *Davidson* v. *Murray* (1784) Mor.761 (poinding is competent).

arrested in the hands of a host or innkeeper[98] and a horse being shod cannot be arrested in the hands of a blacksmith.[99]

The following are not arrestable:

(a) the debtor's tools and wearing apparel;[1]

(b) books, documents and evidents;[2]

(c) stolen property in the hands of the procurator fiscal or police;[3]

(d) the corpus of bills.[4] If the common debtor is payee, the debt can be arrested in the hands of the acceptor. The arrestment can, however, be defeated if the payee indorses the bill to a bona fide holder for value who does not have notice of the arrestment.

(e) the property of the bankrupt's wife held in her own name.[5]

5. Service of Arrestment

The warrant for arrestment in execution is normally an extract of a Court of Session decree, of a sheriff court decree or of a decree proceeding on a deed or protest registered in the Books of Council and Session or sheriff court books.[6] The warrant must be regular. It can, of course, be used for any number of arrestments.[7]

If the arrestee is furth of Scotland an arrestment proceeding on an extract of a Court of Session decree can be served on him edictally[8] but the arrestment is not held to have interpelled such person from paying the common debtor unless it is proved that the arrestee or those having authority to act for him were previously in the knowledge of such arrestment having been so served.[9] An arrestment proceeding on an extract sheriff court decree cannot be served edictally. If the moveables to be arrested are in the territory of a

---

98 *Hume* v. *Baillie* (1852) 14 D.821; *Hutchison* v. *Hutchison,* 1912 1 S.L.T.219.

99 *Neilson* v. *Smiths Gowans & Roy* (1821) Hume 31.

1 *Gassiot,* 12 Nov. 1814, F.C.; *McKay* v. *Highland Rlwy. Co.* 1872 Guth. Sh. Cas. 193; *McMillan* v. *Barrie & Dick* (1890) 6 Sh.Ct.Rep.103 (dressmaker's sewing machine); *Steele* v. *Eagles* (1923) 39 Sh.Ct.Rep.68 (not a photographer's bicycle). See also Chap. 15, para. 4, Chap. 19, para. 6.

2 *Trowsdale's Tr.* v. *Forcett Rlwy Co.* (1870) 9 M.88.

3 *Guthrie* v. *Morren* (1939) 55 Sh.Ct.Rep.172.

4 Erskine, III, 6, 7; Bell, *Comm.*, II, 68; Graham Stewart, p. 78.

5 Married Women's Property (Scotland) Act 1881, s.1(3). But see Chap. 19, para. 17.

6 Debtors (Scotland) Act 1838, ss.2-9; Sheriff Courts (Scotland) Extracts Act 1892, s.7. For the procedure where a person was acquired right to an extract, see *supra,* para. 3. Where he acquires right to a decree before extract he must proceed by letters of arrestment or letters of horning and poinding (Graham Stewart, p.26).

7 Graham Stewart, p.26.

8 1838 Act, s.18.

9 Debts Securities (Scotland) Act 1856, s.1.

sheriff other than the sheriff from whose books the extract was issued a warrant of concurrence must be obtained from the Petition Department of the Court of Session or from the sheriff court in whose jurisdiction the moveables are situated.[10] The common debtor need not be subject to the jurisdiction when the arrestment is used.[11]

No charge is necessary before service of an arrestment.[12] Service must be made by a sheriff officer.[13] The officer must deliver the schedule to the arrestee personally or leave it at his dwelling-house. If it is not personally served, to make it effectual a copy must also be sent by registered post or recorded delivery to the arrestee's last known place of abode, or, if that is unknown, or if the arrestee is a firm or corporation, to the arrestee's principal place of business, if known, or, if that is not known, to any known place of business.[14]

There is no statutory form of schedule.[15] The funds or property to be arrested need not be specified.[16]

6. Types of Arrestee

Where the arrestee is a pupil or *incapax* the arrestment is made in the hands of the tutor, judicial factor or *curator bonis*[17] but in the case of a minor service should be on the minor, not his curator.[18] In the case of trustees the arrestment should be served on all the accepting trustees, or at least a quorum.[19] Where the arrestee holds the fund in a certain capacity—as an executor, for example—the arrestment must be served on him as such.[20] Service is made on a corporation or partnership by putting the notice in the hands of one of their servants at their principal office or branch office.[21] In the

---

10 Debtors (Scotland) Act 1838, s.13.

11 *Wightman* v. *Wilson* (1858) 20 D.779.

12 The doubt as to the position in summary cause decrees (see Gray, 1977 S.L.T. (News) 129) has been resolved by amendment of the form of extract: A.S. (Summary Cause Rules, Sheriff Court) (Amendment) 1978 (S.I. 1978/112).

13 1892 Act, s.8. In a summary cause, service may be postal.

14 S.C.R. 126.

15 Graham Stewart, p.34; see also as to defects in the schedule and execution, *ibid.* pp.35, 36.

16 As to this see *Metzenburg* v. *Highland Rlwy. Co.* (1869) 7 M.919.

17 Erskine, III, 6, 4; Bell, *Prin.*, § 2121.

18 *Binning* v. *Macdoual* (1738) Mor.736.

19 *Black* v. *Scott* (1830) 8 S.367; *Gracie* v. *Gracie*, 1910 S.C.899.

20 *Wilson* v. *Gloag* (1840) 2 D.1233; *Macfarlane* v. *Sanderson* (1868) 40 J.189; *Graham* v. *Macfarlane & Co.* (1869) 7 M.640; *Burns* v. *Gillies* (1906) 8 F.460.

21 *Campbell* v. *Watson's Tr.* (1898) 25 R.690; *Macintyre* v. *Caledonian Rlwy. Co.* (1909) 25 Sh.Ct.Rep. 329; *Abbey National Building Society* v. *Strang*, 1981 S.L.T. (Sh.Ct.) 4. See S.C.R.126.

case of a limited company the notice may be served by leaving it at, or sending it by post to, the registered office or branch office.[22] It seems that where the company is in liquidation, service should be on the company itself and the liquidator as such.[23] While it has been stated that service at a branch of a bank affects only funds held at that branch[24] it is not clear that this is in accordance with principle;[25] the usual practice is to serve on both the head office and the branch at which there is an account.

Where goods are on a ship, instead of service on the owners, the arrestment may be made in the hands of the master[26] and, possibly, if the ship is in harbour, the shipbrokers.[27]

7. Effect of Arrestment

The effect of the arrestment is to interpel the arrestee from paying over the sum attached to the common debtor. If he does so he is liable to the arrester for the loss caused thereby. Similarly, the arrestee cannot pay over the funds to the arrester without either the authority of the court or the consent of the common debtor.[28]

An arrestment of a periodical payment attaches only the payment in respect of the current term which may be only a day.[29] If under the contract, the payment is made in advance, the arrestment cannot attach anything except payments in arrears.[30]

The practice of the Scottish banks is to disclose what sum has been attached by an arrestment in execution.

If they are not pursued or insisted on, arrestments in execution prescribe in three years from the date of service except where the debt is future or contingent when the three years run from the date the debt becomes due and the contingency is purified.[31] In an

---

22 Companies Act 1948, s.437(1); *Hopper & Co.* v. *Walker* (1904) 20 Sh.Ct. Rep.137.

23 *Burns* v. *Gillies, supra.*

24 Graham Stewart, p. 33.

25 See *J. Verrico & Co. Ltd.* v. *Australian Mutual Provident Society,* 1972 S.L.T. (Sh.Ct.) 57.

26 *Kellas* v. *Brown* (1856) 18 D.1089.

27 *Carron Co.* v. *Currie & Co.* (1896) 33 S.L.R.578.

28 *High-Flex (Scotland) Ltd.* v. *Kentallen Mechanical Services Co.,* 1977 S.L.T. (Sh.Ct.) 91.

29 *McAulay* v. *Smith* (1914) 30 Sh.Ct.Rep.162.

30 *Smith* v. *Burns* (1847) 9 D.1344 (annuity); *Morrison* v. *Eastern Brassfounding Co.* (1918) 34 Sh.Ct.Rep.216 (wages).

31 Debtors (Scotland) Act 1838, s.22. From *Jameson* v. *Sharp* (1887) 14 R.643, it would appear that the exemption applies only to what are properly called contingent debts; when the debt is due at a future date but is not yet payable the period runs from the date of service of the arrestment. See Chap. 1, para. 10.

arrestment on the dependence, prescription runs from the date of decree in the action.

8. Furthcoming

The arresting creditor completes his diligence by bringing an action of furthcoming against the arrestee and the common debtor in order to obtain "a decree effectually transferring from the common debtor to the arresting creditor the obligation which was originally prestable to the former by the arrestee."[32] The purposes of the action are to ascertain the existence and extent of the arrestee's obligation to the common debtor and to determine whether the arrester is now in right of that obligation. The action is brought in the Court of Session or in the sheriff court where the fund is situated or to whose jurisdiction the arrestee is subject.[33] The common debtor does not need to be subject to the court's jurisdiction but he must receive fair notice of the action.[34] The usual conclusion or crave is to ordain payment of the sum arrested by the arrestee to the arrester but where the subject arrested is not a pecuniary obligation the summons must be framed so as to be applicable to the subject attached.[35] In the case of corporeal moveables the court will grant a warrant for sale on a conclusion for payment[36] but if the subjects arrested are shares[37] or an insurance policy[38] or an interest in a partnership,[39] a special conclusion is necessary. The maximum amount recoverable by the arrester from the arrested funds is the original debt with interest from the date of arrestment, the expenses of constituting it and the expenses of the arrestment[40] (unless it was an arrestment on the dependence).[41] In the sheriff court the expenses of the furthcoming can be obtained in addition[42] but in the

---

32 *Per* Lord Kinnear, *Lucas's Trs.* v. *Campbell & Scott* (1894) 21 R.1096 at 1103.

33 Sheriff Courts (Scotland) Act 1907, s.6(*g*); S.C.R.128.

34 *Burns* v. *Monro* (1844) 6 D.1352; *Leggat Bros.* v. *Gray,* 1912 S.C.230.

35 *Lucas's Trs.* v. *Campbell & Scott, supra.*

36 *ibid.*

37 *Sinclair* v. *Staples* (1860) 22 D.600; *Valentine* v. *Grangemouth Coal Co.* (1897) 5 S.L.T.47.

38 *Clark* v. *Scottish Amicable Life Assurance Society,* 1922 S.L.T. (Sh.Ct.) 88.

39 *Green* v. *Miller's Debt Recovery Services,* 1954 S.L.T. (Sh.Ct.) 26.

40 *Encyclopaedia of the Laws of Scotland,* Vol. I, p. 548; but *cf.* Graham Stewart, pp. 133 and 229.

41 *Encyclopaedia of the Laws of Scotland,* Vol. I, p. 538; the expenses of arrestment on the dependence cannot be recovered from the common debtor.

42 S.C.R. 129; but not by further arrestment: *Lawsons Ltd.* v. *Campbell* (1925) 41 Sh.Ct.Rep.229.

Court of Session such expenses cannot be claimed from the arrestee unless he opposes the action;[43] such expenses can be awarded against the common debtor. The common debtor may defend the action on the ground that the arrestment was invalid or that he is not indebted to the arrester; the latter course is not open to him if his liability to the arrester has been established in a prior action.[44] The arrestee has no interest to plead that nothing is due by the common debtor to the arrester[45] but he can defend on the grounds that the common debtor has not been duly called,[46] or that the arrestment was invalid, or that nothing was arrested. He may take against the arrester any defence which he could have maintained against the common debtor because the arrester acquires the common debtor's right *tantum et tale*.[47] If the arrestee's liability to the common debtor is contingent upon the result of an arbitration, the furthcoming will be sisted to await the result of the arbitration proceedings.[48] The fact that the common debtor would have been entitled to deduct tax in paying the arrester does not mean that the arrestee is entitled to do so.[49] Any party having an interest in the arrested funds or property can appear in the action. If a prior arrester on the dependence who has not yet obtained decree in his principal action appears, the action of furthcoming will be sisted.[50] If the action is defended it proceeds as an ordinary action.[51] The action is not affected by the death of the arrestee; it proceeds against his representatives.[52] The furthcoming may be raised before the arrested fund is payable and it may be necessary to do this to interrupt the prescription of the arrestment.[53]

---

43 *May* v. *Malcolm* (1825) 4 S.76.

44 *Donaldson* v. *Ord* (1855) 17 D.1053.

45 *Houston* v. *Aberdeen Town & County Banking Company* (1849) 11 D.1490.

46 *Smyth* v. *Ninian* (1826) 5 S.8.

47 *Houston* v. *Aberdeen Town & County Banking Company, supra; Wilson* v. *Carrick* (1881) 18 S.L.R.657 (compensation); *Smith* v. *Chamber's Trs.* (1878) 5 R.97; 5 R.(H.L.)151 (defeasible claim).

48 *Boland* v. *The White Cross Insurance Association,* 1926 S.C.1066; *Palmer* v. *S.E. Lancashire Insurance Co.,* 1932 S.L.T.68; *Cant* v. *Eagle Star Insurance Co.,* 1937 S.L.T.444.

49 *Fletcher* v. *Young,* 1936 S.L.T.572.

50 Graham Stewart, p. 232; *Walker* v. *United Creameries Ltd.,* 1928 S.L.T. (Sh.Ct.) 21.

51 S.C.R. 132.

52 Graham Stewart, p. 228.

53 *Jameson* v. *Sharp* (1887) 14 R.643.

9. Competition: Arrestments inter se

Arrestments rank *inter se* according to priority of service[54] and the arrestment which is executed first is preferred even although the arrester is not the first to obtain a decree of furthcoming[55] or, in the case of arrestment on the dependence, decree of constitution.[56] Priority is determined by the hour shown in the execution.[57] If neither execution mentions the hour, arrestments served on the same day are ranked *pari passu.*[58] If one execution mentions the hour and the other is silent, the former is preferred[59] unless the hour mentioned is late in the day in which case they are ranked *pari passu.*[60] It is probably not competent to prove the hour of service by parole evidence.[61] If there is undue delay in following up the arrestment first served, a subsequent arrester who has obtained and extracted decree in a furthcoming will be preferred.[62] Where an arrestment on the dependence is subsequent to an arrestment to found jurisdiction, the arrester on the dependence cannot enforce a furthcoming until a citation has followed upon the arrestment to found jurisdiction, but once citation has followed he is preferred to the arrestment to found jurisdiction.[63]

A second or subsequent arrestment has effect subject to the prior arrestment and results in a preference over any balance remaining after satisfaction of the claim of the prior arrester.[64]

10. Competition: Other Diligence[65]

In competition with confirmation by an executor-creditor, the arrestment is preferred only if decree of furthcoming has been obtained before the executor has confirmed to the arrested fund.[66] It seems that in competition with an adjudication, the criterion of preference is whether decree of furthcoming was obtained before

---

54 Stair, III, 1, 46; Erskine, III, 6, 18.
55 *Wallace* v. *Scot* (1583) Mor.807.
56 *Baynes* v. *Graham* (1796) Mor.2904; *Mitchell* v. *Scott* (1881) 8 R.875.
57 Erskine, III, 6, 18.
58 Bankton, III, 1, 41; *Sutie* v. *Ross* (1705) Mor.816.
59 Bankton, III, 1, 41; *Hertz* v. *Itzig* (1865) 3 M.813.
60 *Douglas* v. *Palmer* (1777) 5 Brown's Supp. 381.
61 Bankton, III, 1, 41; *Sutie* v. *Ross supra; Hertz* v. *Itzig, supra.*
62 Bankton, III, 1, 41; Graham Stewart, p. 141.
63 *Stillie's Trs.* v. *Stillie* (1898) 6 S.L.T.173.
64 *W. H. Hill & Sons Ltd.* v. *Manning's Tr.,* 1951 S.L.T. (Sh.Ct.) 29.
65 For competition with a poinding of the ground and a heritable creditor collecting rents, see Graham Stewart, p. 163.
66 Bell, *Comm.,* II, 69; *Wilson* v. *Fleming* (1823) 2 S.430.

the date of adjudication.[67] Such a competition could arise only in the limited field where both diligences are competent, *e.g.* heritable bonds not followed by infeftment. A Crown arrestment is preferred if it is served before any other arrester has obtained a decree of furthcoming.[68]

11. Competition: Assignations

In competition with a voluntary assignation an arrestment is preferred if it is executed before the date of intimation of the assignation even if the date of the assignation itself was prior to the arrestment.[69] If the arrestment and intimation are on the same day, priority is determined by the hour.[70] If the hours are not specified, the arrestment and the assignation rank *pari passu.*[71] If either the execution of arrestment or the intimation specified an hour and the other document does not, the former is preferred.[72] Intimation of a transfer of shares in a limited company has the effect of giving the transfer priority over a subsequent arrestment even if the transfer is not registered before the execution of the arrestment.[73]

12. Effect of Insolvency[74]

An arrestment on or after the sixtieth day prior to the common debtor's sequestration is ineffectual in a question with the trustee.[75] It does place a nexus on the fund which prevents the arrestee paying it away to the prejudice of the trustee.[76] The day of sequestration itself is excluded in computing the period so an arrestment on 20 April is affected by a sequestration on 19 June.[77] An arrestment

---

67 Bell, *Comm.*, II, 69; Graham Stewart, p. 161.

68 Exchequer Court (Scotland) Act 1856, s.30; Goudy, p. 538.

69 Stair, III, 1, 43, 44; Erskine, III, 6, 19; *Inglis* v. *Robertson & Baxter* (1898) 25 R.(H.L.)70; Where the arrestment is on the dependence, it does not matter that decree of constitution has not been obtained at the time intimation is made—*A* v. *B* (1618) Mor.2771.

70 *Davidson* v. *Balcanqual* (1629) Mor.2773; presumably this arises only where the intimation is formal.

71 *Inglis* v. *Edward* (1630) Mor.2773.

72 Stair, III, 1, 43.

73 *Thomson* v. *Fullarton* (1842) 5 D.379; *Stillie's Trs.* v. *Stillie* (1898) 6 S.L.T.173; *Harvey's Yoker Distillery* v. *Singleton* (1901) 8 S.L.T.369; *National Bank of Scotland Glasgow Nominees Ltd.* v. *Adamson,* 1932 S.L.T.492. It is arguable that this result is consistent with *Morrison* v. *Harrison* (1876) 3 R.406—see Graham Stewart, p. 143.

74 As to the effect of an English bankruptcy, see Chap. 15, para. 13.

75 B.A., s.104; *Dow & Co.* v. *Union Bank* (1875) 2 R.459.

76 *McKenzie* v. *Campbell* (1894) 21 R.904.

77 *Stiven* v. *Reynolds & Co.* (1891) 18 R.422, *arguendo.*

executed outwith the 60 days is not cut down even although decree in the furthcoming was obtained within the period.[78] An arrestment which was executed before the 60 days but which has not been followed up by a furthcoming prior to sequestration is effectual if there has been no undue delay in bringing the furthcoming;[79] this is so even where the arrestment is on the dependence of an action in which decree on the merits has not yet been obtained before sequestration; in such cases, however, where there has been no furthcoming prior to sequestration, the arrestee does not pay over the funds to the arrester and must make them available to the trustee who then gives a preference to the arrester in the sequestration in respect of the funds recovered.[80] Where the arrestment is executed within the 60 days and decree in a furthcoming has not been obtained before the sequestration, the arrestment is cut down; the arrestee must make the funds available to the trustee and he cannot pay them away to the trustee's prejudice;[81] the arrester is, however, given a preference in the sequestration for the expense bona fide incurred in procuring the warrant for and executing the arrestment.[82] On the other hand, it seems that where the arrestment is executed within the 60 days and the funds have been paid over to the arrester under a decree in a furthcoming prior to sequestration, the diligence is not affected and the arrester can retain the funds.[83] If funds arrested within the 60 days have been paid over to the arrester before the sequestration under a mandate from the common debtor and not under a decree in a furthcoming the arrestment is not affected by s.104[84] but it would appear that such an arrangement is reducible as a fraudulent preference and the arrester

---

78 Graham Stewart, p. 186.

79 It is thought that this is not affected by what was said about the nature of an arrestment in *Lord Advocate* v. *Royal Bank of Scotland Ltd.*, 1977 S.C.155, but see, for the position in a liquidation, para. 13 *infra*.

80 *Mitchell* v. *Scott* (1881) 8 R.875; *Benhar Coal Co.* v. *Turnbull* (1883) 10 R.558 (liquidation); *James Gilmour (Crossford) Ltd.* v. *John Williams (Wishaw) Ltd.*, 1970 S.L.T. (Sh.Ct.) 6.

81 *McKenzie* v. *Campbell* (1894) 21 R.904.

82 See Chap. 15, para 9, *supra* n. 99. Where the arrestment was on the dependence, the following are covered: solicitors' fees taking instructions to sue, preparing initial writ, obtaining warrant to arrest, instructing officer and reporting arrestment; court dues of warrant; officer's fees for arrestment: *Aitken's Seqn.* (1914) 31 Sh.Ct. Rep.27.

83 This seems to follow from *Johnston* v. *Cluny Trs.*, 1957 S.C.184.

84 *Johnston* v. *Cluny Trs.*, *supra*.

will have to repay the funds recovered to the trustee.[85] A payment by the debtor in cash, or by cheque, will not, of course, be a fraudulent preference.[86]

Crown diligence is effectual if the arrestment or poinding is executed before the date of the trustee's Act and Warrant.[87]

As has been indicated above, sequestration has a still wider effect on arrestments by virtue of s.10 of the Bankruptcy Act. Sequestration at its date is equivalent to an arrestment in execution and decree of furthcoming on behalf of all the creditors.[88] Therefore, when sequestration takes place within four months of notour bankruptcy it ranks equally with any arrestment executed within 60 days before, or four months after, notour bankruptcy and the arrestment is, in effect, cut down;[89] the arrester must pay the funds over to the trustee if he has recovered them but he is given a preference for the expenses of his diligence. It seems, however, that where the arrestment is executed within 60 days of notour bankruptcy and sequestration has followed within four months of notour bankruptcy, but the arrested funds have been paid to the arrester under mandate before the sequestration, the trustee cannot recover from the arrester under s.10 because the arrestment has not been "used".[90] An even more complex situation arises where one arrestment is executed within 60 days before notour bankruptcy, a second arrestment is executed within four months after notour bankruptcy, and sequestration follows more than four months after that notour bankruptcy but within 60 days of the second arrestment. It seems that the arrestments are equalised but the second arrester's share goes to the trustee.[91]

An arrestment executed by a pre-sequestration creditor after the award of sequestration but before the appointment of a trustee attaches nothing.[92]

---

85 *Newton & Sons' Tr.* v. *Finlayson & Co.*, 1928 S.C.637; *Robertson's Tr.* v. *P. & W. Maclellan Ltd.*, 1957 S.L.T. (Sh.Ct.) 65; but see *Walkraft Paint Co. Ltd.* v. *Lovelock*, 1964 S.L.T.103; *Richmond v. United Collieries Ltd.* (1905) 13 S.L.T.458; on this topic see also Antonio, 1958 S.L.T. (News) 121.

86 See Chap. 20, para. 10.

87 *Admiralty* v. *Blair's Tr.*, 1916 S.C.247.

88 B.A., s.104.

89 *Stewart* v. *Jarvie*, 1938 S.C.309. See also Chap. 15, para. 10.

90 *Millar* v. *Forage Supply Co. Ltd.*, 1955 S.L.T. (Sh.Ct.) 18.

91 Goudy, p. 243; Wardhaugh, p. 9.

92 *Hodgson & Son* v. *United Thread Mills Ltd.* (1935) 51 Sh.Ct.Rep.69; *cf.* *McLardy & Co.* v. *Mutter Howey & Co.* (1934) 50 Sh.Ct.Rep.100.

Any creditor judicially producing in a process relative to the subject of an arrestment used within 60 days before or four months after notour bankruptcy liquid grounds of debt or a decree of payment within such period is entitled to rank as if he had executed an arrestment; if the first or any subsequent arrester has in the meantime obtained a decree of furthcoming and has thereupon recovered payment he is accountable for the sum received to the other creditors entitled to a *pari passu* ranking after allowing for the expenses of recovering the same.[93] Arrestments on the same subject after the four months may rank on the reversion. The procedure applies to the arrestment of a ship.[94]

13. Liquidation

The Companies Act 1948, s.327(1) provides that a liquidation "shall, as at the date of commencement thereof, be equivalent to an arrestment in execution and decree of furthcoming, and to an executed or completed poinding, and no arrestment or poinding of the funds or effects of the company executed on or after the sixtieth day prior to that date shall be effectual, and those funds or effects or the proceeds of these effects if sold shall be made forthcoming to the liquidator . . .". This is in terms almost identical to those of s.104 of the Bankruptcy (Scotland) Act 1913 and it has been indicated that the two sections should be interpreted alike.[95] It would follow that the effect of a liquidation on an arrestment would be the same as that of a sequestration already explained.[96] In a recent case,[97] the First Division held that an arrestment which has not been followed up by a furthcoming was not "effectually executed diligence" in terms of the Companies (Floating Charges and Receivers) (Scotland) Act 1972, s.15 (2) (*a*), and accordingly did not prevail against a receiver subsequently appointed under a floating charge. The expression "effectually executed diligence" also occurs in s.1(2) of the Act of 1972 in relation to the attachment of a floating charge on the liquidation of the company. If effect is given to the presumption that the same meaning is to be given to the same words in different

93 B.A., s.10.

94 *Harvey* v. *McAdie* (1888) 4 Sh.Ct.Rep.254; *Munro* v. *Smith,* 1968 S.L.T. (Sh.Ct.) 26.

95 *Johnston* v. *Cluny Trs.,* 1957 S.C.184, *per* Lord Sorn at p. 194.

96 See *supra,* para. 12.

97 *Lord Advocate* v. *Royal Bank of Scotland Ltd.,* 1977 S.C.155. See *infra,* para. 14.

sections of an Act,[98] this means that an arrestment executed more than 60 days before liquidation and not followed by a furthcoming does not prevail against the rights of the holder of a floating charge over the arrested property but would prevail against the general creditors if there were no floating charge. Where a liquidator was appointed on the common debtor company between the raising of the furthcoming and the granting of decree therein, and the liquidator intimated that he claimed the arrested funds, the court granted a sist of execution to prevent the arrester proceeding to do diligence against the arrestees on the furthcoming decree.[99] It has been held that the provisions of the Bankruptcy Act relating to the equalisation of diligence apply to companies registered under the Companies Acts.[1]

The foregoing provision as to the effect of liquidation applies to the estate in Scotland of a company registered in England.[2] Where an arrester has obtained payment of the sum arrested before presentation of the winding-up petition, the sum cannot be recovered by the liquidator by virtue of what is now s.228 of the Companies Act 1948.[3]

14. Appointment of Receiver

When a receiver is appointed by virtue of a floating charge, his powers are subject to, *inter alia,* "the rights of any person who has effectually executed diligence on all or any part of the property of the company" prior to the appointment of the receiver.[4] In *Lord Advocate* v. *Royal Bank of Scotland Ltd.*[5] the First Division held that an arrestment which had not been followed by a furthcoming was not effectually executed diligence and that the receiver was entitled to the sum arrested. It was suggested that a case in which an arrester would have a preference over property of the company would be where a decree of furthcoming has proceeded on an arrestment of corporeal moveables. It is submitted that this decision is clearly wrong; it makes arrestment on the dependence of an action against a company almost useless; it leads to a circuitous

---

98 *Littlewoods Mail Order Stores Ltd.* v. *I.R.C.* [1963] A.C.135.
99 *Parkinson & Co. Ltd.* v. *Bowen & Sons Ltd.*, 1951 S.L.T.393.
1 *Clark* v. *Hinde Milne & Co.* (1884) 12 R.347.
2 Companies Act 1948, s.327(2).
3 *Inshaw Tubes Ltd.* v. *Smith Roberts & Co. Ltd.* (1912) 28 Sh.Ct.Rep.171.
4 Companies (Floating Charges and Receivers) (Scotland) Act 1972, s.15(2).
5 1977 S.C.155.

situation if an arrestment has been followed by intimation of an assignation of the fund which in turn has been followed by the receiver's appointment; it is suggested that the correct meaning of the Act is that effectually executed diligence is diligence which has not been rendered ineffectual under the Companies Act 1948, s.327(1)(*a*), by reason of liquidation commencing within 60 days thereafter.

It is clear that the appointment of a receiver under a floating charge created by a company registered in England renders ineffectual any subsequent arrestment of assets in Scotland.[6] The validity of prior diligence would seem to be the same as in the case of a Scottish receiver as the English receiver may exercise his powers "so far as their exercise is not inconsistent with the law applicable" in Scotland.[7]

15. Preventing Arrestment

It is possible to prevent, by interdict, a threatened use of arrestment in execution if caution is offered or if malice and oppression can be instantly verified.[8] When arrestments have been used, it is possible to have an arrestment in execution recalled by the statutory procedure available in the case of arrestment on the dependence.[9] The sheriff may recall or restrict arrestments proceeding on a warrant issued from his books with or without caution as appears just, his judgment being subject to review in the Court of Session.[10] A contention that the subjects are not arrestable can be raised in a petition for recall if there is a delay in bringing the furthcoming.[11] The suspension of a charge on the decree on which the arrestment has been used is a ground for recall of the arrestment on caution.[12]

16. Arrestment of Ships

Arrestment is the appropriate diligence to attach a ship.[13] This

[6] *Gordon Anderson (Plant) Ltd.* v. *Campsie Construction Ltd.*, 1977 S.L.T.7 (decided under s.15(4) of the 1972 Act).

[7] Administration of Justice Act 1977, s.7, replacing Companies (Floating Charges and Receivers) (Scotland) Act 1972, s.15(4).

[8] *Beattie & Son* v. *Pratt* (1880) 7 R.1171.

[9] *Gillies* v. *Bow,* 1877, Guthrie's Select Cases I, 196; See Chap. 11, para. 10.

[10] Debtors (Scotland) Act 1838, s.21.

[11] *Lord Ruthven* v. *Drummond,* 1908 S.C.1154.

[12] *Smith* v. *Macintosh* (1848) 10 D.455.

[13] See generally Graham Stewart, pp. 23-24, 41-42, 242-245; Dobie, *Sheriff Court Practice,* pp. 272, 275. Anomalous provisions for the poinding of ships are found in Merchant Shipping Act 1894, s.693, and Prevention of Oil Pollution Act 1971, s.20(1).

differs from other forms of arrestment in that it is not used in the hands of a third party but is used as a real diligence against the ship itself.[14] The ship must be in harbour or lying in a roadstead before it is subject to arrestment. The schedule is attached to the mast and the Royal initials are chalked above it. Special authority to dismantle the ship may be obtained. The diligence is completed by an action of sale.

---

14 See *Clan Line Steamers Ltd.* v. *Earl of Douglas Steamship Co. Ltd.*, 1913 S.C.967.

CHAPTER 17

OTHER DILIGENCE

1. Inhibition

An inhibition is "a writ passing under the signet, prohibiting the debtor from alienating any part of his estate, and from contracting debt by means of which it may be carried off, to the prejudice of the creditor inhibitor; and interdicting third parties from taking conveyances of the heritage."[1] It affects only the heritable estate of the debtor. It is not a complete diligence and its effect is merely prohibitory and preventive.

Inhibition may proceed on a decree of the Court of Session or the ordinary sheriff court.[2] It may also proceed on a liquid document of debt such as a bond or bill and it is not necessary that the document should be capable of registration for execution.[3]

2. Procedure

Even in the case of a sheriff court decree, an inhibition must be effected through the Petition Department of the Court of Session. A Bill for Letters of Inhibition is presented with the decree or document of debt in the Petition Department. A *fiat* is obtained and Letters of Inhibition can then be signeted. The Letters authorise a messenger-at-arms to serve a copy of them on the debtor. Before service, it is competent to register in the Register of Inhibitions and Adjudications a Notice of Inhibition. After service, the execution, together with the Letters, is registered and, if this is done not later than 21 days from the date of registration of the notice, the inhibition takes effect from the date of registration of the notice; otherwise, the effective date is the date of registration of the Letters.[4] An inhibition prescribes on the lapse of five years from its effective date.[5]

---

1 Bell, *Prin.*, §2306.

2 Graham Stewart, p.527.

3 Graham Stewart, *loc. cit.*

4 Titles to Land Consolidation (Scotland) Act 1868, s.155. Under registration of title, on registration of an interest, any subsisting entry in the Register of Inhibitions and Adjudications adverse to the interest is entered in the title sheet; the mode of entry of subsequent inhibitions is not yet clear: Land Registration (Scotland) Act 1979, s.6(1)(*c*) (as to indemnity by the Keeper, see s.12(3)(*k*)).

5 Conveyancing (Scotland) Act 1924, s.44(3)(*a*).

3. Effect of Inhibition

The inhibition affects all heritage owned by the debtor whether or not he is infeft therein;[6] it also affects heritable securities if notarial intimation is made to the debtor in the security;[7] it does not affect *acquirenda* except in certain special circumstances.[8] The effect of the inhibition is to prohibit the debtor from granting future voluntary deeds to the inhibitor's prejudice. This does not affect the recording of a deed already granted;[9] nor does it affect the granting of a disposition in implement of missives completed prior to the inhibition because this is not a voluntary act.[10] It did not affect further advances made on a bond of cash credit.[11] Acts of ordinary administration, *e.g.* the granting of a lease of ordinary duration, are not struck at.[12] A deed which is affected by the inhibition may be reduced *ex capite inhibitionis* by the inhibitor; the right transmits to his representatives and assignees.[13] The inhibition operates only against the debtor; his successors are not constrained by it.[14] Where the debtor has granted a heritable security and another creditor has then inhibited, on the sale of the security subjects, the heritable creditor is entitled to be paid in full from the proceeds and the inhibiting creditor is entitled to the balance in preference to creditors whose debts were contracted after the date of the inhibition but not, it would seem, in preference to other creditors whose debts were contracted before the date of the inhibition.[15] An inhibition also has an effect on the ranking on the heritable estate in the debtor's sequestration.[16]

4. Adjudication

Adjudication is the appropriate diligence to attach the heritable

---

6 *Dryburgh* v. *Gordon* (1896) 24 R.1, *per* Lord Kincairney at p.3.

7 Graham Stewart, p.549; but see *Mackintosh's Trs.* v. *Davidson & Gordon* (1898) 25 R.554.

8 Titles to Land Consolidation (Scotland) Act 1868, s.157.

9 Graham Stewart, p.563.

10 *Livingstone* v. *McFarlane* (1842) 5 D.1.

11 *Campbell's Tr.* v. *De Lisle's Exrs.* (1870) 9 M.252.

12 Bell, *Comm.*, II, 142.

13 Bankton, I, 7, 140; Graham Stewart, p.552.

14 Erskine, II, 11, 2; *Menzies* v. *Murdoch* (1841) 4 D.257.

15 *Bank of Scotland* v. *Lord Advocate,* 1977 S.L.T.24; Love *et al.* (1977) 22 J.L.S.424; Gretton (1979) 24 J.L.S.101; *McGowan* v. *A. Middlemàs & Sons Ltd.*, 1977 S.L.T.(Sh.Ct.)41 is wrongly decided. See also *Abbey National Building Society* v. *Shaik Aziz,* 1981 S.L.T.(Sh.Ct.)29.

16 See Chap. 21, para. 5.

property of the debtor.[17] The subjects of the diligence are: land and heritable rights generally including liferents, annuities and rights having a *tractum futuri temporis;* heritable securities; a heritable interest in a trust;[18] bank stock where the charter excludes arrestment.[19] Where a security over heritage has been constituted by *ex facie* absolute disposition, the disponer's reversionary right is adjudgeable.[20] A *spes successionis* cannot be adjudged.[21] The procedure is by an action which can be raised only in the Court of Session. Service of the summons together with registration of a notice in the Register of Inhibitions and Adjudications makes the subjects litigious and prevents voluntary conveyances by the debtor to the prejudice of the creditor. Decree in the action when recorded in the Sasine Register vests the property in the adjudger subject to the debtor's right of redemption. Redemption may be effected at any time until *either* a period of ten years (the "legal") has expired and the adjudger has obtained decree in an action of declarator of expiry of the legal *or* the legal has expired and possession for the period of 10 years of positive prescription has followed upon the recording of the decree of adjudication.[22] Adjudications within a year and a day of the first are equalised.[23] The adjudication is cut down by sequestration or liquidation within a year and a day.[24]

5. Summary Diligence

If a document of debt incorporates a clause of consent to registration for execution, the creditor may do diligence against the debtor without first resorting to a court action. The document is registered in the court books and an extract therefrom is a warrant for diligence. In other words, the clause is "a consent given *ab ante* that the Court of Session may issue a decree which is to have the same effect as if the parties had entered into a suit before the Court, and decree had been pronounced in that action."[25] The extract is "a constructive decree".

---

17 As adjudication is not a satisfactory form of diligence in the general case, it is dealt with here in a summary fashion.

18 *Learmonts* v. *Shearer* (1866) 4 M.540.

19 *Royal Bank* v. *Fairholm* (1770) Mor.App.'Adjudication' No. 3.

20 Graham Stewart, p.606.

21 *Reid* v. *Morison* (1893) 20 R.510.

22 Prescription and Limitation (Scotland) Act 1973, s.1(3).

23 Diligence Act 1661; Adjudications Act 1672.

24 Bankruptcy (Scotland) Act 1913, s.103; Companies Act 1948, s.327(1)(*b*).

25 Wood, *Lectures,* p.160.

The document of debt must be probative.[26] It must contain the clause "I consent to registration for execution"[27] although this is not necessary in a bond in favour of the Crown.[28] The sum due must be definitely ascertainable on the face of the document or the document must state the mode in which the sum due is to be ascertained. For example, the sum may be ascertained by a separate certified account which need not be registered.[29]

If the debtor resides anywhere in Scotland, registration may be made in the Books of Council and Session. Registration may be made in the books of a sheriff court if the debtor is designed in the document as residing within the appropriate sheriff court district. Anyone may lodge the document for registration. An extract is then issued with a warrant for diligence endorsed on it. The warrant authorises diligence by poinding after a charge of six days and arrestment.[30] In the case of a sheriff court extract, if the debtor has changed his residence to another jurisdiction, diligence may be done against him there after presenting the extract with a minute endorsed thereon either to the Petition Department of the Court of Session or to the sheriff within whose jurisdiction the debtor is now residing and obtaining a warrant of concurrence.[31]

If the original creditor assigns the debt or dies before registration of the document, the assignee or executor must register the document and apply to the Petition Department for letters of horning and poinding. If the assignation or death occurs after registration, the assignee or executor presents the extract together with the assignation or confirmation and a minute to the Petition Department (or sheriff clerk) and a deliverance is written on the extract which forms a warrant for diligence at the instance of the assignee or executor.[32] If the original debtor has died, summary diligence is incompetent and the debt must be constituted against his representatives by an action[33] except where, in the case of a heritable

[26] *Carnoway* v. *Ewing* (1611) Mor.14988.

[27] *Erskine* (1710) Mor.14997; Titles to Land Consolidation (Scotland) Act 1868, s.138.

[28] Exchequer Court (Scotland) Act 1856, s.38.

[29] *Fisher* v. *Stewart* (1828) 7 S.97; *Paisley Union Bank* v. *Hamilton* (1831) 9 S.488; *Keith* v. *Cairney*, 1917 1 S.L.T.202.

[30] Debtors (Scotland) Act 1838, s.9; Titles to Land Consolidation (Scotland) Act 1868, s.138; Writs Execution (Scotland) Act 1877, ss.1 and 2; Court of Session (Extracts) Act 1916.

[31] Debtors (Scotland) Act 1838, s.13.

[32] *ibid.*, ss.7, 12. See *Mitchell* v. *St. Mungo Lodge of Ancient Shepherds*, 1916 S.C.689.

[33] *Kippen* v. *Hill* (1822) 2 S.105.

security, a person taking the security subjects by conveyance, succession, gift or bequest has executed an agreement to the transmission of the personal obligation.[34]

6. On Bills of Exchange

Summary diligence may also be done on a bill of exchange or a promissory note[35] but not on a cheque.[36] On non-acceptance or non-payment the protest is registered in the books of a court having jurisdiction over the party against whom diligence is to be executed.[37] In the case of non-acceptance the registration must be within six months from the date of the bill; in the case of non-payment within six months from the date it fell due.[38] If the bill is payable on demand, the six months runs from the date of presentation for payment.

A bill may be a valid document of debt and yet not be a valid ground of summary diligence, "the whole grounds and warrants of the diligence must be entire, and must be apparently and manifestly entire."[39] The bill must itself prove liability and require no extrinsic evidence to support it or to identify the parties.[40] The debt must be exigible without any qualification or condition whatsoever.[41] The bill must be *ex facie* complete and regular. Summary diligence cannot follow upon a bill which is signed with initials[42] or a mark,[43] or which is undated[44] or unstamped[45] or which has been torn up and pasted together.[46] It is vitiated if the date[47] or date of payment[48] is written upon an erasure. A procuration signature is not objectionable if the procuration is notorious.[49]

---

34 Conveyancing (Scotland) Act 1874, s.47; Conveyancing (Scotland) Act 1924, s.15.

35 Bills of Exchange Act 1681; Inland Bills Act 1696; 12 Geo.III, c.72, s.42; Bills of Exchange Act 1882, s.98.

36 *Glickman* v. *Linda,* 1950 S.C.18.

37 The diligence may proceed on a householder's certificate in place of a protest: Bills of Exchange Act 1882, s.94; *McRobert* v. *Lindsay* (1898) 14 Sh.Ct.Rep.89.

38 *McNeill* v. *Innes Chambers & Co.,* 1917 S.C.540.

39 *per* Lord Gillies, *Smith* v. *Selby* (1829) 7 S.885 at 886.

40 *Summers* v. *Marianski* (1843) 6 D.286; *Fraser* v. *Bannerman* (1853) 15 D.756.

41 Bell, *Prin.,* §316; *Hughson* v. *Cullen* (1857) 20 D.271.

42 *Munro* v. *Munro* (1820) Hume 81.

43 *Stewart* v. *Russell,* 11 July 1815, F.C.; *Mackintosh* v. *Macdonald* (1828) 7 S.155.

44 Bell, *Prin.,* §343.

45 Bell, *Comm.,* I, 415.

46 *Thomson* v. *Bell* (1850) 12 D.1184.

47 *Armstrong* v. *Wilson* (1842) 4 D.1347; *McRostie* v. *Halley* (1850) 12 D.816.

48 *Hamilton* v. *Kinnear & Sons* (1825) 4 S.102.

49 *Turnbull* v. *McKie* (1822) 1 S.353.

The extract registered protest contains a warrant for arrestment and poinding.[50]

7. Recovery of Rates

There is a special summary procedure for the recovery of rates. On a petition by the collector of rates containing a certificate that notice has been given to the debtor requiring payment within 14 days thereafter, that this period has expired and that the amount is still unpaid, the sheriff grants a summary warrant for the recovery of the rates due and unpaid with an addition of 10 per cent.[51] The warrant decerns and ordains instant execution by arrestment and authorises sheriff officers to enter premises occupied by the debtor to poind and remove goods belonging to the debtor and, after four days, to sell the goods by public auction on three days' notice. Goods on hire-purchase cannot now be poinded.[52] There is no provision for delivery of goods to the creditor in default of sale.

The sum realised by the sale, under deduction of expenses, is paid over to the collector who must account to the debtor for any balance remaining after payment of the arrears and the 10 per cent. addition.

The owner of any goods which have been poinded or sold who feels aggrieved by the proceedings may present an application to the sheriff who determines summarily the dispute or claim for damages raised by the application.[53]

The warrant can be executed beyond the area of the rating authority if it is endorsed by the sheriff of the county concerned.[54]

If the rating authority has obtained decree for the rates unpaid in other competent proceedings the summary warrant procedure cannot be followed.[55] If a summary warrant has been obtained the authority may subsequently proceed by ordinary action provided that the warrant has not been enforced and is abandoned before decree is given.[56]

---

50 Writs Execution (Scotland) Act 1877, s.3.

51 Local Government (Scotland) Act 1947, s.247(2).

52 Local Government (Miscellaneous Provisions) (Scotland) Act 1981, s.12.

53 s.249.

54 s.251.

55 s.247(2).

56 s.247(1).

8. Recovery of Tax

There is also a special procedure for recovery of income tax and petroleum revenue tax.[57] If the collector of taxes certifies that tax is due and not paid, the General Commissioners of Income Tax or the sheriff may issue a warrant for recovery of the tax by poinding. The poinded goods are detained in the house where they were poinded in custody of the sheriff officer for five days unless the owner redeems them by payment of the tax and "costs". Thereafter they are valued and sold at a sum not less than the value and the proceeds are applied towards the tax due and payment for the officer's trouble at 10p per pound of tax. If the debtor is sequestrated before the sale takes place, the sheriff officer cannot claim a preferred ranking in the sequestration for the statutory fee and indeed, is not a creditor of the bankrupt.[58] If no purchaser appears the goods are lodged in the hands of the sheriff and are sold by his order. The expenses of preserving the goods are recoverable. Auctioneers selling any goods by any mode of sale at auction must give three days' notice of the sale to the collector of taxes specifying the name and residence of the person whose goods are to be sold.

There are similar procedures for recovery of value added tax,[59] and car tax,[60] and betting and gaming duties.[61]

An arrestment for a debt due to the Crown transfers the fund to the Crown preferably to all other creditors and the arrestee may safely pay the fund to the Crown.[62]

9. Civil Imprisonment

Imprisonment in respect of non-payment of debt is competent only in the following cases:

(a) failure to pay rates, the maximum period being six weeks;[63]

(b) wilful failure to pay aliment, the maximum period being six

---

57 Taxes Management Act 1970, s.63; Oil Taxation Act 1975, s.1, Sched. 2. See *Rutherford* v. *Lord Advocate,* 1931 S.L.T.405; *Norman* v. *Dymock,* 1932 S.C.131.

58 *Cuthbert & Wilson* v. *Shaw's Tr.,* 1955 S.C.8.

59 Value Added Tax (General) Regulations 1980 (S.I. 1980/1536), reg.59.

60 Car Tax Regulations 1972 (S.I. 1972/1345), reg.12.

61 Betting and Gaming Duties Act 1972, Sched. 1, para. 13, Sched. 2, para. 10, Sched. 3, para. 15.

62 Exchequer Court (Scotland) Act 1856, s.30, which subsists notwithstanding Crown Proceedings Act 1947, s.26(1).

63 Civil Imprisonment (Scotland) Act 1882, s.5; Local Government (Scotland) Act 1947, s.247(5).

weeks.[64] The failure is presumed to be wilful until the contrary is proved but the warrant will not be granted if it is proved that the debtor has not since the commencement of the action possessed or been able to earn the means of paying the sums due or such instalments thereof as are considered reasonable. The warrant may be granted of new at intervals of not less than six months in respect of failure to pay the same sums or sums afterwards accruing. Imprisonment does not extinguish the debt or interfere with other remedies. The creditor is not liable for the debtor's aliment;

(c) wilful refusal to comply with a decree *ad factum praestandum* the maximum period being six months.[65] Imprisonment does not operate to extinguish the obligation.

---

64 Civil Imprisonment (Scotland) Act 1882, s.4 (as to means, see Social Security Act 1975, s.87(3)).

65 Law Reform (Miscellaneous Provisions) (Scotland) Act 1940, s.1.

CHAPTER 18

SEQUESTRATION

1. The Process

"The principle of sequestration is that it is a process by which the whole property of a bankrupt person is ingathered by a trustee for the purpose of division *pari passu* among the creditors."[1]

To be sequestrated, the debtor must be subject to the jurisdiction of the supreme courts of Scotland and he must have at some time during the year before the date of presentation of the petition resided or had a dwelling-house or place of business in Scotland.[2] He must also be notour bankrupt.[2] Notour bankruptcy is constituted[3]:

(1) By sequestration, or by the issuing of an adjudication of bankruptcy or the granting of a receiving order in England or Ireland; or

(2) By insolvency, concurring:

(A)—(1) with a duly executed charge for payment, where a charge is necessary, followed by the expiry of the days of charge without payment;[4]

(2) where a charge is not necessary, with the lapse without payment of the days which must elapse before poinding or imprisonment can follow on a decree or warrant for payment of a sum of money;

(3) with a poinding or seizure of any of the debtor's moveables for non-payment of rates or taxes;

(4) with a decree of adjudication of any part of his heritable estate for payment or in security; or

(B) with a sale of any effects belonging to the debtor under a sequestration for rent.

Insolvency in this connection means inability to meet current

---

[1] *per* Lord Dunedin, *Caldwell* v. *Hamilton,* 1919 S.C.(H.L.)100 at 107.

[2] Bankruptcy (Scotland) Act 1913 (hereinafter "B.A."), s.11 as amended by Law Reform (Miscellaneous Provisions) (Scotland) Act 1980, s.12. The sequestration of the estate of a deceased debtor is dealt with elsewhere—see Chap. 26, para. 12.

[3] B.A., s.5.

[4] The withdrawal of the charge during its currency does not prevent the constitution of notour bankruptcy: *Brown & Co.* v. *Martin* (1888) 4 Sh.Ct.Rep.281.

obligations. The fact that the assets, if realised, would exceed the liabilities does not constitute solvency.[5]

The petition[6] must be at the instance or with the concurrence of one or more creditors whose debt or debts together amount to not less than £200. The debts may be liquid or illiquid provided they are not contingent.[7] A contingent debt is "a debt which has no existence now but will only emerge and become due upon the occurrence of some future event."[8] It means "only some element in the debt itself, and which covers only some 'contingency' arising, *ex facie,* upon the documents of debt, or which can be instantly verified."[9] The marking of an appeal after the expiry of a charge does not make the debt contingent.[9] Liability for future rent is not contingent.[10] The petition is presented in the Court of Session or in the sheriff court of any sheriffdom within which the debtor—

(*a*) resided or had a dwelling house or place of business at the date of the presentation of the petition for sequestration; or

(*b*) resided or carried on business for any period of forty or more days during the year before the said date.[11]

The petition must be lodged with the court office within four months of the date of notour bankruptcy.[12] Where sequestration is awarded in the Court of Session it is subsequently remitted to such sheriff court as is deemed expedient for further procedure.[13] With the petition there must be produced the creditor's oath with account and vouchers for his debt.[14] The oath to the verity of the debt must specify any co-obligants and any securities held by the creditor for the debt;[15] where the creditor is a corporation or firm the oath is

---

5 *Teenan's Tr.* v. *Teenan* (1886) 13 R.833; *Mackenzie* v. *Tod Brothers & Co. Ltd.*, 1912 1 S.L.T.464.

6 Where the debtor's assets do not exceed £4,000 in value a petition for summary sequestration is appropriate—see Chap. 21, para. 13.

7 s.12. The debtor may himself petition with the concurrence of creditors. He need not be notour bankrupt and sequestration will be awarded forthwith: s.28. He may have a duty to petition: *Sieber's Seqn.* (1894) 10 Sh.Ct.Rep.237.

8 *per* Lord Watson, *Fleming* v. *Yeaman* (1884) 9 A.C.966 at 976.

9 *British General Insurance Co.* v. *Borthwick* (1924) 40 Sh.Ct.Rep.198.

10 *Strathdee* v. *Paterson,* 1913 1 S.L.T.498.

11 s.16 as amended by Law Reform (Miscellaneous Provisions) (Scotland) Act 1980, s.127. For Court of Session procedure see McBryde, 1978 S.L.T.(News)265, 1979 S.L.T.(News)117; McBryde and Dowie, *Petition Procedure in the Court of Session,* pp.56-66.

12 s.13; *Burgh of Millport, Ptnrs.*, 1974 S.L.T.(Notes)23.

13 s.17. Notice of the remit in the *Gazette* is not necessary where there is only one award of sequestration: *West of Scotland Refractories Ltd.*, 1969 S.C.43.

14 s.20.

15 s.21.

sworn by a principal officer; and in the case of a firm by a partner; where the creditor is under age or otherwise *incapax* the oath is by his authorised agent, factor, guardian or manager.[16] The vouchers must afford such *prima facie* evidence of debt as is appropriate to its nature.[17] A document of debt should be produced for a loan. Where the debt runs into an account, an account and vouchers are necessary. If the debt is an open trading account, an account in the form of an extract from the creditor's books is sufficient provided that the items are specified.

On presentation of the petition the court makes the first deliverance granting warrant to cite the debtor[18] on an *induciae* of not less than six and not more than 14 days[19] and directing intimation of the warrant and diet of appearance in the *Edinburgh Gazette*.[19] The court also has power at this stage to grant diligence to recover evidence of notour bankruptcy[20] and to grant warrant to take possession of cash, bonds, bills and other moveables of the debtor and to open lockfast places and search premises;[21] and it may appoint a judicial factor or take other measures for the interim preservation of the estate.[22] The sequestration is held to commence and take effect on and from the date of this first deliverance which is held to be the date of sequestration even although sequestration is not awarded till a later date.[23] The petitioner must post before the expiry of the second lawful day after the first deliverance an abbreviate of the petition and deliverance to the Keeper of the Register of Inhibitions and Adjudications for recording.[24] The abbreviate when recorded has the effect from the date of the deliverance of an inhibition and a citation in an adjudication at the instance of the creditors afterwards ranked and this effect is not stopped by the debtor's paying the debts in respect of which sequestration was applied for.[24] If the petitioner withdraws, goes

---

16 s.24.

17 Goudy, p.172. The account must be specific: *Riddell* v. *Galbraith* (1896) 24 R.51.

18 s.25; if the petition is presented by or with the concurrence of the debtor sequestration is awarded forthwith: s.28.

19 s.27.

20 s.25.

21 s.15.

22 s.14.

23 s.41; *British General Insurance Co. Ltd.* v. *Borthwick* (1924) 40 Sh.Ct.Rep.198.

24 s.44; the effect expires in five years—see *Kippen's Tr.*, 1966 S.C.3.

bankrupt, or dies after presentation of the petition, any other creditor may be sisted in his place and follow out the proceedings.[25]

The debtor may appear at the next diet and show cause why sequestration cannot competently be awarded. If the statutory conditions are satisfied, however, the court has no discretion and is bound to award sequestration.[26] Consequently the valid grounds of objection are restricted to questions of jurisdiction and defects in the documents produced with the petition.[27] It is not an answer to state that the creditor has a security for his debt[28] or for the debtor to offer to prove his general solvency.[29] It is the practice to dispose of objections without proof and on *ex parte* statements.[30] The debtor may alternatively avoid sequestration by instantly paying the debt or debts in respect of which he was made bankrupt or by showing by written evidence that such debts and the debts of the petitioner and the other creditors appearing or concurring have been paid or satisfied.[31] In certain circumstances, consignation may be allowed instead of payment.[32] Interest on the debt must be paid or consigned but not the petitioner's expenses although these will be awarded against the debtor.[33] If the petition is dismissed because of payment of the debt the petitioner is awarded expenses unless the petition was unwarranted.[32] If the debtor does not appear at the diet or if he appears but does not advance a valid objection to the petition, the court, on production of evidence of citation and other requisites, makes an award of sequestration of the estates which then belong or shall thereafter belong to the debtor before the date of discharge and declares the estates to belong to the creditors for the purposes of the Bankruptcy Act.[34] In the same deliverance the court appoints a creditors' meeting at a specified day and time not less than six or more than 12 days from the date of appearance in the *Edinburgh Gazette* of a notice of award of sequestration for the purpose of, *inter alia*, electing a trustee.[35] The court may also take measures for

---

25 s.33.

26 s.28; *Joel* v. *Gill* (1859) 21 D.929; *Stuart & Stuart* v. *Macleod* (1891) 19 R.223.

27 *Riddell* v. *Galbraith* (1896) 24 R.51.

28 Maclaren, *Bill Chamber Practice*, p.258.

29 *Scottish Milk Marketing Board* v. *Wood*, 1936 S.C.604.

30 *Scottish Milk Marketing Board* v. *Wood*, *supra*, *per* L.P. Normand at p.611.

31 s.29.

32 *Laird* v. *Scott*, 1914 1 S.L.T.368; *McCumiskey Bros.* v. *MacLaine*, 1922 S.L.T.104; *Elliot & Stuart* v. *McDougall*, 1956 S.C.241.

33 *McCumiskey Bros.* v. *MacLaine*, (O.H.) 1922 S.L.T.104.

34 ss.28, 29.

35 s.63; see *Law Society of Scotland, Ptnrs.*, 1974 S.L.T.(Notes)66.

the safe custody of the bankrupt's books and papers and for the locking up of his repositories.[36]

Section 29, under which sequestration is awarded, is purely declaratory and not operative; it in effect declares that the debtor holds his property as trustee for his creditors until a trustee in the sequestration is appointed; the operative sections are 97 and 98 under which the Act and Warrant vests the property in the trustee in the sequestration.[37]

The petitioner must, within four days of an award in the Court of Session, or, in other cases, within four days after a copy of the deliverance could be received in course of post in Edinburgh, insert a notice[38] in the *Edinburgh Gazette* and within six days a similar notice in the *London Gazette*.[39]

The petitioning and concurring creditors are entitled to the expenses incurred in obtaining the sequestration and in doing the other acts required prior to the election of the trustee from the trustee out of the first of the funds which shall come into his hands.[40]

2. Conspectus of Further Procedure

The meeting of creditors appointed by the court elects a trustee, fixes the amount of caution to be found by him and elects three commissioners to advise him in the conduct of the sequestration.[41] Creditors are qualified to vote at the meeting by production of a notice of claim, account and vouchers;[42] a postponed creditor has no vote;[43] questions are generally decided by a majority in value of those present and entitled to vote. The preses reports the proceedings to the sheriff who then declares the person elected to be trustee. On the bond of caution being lodged, the election is confirmed and the sheriff clerk issues to the trustee an Act and Warrant which is an effectual title to the trustee to perform his duties and

---

36 s.15.

37 *Caldwell* v. *Hamilton*, 1919 S.C.(H.L.)100, *per* Lord Dunedin at p.107.

38 Sched. B.

39 s.44.

40 s.40.

41 ss.64, 69 and 72. If the creditors fail to elect a trustee, a petition to the *nobile officium* to fix another meeting is necessary: *Gilbey Ltd.* v. *Franchitti*, 1969 S.L.T. (Notes) 18. As to the bankrupt's discharge where no creditors attend the meeting, see *Fraser* v. *Glasgow Corporation*, 1967 S.C.120.

42 s.45; see *Whitelaw's Seqn.* (1917) 33 Sh.Ct.Rep.253.

43 *Crann & Co.'s Seqn.* (1909) 25 Sh.Ct.Rep.238.

evidence of his right and title to the sequestrated estate.[44] The trustee then proceeds to take possession of the estate and convert it into money.[45] On application by the trustee to the sheriff, a date is appointed for the examination of the bankrupt and, if desired, of his wife, family and servants.[46] The trustee thereafter prepares a report on the state of the bankrupt's affairs and presents it to another meeting of creditors.[47] When the estate has been reduced into money, the trustee, after paying all necessary charges, divides it among the creditors of the bankrupt at the date of sequestration ranked according to their several rights and interests.[48] If, after payment of the debt with interest and of the charges of recovering and distributing the estate, there is a surplus of the estate and effects, it is paid to the bankrupt or to his successors or assignees.[49] The trustee eventually applies for his discharge.

If additional estate emerges after the trustee's discharge a commissioner or creditor can apply to the court for an order to hold a meeting to elect a new trustee;[50] if both the trustee and the bankrupt have been discharged, a petition to the *nobile officium* is necessary.[51]

3. Recall of Sequestration

The deliverance awarding sequestration is not subject to review but within 40 days of the award the debtor or any creditor can petition the Court of Session for recall of the sequestration.[52] The petition is served on the creditor who petitioned for sequestration and any concurring creditors. Answers must be lodged within a specified time. Notice of the recall petition must be given in the *Edinburgh Gazette*. The presentation of the petition does not stay the sequestration proceedings.[53]

---

44 s.70. The bankrupt may have to resort to the *nobile officium* if the trustee fails to lodge the bond of caution (*Black, Ptnr.*, 1964 S.C.276) or if the sheriff refuses to confirm the election: *Aitken* v. *Robson*, 1914 S.C.224; *Laings, Ptnrs.*, 1962 S.C.168.

45 ss.76-78.

46 s.83. "The whole scope of those sections is to trace property which the bankrupt may otherwise have concealed": *Jacks' Tr.* v. *Jacks' Trs.*, 1910 S.C.34.

47 s.92.

48 s.117.

49 s.155.

50 s.71.

51 *Cockburn's Trs.*, 1941 S.C.187.

52 s.30.

53 s.32.

The grounds of recall are those which were, or might have been, stated to oppose the petition for sequestration.[54] The most important are:

(a) Defects in the proceedings. If the defect appears *ex facie* of the proceedings—for example, if the account produced by a concurring creditor was not sufficiently specific in its terms[55]—the court must recall the sequestration. If the defect is latent—for example, if the petitioning creditor's affidavit was invalid because the granter had not been put on oath[56]—the granting of the petition for recall is in the discretion of the court.[57] The matters to be considered in the exercise of this discretion are whether the defect was substantial, whether the irregularity was due to the fraud of the petitioning creditor, whether creditors not responsible for the irregularity would be prejudiced by recall and whether the bankrupt suffered prejudice because of the irregularity.[58] Where the defect is latent a creditor who has taken part in the sequestration proceedings may be barred by acquiescence if he petitions for recall.[59]

(b) Solvency: The court has a discretion to recall the sequestration if the bankrupt shows that he was at the time of the award in a position to meet his current obligations,[60] but the court can take into account the bankrupt's situation at the date of the hearing for recall.[61]

(c) That the debt founded on by the petitioning creditor was not due. The court's power is again discretionary,[62] but will not normally be exercised if no steps have been taken to reduce the decree for the debt.[61]

(d) That the award of sequestration was obtained by fraud or an unfair use of process.[63]

Considerations of equity and expediency are not grounds for recall.[64]

---

54 *Menzies* v. *Poutz,* 1916 S.C.143.
55 *Riddell* v. *Galbraith* (1896) 24 R.51.
56 *Blair* v. *North British and Mercantile Insurance Co.* (1889) 16 R.325.
57 *Ballantyne* v. *Barr* (1867) 5 M.330; *Mitchell* v. *Motherwell* (1888) 16 R.122.
58 *Nakeski-Cumming* v. *Gordon,* 1924 S.C.217.
59 *Ure* v. *McCubbin* (1857) 19 D.758; *Tennent* v. *Martin & Dunlop* (1879) 6 R.786.
60 *Aitken* v. *Kyd* (1890) 28 S.L.R.115; *Michie* v. *Young,* 1962 S.L.T.(Notes)70.
61 *Murdoch* v. *Newman Industrial Control Ltd.*, 1980 S.L.T.13.
62 *Pert* v. *Bruce,* 1937 S.L.T.475.
63 *Joel* v. *Gill* (1859) 22 D.6; *Gardner* v. *Woodside* (1862) 24 D.1133.
64 *Joel* v. *Gill, supra.*

Even after the expiry of the 40 days nine-tenths in number and value of the creditors ranked on the estate may apply to the Court of Session for recall of the sequestration.[65] The onus is on those opposing this application to show why it should not be granted.[66]

Within three months of the date of sequestration, the Accountant of Court or any creditor or other person having interest may petition for recall on the ground that a majority of the creditors in number and value reside in England or Ireland and that from the situation of the bankrupt's property or other causes his estate ought to be distributed among the creditors under the laws of England or Northern Ireland. The court, after such inquiry as to them shall seem fit may recall the sequestration.[67]

4. The Bankrupt

The effect of the award of sequestration is that all payments and preferences or securities obtained by or granted to prior creditors and all acts done and deeds granted by the bankrupt after the date of sequestration and before his discharge out of or in relation to his estate (unless with the consent of the trustee) are null and void,[68] and the trustee can recover the sums paid or property transferred under deduction of expenses bona fide incurred but: (a) if a bona fide purchaser is in possession of moveable effects which he recêived after the sequestration and in ignorance thereof for a price which he has paid or is ready to pay, he is not obliged to restore them; (b) if a debtor has, in ignorance of the sequestration, paid the debt bona fide to the bankrupt, he is not obliged to pay a second time to the trustee; (c) the possessor of a bill or promissory note payable by the bankrupt with recourse on other persons or the holder of a security for a debt due by the bankrupt who has received payment in ignorance of the sequestration and has given up the bill, promissory note or security to the bankrupt is not liable to repay the sum received to the trustee unless he is replaced in the situation in which he stood before or is reimbursed for any loss or damage. The bankrupt may carry on business after sequestration,[69] but it is a criminal offence if he obtains credit to the extent of £50 or more from any person without informing him that he is an undischarged

---

65 s.31; *Craig & Co. Ltd.*, 1946 S.C.19 (where creditors had not been ranked).

66 *Livingstone's Crs.* v. *Livingstone's Tr.*, 1937 S.L.T.391.

67 s.43.

68 s.107.

69 Goudy, p.359.

bankrupt.[70] The profits of the business will be available to the trustee. The assets of the business are available for the diligence of the creditors of the business.[71] The trustee cannot, after a long interval, claim them as *acquirenda*.[72] If the bankrupt earns wages they cannot be arrested by a prior creditor.[73] The bankrupt cannot insist in any action raised by him which the trustee wishes to take up unless it is of a personal character.[74] An action may be brought against the bankrupt but it is not *res judicata* in a question with the trustee.[75] The creditors may grant an allowance to the bankrupt during the course of the sequestration.[76] The bankrupt has right to any property abandoned by his creditors[77] and to the surplus of his estate after the creditors have been paid in full with interest and the expenses of sequestration have been met.[78] An undischarged bankrupt is disqualified from holding certain public offices[79] and cannot be a company director without the consent of the court.[80] Certain criminal offences may arise out of the bankrupt's conduct before and during the sequestration.[81] A bankrupt who raises an action may be required to find caution for expenses.[82] A bankrupt defender is not normally required to find caution.[83]

5. Bankrupt's Discharge

The bankrupt may apply to the court for his discharge after the creditors' meeting following his examination if all the creditors concur; after six months from the date of sequestration if four-fifths of the creditors in value concur; after 12 months, if two-thirds concur; after 18 months, if a majority concur; and after two years

---

70 s.182. The section applies only to a person rendered bankrupt in Scotland: *Kaye* v. *H.M. Advocate,* 1957 J.C.55.

71 *Abel* v. *Watt* (1883) 11 R.149.

72 *M. P. Thomas* v. *Baird* (1897) 13 Sh.Ct.Rep.291.

73 *Gomm* v. *McKellar* (1895) 11 Sh.Ct.Rep.97; *Parish Council of Glasgow* v. *Steel Co. of Scotland* (1908) 24 Sh.Ct.Rep.37; *cf. Duff* v. *Gilmour* (1902) 18 Sh.Ct.Rep.198.

74 Goudy, p.364.

75 Goudy, p.372.

76 s.74; Goudy, p.360.

77 Goudy, p.371.

78 s.155.

79 ss.183-4.

80 Companies Act 1948, s.187.

81 B.A., s.178.

82 *Weepers* v. *Pearson and Jackson* (1859) 21 D.305; *Maltman* v. *Tarmac Civil Engineering Ltd.,* 1967 S.L.T.(Notes)102.

83 *Mackay* v. *Boswall-Preston,* 1916 S.C.96.

without the concurrence of his creditors. Before the application the trustee must prepare a report with regard to the conduct of the bankrupt, and as to how far he has complied with the provisions of the Bankruptcy Act and, in particular, whether the bankrupt has made a fair discovery and surrender of his estate and whether he has been guilty of collusion and whether the bankruptcy arose from "innocent misfortunes or losses in business, or from culpable or undue conduct." The report is not demandable from the trustee till five months after the deliverance awarding sequestration. The court may hear objections and may grant, refuse, or defer consideration of, the application or may annex to the discharge such conditions as the justice of the case may require.[84] The matters dealt with in the trustee's report suggest relevant grounds of objection. When two years have elapsed since the sequestration, the onus is on the creditors to show cause why discharge should be refused.[85] Objections by only one of a large body of creditors must be closely scrutinised.[86] Even if there are no objections, the application may be refused if the bankrupt has fraudulently concealed any part of his estate or has wilfully failed to comply with the Bankruptcy Act.[87] Discharge will not be granted on payment of a dividend if the bankrupt has funds which will enable him to make payment in full.[88] Moreover, if a dividend of at least 25p in the pound has not been paid, the bankrupt is not entitled to his discharge unless his failure to pay such a dividend has, in the opinion of the court, "arisen from circumstances for which the bankrupt cannot justly be held responsible."[89] The onus is on the bankrupt. He must establish the circumstances of the failure and show that he is not responsible therefor.[90] This may be done, for example, by showing that the deficiency was caused by the trustee's maladministration or that it was due to the trustee's method of administration, however prudent

---

84 s.143; see *Millar* (1877) 5 R.144; *Mackenzie* v. *Keith* (1925) 41 Sh.Ct.Rep.340; *Down's Seqn.* (1927) 43 Sh.Ct.Rep.282.

85 *Wilson's Seqn.* (1916) 32 Sh.Ct.Rep.148.

86 *Alexander's Seqn.* (1918) 34 Sh.Ct.Rep.277.

87 s.149.

88 *Hurst* v. *Beveridge* (1900) 2 F.702.

89 s.146.

90 *Greer, Applicant,* 1960 S.L.T.(Sh.Ct.)13; a discharge can be granted even although the funds were insufficient to meet the fees and outlays of the trustee: *Spark, Ptnr.*, 1974 S.L.T.(Sh.Ct.)10; see also *Clarke* v. *Crockatt & Co.* (1883) 11 R.246; *Shand* (1882) 19 S.L.R.562; *Boyle* (1885) 22 S.L.R.767; *Bell* v. *Bell's Tr.*, 1908 S.C.853; *Evans' Seqn.*, 1925 S.L.T.(Sh.Ct.)43.

it appeared at the time.[91] It seems that refusal is obligatory only where the failure has arisen wholly or mainly from the bankrupt's fault. If the bankrupt's negligence or imprudence contributed to the failure, but other causes have contributed to a greater degree, the discharge may be granted.[92]

After the court has found him entitled to his discharge, the bankrupt must make a declaration that he has made a full and fair surrender of his estate, that he has not granted or promised any security nor made or promised any payment nor entered any agreement or transaction to obtain the concurrence of any creditor in the discharge.[93] The court then pronounces a deliverance discharging the bankrupt of all debts and obligations contracted by him or for which he was liable at the date of sequestration.[93]

The discharge covers debts present, future or contingent "in every imaginable shape"[94] but not aliment accruing after the date of sequestration, even where the obligation has been reduced to writing.[95] It does cover the personal obligation under a feu or contract of ground annual.[96] The bankrupt may remain liable for the debts of a firm of which he was a partner where his interest in the firm was not affected by the sequestration.[97]

The discharge does not justify the removal of the bankrupt's name from a register of shareholders where the shares were only partly paid up.[98] The discharge does not cover Crown debts unless the Treasury consents.[99]

The discharge covers debts contracted in England or Northern Ireland and is a bar to recovery in these jurisdictions.[1]

---

91 *Inglis, Ptnr.*, 1937 S.L.T.619. Slumps in trade or catastrophes may provide excuse: *Cohen* (1944) 60 Sh.Ct.Rep.59. Reckless trading is fault: *Reid & Sons* (1939) 55 Sh.Ct.Rep.287. See also *McColl's Seqn.* (1913) 29 Sh.Ct.Rep.278; *Wilson's Seqn., supra; Alexander's Seqn., supra; Marwick* (1926) 42 Sh.Ct.Rep.53 (no estate — one debt).

92 *Shand* (1882) 19 S.L.R.562. See also *Bremner* (1900) 2 F.1114.

93 s.144.

94 Bell, *Comm.*, II, 372.

95 *Marjoribanks* v. *Amos* (1831) 10 S.79.

96 *Anderson* v. *Buchanan* (1894) 10 Sh.Ct.Rep.31; *Shaw* v. *Emery* (1908) 24 Sh.Ct.Rep.333.

97 *Woolley & Son* v. *Mason* (1894) 10 Sh.Ct.Rep.210.

98 *Taylor* v. *Union Heritable Securities Co. Ltd.* (1889) 16 R.711.

99 s.147.

1 ss.137, 144; *Sidaway* v. *Hay* (1824) 3 B. & C. 12; *Re Nelson* [1918] 1 K.B.459; Anton, *Private International Law* (1967), p.443; Cheshire & North, *Private International Law* (10th ed., 1979), p.570; Williams and Muir Hunter, *Bankruptcy* (19th ed., 1979), p.144.

6. Death of Bankrupt

There is provision for a discharge of all debts and the vesting of the estates in the personal representatives of the bankrupt where there has been a composition but the case of the deceased bankrupt is not covered by the fasciculus of sections (143-149) of the Act of 1913 dealing with discharges without composition. However, where creditors had been paid in full the Lord Ordinary discharged the representatives and estate of the bankrupt, declared the sequestration at an end and declared the representatives entitled to obtain themselves invested in the estate.[2]

---

[2] *Gray's Exrs.*, 1928 S.L.T.558.

CHAPTER 19

SEQUESTRATION: THE ESTATE

1. Vesting in Trustee

The Act and Warrant transfers to and vests in the trustee *ipso jure* absolutely and irredeemably as at the date of sequestration the moveable estate and effects of the bankrupt wherever situated so far as attachable for debt or capable of voluntary alienation by the bankrupt to the same effect as if actual delivery or possession had been obtained or intimation made at that date and the heritable estate as if a decree of adjudication in implement of sale as well as a decree of adjudication for payment and in security of debt subject to no legal reversion had been pronounced in favour of the trustee and recorded as at the date of sequestration.[1] "A bankrupt may have had property scattered in his own name all over the world. But the sequestration vests it all in the trustee."[2]

2. Trust Property

Property held by the bankrupt on trust does not pass to the trustee. This is so even where heritage is held on an unqualified feudal title subject to a latent trust.[3] A trust obligation must, however, be distinguished from a mere liability created by personal contract.[4] Trust property cannot be recovered if it has been so mixed with the bankrupt's own funds as to be indistinguishable.[5] The fact that shares have been pledged with other securities under a general letter of hypothecation does not make them unidentifiable.[6]

The terms of a building contract may be such that payments made by the employer to the principal contractor in respect of work done by a sub-contractor are held in trust by the principal contractor.[7]

---

[1] B.A., s.97.

[2] *Per* Lord Cockburn, *Adam* v. *McRobbie* (1845) 7 D.276 at 282.

[3] *Heritable Reversionary Co.* v. *Millar* (1892) 19 R.(H.L.)43.

[4] *Bank of Scotland* v. *Liquidators of Hutchison Main & Co. Ltd.*, 1914 S.C. (H.L.)1. See also *Export Credits Guarantee Department* v. *Turner*, 1981 S.L.T. 286; *Clark Taylor and Co. Ltd.* v. *Quality Site Development (Edinburgh) Ltd.* (First Division, 8 January 1981, unreported).

[5] Goudy, p.289. As to a solicitor's client bank account, see Solicitors (Scotland) Act 1980, s.42.

[6] *Newton's Exix.* v. *Meiklejohn's J.F.*, 1959 S.L.T.71.

[7] *Tout and Finch Ltd.* [1954] 1 All E.R. 127; *Veitchi Co.* v. *Crowley Russell & Co.*, 1972 S.C.225; *Dunbarton C.C.* v. *George W. Sellars & Sons Ltd.*, 1973 S.L.T. (Sh.Ct.)67.

Money representing the price of goods sent in with an order may be treated by the recipient in such a way as to create a trust of it, *e.g.* by putting it into a bank account denominated as a trust account.[8]

3. Ex facie Absolute Disposition

Property held by the bankrupt on a disposition *ex facie* absolute but truly in security does not vest in the trustee.[9]

4. Special Appropriation

Property which has been lodged with the bankrupt for a specific purpose does not pass to the trustee if it can be identified in the bankrupt's hands.[10] If the bankrupt has mixed the deposited funds with his own in a bank account and has later made a withdrawal, he is presumed to have withdrawn his own funds.[11]

5. Acquisitions by Fraud

The trustee cannot take advantage of the bankrupt's fraud and property acquired by fraud can be recovered if it can be identified.[12]

6. Corporeal Moveables

Corporeal moveables vest in the trustee as if possession had been obtained at the date of sequestration.[13] The necessary wearing apparel of the bankrupt, his wife and family and the bankrupt's tools do not vest in the trustee.[14] What is a tool is a question of fact.[15]

7. Sales of Goods

Where the bankrupt has in his possession goods which he has bought but not paid for, the disposal of the goods depends largely on whether the property has passed.[16] If the property had not passed

---

8 *Re Kayford Ltd.* [1975] 1 W.L.R.279.

9 *Heritable Reversionary Co.* v. *Millar, supra; Forbes' Trs.* v. *Macleod* (1898) 25 R.1012.

10 *Macadam* v. *Martin's Tr.* (1872) 11 M.33.

11 *Jopp* v. *Johnston's Tr.* (1904) 6 F.1028; but see *Hofford* v. *Gowans,* 1909 1 S.L.T.153.

12 *Colquhouns' Tr.* v. *Campbell's Trs.* (1902) 4 F.739.

13 s.97.

14 *Gassiot,* 12 Nov. 1814, F.C.

15 *Macpherson* v. *Macpherson's Tr.* (1905) 8 F.191. See also *Pennell* v. *Elgin,* 1926 S.C.9, Chap. 15, para. 4, Chap. 16, para. 4.

16 For the rules as to passing of property, see Sale of Goods Act 1979, ss.16-19.

to the bankrupt, the seller can recover them.[17] If there is an appropriate clause in the contract the seller may be able to recover the proceeds of a sub-sale of the goods if they can be identified.[18] If the property has passed he cannot recover the goods,[19] except, possibly, where the buyer induced the contract of sale by fraudulent representations as to his solvency and the seller has raised an action of rescission prior to the sequestration;[20] or where the buyer fraudulently took delivery on the eve of sequestration or after the presentation of the sequestration petition; but mere knowledge of insolvency does not constitute fraud.[21] If the buyer before sequestration rejected the goods the seller can recover them.[22] If the goods are not in the bankrupt's possession at the sequestration the seller can exercise his rights of lien[23] or stoppage *in transitu*[24] if the property has passed or his co-extensive right of withholding delivery if the property has not passed.[25]

Where the bankrupt has sold goods and received payment of the price the buyer can recover the goods if the property has passed to him[26] unless the transaction was in substance a security in the form of a sale.[27]

In the case of goods on hire-purchase the goods do not pass to the hirer's trustee.[28] If the goods were originally owned by the bankrupt and the hire-purchase transaction was preceded by a purported sale, the transaction may be struck at by s.62(4) of the Sale of Goods Act 1979.[29]

If goods have been let on hire-purchase by the bankrupt, the trustee acquires the property in the goods and the right to receive

---

17 *Ross & Co.* v. *Plano Manufacturing Co.* (1903) 11 S.L.T.7 (sale or return).

18 See Chap. 2, para. 3.

19 *London Scottish Transport Ltd.* v. *Tyres (Scotland) Ltd.*, 1957 S.L.T. (Sh.Ct.)48.

20 *A. W. Gamage Ltd.* v. *Charlesworth's Tr.*, 1910 S.C.257. The many reservations in the opinions should be noted.

21 Goudy, p.281; *Allan* v. *Murray* (1894) 10 Sh.Ct.Rep.103; *Primrose's Seqn.* (1894) 10 Sh.Ct.Rep.238.

22 Goudy, p.281; and see *Nelson* v. *Chalmers & Co. Ltd.*, 1913 S.C.441.

23 ss.41-43; *Paton's Trs.* v. *Finlayson*, 1923 S.C.872.

24 ss.44-46.

25 s.39(2).

26 *Hayman & Son* v. *McLintock*, 1907 S.C.936.

27 See Chap. 7, para. 3.

28 *Murdoch & Co. Ltd.* v. *Greig* (1889) 16 R.396; *McLaren's Tr.* v. *Argylls Ltd.*, 1915 2 S.L.T.241.

29 *Newbigging* v. *Ritchie's Tr.*, 1930 S.C.273; *Scottish Transit Trust* v. *Scottish Land Cultivators*, 1955 S.C.254; *G. & C. Finance Corporation Ltd.* v. *Brown*, 1961 S.L.T.408.

payments under the contract. It is thought that the trustee cannot prevent the hirer completing the contract and obtaining property in the goods.[30]

Corporeal moveables vest in the trustee subject to such preferable securities as existed at the date of sequestration and are not null and reducible.[31]

8. Incorporeal Moveables

Incorporeal moveable property vests in the trustee as if intimation had been made at the date of sequestration.[32] So where a life insurance policy was assigned for value but the assignation not intimated to the insurance company before the cedent's sequestration, the trustee had a right to the policy preferable to that of the assignee;[33] the result was the same where the unintimated assignation was of a trust fund.[34] A bank draft in favour of a creditor which is still in the bankrupt's possession falls to the trustee.[35]

Alimentary Provisions: Alimentary provisions to the bankrupt made by a deed of a third party do not vest in the trustee,[36] but the court may determine whether the amount is in excess of suitable aliment to the bankrupt in view of his existing circumstances and, if it is so determined, order the excess to be paid to the trustee.[37] The trustee in the sequestration has a direct right of action against the trustees holding the alimentary fund. The *excessum* must be declared by the court.[38] The trustee has no right to claim on behalf of alimentary creditors.[39]

9. State Pensions

Certain state pensions, by statute, do not vest in the trustee, *e.g.* pensions under the Police Pensions Act 1976, social security

---

30 Gow, *Law of Hire-Purchase,* 2nd ed., p.223.

31 s.97. See, as to ships, n.49, *infra*.

32 s.97.

33 *Wood* v. *Weir* (1900) 16 Sh.Ct.Rep.356.

34 *Tod's Trs.* v. *Wilson* (1869) 7 M.1100 (but see *Watson* v. *Duncan* (1879) 6 R. 1247, *per* Lord Deas at p.1252).

35 *Brown* v. *Hunter-Arundell's Trs.* (1899) 15 Sh.Ct.Rep.281.

36 Bell, *Comm.,* I, 125.

37 s.98(2); *Caldwell* v. *Hamilton,* 1919 S.C.(H.L.)100, *per* Lord Dunedin at p.110; *Inglis's Tr.* v. *Inglis,* 1924 S.C.226.

38 *Wilson* v. *Shaw* (1926) 42 Sh.Ct.Rep.133, 165. See also *Simmers* v. *Ballantyne's Trs.* (1924) 40 Sh.Ct.Rep.283.

39 *Corbet* v. *Waddell* (1879) 7 R.200.

benefits and supplementary benefit.[40] They may, however, be treated as alimentary provisions so that any excess is recoverable by the trustee.[41]

10. Rights of Action

The trustee has a title to sue for patrimonial loss suffered by the bankrupt's estate but he cannot raise an action to recover *solatium* for personal injuries suffered by the bankrupt because the claim, being personal in character, does not transmit to him.[42] Where the bankrupt has raised an action, however, the trustee can have himself sisted as pursuer and acquire for the creditors any sum recovered.[43] But if he is unsuccessful he will be personally liable for the expenses before, as well as after, the sist.[44] Once decree has been granted in an action by the bankrupt for *solatium* in respect of an injury sustained after the sequestration, the trustee can apply for a vesting order to obtain the damages for the creditors.[45]

11. Rights against Insurers

Where the bankrupt is insured against liabilities to third parties which he may incur and such a liability is incurred before or after sequestration, his rights against the insurer are transferred to the third party.[46]

The proceeds of a claim under a personal accident policy are *acquirenda* but the bankrupt has a right to be indemnified co-extensive with the amount of the proceeds.[47]

12. Building Contracts

Where a building contract provided that the principal contractor could not obtain an architect's certificate for payment until he had paid the sums due to sub-contractors under previous certificates, it was held that on the liquidation of the principal contractor the provision was still operative.[48]

---

40 Social Security Act 1975, s.87(1); Supplementary Benefits Act 1976, s.16.

41 *Macdonald's Tr.* v. *Macdonald*, 1938 S.C.536. See also s.148.

42 *Muir's Tr.* v. *Braidwood*, 1958 S.C.169.

43 *Thom* v. *Bridges* (1857) 19 D.721.

44 *Torbet* v. *Borthwick* (1849) 11 D.694.

45 *Jackson* v. *McKechnie* (1875) 3 R.130.

46 Third Parties (Rights against Insurers) Act 1930, s.1.

47 *Railway Passengers' Assurance Co.* v. *Kyd* (1894) 10 Sh.Ct.Rep.138.

48 *Veitchi Co.* v. *Crowley Russell & Co.*, 1972 S.C.225. As to contracts in general, see *Anderson* v. *Hamilton & Co.* (1875) 2 R.355; *Asphaltic Limestone Co. Ltd.* v. *Glasgow Corporation*, 1907 S.C.463; *Sturrock* v. *Robertson's Tr.*, 1913 S.C.582.

13. Registered Titles

Where property is held on a registered title (*e.g.* shares in a limited company), the Act and Warrant does not confer a real right on the trustee as at the date of sequestration and his title is not complete until he is placed on the register. An assignee whose transfer was granted before and registered after the date of sequestration but before registration of the trustee's title is preferred.[49] The rule applies not only to shares, but also to heritage, ships, patents, copyrights and trade-marks.[50]

14. Copyrights

Where the estate includes a copyright or an interest therein and the bankrupt was liable to pay the author royalties or a share of profits, the trustee cannot utilise the copyright in any way without making such payments in the same way and he cannot assign the right or transfer the interest except upon terms securing to the author payments at the same rate.[51]

15. Spes successionis

A non-vested contingent right of succession in favour of the bankrupt under a will or marriage contract vests in the trustee as if an assignation by the bankrupt had been intimated at the date of sequestration.[52]

16. Heritage

Heritage vests in the trustee at the date of sequestration but the holder of an unrecorded disposition or security deed is preferred to the trustee if he records his deed first.[53]

---

[49] *Morrison* v. *Harrison* (1876) 3 R.406.

[50] Goudy, p.254. There is more than one principle underlying this rule. In the case of shares, the rationale is that the bilateral character of membership of a company which involves both rights and liabilities requires entry on the register to complete the transfer (see the opinions in *Morrison*); in the case of heritage the reason is to give heritable creditors a reasonable time in which to complete their securities (see Bell, *Comm.*, II, 33).

[51] B.A., s.102.

[52] s.97(4).

[53] Bell, *Comm.*, II, 338; *Cormack* v. *Anderson* (1829) 7 S.868; *Melville* v. *Paterson* (1842) 4 D.1311, *per* Lord Ivory at p.1315; *Smith* v. *Frier* (1857) 19 D.384; Bell, *Lectures on Conveyancing*, 3rd ed., p.812; Craigie, *Scottish Law of Conveyancing: Heritable Rights*, 3rd ed., p.514; Wallace, *Bankruptcy*, 2nd ed., p.238; Burns, *Conveyancing Practice*, 4th ed., p.409.

Where the bankrupt has concluded missives for the sale of heritage, has received payment of the price and has given possession to the purchaser, but no disposition has been granted prior to sequestration, the subjects pass to the trustee, the purchaser having only a *jus crediti* and not a real right.[54]

The trustee can have the bankrupt ejected from the heritable property.[55] When the bankrupt has constituted a security over the subjects by *ex facie* absolute disposition the trustee acquires the right to redeem the property, and is entitled to an accounting.[56]

17. Property of the Bankrupt's Wife

A wife's property is not in general liable for her husband's debts provided that the moveable estate is placed in her name or otherwise distinguished except in the case of such corporeal moveables as are usually possessed without a written title.[57] However, any money or estate lent or entrusted to the husband, or inmixed with his funds, is treated as assets of the husband subject to the wife's postponed claim in the sequestration.[58] The wife's executor or assignee has no higher right than the wife[59]; a security to the wife is not affected.[60] A woman, who on marriage, brings her furniture to furnish the matrimonial home does not thereby lend or entrust it to the husband.[61] A husband may deliver furniture to his wife by taking her to live with him in the house where the furniture is or by bringing furniture to the matrimonial home.[62]

Contributions made by children towards a fund for the maintenance of the household administered by the wife are nevertheless the husband's property.[63]

---

54 *Gibson and Hunter Home Designs Ltd.*, 1976 S.C.23. See *Napier and Ettrick's Tr.* v. *De Saumarez* (1900) 2 F.882, *per* Lord McLaren at p.886.

55 *White* v. *Stevenson*, 1956 S.C.84.

56 *Hay's Tr.* v. *Davidson* (1853) 15 D.583.

57 Married Women's Property (Scotland) Act 1881, s.1(3).

58 *ibid.*, s.1(4); *National Bank* v. *Cowan* (1893) 21 R.4.

59 *Mitchell's Exor.* v. *Mitchell's Tr.*, 1908 S.C.1046; *Cochrane* v. *Lamont's Tr.* (1891) 18 R.451.

60 *Commercial Bank* v. *Wilson*, 1909 1 S.L.T.273.

61 *Adam* v. *Adam's Tr.* (1894) 21 R.676. *Cf. Anderson* v. *Anderson's Tr.* (1892) 19 R.684.

62 *Mitchell's Trs.* v. *Gladstone* (1894) 21 R.586; *Rubin* v. *Walker* (1929) 45 Sh.Ct.Rep.109.

63 *Smith* v. *Smith*, 1933 S.C.701.

18. Acquirenda

Estate which is acquired by or reverts or descends to the bankrupt after his sequestration and before his discharge *ipso jure* falls under the sequestration and is transferred to and vested in the trustee as at the date of acquisition or succession.[64] The trustee, on learning of the acquisition, must present a petition to the court for a declaration of vesting.[65] Until this is done, the *acquirenda* remain open to the diligence of creditors whose debts have been incurred after the sequestration. The trustee takes every interest *tantum et tale* as it stood in the bankrupt, *i.e.* s.98 places the trustee in the same position regarding property subsequently coming to the bankrupt as s.97 does as to the property belonging to him at the date of sequestration.[66]

19. Earnings

The bankrupt cannot be forced to work for the benefit of his creditors but, if he is employed, the instalments of salary as they accrue vest in the trustee as *acquirenda* in so far as they exceed the *beneficium competentiae*—what is reasonably required for the bankrupt's maintenance. The needs and resources of the bankrupt's wife must be taken into account.[67] The court can pronounce an order under s.98(1) of the Act of 1913 for payment to the trustee of the instalments receivable *in futuro* under reservation to the trustee, the bankrupt or any other persons interested of the right to apply to the court in the event of a change of circumstances.[68]

20. Property in England

Personal estate in England vests in the trustee as "moveable estate . . . wherever situated." Real estate in England is vested in the trustee to the same extent as if the bankrupt had been adjudicated bankrupt in England.[69] The Act and Warrant must be registered in the English court. The orders of the Scottish court have to be enforced in England and the English courts have to act in aid of the orders of the Scottish court.[70]

---

64 B.A., s.98(1); *Taylor* v. *Charteris and Andrew* (1879) 7 R.128.

65 *Grant* v. *Green's Tr.* (1901) 3 F.1016.

66 *Lord Napier's Tr.* v. *Lord de Saumarez* (1899) 1 F.614.

67 *Birrell's Tr.* v. *Birrell,* 1957 S.L.T.(Sh.Ct.) 6; *A. M. Cochran's Tr.* v. *Cochran* (1958) 74 Sh.Ct.Rep.75.

68 *Caldwell* v. *Hamilton,* 1919 S.C.(H.L.)100.

69 B.A., s.97(3).

70 Bankruptcy Act 1914, ss.121, 122.

A sequestration does not affect a prior garnishee order attaching the bankrupt's property in England; s.104 of the Scottish Act has no effect in England and the English doctrine of relation back applies only in an English bankruptcy.[71]

---

[71] *Galbraith* v. *Grimshaw* [1910] A.C.508. Anton (*Private International Law*, p.442) suggests that the position may be changed by s.122 of the Bankruptcy Act 1914, which would allow the English court in response to a request from the Scottish court to exercise such jurisdiction as it could exercise within its own jurisdiction or such jurisdiction as the Scottish court could exercise. However, it can be argued that both s.104 of the 1913 Act and s.40 of the 1914 Act (which restricts the rights of creditors on the making of a receiving order) do more than confer jurisdiction. Section 122 of the 1914 Act is a re-enactment of s.118 of the Bankruptcy Act 1883. In *Singer & Co.* v. *Fry* (1915) 113 L.T.552, it was held that an English receivership order affecting real estate in England was not affected by a sequestration. That case was decided under the 1856 Act and the result might now be different so far as real estate is concerned because the words "as would have happened if the bankrupt had been adjudicated bankrupt in England or Ireland" have been added to s.97(3) of the 1913 Act; see Williams and Muir Hunter, *Bankruptcy*, 19th ed., p.474.

CHAPTER 20

ANTECEDENT TRANSACTIONS

Certain antecedent transactions can be reduced by the trustee to the effect of recovering assets for the benefit of the creditors. The principal transactions affected are (a) gratuitous alienations, (b) fraudulent preferences, (c) *inter vivos* trusts and donations *inter virum et uxorem*.

GRATUITOUS ALIENATIONS

1. Common Law

At common law, the trustee, or any onerous creditor, can challenge a gratuitous alienation made by the debtor when he was insolvent. The onus is on the challenger to show that the alienation was gratuitous, that the debtor was insolvent at the date of the alienation, that the debtor is still insolvent, and that the alienation was made to the prejudice of creditors. The difficulty of proving these matters is such that in practice resort is usually made to the Bankruptcy Act 1621, which strikes at gratuitous alienations to conjunct and confident persons.

2. Bankruptcy Act 1621

The Bankruptcy Act 1621, renders null and void "all alienations, dispositions, assignations and translations whatsoever made by the debtor of any of his lands, teinds, reversions, actions, debts or goods whatsoever to any conjunct or confident person without true just and necessary causes and without a just price really paid the same being done after the contracting of lawful debts from true creditors." It is necessary to establish: (i) that the debtor is insolvent at the date of challenge, (ii) that the debtor has made an alienation of his property to a conjunct and confident person, (iii) that the alienation was without true just and necessary cause, (iv) that the debtor was insolvent at the date of the alienation. If, however, the challenger proves (i) and (ii), (iii) and (iv) are presumed unless the contrary is proved.

The challenge is primarily at the instance of prior creditors, *i.e.* those whose debts were contracted before the date of alienation.[1] Where the debt arises from a verbal transaction the date of contracting it is the date of the transaction and not the date of the document or decree constituting it.[2] The trustee in the debtor's sequestration however, whether representing prior creditors or not, has a title to challenge for behoof of the whole body of creditors.[3] This does not evacuate the title of a prior creditor.[4] The syndic in a French bankruptcy has been allowed to challenge[5] and so has a liquidator in a voluntary liquidation.[6] The trustee under a voluntary trust deed can challenge only if the deed empowers him to do so and some creditors having a title to challenge accede to the trust deed.[7] A purchaser of the bankrupt's estate cannot challenge unless the right to do so is specially assigned to him.[8] Postponed[9] and gratuitous[10] creditors may challenge. Creditors whose claims are contingent or conditional may challenge but this is not effectual till the condition is purified.[11]

3. Alienations

The Act applies to "all alienations, dispositions, assignations, and translations, whatsoever made by the debtor of any of his lands, teinds, reversions, actions, debts, or goods whatsoever." The subjects of the alienation must be attachable by the diligence of creditors.[12] The following are alienations: the assignation of a life interest or life insurance policy; a lease;[13] the granting of a bill[14] or promissory note;[15] the discharge of a claim;[16] the abandonment of

---

1 Bell (*Comm.*, II, 172-3) suggests that posterior creditors may challenge but they must prove the debtor's insolvency at the date of alienation, *i.e.* they do not have the benefit of any presumption.

2 *Pollock's Crs.* v. *Pollock* (1669) Mor.1002; *Street* v. *Masson* (1669) Mor.1003.

3 B.A. 1913, s.9.

4 *Brown & Co.* v. *McCallum* (1890) 18 R.311.

5 *Obers* v. *Paton's Trs.* (1897) 24 R.719.

6 *Abram S.S. Co. Ltd.* v. *Abram*, 1925 S.L.T.243.

7 *Fleming's Trs.* v. *McHardy* (1892) 19 R.542.

8 *Smith & Co.* v. *Smyth* (1889) 16 R.392.

9 Goudy, p.52.

10 Erskine, IV, 1, 28.

11 Bell, *Comm.*, II, 173.

12 Bell, *Comm.*, II, 178-9.

13 *Gorrie's Tr.* v. *Gorrie* (1890) 17 R.1051.

14 Bell, *Comm.*, II, 177.

15 *Thomas* v. *Thomson* (1865) 3 M.1160; but a mere voucher is not an alienation. The point seems to be that a voucher neither attaches a fund nor gives a right to do diligence.

16 *Laing* v. *Cheyne* (1832) 10 S.200.

an action;[17] a decree allowed to pass in absence.[18] At one time it was considered that the Act applied only to transactions in writing but it seems that its effect now extends to the delivery of goods unaccompanied by writing.[19] The conveyance may be direct or indirect.[20] So, a conveyance from the seller to the conjunct or confident person, the price being paid by the insolvent, is an alienation.[21] In the insolvency of a partnership where one partner exercised a power of appointment under an ante-nuptial marriage contract so as to divert a *spes successionis* from her partner to her grandchild, it was held that there had been an alienation because the creditors of the appointer were prejudiced.[22] Cash payments are not alienations under the Act[23] but they are under the common law.[24]

4. Conjunct and Confident Persons

The onus is on the challenging creditor to show that the grantee is a conjunct or confident person.[25] Conjunct and confident persons are described in the preamble to the Act as "wives, children, kinsmen, allies and other confident and interposed persons." Conjunct persons are those closely related to the bankrupt by blood or affinity. They include parents, children, grandchildren,[26] brothers, sisters, uncles,[27] aunts, nephews and nieces, parents-in-law, brothers and sisters-in-law,[28] sons-in-law,[29] a stepson,[30] an illegitimate child,[31] a paramour[31] and an intended spouse.[32] The following are not conjunct persons: the husband of a sister of the bankrupt's

---

17 *Wilson* v. *Drummond's Reps.* (1853) 16 D.275.

18 Mackenzie, *Works,* II, p.8.

19 *N.B. Rlwy. Co.* v. *White* (1882) 20 S.L.R.129; see *Encyclopaedia of the Laws of Scotland,* Vol. II, p.108.

20 Bell, *Comm.*, II, 174.

21 *Ross* v. *Hutton* (1830) 8 S.916; *Bolden* v. *Ferguson* (1863) 1 M.522.

22 *Thomson* v. *Spence,* 1961 S.L.T.395.

23 *Gilmour Shaw & Co.'s Tr.* v. *Learmonth,* 1972 S.C.137.

24 *Dobie* v. *Mitchell* (1854) 17 D.97; *Main* v. *Fleming's Trs.* (1881) 8 R.880.

25 Bell, *Comm.*, II, 175.

26 *Thomson* v. *Spence,* 1961 S.L.T.395.

27 *Tarpersie's Crs.* v. *Kinfauns* (1673) Mor.900.

28 *McKenzie* v. *Fletcher* (1712) Mor.924; *Hume* v. *Smith* (1673) Mor.899.

29 *Skeen* v. *Betson* (1632) Mor.896.

30 *Mercer* v. *Dalgardno* (1694) Mor.12563.

31 *Ballantyne* v. *Dunlop,* 17 Feb. 1814, F.C.

32 *McLay* v. *McQueen* (1899) 1 F.804.

wife,[33] uncles and nephews by affinity.[34] The position of cousins is doubtful.[35]

Confident persons are "those in whom the grantor is presumed to place an uncommon trust, from his employing them in certain offices about his person or estate, as a doer, steward or domestic servant."[36] It is in each case a question of circumstances but the following have been held to fall within the category: servants, factors, business partners, confidential men of business,[37] a confidential clerk,[38] a tutor or curator,[39] a joint adventurer,[40] the bankrupt's wife's maternal aunt and next-of-kin to whom the bankrupt was law-agent, confidential adviser and intimate friend.[41] A trustee is not confident with the beneficiaries[42] nor is the insurer confident with the insured.[43] The constituent is not confident with his factor, although the factor may be with the constituent.[44]

5. True, Just and Necessary Cause

The onus is on the grantee or receiver to show that there was a true, just and necessary cause for the alienation.[45] The "and" is construed disjunctively so the requirement is satisfied if there is a true and just cause but no prior obligation.[46] The cause must be "existing and operating on the bankrupt at the date of the deed."[47] The proof may be by parole evidence.[48] Something more than the grantee's oath and the terms of the deed itself is required.[49] The production of a

---

33 *McGowan* v. *McKellar* (1826) 4 S.498.
34 *Elibank* v. *Adamson* (1712) Mor.12569.
35 *Sinclair* v. *Dickson* (1680) Mor.12562; *McDowal* v. *Fullerton* (1714) Mor.12569.
36 Erskine, IV, 1, 31.
37 Erskine, IV, 1, 31; Bell, *Comm.*, II, 175.
38 *Bank of Scotland* v. *Gardiner* (1906) 14 S.L.T.146; 15 S.L.T.229.
39 *Laing* v. *Cheyne* (1832) 10 S.200.
40 *Witham* v. *Teenan's Tr.* (1884) 11 R.776.
41 *Edmond* v. *Grant* (1853) 15 D.703.
42 *Young* v. *Darroch's Trs.* (1835) 13 S.305; *Watson* v. *Grant's Trs.* (1874) 1 R.882. *Cf. McLay* v. *McQueen* (1899) 1 F.804.
43 *Ritchie* v. *Scottish Automobile and General Insurance Co.* 1931 S|N.83; *Todd* v. *Anglian Insurance Co. Ltd.*, 1933 S.L.T.274.
44 *Buccleuch* v. *Sinclair* (1728) Mor.12573.
45 *Napier* v. *Gordon* (1670) Mor.3755; Bell, *Comm.*, II, 179; *Dawson* v. *Thorburn* (1888) 15 R.891; *Gilmour Shaw & Co.'s Tr.* v. *Learmonth*, 1972 S.C.137.
46 *Grant* v. *Grant* (1748) Mor.949; *Gilmour Shaw & Co.'s Tr.* v. *Learmonth*, 1972 S.C.137.
47 *per* L.J.-C. Hope, *Horne* v. *Hay* (1847) 9 D.651 at 665.
48 *per* L.P. Inglis, *Matthew's Tr.* v. *Matthew* (1867) 5 M.957 at 961.
49 *Dawson* v. *Thorburn, supra; Rule* v. *Purdie* (1711) Mor.12566.

deed instructing a prior obligation is probably sufficient.[50] If there has been delay on the part of the challenging creditor, slight evidence of onerosity may suffice.[51]

There is a true just and necessary cause if money or money's worth has been given.[52] An IOU cannot be challenged if the money in fact passed.[53] In the case of sale, it is sufficient if a fair price was really and bona fide paid.[54] Again, it is sufficient if the alienation is in implement of a prior obligation.[55] The implement may be specific or in another form.[56] The alienation may give security for implement.[57] There is also a true, just and necessary cause if an obligation is undertaken by the grantee. Marriage is itself a consideration in an ante-nuptial marriage contract or where a fiancée is given money with which to purchase the matrimonial home.[58] It is doubtful to what extent a natural obligation constitutes a true cause.[59] A policy taken out by a person under the Married Women's Policies of Assurance (Scotland) Act 1880 expressed to be for the benefit of his or her spouse or children is protected from challenge by creditors but if it is proved that it was effected and the premiums paid with intent to defraud creditors or if the person is made bankrupt within two years of the date of the policy, the creditors can recover the premiums from the proceeds.[60]

6. Insolvency

For the Act to apply, the bankrupt must be insolvent at the date of alienation,[61] and an averment to this effect must be made.[62] The date of alienation of heritage is the date of recording of the disposition.[63] It is sufficient to show that the bankrupt was made insolvent

---

50 *McKies* v. *Agnew* (1739) Mor.12574.

51 Bell, *Comm.*, II, 181; *Guthrie* v. *Gordon* (1711) Mor.1020.

52 *Hodge* v. *Morrisons* (1883) 21 S.L.R.40.

53 *Williamson* v. *Allan* (1882) 9 R.859.

54 Bell, *Comm.*, II, 179-180; *Tennant* v. *Miller* (1897) 4 S.L.T.318.

55 *Horne* v. *Hay* (1847) 9 D.651.

56 *Birkinbog* v. *Grahame* (1671) Mor.881.

57 *Thomas* v. *Thomson* (1866) 5 M.198.

58 Erskine, IV, 1, 33; *Carphin* v. *Clapperton* (1867) 5 M.797; *Watson* v. *Grant's Trs.* (1874) 1 R.882; *McLay* v. *McQueen* (1899) 1 F.804; *Gilmour Shaw & Co.'s Tr.* v. *Learmonth, supra.*

59 Goudy, p.49.

60 1880 Act, s.2; see *Stewart* v. *Hodge* (1901) 8 S.L.T.436.

61 *Garthland* v. *Ker* (1632) Mor.915; *Clerk* v. *Stewart* (1675) Mor.917; *Ballantyne* v. *Dunlop,* 17 Feb. 1814, F.C.

62 *Bolden* v. *Ferguson* (1863) 1 M.522.

63 *McManus's Tr.* v. *McManus,* 1978 S.L.T.255.

by the alienation.[64] But if the creditor proves insolvency at the date of challenge, insolvency at the date of alienation is presumed and it is for the bankrupt to rebut the presumption.[65] The creditor may prove insolvency *prout de jure*.[66] Insolvency here means absolute insolvency.[67] The onus on the bankrupt is to prove "that upon a balance of his assets and liabilities according to their fair worth at the time, he would have been able to pay all his creditors 20s. in the pound."[68] Allowance must be made for changes in value since the date of the alienation.[69] If the challenging creditor has delayed, the presumption in his favour is of less weight.[70]

7. Challenge

The challenge may be taken by action or exception in the Court of Session or the sheriff court.[71]

The effect of successful challenge is that the subject of the alienation becomes an asset of the debtor's estate and may be attached by the diligence of any creditor.[72] The challenging creditor is not entitled to delivery of the asset and, indeed, the result may be a preference to another creditor.[73] Where the grantee has transferred the asset to a third party for an onerous consideration the property cannot be recovered from the third party[74] unless he knew of the gratuitous alienation[75] but the price can be recovered from the grantee.

---

64 *Queensberry* v. *Mouswell,* (1677) Mor.961. *Cf. McLay* v. *McQueen* (1899) 36 S.L.R.568, *per* Lord McLaren at p.572.

65 Bell, *Comm.*, II, 180; *Cult's Crs.* v. *Younger Children* (1783) Mor.974; *Holwell* v. *Cuming* (1796) Mor.11583.

66 *Hodge* v. *Morrisons* (1883) 21 S.L.R.40.

67 Erskine, IV, 1, 32; *McKell* v. *Jamieson* (1680) Mor.920; *McKenzie* v. *Fletcher* (1712) Mor.924; *Salaman* v. *Rosslyn's Trs.* (1900) 3 F.298.

68 *per* Lord McLaren, *Hodge* v. *Morrisons, supra,* at 42. See as to the valuation of future debts in the computation, Bell, *Comm.*, II, 181, n.2; *Taylor* v. *Russo* 1977 S.L.T.(Sh.Ct.)60.

69 *Remington* v. *Bruce* (1829) 8 S.215.

70 Bell, *Comm.*, II, 181; *Spence* v. *Dick's Crs.* (1692) Mor.1014.

71 B.A. 1913, s.8.

72 *Cook* v. *Sinclair & Co.* (1896) 23 R.925. Under registration of title, there is no indemnity in respect of the reduced title: Land Registration (Scotland) Act 1979, s.12(3)(*b*).

73 *Bell* v. *Gow* (1862) 1 M.183.

74 The Bankruptcy Act 1621.

75 *Hay* v. *Jamieson* (1672) Mor.1009; see *Caird* v. *Key* (1857) 20 D.187.

FRAUDULENT PREFERENCES

8. Bankruptcy Act 1696

A fraudulent preference arises where a debtor "after his funds have become inadequate to the payment of all his debts, intentionally, and in contemplation of his failing, confers on favourite creditors a preference over the rest."[76] Such fraudulent preferences are challengeable at common law if they are made by the debtor (i) voluntarily (ii) during insolvency, and (iii) while conscious of his insolvency. It seems that the challenge can be at the instance of any creditor who is prejudiced by the transaction, whereas the challenge under the Bankruptcy Act 1696, can only be at the instance of a prior creditor.[77] Most challenges are effected under the statute.

The Bankruptcy Act 1696[78] provides: "All and whatsomever voluntar dispositions, assignations or other deeds which shall be found to be made or granted, directly or indirectly, by the foresaid dyvour or bankrupt, either at or after his becoming bankrupt, or in the space of sixty days of before, in favour of his creditors, either for their satisfaction or farder security, in preference to other creditors, to be void and null." The period of 60 days has been increased to six months.[79] Accordingly, any fraudulent preference within six months of notour bankruptcy can be reduced.

9. Transactions Affected

The statute strikes at "any act whatever affecting the bankrupt's estate, whereby the equality of distribution may be disturbed."[80] It has been applied to: a disposition of heritage;[81] the granting of a lease;[82] the transfer of moveables;[83] the return of moveables bought but not paid for under an arrangement made in view of the buyer's insolvency;[84] the granting of a delivery order for moveables;[85] an

---

76 Bell, *Comm.*, II, 226.

77 Goudy, p.42. The trustee has a title.

78 1696, c.5.

79 Companies Act 1947, s.115(3); see Antonio, 1965 S.L.T.(News) 145.

80 *per* Lord Young, *Nicol* v. *McIntyre* (1882) 9 R.1097 at 1100.

81 *Hill's Tr.* v. *Macgregor* (1901) 8 S.L.T.484. Under registration of title, there is no indemnity in respect of the reduced title: Land Registration (Scotland) Act 1979, s.12(3)(*b*).

82 *Gorrie's Tr.* v. *Gorrie* (1890) 17 R.1051.

83 *Dawson* v. *Lauder* (1840) 2 D.525; *Rhind's Tr.* v. *Robertson & Baxter* (1891) 18 R.623; *Walker* v. *Coyle* (1891) 19 R.91.

84 *Watson & Sons Ltd.* v. *Veritys Ltd.* (1908) 24 Sh.Ct.Rep.148.

85 *Wright* v. *Mitchell* (1871) 9 M.516; *Price & Pierce Ltd.* v. *Bank of Scotland*, 1910 S.C.1095; 1912 S.C.(H.L.)19.

assignation;[86] a mandate for payment;[87] the indorsation of a bill or cheque;[88] a bond and disposition in security;[89] a security constituted by an *ex facie* absolute disposition of heritage;[90] a mortgage of a ship;[91] a trust deed for creditors;[92] the discharge of a right;[93] the renunciation of a lease;[94] the abandonment of a competent defence;[95] the allowance of decree by default;[96] possibly, an agreement to pay several creditors by instalments provided they did not sue for recovery of their debts;[97] It applies even where the creditor is given an advantage by means of a circuitous device. It appears that the granting of a mere acknowledgment of a subsisting debt is not affected at least where effectual diligence has not followed upon it.[98]

There are, however, certain transactions which are not affected by the statute, *viz:* cash payments, transactions in the ordinary course of business and *nova debita*.

10. Cash Payments

A cash payment in ordinary course of business made to extinguish a debt already due does not fall under the Act and is not challengeable unless it is collusive.[99] An insolvent debtor can prefer which creditors he pleases by paying their due debts in cash until the eve of sequestration, although he cannot give them securities for their debts.[1] Cash payments for this purpose include not only currency but also cheques drawn by the debtor,[2] bank drafts,[2] bills drawn by the debtor on his banker[3] and orders for payment signed by the debtor and addressed to persons who are obliged, or have agreed,

86 Bell, *Comm.*, II, 196.
87 *Dods* v. *Welsh* (1904) 12 S.L.T.110.
88 *Nicol* v. *McIntyre* (1882) 9 R.1097; *Carter* v. *Johnstone* (1886) 13 R.698.
89 *Neil's Tr.* v. *British Linen Co.* (1898) 6 S.L.T.227.
90 *MacArthur* v. *Campbell's Tr.*, 1953 S.L.T.(Notes)81.
91 *Anderson* v. *Western Bank* (1859) 21 D.230.
92 *Douglas* v. *Gibson-Craig* (1832) 10 S.647; *Mackenzie* v. *Calder* (1868) 6 M.833.
93 *Keith* v. *Maxwell* (1795) Mor.1163.
94 *Morrison* v. *Carron Co.* (1854) 16 D.1125.
95 *Wilson* v. *Drummond's Reps.* (1853) 16 D.275.
96 *Lauries' Tr.* v. *Beveridge* (1867) 6 M.85.
97 *Munro* v. *Rothfield,* 1920 S.C.118.
98 *Matthew's Tr.* v. *Matthew* (1867) 5 M.957.
99 *Forbes* v. *Brebner* (1751) Mor.1128; *per* L.P. McNeill, *Guild* v. *Orr Ewing & Co.* (1858) 20 D.392 at 397.
1 *per* Lord Young, *Coutts' Tr. and Doe* v. *Webster* (1886) 13 R.1112 at 1116.
2 *per* Lord Shand, *Carter* v. *Johnstone* (1886) 13 R.698 at 707.
3 *Dixon* v. *Cowan* (1828) 7 S.132.

to honour the debtor's drafts.[4] Consignation may be a cash payment.[5] On the other hand, a bill of exchange drawn on an ordinary debtor,[6] and a bill[7] or cheque[8] *indorsed* to a creditor (whether by the debtor or his agent[9]) are assignations, not cash payments, and are struck at by the Act. Where, however, the debtor has indorsed a bill to his banker[10] or has indorsed a cheque to his bank as an agent for collection,[11] the transaction is regarded as a cash payment. As a rule the debt must be due at the time of payment and anticipatory payments are not protected,[12] but there may be circumstances where this does not hold.[13]

A cash payment is not protected if the transaction is simulate or collusive.[14] It is not collusive by reason only of the fact that both debtor and creditor knew of the debtor's insolvency.[15] To establish collusion it must be shown that the creditor was "participant in a fraudulent design."[16] It seems that reduction of a collusive payment should be effected under the common law and not under the Act.[17]

11. Transactions in the ordinary course of business

The second exception is transactions in the ordinary course of business. This operates "wherever the transaction is in the ordinary course of dealing, and requisite or suitable to the fair purpose of the debtor proceeding with his trade, and unaccompanied by indications of collusion or notice of insolvency."[18] The transaction must

---

4 *Miller* v. *Philip & Son* (1883) 20 S.L.R.862; *Craig* v. *Hunter & Son* (1905) 13 S.L.T.525.

5 *Gordon* v. *Brock* (1838) 1 D.1; *Littlejohn* v. *Reynolds* (1890) 6 Sh.Ct.Rep.321.

6 *Carter* v. *Johnstone, supra*.

7 *Nicol* v. *McIntyre* (1882) 9 R.1097.

8 *Carter* v. *Johnstone, supra*.

9 *Anderson's Tr.* v. *John Somerville & Co. Ltd.* (1899) 36 S.L.R.833.

10 *Blincow's Tr.* v. *Allan & Co.* (1828) 7 S.124; (1833) 7 W. & S.26.

11 *Whatmough's Tr.* v. *British Linen Bank*, 1934 S.C.(H.L.)51.

12 *Speir* v. *Dunlop* (1827) 5 S.729; *Blincow's Tr.* v. *Allan & Co., supra*.

13 *Per* L.P. McNeill, *Guild* v. *Orr Ewing & Co.* (1858) 20 D.392 at 397; any such cases can be regarded as falling under the next exception—transactions in the ordinary course of business.

14 *Whatmough's Tr.* v. *British Linen Bank, supra; Jones' Tr.* v. *Jones* (1888) 15 R.328; *Neil's Tr.* v. *British Linen Co.* (1898) 36 S.L.R.139; *Angus' Tr.* v. *Angus* (1901) 4 F.181; *Newton & Sons' Tr.* v. *Finlayson & Co.* 1928 S.C.637. See also the exhaustive analysis of the law in *Nordic Travel Ltd.* v. *Scotprint Ltd.*, 1980 S.L.T.189.

15 *Coutts' Tr. and Doe* v. *Webster, supra; Pringle's Tr.* v. *Wright* (1903) 5 F.522.

16 Bell, *Comm.*, II, 226; *Whatmough's Tr.* v. *British Linen Bank, supra*.

17 Goudy, p.86 n.(f); *Whatmough's Tr.* v. *British Linen Bank, supra*.

18 Bell, *Comm.*, II, 205.

be "the natural and ordinary course"[19] for the debtor to pursue and "incident to transactions in which the parties are ordinarily engaged."[20] Accordingly, if a debtor enters into such a transaction with his creditor, any security which the creditor obtains as an incidental result is not struck at by the Act. So, where goods were sent to bleachers in the ordinary course of trade and the bleachers thereby acquired a lien on the goods for prior debts, the security was not affected by the Act.[21] A similar result followed where a farmer sent goods to an auctioneer to be sold and the auctioneers thereby acquired a right to withhold part of the proceeds against a prior debt due to them;[22] where a merchant indorsed a bill to his bankers;[23] and where a purchaser returned an article for which he had not paid to the seller on the ground that he no longer required it.[24] Cash payment of a debt which is not yet due may be a transaction in the ordinary course of business.[25]

It is, however, necessary to prove that the transaction was in the ordinary course of business and if this is not proved the transaction will be reduced.[26] A transaction is obviously not in the ordinary course of business where its main object is to give the creditor a security, as where the debtor sells goods to the creditor to set off a prior debt,[27] or where the debtor hands over goods to the creditor to be sold for payment of the debt.[28] A transaction is not in the ordinary course of business only because it has become the debtor's habitual method of conducting business in a prolonged state of insolvency.[29] It seems that a transaction which takes place after the debtor's notour bankruptcy cannot be in the ordinary course of business.[30]

---

19 *per* Lord Guthrie, *Crockart's Tr.* v. *Hay & Co. Ltd.*, 1913 S.C.509 at 521.

20 *per* L.P. Inglis, *Loudon Bros.* v. *Reid & Lauder's Tr.* (1877) 5 R.293 at 301.

21 *Anderson's Trs.* v. *Fleming* (1871) 9 M.718.

22 *Crockart's Tr.* v. *Hay & Co. Ltd., supra.*

23 *Stein's Crs.* v. *Forbes Hunter & Co.* (1791) Mor.1142.

24 *Loudon Bros.* v. *Reid & Lauder's Tr., supra;* Goudy, p.87, considers this decision open to criticism on its facts. See also *Watson & Sons Ltd.* v. *Veritys Ltd.* (1907) 24 Sh.Ct.Rep.148.

25 *McLaren's Tr.* v. *National Bank* (1897) 24 R.920; *cf. McFarlane* v. *Robb & Co.* (1870) 9 M.370.

26 *Scougall* v. *White* (1828) 6 S.494; *White* v. *Briggs* (1843) 5 D.1148; *Carter* v. *Johnstone* (1886) 13 R.698; *Craig's Tr.* v. *Macdonald Fraser & Co. Ltd.* (1902) 4 F.1132; *Craig's Tr.* v. *Craig* (1903) 10 S.L.T.556; *Dods* v. *Welsh* (1904) 12 S.L.T.110; *Walkraft Paint Co. Ltd.* v. *James Kinsey & Co. Ltd.*, 1964 S.L.T.104.

27 *Stewart* v. *Scott* (1832) 11 S.171; *Dawson* v. *Lauder* (1840) 2 D.525.

28 *Morton's Tr.* v. *Fifeshire Auction Co. Ltd.*, 1911 1 S.L.T.405.

29 *Horsbrugh* v. *Ramsay & Co.* (1885) 12 R.1171.

30 *Jackson* v. *Fenwick's Tr.* (1899) 6 S.L.T.319.

12. Nova Debita

The third exception is *nova debita:* "all those cases in which a fair and present value is given for the conveyance or other deed executed by the bankrupt."[31] Obviously, the creditors are not prejudiced if the bankrupt transfers property in return for a fair consideration because the consideration becomes part of the assets available to the creditors. Accordingly, a conveyance within the period of property which has been sold for a fair price is not struck at by the Act.[32] Similarly, where money has been advanced to the bankrupt in reliance upon a security to be granted by him, the granting of the security within the period is not affected by the Act.[33] On the same principle the substitution of one security for another security is not affected;[34] and where a security had been granted within the period for a prior debt which was subsequently paid, and a further advance was then made on the strength of the security, it was held that the security was valid.[35]

Considerable difficulties arise where there is an interval of time between the making of the advance and the granting of the security. To come within the exception, the advance must be made in reliance upon the security[36] which is to be granted and the whole transaction must be carried out *unico contextu*.[37] There is the further difficulty that in many cases the creation of a security is effected in two stages, one prior to the period and one within the period. Where the security deed is granted outwith the period in consideration of advances made at that time, the security is valid even although it is completed within the period by, for example, the recording of a deed in the Sasine Register,[38] the registration of a transfer,[39] or the intimation of an assignation.[40] A more extreme

---

31 Bell, *Comm.*, II, 205.

32 *Brugh* v. *Gray* (1717) Mor.1125; *Cranstoun* v. *Bontine* (1830) 8 S.425; (1832) 6 W. & S.79; *Taylor* v. *Farrie* (1855) 17 D.639; *Miller's Tr.* v. *Shield* (1862) 24 D.821.

33 *Bank of Scotland* v. *Stewart & Ross,* 7 Feb. 1811, F.C.; *Renton & Gray's Tr.* v. *Dickison* (1880) 7 R.951.

34 *Roy's Tr.* v. *Colville & Drysdale* (1903) 5 F.769.

35 *Robertson* v. *Ogilvie* (1798) Mor. *s.v.* "Bills of Exchange" App. No. 6; *Robertson's Tr.* v. *Union Bank of Scotland,* 1917 S.C.549.

36 *White* v. *Briggs* (1843) 5 D.1148, *per* Lord Fullerton at p.1164; *MacArthur* v. *Campbell's Tr.*, 1953 S.L.T.(Notes)81.

37 *Cowdenbeath Coal Co. Ltd.* v. *Clydesdale Bank Ltd.* (1895) 22 R.682.

38 *Cormack* v. *Anderson* (1829) 7 S.868.

39 *Guild* v. *Young* (1884) 22 S.L.R.520.

40 *Scottish Provident Institution* v. *Cohen & Co.* (1888) 16 R.112; *Caledonian Insurance Co.* v. *Beattie* (1898) 5 S.L.T.349.

case is where the advances have been made before the period on the strength of an undertaking by the debtor to grant a security at a later date and the security deed is executed within the period. It seems that the security is valid if the undertaking creates an immediate and unconditional obligation relating to specific property so that the debtor in granting the security deed is fulfilling a legal obligation and doing "the very thing he is bound to do"[41]—something which could be enforced by an action *ad factum praestandum* and which was part of the contract under which the loan was made.[42] On the other hand, if the obligation is of a general kind or is qualified by such phrases as "at any time required," "if you desire it", "in due course", the security is struck at by the Act.[43]

The law on this whole subject is in a state of confusion[44] and it is necessary to mention two further principles which are stated by some authorities but which must respectfully be questioned. It has been suggested that the rule about the completion of a security within the period by registration and so on is not confined to cases where the security is granted in respect of advances made *simul et semel* but extends to cases where the security has been granted before the period in respect of prior debts;[45] it is doubtful if this is correct.[46] Secondly, it has been suggested that the effect of completion of the security within the period depends on whether the act of completion is that of the debtor or that of the creditor;[47] the preferable view is that this does not matter and the only question is whether the transaction is truly a *novum debitum*;[48] the only significance of the question of who completed the security is that the bankrupt cannot act after the date of sequestration while, in the case of registered titles, the creditor can.

13. Trusts and Donations

The funds of an *inter vivos* trust constituted by the bankrupt may be

---

41 *Bank of Scotland* v. *Stewart & Ross, supra; Taylor* v. *Farrie, supra.*

42 *T.* v. *L.*, 1970 S.L.T.243.

43 *Moncrieff* v. *Hay* (1851) 14 D.200; *Stiven* v. *Scott & Simson* (1871) 9 M.923; *Gourlay* v. *Hodge* (1875) 2 R.738; *Gourlay* v. *Mackie* (1887) 14 R.403; *Price & Pierce Ltd.* v. *Bank of Scotland,* 1910 S.C.1095; *affd.* 1912 S.C.(H.L.)19; *Barclay* v. *Cuthill,* 1961 S.L.T.(Notes)62; *T.* v. *L.*, 1970 S.L.T.243.

44 See Antonio, 1957 S.L.T.(News) 13; Gloag and Irvine, pp.9-14.

45 *Lindsay* v. *Adamson & Ronaldson* (1880) 7 R.1036, *per* L.P. Inglis at p.1041.

46 *Encyclopaedia of the Laws of Scotland,* Vol. II, p.140.

47 Goudy, p.91.

48 *Encyclopaedia of the Laws of Scotland,* Vol. II, p.140.

available to creditors if the trust is revocable in character.[49] Where a trust has been constituted under the Married Women's Policies of Assurance (Scotland) Act 1880, if it is proved that the policy was effected and the premiums paid thereon with intent to defraud the creditors, or if the bankruptcy occurs within two years of the date of the policy, the creditors may claim repayment of the premiums so paid from the trustee of the policy out of the proceeds thereof.[50] A trust deed for creditors is superseded, or, at least, suspended, by the grantor's sequestration (or English bankruptcy) and the trustee under the deed must denude in favour of the trustee in the sequestration.[51] A donation by the bankrupt to his spouse completed within a year and a day before his sequestration is revocable at the instance of his creditors.[52]

---

49 *Scott* v. *Scott,* 1930 S.C.903; *Lawrence* v. *Lawrence's Trs.*, 1974 S.L.T.174.

50 s.2; *Stewart* v. *Hodge* (1901) 8 S.L.T.436; *Chrystal's Tr.* v. *Chrystal,* 1912 S.C.1003.

51 Bell, *Comm.*, II, 391; *Salaman* v. *Rosslyn's Trs.* (1900) 3 F.298.

52 Married Women's Property (Scotland) Act 1920, s.5.

CHAPTER 21

THE CLAIM

1. Procedure

In general, a creditor must proceed by lodging a claim in the sequestration.[1] After sequestration, an action against the bankrupt for recovery of a debt due at the date of sequestration is not incompetent but it is of small practical value as there are no assets which can be attached by diligence on the decree. As a general rule, it is not proper to bring an action for recovery of a debt due by the bankrupt against the trustee in his sequestration although there may be exceptional cases where it is a correct procedure in order to obtain a decree of constitution of the debt.[2] Where a decree for payment has been granted against the trustee in a sequestration, as such trustee, it can be enforced only if it is in respect of a matter for which the trustee has come under personal obligation to pay. If the decree is in respect of a prior debt due by the bankrupt at the date of sequestration, it cannot be enforced against the trustee and the holder is entitled only to rank for a dividend in the sequestration.[3] A judicial factor who has been appointed on the estate of a solicitor under the Solicitors (Scotland) Act 1980, s.41, is not in the position of a trustee in a sequestration and can be sued for a debt due by the solicitor.[4]

To obtain payment of the first dividend the creditor must produce his notice of claim and grounds of debt at least two months before the date fixed for payment, or one month before the time fixed if it has been accelerated.[5] The date of payment is the first lawful day after the expiration of six months from the date of the deliverance actually awarding sequestration.[6] The second dividend is payable after 10 months from the same deliverance and subsequent dividends at intervals of three months thereafter.[7] These dates may be

1 Goudy, p.373.

2 *Crichton's Tr.* v. *Stewart* (1866) 4 M.689; *Adam & Winchester* v. *White's Tr.* (1884) 11 R.863; *Martin's Tr.* v. *Wilson* (1904) 12 S.L.T.112; *Legal and General Assurance Society Ltd.* v. *Carter,* 1926 S.L.T.63; *Dow* v. *Pennell's Tr.,* 1929 S.L.T.674.

3 *Thomson & Co.* v. *Friese-Greene's Tr.,* 1944 S.C.336.

4 *Ross* v. *Gordon's J.F.,* 1973 S.L.T.(Notes)91.

5 B.A., s.119.

6 s.126.

7 ss.128, 129.

accelerated but the first dividend cannot be paid earlier than four months from the date of the deliverance actually awarding sequestration.[8]

A creditor who has not claimed before the first dividend can obtain payment of the second or a subsequent dividend by producing his notice of claim and grounds of debt at least two months before the appropriate date of payment. He is entitled on the occasion of the second or subsequent dividend to receive out of the first of the fund (if there is sufficient) an equalising dividend corresponding to the dividend he would have drawn if he had claimed in time for the prior dividends.[9] If a claim has been rejected before the first dividend but another claim is made for the same debt thereafter and is allowed, the creditor is entitled to a second dividend and an equalising dividend.[10]

2. Claim for Ranking

To claim for a ranking in the sequestration the creditor must produce a notice of claim together with an account and vouchers.[11] The notice states the creditor's name, occupation and address, the total amount of the claim, particulars of the debt including its nature and the date on which it was incurred, the nature of any security, the date it was granted and its value. It may be signed by the creditor or his solicitor. A partner can sign for a firm, and a director, secretary or principal officer for a company.[12] If the debt is in respect of the supply of goods or services and the creditor intends to reclaim value added tax already paid from the Commissioners of Customs and Excise he should deduct the amount of the refund from his claim in the sequestration.[13] The vouchers are those necessary to prove the debt. The evidence required is that which would be necessary to prove the debt in an action of constitution.[14] For example, a bank claiming in respect of an overdraft must produce bills, cheques and docquets vouching the debt although a copy of a docquet will suffice if it is authenticated in accordance with the Bankers' Books

---

8 s.130.

9 s.119.

10 *Stewart's Seqn.* (1901) 17 Sh.Ct.Rep.253.

11 s.45 (Amended Insolvency Act 1976, s.5(3)); the trustee may require an oath.

12 Notice of Claim (Scotland) Regulations 1977 (S.I. 1977/1495).

13 Finance Act 1978, s.12; Value Added Tax (Bad Debt Relief) Regulations 1978 (S.I.1978/1129), reg.9.

14 Goudy, p.315.

Evidence Act 1879.[15] The debt cannot be proved by reference to the bankrupt's oath.[16] If the creditor is not at the time for lodging claims in possession of the necessary vouchers, he must state in his notice of claim the cause of the vouchers not being produced and in whose hands, to the best of his knowledge, they are.[17] A dividend must then be set apart till a reasonable time be afforded for production of the vouchers but the creditor cannot vote until the debt is established. If a preference is claimed, evidence to establish the right must be produced but it is not necessary to claim the preference specifically in the notice of claim if informal intimation of the claim to a preference is made.[18]

Interest can be claimed only to the date of sequestration but if there is any residue of the estate after discharge of the debts ranked, the creditor is entitled to any interest on his debt in terms of law from such residue.[19] If the debt is not payable until after the date of sequestration, interest from the date of sequestration must be deducted as must also any discount beyond legal interest to which his claim is liable by the usage of trade applicable to it or by the contract or course of dealing between the creditor and the bankrupt.[20]

Aliment to become due under a decree of separation and aliment, whether granted before or after the husband's sequestration, is not a valid claim.[21] Similarly, amounts to become due under an award of aliment to a wife in a divorce action for the legitimate child in her custody cannot be given ranking.[22] On the other hand, the mother of an illegitimate child can rank on the sequestrated estate of the father for its future aliment, the claim being treated as a contingent debt.[23]

3. Adjudication of Claims

Within 14 days after the expiration of four months from the date

---

15 *Forrest* v. *Borthwick* (1848) 11 D.308; *Warden's Seqn.* (1908) 24 Sh.Ct.Rep.301; *Maitland's Seqn.* (1912) 28 Sh.Ct.Rep.354; *Whitelaw's Seqn.* (1917) 33 Sh.Ct.Rep.253.

16 *Adam* v. *Maclachlan* (1847) 9 D.560.

17 s.46.

18 *Crerar* v. *Clement's Tr.* (1905) 7 F.939.

19 s.48; see Goudy, p.318, as to questions arising under this section.

20 *Ibid.*

21 *Matthew* v. *Matthew's Tr.* (1907) 15 S.L.T.326; *McNaught* v. *Miller* (1917) 33 Sh.Ct.Rep.68.

22 *Barnes* v. *Tosh* (1913) 29 Sh.Ct.Rep.340.

23 *Downs* v. *Wilson's Tr.* (1886) 13 R.1101.

of the deliverance actually awarding sequestration (unless the dividend is accelerated), the trustee must examine the notices of claim and grounds of debt and in writing admit or reject them or require further evidence in support of them.[24] "The trustee is expected to take all reasonable means of obtaining satisfactory information, and to exercise the powers conferred on him so far as necessary. If he is satisfied that the debt claimed is due, he is entitled to admit it, and rank the creditor accordingly. If not satisfied, it is his duty to reject the claim, and refuse to rank the claimant."[25] In the case of rejection he must state his grounds. He must then compose a list of creditors entitled to draw dividend and on or before the first lawful day after the 14 days send a letter to each creditor specifying the amount of the claim and the proposed dividend thereon or, if the claim is rejected, he must enclose a copy of his deliverance thereon.[26] A creditor may appeal to the sheriff against the trustee's decision (including a decision calling for further evidence)[27] by a short written note within 14 days of the publication by the trustee in the *Edinburgh Gazette* of a notice of the time and place of payment of the dividend. A creditor can appeal against the admission or preference of another creditor's claim but the appeal should be intimated to the creditor concerned as well as to the trustee.[28] An appeal against a deliverance on a claim brings the general scheme of ranking under review and it is not necessary to appeal against the deliverances on other claims.[29]

4. Secured Creditors

Where a creditor holds a security,[30] over part of the bankrupt's estate, he must before voting put in his notice of claim a specified value on his security (or if the security subjects have been sold the proceeds received therefrom), deduct the stated sum from his debt and specify the balance. He is entitled to vote only in respect of that balance, except in questions as to the disposal or management of the

---

24 s.123.

25 *per* L.P. Inglis, *Phosphate Sewage Co.* v. *Molleson* (1874) 1 R.840 at 846.

26 s.124.

27 *Brown* v. *Brown's Tr.* (1859) 21 D.1133.

28 *Skinner's Tr.* v. *Keith* (1887) 14 R.563.

29 *Baird & Brown* v. *Stirrat's Tr.* (1872) 10 M.414.

30 A "security" includes rights of lien, retention or preference: B.A., s.1. A deposit is a security: *British Marine Mutual Insurance Association Ltd.* v. *Adamson* (1932) 48 Sh.Ct.Rep.3.

security subjects where he can vote for the full amount of his debt.[31] Where more than one such security is held each must be valued separately. Within two months after the use of such a notice of claim for voting purposes the trustee (or the majority of the creditors) may require the creditor holding the security to convey it to the trustee at the expense of the estate on payment of the specified value with the addition of 20 per cent.[32] The creditor can, after 21 days from the date of the voting and before he has been required to convey the security, correct the valuation by a new notice of claim.

In the same way, the creditor holding a security must, in claiming a ranking, in his notice of claim put a specified value on the security and deduct the value from his debt. The trustee may then require a conveyance of the security to him on payment of the specified value out of the first of the common fund or he may reserve to the creditor the full value of the security and in either case the creditor receives a dividend only on the balance.[33] The creditor may re-value the security between the first and the second dividend or at any time while the trustee is undischarged and holds undistributed assets but he may not claim an equalising dividend.[34] If he first lodges a claim after payment of the first dividend, he values the security as at the date of the lodging of the claim.[35]

If the trustee intimates that he wishes to take over the security, the creditor cannot defeat this by withdrawing his claim.[36] If the trustee does not offer to take over the security the creditor is free to realise it.[37] If he recovers less than the specified value he may substitute the sum realised for the specified value and rank for the balance. If he recovers more than the specified value the trustee is entitled to substitute the sum realised for the specified value and rank the creditor only for the balance of his claim so far as subsequent dividends are concerned but the trustee cannot restrict the subsequent dividends to the creditor so as to take into account the over-payment in the earlier dividends.[38] The creditor in a question

---

31 s.55.

32 s.58.

33 s.61; the trustee must tender payment: *Maclachlan* v. *Maxwell*, 1910 S.C.87.

34 *Commercial Bank of Scotland Ltd.* v. *Speedie's Tr.* (1885) 13 R.257; *Wood* v. *MacKay's Tr.*, 1936 S.C.93.

35 *Commercial Bank of Scotland* v. *Muirhead's Tr.*, 1918 1 S.L.T.132.

36 *Macdougall's Tr.* v. *Lockhart* (1903) 5 F.905.

37 *Henderson's Tr.* v. *Auld and Guild* (1872) 10 M.946; *Maclachlan* v. *Maxwell*, *supra*.

38 *Union Bank of Scotland* v. *Calder's Tr.*, 1937 S.C.850.

with the trustee must apply the sum realised *primo loco* towards the principal debt and not towards the interest accrued thereon from the date of sequestration.[38] If the sum realised is more than the creditor's claim, he must account to the trustee or the debtor for the balance.[39]

Ineffectual diligence does not create a security for purposes of these provisions.[40] Bills indorsed to a bank for collection are securities and their value must be deducted.[41]

The foregoing provisions apply only where the security subjects form part of the bankrupt's estate—where the subject "were it not for the creditor's nexus, would go to increase the divisible fund."[42] They do not apply to a collateral security. Such securities must be specified in the creditor's oath or notice of claim and must be valued and deducted for purposes of voting but not for ranking.[43] The creditor can realise them and receive a dividend on the full amount of the debt so long as he does not receive more than 100p in the pound.

5. Effect of Inhibition

Where a creditor has used an inhibition, he is entitled to a preference in the ranking on the heritable estate.[44] The mode of giving this preference is regulated by Professor Bell's five canons of ranking.[45] The general principle is that the inhibitor obtains a preference over creditors whose debts were contracted after the inhibition (posterior creditors), but does not obtain a preference over creditors whose debts were contracted before the inhibition (anterior creditors) and the anterior creditors obtain no preference over the posterior creditors.[46] The procedure is that the proceeds of the heritable estate are firstly divided among all the creditors *pari passu;* the anterior creditors receive a dividend on this basis; the

38 *Union Bank of Scotland* v. *Calder's Tr.*, 1937 S.C.850.

39 *Kinmond Luke & Co.* v. *James Finlay & Co.* (1904) 6 F.564; *Clydesdale Bank Ltd.* v. *McIntyre,* 1909 S.C.1405.

40 *Dow & Co.* v. *Union Bank* (1875) 2 R.459.

41 *Clydesdale Bank* v. *Liqrs. of James Allan Senior & Son,* 1926 S.C.235.

42 Goudy, p.319. See *McClelland* v. *Bank of Scotland* (1857) 19 D.574; *British Linen Bank* v. *Gourlay* (1877) 4 R.651; *Royal Bank* v. *Purdom* (1877) 15 S.L.R.13; *University of Glasgow* v. *Yuill's Tr.* (1882) 9 R.643; *Royal Bank of Scotland* v. *Millar & Co.'s Tr.* (1882) 9 R.679.

43 ss.21, 45; Goudy, p.168.

44 s.97.

45 Bell, *Comm.*, II, 413.

46 *Baird & Brown* v. *Stirrat's Tr.* (1872) 10 M.414.

ranking is then calculated on the basis that the posterior debts did not exist; the inhibitor then draws back from the posterior creditors the difference between what he would receive on the first basis and what he would receive on the second. For example, if the debts of each of the three classes are equal in amount and the dividend on a *pari passu* ranking is 50p per pound, the anterior creditors receive 50p. If there had been no posterior debts the *pari passu* dividend would have been 75p. The inhibitor therefore draws 25p from the posterior creditors so that he obtains 75p and they receive 25p.

It has been held that where the debtor entered into a lease prior to the inhibition, the rent payable for a period after the inhibition, and damages for breach of the lease arising when the trustee in the sequestration failed to adopt it, were anterior debts.[47]

In the ranking on the moveable estate the inhibitor is not obliged to deduct what he has drawn from the heritable estate affected by the inhibition.[48]

6. Co-obligants

The creditor must in his notice of claim put a specified value on the obligation of any co-obligant who is liable in relief to the bankrupt and on any security which he holds from an obligant liable in relief to the bankrupt or from which the bankrupt has a right of relief.[49] The value is deducted from the claim for purposes of voting, but not of ranking, and the trustee can require an assignation of the obligation or security on payment of the specified value plus 20 per cent.[50]

A co-obligant is not freed from liability by the payment of a dividend to the creditor or by the creditor's assent to the discharge of the bankrupt, a composition or a deed of arrangement.[51] If the co-obligant pays the debt in full he may require the creditor to grant an assignation of the debt to him and he may then rank on the estate for the relief to which he is entitled. If, however, the creditor draws a dividend from the bankrupt's estate and then obtains payment of the deficiency from a co-obligant, the latter cannot rank on the estate because of the rule against double ranking.[52] If all the obligants are bankrupt, the creditor can rank on each of the estates so

[47] *Scottish Waggon Co. Ltd.* v. *James Hamilton's Tr.* (1906) 13 S.L.T.779.

[48] *Scottish Waggon Co. Ltd.* v. *James Hamilton's Tr., supra; cf. Baird & Brown* v. *Stirrat's Tr., supra.*

[49] s.56.

[50] s.58.

[51] s.52.

[52] Bell, *Comm.*, II, 420. See *Mackinnon* v. *Monkhouse* (1881) 9 R.393, *per* L.P. Inglis at p.401.

long as he recovers no more than 100p in the pound in all. There can then be no relief between the estates because of the double ranking rule. The creditor must deduct from his claim any payments made to him by any co-obligant and any dividends received from the estates of co-obligants prior to the sequestration.[53] However, payments and dividends received from co-obligants or their estates after bankruptcy do not require to be deducted.

7. Cautionary Obligations

Where there is a cautionary obligation the position is complicated because the creditor usually has alternative courses of action. One general point to be made *in limine* is that the creditor's claim against any estate must be made under deduction of securities held from the principal debtor and of all payments or dividends received from the debtor or cautioners or their estates prior to the date of sequestration of the estate against which the claim is being made but no adjustment is required in respect of payments and dividends subsequently received.[53]

Three cases can be distinguished:

(1) Where the debtor is bankrupt and the cautioners solvent. The creditor may (a) claim in the debtor's sequestration and then require the cautioners to pay the deficiency, or, (b) simply demand payment from the cautioners without resorting to the debtor's estate.

In (a) the creditor does not need to value the cautionary obligation because the cautioner is not a co-obligant against whom the bankrupt has a right of relief. With regard to the deficiency, if the cautionary obligation is proper (*i.e.* appears *ex facie* of the instrument), each cautioner is liable only for a *pro rata* share;[54] but in the case of improper cautionry, each is liable for the full amount of the deficiency. Any cautioner who pays more than his *pro rata* share has a right of relief against his co-cautioners for the excess. The cautioners cannot claim against the debtor's estate because of the rule against double ranking but they may be able to rank in respect of payments made before the sequestration.

---

53 *Hamilton* v. *Cuthbertson* (1841) 3 D.494; *Royal Bank of Scotland* v. *Commercial Bank of Scotland* (1881) 8 R.805, *per* L.P. Inglis at p.817.

54 Bell, *Prin.*, §267.

In (b) the distinction between proper and improper cautionry determines the nature of the cautioner's liability as in (a). The cautioners have a *pro rata* right of relief *inter se* and have a right of relief against the debtor's estate as they stand in the position of the creditor. The right of relief is not dependent upon an assignation by the creditor to them but in some circumstances it may be advantageous to have such an assignation.[55] Where the limit of the cautioner's liability is less than the debtor's liability to the creditor, it is a question of construction of the cautionary obligation whether the cautioner has guaranteed a part of the total debt and is thus entitled to rank on the debtor's estate in respect of the proportion which he has paid, or whether he has guaranteed the whole debt and placed a limitation on his liability and is thus not entitled to rank on the debtor's estate.[56]

(2) Where the debtor and some of the cautioners are bankrupt and some of the cautioners solvent.

The creditor may (a) claim for the whole amount of the debt on each of the estates of the debtor and the insolvent cautioners and then require payment of the deficiency from the solvent cautioners, or (b) simply demand payment from the solvent cautioners.

(a) The solvent cautioners are liable *pro rata inter se* and have no right of relief against the estates of the debtor and insolvent cautioners because of the rule against double ranking. If the creditor has received in dividends (not in ranking) from the estate of an insolvent cautioner more than the cautioner's *pro rata* share, the estate has a right of relief against the solvent cautioners for the excess.[57]

(b) The solvent cautioners are again liable *pro rata inter se.* They have a right of relief against the debtor's estate. They also have jointly a right of relief against the estate of each insolvent cautioner for the excess of what they have paid over their original *pro rata* share.[58]

(3) Where the debtor and all the cautioners are insolvent the creditor can rank for the full amount of his debt on each estate

---

55 Gloag & Irvine, p.806.

56 *Harvie's Trs.* v. *Bank of Scotland* (1885) 12 R.1141; *Veitch* v. *National Bank of Scotland,* 1907 S.C.554.

57 Bell, *Comm.*, I, 373.

58 *ibid.*

although he cannot obtain more than 100p in the pound in all. Because of the double ranking rule the cautioners have no right of relief *inter se* or against the debtor's estate. If the creditor obtains more than 100p in the pound, an estate which has paid more than its share of the debt is entitled to the benefit of the creditor's ranking on the other estates.[59]

8. Cautioner's Securities

Where a cautioner holds securities from the principal debtor, it is to his advantage if the creditor ranks on the debtor's estate, because if the cautioner has to rank for relief he must deduct the value of the security. If the creditor has ranked on the debtor's estate and then recovered the deficiency from the cautioner, the cautioner can apply the security towards what he has paid under the cautionary obligation and can rank on the debtor's estate in respect of other debts which are also covered by the security.[60]

A cautioner must, however, share the benefit of his security with his co-cautioners.[61]

Where there are two bankrupt co-obligants, one of whom is cautioner for the other and holds a security from the other, the security is applied first to indemnifying the cautioner's estate in respect of the dividends paid to the creditor. The sum obtained by this is then used to pay a further dividend to all the cautioner's creditors, including the creditor in the cautionary obligation. The process is repeated until the security is exhausted.[62]

9. Bills of Exchange

If the bankrupt has given a creditor a bill for an amount larger than the debt, the creditor cannot rank for more than the amount of the debt either on the estate of the bankrupt or on the estate of a cautioner but if the bill has been negotiated a holder in due course can rank for the full amount.[63] Similarly, if the bankrupt has negotiated bills to his creditor in security of the debt, the creditor can rank for the full amount on the estates of the parties liable thereon. An accommodation party is treated as a cautioner and so, while on the one hand he may rank on the debtor's estate for relief if

59 Gloag & Irvine, p.841.
60 *Jamieson* v. *Forrest* (1875) 2 R.701.
61 Gloag & Irvine, pp.819-824.
62 *Royal Bank of Scotland* v. *Saunders & Sons' Trs.* (1882) 9 R.(H.L.)67.
63 *Jackson* v. *McIver* (1875) 2 R.882.

he has paid the bill, on the other hand, if he and the debtor are bankrupt, the creditor can rank for the full amount on both estates but the trustee of the accommodation party cannot rank for relief on the debtor's estate.[64] Where the accommodation party holds funds or property of the debtor and both parties are bankrupt it seems that the trustee on the estate of the accommodation party cannot plead retention or compensation if the funds or property were not appropriated as security for the liability on the bill.[65] If there is such a specific appropriation the trustee can plead retention or compensation.

10. Distribution

The realised estate is applied in payment of the bankrupt's debts in the following order, each class being paid in full before the succeeding class becomes entitled to any payment:

(1) the expenses of the petitioning and concurring creditors,[66]
(2) the commission and expenses of the trustee,[67]
(3) privileged and preferable debts,
(4) ordinary and contingent debts. These rank *pari passu* but if a contingent debt is valued the dividend is paid only on the value; if it is not valued a dividend is set aside until the contingency is purified,
(5) the debts of postponed creditors, *e.g.* debts falling under s.3 of the Partnership Act 1890,[68] and the claim of the bankrupt's wife in respect of her estate lent to the husband or inmixed with his funds which is postponed to the claims of creditors for valuable consideration.[69] A wife who has lent money to a firm of which her husband is a partner is not a postponed creditor of the firm.[70]

11. Privileged and Preferable Debts

Deathbed and funeral expenses are privileged debts and are paid before all ordinary debts, debts secured by diligence and debts

---

64 *Anderson* v. *Mackinnon* (1876) 3 R.608; For the position as to cross-accommodation bills see Goudy, pp.574-576 and *Encyclopaedia of the Laws of Scotland*, Vol. II, p.253.
65 *Royal Bank of Scotland* v. *Saunders & Sons' Trs., supra*.
66 s.40.
67 s.117.
68 *Crann & Co.'s Seqn.* (1909) 25 Sh.Ct.Rep.238.
69 Married Women's Property (Scotland) Act 1881, s.1(4).
70 *Lumsden* v. *Sym* (1912) 28 Sh.Ct.Rep.168.

secured over the general estate.[71] *Inter se* they rank *pari passu.* Deathbed expenses include medical fees and expenses incurred during the last illness. Funeral expenses include the cost of family mournings.

Thereafter the following are paid in priority to all other debts, rank equally among themselves and are paid in full unless the assets are insufficient to meet them in which case they abate in equal proportions:[72]

(a) all poor or other local rates due by the bankrupt at the date of sequestration[73] and having become due and payable[74] within 12 months next before that date and all assessed taxes[75] assessed on the bankrupt up to 5 April next before that date and not exceeding in the whole one year's assessment.[76] The Crown has no preference at common law.[77] The preference is extended to include Class 4 social security contributions,[78] and sums which an employer should have deducted as income tax on employees' emoluments.[79]

(b) all wages or salary of any clerk or servant in respect of service rendered to the bankrupt during four months before the date of sequestration[73] not exceeding £800 to any one clerk or servant.

(c) all wages of any workman or labourer, not exceeding £800 to any one, whether payable for time or piecework, in respect of services rendered to the bankrupt during four months before the date of sequestration.[73] Where a labourer in husbandry has contracted for a portion of his wages in a lump sum, the priority extends to the whole sum or such part as the court decides to be due proportionate to the time of service up to the sequestration.

---

71 Erskine, III, 9, 43.

72 s.118, as amended by Companies Act 1947, s.115(1).

73 *i.e.* the date of actual award of sequestration. In the sequestration of a deceased debtor the relevant date is the date of death: s.118(4).

74 Rates levied under a resolution made after the date of sequestration are not "payable" at the date of sequestration even although the premises were occupied during the year of assessment: *Mitchell* v. *Smith* (1936) 52 Sh.Ct.Rep.39.

75 Development Land Tax 1976, s.42; Betting and Gaming Duties Act 1972, Sched. 1, para. 14, Sched. 2, para. 11, Sched. 3, para. 16; Finance Act 1972, s.41 (value added tax); Finance Act 1972, s.52, Sched. 7, para. 18 (car tax).

76 The Revenue may select different years for different taxes: *Lord Advocate* v. *Liqrs. of Purvis Industries Ltd.*, 1958 S.C.338.

77 *Admiralty* v. *Blair's Tr.*, 1916 S.C.247.

78 Social Security (Consequential Provisions) Act 1975, Sched. 2, para. 1.

79 Finance Act 1952, s.30(6).

(d) debts in respect of social security contributions and other debts specified in Social Security Act 1975, s.153(2), Social Security Pensions Act 1975, Sched. 3 and any corresponding Northern Irish provisions.[80]

Certain payments due under employment legislation are treated as if they were wages payable by the employer to the employed in respect of the periods for which they are payable.[81]

The trustee, with the commissioners' consent, may dispense with the lodging of oaths or notices of claim relative to these debts and may pay them before the period for payment of the first dividend.[82]

12. Ancestor's Creditors

The creditors of the bankrupt's ancestor have a preferential right in respect of items of the ancestor's estate which can be distinguished and identified.[83] The trustee in the bankrupt's estate is trustee also for the ancestor's creditors and it is unnecessary and incompetent to sequestrate the ancestor's estates to effectuate this preference.[84]

13. Summary Sequestration

A summary form of sequestration is competent where the debtor's assets of every description do not in the aggregate exceed £4,000 in value. The modifications appropriate to this process are set forth in ss.175[85] and 176 of the Act of 1913. It seems that the court has a discretion as to the awarding of summary sequestration.[86]

---

80 B.A. s.118(1)(*f*) substituted by Social Security Pensions Act 1975, Sched. 4, para. 1.

81 Employment Protection (Consolidation) Act 1978, ss.121, 125. See Chap. 23, para. 8.

82 B.A., s.118(3), (3A) (substituted by Insolvency Act 1976, s.5).

83 See Chap. 26, para. 6; B.A., s.97.

84 *Menzies* v. *Poutz,* 1916 S.C.143.

85 As amended by Law Reform (Miscellaneous Provisions) (Scotland) Act 1980, s.12.

86 *Mackay's Seqn.* (1918) 34 Sh.Ct.Rep.152; *Reading Trust Ltd.* v. *Adamson* (1936) 52 Sh.Ct.Rep.225. *Cf. Montgomery* v. *MacCallum* (1936) 52 Sh.Ct.Rep.227.

CHAPTER 22

ALTERNATIVES TO SEQUESTRATION

1. Composition

At the first meeting of creditors,[1] or at any subsequent meeting,[2] the bankrupt or his friends may offer a composition, *i.e.* offer to pay the expenses of sequestration, the remuneration of the trustee and the preferable debts in full and to pay a rateable proportion of the ordinary debts. Security for the payment must also be offered. If a majority of the creditors in number and a majority of three-quarters in value resolve that the offer shall be entertained, the offer is advertised in the *Gazette* and a subsequent meeting of creditors appointed. If the same majority accepts the offer at the next meeting, a bond of caution is lodged with the trustee, the trustee makes a report of the resolution of the meeting to the sheriff clerk and application is made to the court for approval. The court may hear objections. The condition imposed by s.146 as to payment of at least 25p in the pound must be satisfied. If the offer is approved, the bankrupt makes the declaration required by s.144.[3] The court then discharges him of all debts and obligations contracted by him and declares the sequestration at an end and the bankrupt reinvested in his estate, but reserving the claims of the creditors for the composition against the bankrupt and the cautioner.[4]

The bankrupt and the cautioner cannot object to debts listed in the composition offer or in the state of affairs unless the entry was appropriately qualified and notice of the objection given to the creditor.[5] No person who has not produced an oath as creditor before the date of the deliverance approving the composition is entitled to demand payment from the cautioner after two years from the date of the deliverance but the claim for composition of such a creditor against the bankrupt and his estate is reserved.[6]

If the composition offer is refused by the meeting of the creditors, no subsequent offer is entertained unless nine-tenths of the creditors in number and value agree.[7]

---

1 B.A., s.134.
2 s.136.
3 s.137.
4 s.137.
5 s.140.
6 s.141.
7 s.142.

It is possible to have an extra-judicial composition contract.[8] This is a purely contractual arrangement in which the debtor offers a composition on the debts in exchange for a discharge. It is not binding on a creditor who has not assented to it. Accession is a matter of fact and no obligatory writing is necessary.[9] If the composition is not paid, the original debt revives.[10]

2. Deed of Arrangement

A sequestration may be terminated by a deed of arrangement. At the meeting for the election of the trustee or at any subsequent meeting called for the purpose, a majority in number and three-fourths in value of the creditors present or represented at the meeting may resolve that the estate ought to be wound up under a deed of arrangement and that an application should be presented to the Lord Ordinary or sheriff to sist procedure in the sequestration for a period not exceeding two months.[11] The creditors who vote must support their claims by vouchers and a creditor whose claim does not amount to £20 is not entitled to vote.[12] The bankrupt's wife, if she is a creditor, is entitled to vote.[13] The creditors cannot at this meeting determine the terms of the deed of arrangement.[14]

If the resolution is carried at the first meeting of creditors, it is not necessary to elect a trustee. The bankrupt, or any person appointed by the meeting, may report the resolution to the Lord Ordinary or sheriff within four days of its date and apply for a sist of the sequestration in terms thereof. The Lord Ordinary or sheriff, after hearing any interested party, may grant the application if he finds that the resolution was duly carried and that the application is reasonable.[15] If the application is granted, he may also make any necessary arrangements for the interim management of the estate but he should not appoint a judicial factor for this purpose if a trustee has already been appointed.[16]

---

8 See Goudy, Chap. XXXVI.

9 *Henry* v. *Strachan & Spence* (1897) 24 R.1045.

10 *Woods Parker & Co.* v. *Ainslie* (1860) 22 D.723.

11 s.34. If the deed is not produced within the period of sist, the sequestration proceeds: *Hunter's Seqn.* (1930) 46 Sh.Ct.Rep.52.

12 s.96; *North of Scotland Banking Co.* v. *Ireland* (1880) 8 R.117.

13 *MacNaught* v. *Sievwright,* 1927 S.C.285.

14 *Dixon* v. *Greenock Distillery Co.* (1867) 5 M.1033.

15 s.35.

16 s.36; *Brown* v. *Bayley's Trs.,* 1910 S.C.76.

If the sequestration is sisted, the creditors may at any time within the period of the sist produce to the Lord Ordinary or sheriff a deed of arrangement signed by the bankrupt and subscribed by, or by authority of, a majority in number and three-fourths in value of the whole creditors claiming on the estate.[17] It is not necessary that there should be a further meeting of creditors to adopt the deed but it has been said that the statute contemplates this.[18] If there is subsequently opposition, the signing creditors must produce their claims and vouchers. The Lord Ordinary or sheriff considers the deed, makes such intimation thereof as he thinks proper, including intimation to non-concurring creditors,[19] hears parties having an interest and makes any inquiry he thinks necessary.

There are no prescribed provisions for a deed of arrangement. It may provide for the realisation and distribution of the estate by the creditors or by a trustee. The arrangement may be by way of a composition in which event it may be accepted without caution.[20] Before he can approve the deed, the Lord Ordinary or sheriff must be satisfied that it has been duly entered into and executed and is reasonable, *i.e.* that its terms are of "such a kind as may fairly be forced on a dissentient minority."[21] It is for those proponing the deed to show that it is reasonable.[22] The fact that it is subscribed by creditors to the requisite number and value is in no way conclusive. A proper explanation of the cause of the deficiency in the estate should be given by evidence on oath or otherwise. The public interest must also be considered because the effect of the deed may be that the bankrupt can immediately set up in a new business under a different trading name without having to make any disclosures of his previous history. Failure to pay 25p in the pound may raise a prima facie case of unreasonableness.

If the Lord Ordinary or sheriff approves of the deed, he declares the sequestration at an end and the judgment declaring same is recorded in the same manner as if the sequestration had been

---

[17] s.37; creditors for under £20 are not taken into account: *Cassils & Co.'s Seqn.* (1899) 15 Sh.Ct.Rep.231.

[18] *per* Lord Shand, *North of Scotland Banking Co.* v. *Ireland, supra,* at p.119; *per* Lord Deas, *Dixon* v. *Greenock Distillery Co., supra,* at p.1036.

[19] *per* Lord Shand, *North of Scotland Banking Co.* v. *Ireland, supra,* at p.119.

[20] s.34.

[21] Goudy, p.421. See *Tait's Seqn.* (1913) 29 Sh.Ct.Rep.94; *Fraser's Seqn.* (1935) 51 Sh.Ct.Rep.225.

[22] *Stone* v. *Woodhouse Hambly & Co.,* 1937 S.C.824.

recalled.[23] The deed is then binding on all the creditors as if they had acceded thereto.[24] If the bankrupt wishes to be discharged he must stipulate for his discharge as a part of the arrangement. If the arrangement is in the form of a composition and the bankrupt defaults in payment the creditor may sue for his whole debt.[25] A creditor whose debt is incurred after the award of sequestration may sequestrate the bankrupt *de novo* but the trustee under the deed of arrangement is only bound to denude subject to such rights as he may have acquired on behalf of the creditors under the former sequestration.[26]

Although the sequestration has been recalled, it still has effect for the purpose of preventing, challenging or setting aside preferences over the estate.[27] Where the deed of arrangement transfers the estate to a purchaser the right to challenge is not carried.[28]

If the original resolution is not duly reported, or if a sist is refused, or if the deed is not duly produced, or if it is not approved of, the sequestration proceeds and the court makes all necessary orders, by appointing meetings of creditors and otherwise, for resuming the necessary procedure.[29] The period of time subsequent to the resolution is not reckoned in calculating the various periods prescribed for the sequestration procedure. It has been held that the time limit of two months applies to the production of the deed and not to the judicial approval of the deed.[30]

3. Trust Deeds

A trust deed may be adopted as a quick and cheap alternative to sequestration. This is a voluntary extra-judicial arrangement in which the insolvent grants in favour of a trustee a deed transferring his property to the trustee for behoof of his creditors for their several rights and preferences. The deed usually provides that the trustee shall be judge of the creditors' claims; that the trustee shall have power to reduce voluntary dispositions and illegal or fraudulent preferences;[31] that the estate shall be distributed in

---

23 ss.37, 39.

24 s.37.

25 *Alexander and Austin* v. *Yuille* (1873) 1 R.185.

26 *A.* v. *B,* 1912 2 S.L.T.498.

27 s.37.

28 *Smith & Co.* v. *Smyth* (1889) 16 R.392.

29 s.38.

30 *Williamson's Sequestration,* 1923 S.L.T.122.

31 The trustee does not have the power if there is no provision in the deed: *Fleming's Trs.* v. *McHardy* (1892) 19 R.542.

accordance with the rules pertaining in a sequestration;[32] and that acceptance of a dividend by a creditor is to import a discharge.[33] The trustee completes title to the estate and realises it; the creditors lodge claims which are adjudged by the trustee;[34] the trustee distributes the estate among the creditors in accordance with their rights and preferences; and any surplus is returned to the insolvent. The trustee must complete title to shares by obtaining and registering a transfer in the ordinary form.[35]

The insolvent may revoke the deed at any time before the creditors are aware of it.[36] A creditor who accedes to the trust deed[37] cannot do diligence against the estate or petition for the sequestration of the insolvent unless a non-acceding creditor is obtaining a preference by doing diligence.[38] If, however, the trustee rejects his claim, he can raise an action against the truster and the trustee to constitute his claim.[39] A non-acceding creditor can execute effectual diligence against the assets of the estate until the trustee has completed his title thereto; after completion the assets are not liable to diligence.[40] A non-acceding creditor can reduce the trust deed as a fraudulent preference within six months of its date[41] and he can also petition for sequestration.[42] He can, alternatively, without resorting to sequestration, render the truster notour bankrupt within six months of the deed, arrest in the trustee's hands within four months and recover his debt in a subsequent furthcoming in which the trust deed is reduced *ope exceptionis*.[43] Sequestration, at any subsequent time, supersedes the trust deed and the trust estate must

---

32 This does not affect a non-acceding creditor, *e.g.* the trustee's wife: *Mitchell* v. *Hunter* (1901) 17 Sh.Ct.Rep.208. For the common law rules which apply in the absence of such a provision, see *Encyclopaedia of the Laws of Scotland,* Vol. XV, p. 293.

33 *Larkin* v. *Morrow* (1932) 48 Sh.Ct.Rep.59.

34 An affidavit is not required; a statement suffices. The lodging of a claim does not interrupt prescription: *Blair* v. *Horn* (1858) 21 D.45.

35 *Walker* v. *Hunter* (1933) 49 Sh.Ct.Rep.139.

36 *per* Lord Cranworth, *Synnot* v. *Simpson* (1854) 5 H.L.C.121 at 133; *per* Lord Dunedin, *Carmichael* v. *Carmichael's Exix.,* 1920 S.C.(H.L.)195 at 201.

37 As to proof of accession, see Goudy, pp.477-479.

38 *Jopp* v. *Hay* (1844) 7 D.260; *Campbell & Beck* v. *Macfarlane* (1862) 24 D.1097.

39 *Crerar* v. *Dow* (1906) 22 Sh.Ct.Rep.311.

40 *Gibson* v. *May* (1841) 3 D.974; *Ogilvie & Son* v. *Taylor* (1887) 14 R.399, *per* Lord Young at p.401; *Doughty* v. *Wells* (1906) 14 S.L.T.299.

41 *Mackenzie* v. *Calder* (1868) 6 M.833; *Nicolson* v. *Johnstone & Wright* (1872) 11 M.179; but not after six months: *Lamb's Trs.* v. *Reid* (1883) 11 R.76.

42 *per* Lord Gifford, *Kyd* v. *Waterson* (1880) 7 R.884 at 886.

43 *Gray & Sons* v. *Steel* (1891) 7 Sh.Ct.Rep.137.

be handed over to the trustee in the sequestration.[44] A non-acceding creditor is entitled to a dividend from the trust estate without giving a discharge and he can sue the trustee for his dividend.[45] A creditor cannot bring an action against the trustee for declarator that he is entitled to a ranking.[46]

The insolvent retains a radical right in the estate and, when the creditors are satisfied, he can call on the trustee to account for and to reconvey the surplus.[47] He is not, however, entitled to a retrocession of the estate unless full satisfaction has been made or the creditors consent to abandon some portion of it or a discharge or composition is given.[48] Whether the discharge is in effect a discharge on composition depends on its terms and on the provisions of the trust deed.

---

44 Bell, *Comm.*, II, 391; *Nicolson* v. *Johnstone & Wright, supra; Salaman* v. *Rosslyn's Trs.* (1900) 3 F.298. As to the position of the trustee under the trust deed where no creditor has acceded, see *Mess* v. *Hay* (1898) 1 F.(H.L.)22. *McAlister* v. *Swinburne & Co.* (1874) 1 R.958 (sequestration on debtor's petition).

45 *Ogilvie & Son* v. *Taylor* (1887) 14 R.399; *Athya* v. *Clydesdale Bank* (1881) 18 S.L.R.287; *Davidson* v. *Union Bank of Scotland* (1881) 19 S.L.R.15; *Heritable Securities Investment Association Ltd.* v. *Wingate & Co.* (1891) 29 S.L.R.904.

46 *Mackie* v. *McMillan* (1925) 41 Sh.Ct.Rep.339.

47 *Gilmour* v. *Gilmours* (1873) 11 M.853; *Edmond* v. *Dingwall's Trs.* (1860) 23 D.21; *Buttercase & Geddie's Tr.* v. *Geddie* (1897) 24 R.1128.

48 *Flett* v. *Mustard*, 1936 S.C.269.

CHAPTER 23

LIQUIDATION

1. The Process

A company registered under the Companies Acts cannot be sequestrated.[1] The legal process corresponding to sequestration in the case of companies is winding-up or, as it is more usually known in Scotland, liquidation.[2] An official known as a liquidator is appointed to distribute the assets of the company to the creditors in accordance with their rights and to distribute any balance among the contributories. A liquidator, however, differs from the trustee in a sequestration in that there is no transfer of the company's property to him; he is not vested in the estate to the exclusion of the company; he has no new or independent title; he is a mere administrator for the statutory purposes and the doctrine of *tantum et tale* has no application in relation to him.[3]

2. The Petition

A creditor of a company may petition for its liquidation if the company is unable to pay its debts.[4] The company is deemed to be unable to pay its debts if (a) a creditor for a sum exceeding £200 then due has served on the company at its registered office a demand under his hand requiring payment of the sum and the company has for three weeks thereafter neglected to pay the sum or to secure or compound for it to the creditor's satisfaction[5] or (b) the *induciae* of a charge for payment on an extract decree, an extract registered bond or an extract registered protest have expired without payment being made[6] or (c) it is proved to the satisfaction of the court that the company is unable to pay its debts, contingent and prospective

---

1 *Standard Property Investment Co. Ltd.* v. *Dunblane Hydropathic Co. Ltd.* (1884) 12 R.328.

2 *Haig and Others* v. *Lord Advocate,* 1976 S.L.T.(Notes)16.

3 *Gray's Trs.* v. *Benhar Coal Co. Ltd.* (1881) 9 R.225; *Clark* v. *West Calder Oil Co.* (1882) 9 R.1017; *Bank of Scotland* v. *Liquidators of Hutchison Main & Co. Ltd.,* 1914 S.C.(H.L.)1. See also *Smith* v. *Lord Advocate,* 1978 S.C.259.

4 Companies Act 1948, ss.224, 222(*e*). As to procedure, see McBryde and Dowie, *Petition Procedure in the Court of Session,* pp.19-30.

5 s.223(*a*). There must be 21 clear days between the day of demand and the presenting of the petition: *Re Lympne Investments Ltd.* [1972] 1 W.L.R.523.

6 s.223(*c*).

liabilities being taken into account.[7] A contingent creditor may petition but there will be no hearing until he finds security for costs and a prima facie case is established.[8] A creditor who holds a floating charge over property comprised in the company's property and undertaking may petition for liquidation if his security is in jeopardy, *i.e.* if events have occurred or are about to occur which render it unreasonable in the interests of the creditor that the company should retain power to dispose of the property subject to the floating charge.[9]

The Court of Session has jurisdiction to wind up any company registered in Scotland.[10] If the share capital paid up or credited as paid up does not exceed £120,000 the petition may be presented to the sheriff court in whose jurisdiction the registered office is situated.[11] If any company or a holder of shares or debentures has lodged a *caveat* no order is made by the court on presentation of the petition except after hearing parties.[12] Otherwise, the court orders such intimation service and advertisement as it thinks fit.[13] There must be advertisement in the *Edinburgh Gazette* and as the court directs in one or more newspapers circulating in the district where the registered office is situate.[14] The court may also, on presentation, or at any time before the first appointment of liquidators, appoint a provisional liquidator.[15] Whether such an appointment should be made is in the discretion of the court.[16] The provisional liquidator has to take into his custody and control all the property and things in action to which the company is, or appears to be, entitled.[17] His powers may be limited or restricted by the order appointing him.[18] He may be granted further powers.

The liquidation is deemed to commence at the time of the presentation of the petition for winding-up unless the company has

[7] s.223(*d*).

[8] s.224(1).

[9] Companies (Floating Charges and Receivers) (Scotland) Act 1972, s.4.

[10] 1948 Act, s.220(1). As to the petition, see R.C.202.

[11] s.220(3).

[12] R.C.202(*c*); A.S., 20 March 1930, para. 5, as amended by A.S. (Sheriff Court Liquidations) 1948, para. 3.

[13] R.C.202(*c*).

[14] R.C.202(*d*).

[15] s.238; R.C.202(*e*).

[16] Buckley on the *Companies Acts* (13th ed.), pp.505-6; *Levy* v. *Napier,* 1962 S.L.T.264; *McCabe* v. *Andrew Middleton (Enterprises) Ltd.*, 1969 S.L.T.(Sh.Ct.) 29.

[17] s.243(1). See McBryde, 1977 S.L.T.(News)145.

[18] s.238(4).

previously passed a resolution for voluntary liquidation in which case the liquidation commences at the time of passing of the resolution.[19]

Generally, a petitioning creditor whose debt is unpaid is entitled to a winding-up order *ex debito justitiae*.[20] A letter from the company's solicitors stating that the company had no assets on which execution could be levied is evidence that the company is unable to pay its debts.[21] If the company shows that the debt is bona fide disputed the petition will be dismissed because the purpose of the petition is not to constitute a debt.[22] If the matter is in doubt, the petition will be sisted to allow constitution.[23] The dispute, however, must be as to the existence of the debt and not merely as to its precise amount.[24] It may be an answer for the company to show that the petitioner has security for his debt if it is clear that the security commands in the market the amount of the debt.[25] The petition may be refused if the general voice of the creditors is against the application or if it is shown that refusal of the order would not prejudice the petitioner.[26] If a petitioner is found not entitled to present the petition or if he fails to proceed with the petition, another creditor can be sisted in his place.[27]

3. Conspectus of Procedure

The making of the winding-up order is intimated to the Register of Companies and advertised in the *Edinburgh Gazette*.[28] The liquidator has to find caution. Within one month of the *Gazette* advertisement the liquidator must call by advertisement, meetings of creditors and contributories to appoint a committee of inspection.[29] The liquidator takes into his custody or under his control all

---

19 s.229(2); *Haig and Others* v. *Lord Advocate*, 1976 S.L.T.(Notes)16.

20 *Smyth & Co.* v. *Salem Flour Mills Co. Ltd.* (1887) 14 R.441.

21 *Re Douglas Griggs Engineering Ltd.* [1963] Ch.19.

22 *Cuninghame* v. *Walkinshaw Oil Co. Ltd.* (1886) 14 R.87; *W. & J. C. Pollok* v. *The Gaeta Pioneer Mining Co.*, 1907 S.C.182; *Mann* v. *Goldstein* [1968] 1 W.L.R. 1091; *Holt Southey Ltd.* v. *Catnic Components Ltd.* [1978] 1 W.L.R.630.

23 *Landauer & Co.* v. *Alexander & Co.*, 1919 S.C.492.

24 *Re Tweeds Garages Ltd.* [1962] Ch.406.

25 *Commercial Bank of Scotland Ltd.* v. *Lanark Oil Co. Ltd.* (1886) 14 R.147.

26 *Smyth & Co.* v. *Salem Flour Mills Co. Ltd.*, *supra; Bouboulis* v. *Mann Macneal & Co.*, 1926 S.C.637. See also *Foxhall & Gyle (Nurseries) Ltd. Ptrs.*, 1978 S.L.T. (Notes)29.

27 R.C.204.

28 R.C.205.

29 s.252; R.C.208.

the property and things in action to which the company is, or appears to be entitled. If and so long as there is no liquidator, all the company's property is deemed to be in the custody of the court.[30] The liquidator has power *inter alia* to bring or defend actions and compromise debts with the sanction of the court or committee of inspection.[31] Subject to general rules, he has the same powers as the trustee on a bankrupt estate.[32] The court fixes the time or times within which creditors must prove their debts or be excluded from any distribution made before the debts are proved.[33]

The court must cause the assets of the company to be collected and applied in discharge of its liabilities.[34]

The assets of the company are applied first to payment of the preferential debts, then in satisfaction of its liabilities *pari passu* and then, unless the articles otherwise provide, to a distribution among the members according to their rights and interests in the company.[35]

Any disposition of the property of the company, including "things in action" and any transfer of shares or alteration in the status of the members of the company, made after the commencement of the liquidation is void, unless the court otherwise orders.[36] Payments by the company into its overdrawn bank account after the presentation of the winding-up petition are accordingly void unless validated by the court.[37]

On an application being made, the court may stay proceedings against the company. Where the action is in an English or Northern Irish court application must be made to that court.[38]

When the company's affairs have been completely wound up, the court, on the liquidator's application, makes an order dissolving the company.[39]

---

30 s.243.

31 s.245(1).

32 s.245(5).

33 s.264; *Dickey* v. *Ballantine,* 1939 S.C.783.

34 s.257(1).

35 s.302.

36 s.227.

37 *Re Gray's Inn Construction Co.* [1980] 1 W.L.R.711. See also *Millar* v. *National Bank* (1891) 28 S.L.R.884.

38 s.308. See *Re Dynamics Corporation of America* [1973] 1 W.L.R.63.

39 s.274. In practice, the registrar strikes the company off the register under s.353(4); Gower, *Company Law* (4th ed.), p.724.

4. Effect on Property

As has already been mentioned, there is no transference of the property of the company to the liquidator[40] but liquidation has an effect on property similar to that of sequestration. The basis of this has not been the subject of much discussion but it seems to be founded on the liquidator's duty to administer the property for distribution among the creditors *pari passu*[41] and on the cumulative effect of a number of the sections of the Companies Acts.[42]

It is clear that property held by the company on trust must be delivered up by the liquidator if it can be identified.[43] Moveable property is affected by the provision that winding-up is equivalent to an executed or completed poinding and arrestment and decree in a furthcoming.[44] It is also equivalent to a decree of adjudication of the heritage[45] and so where missives of sale have been concluded by the company and the price has been received but no disposition delivered, on liquidation the heritage is still the company's property and the buyer's only remedy is to claim in the liquidation.[46] Similarly, where the company has delivered the disposition the buyer's title will be defective if the liquidator completes title first.[47]

The liquidator may adopt or abandon a contract made by the company. If he is to adopt it he must intimate his intention to do so within a reasonable time. If he abandons it, the other party can claim damages for breach of contract in the liquidation.[48]

5. Effect on Antecedent Transactions

Any conveyance, mortgage, delivery of goods, payment, execution or other act relating to property made or done by or against a company within six months before the commencement of its

---

40 *Gray's Trs.* v. *Benhar Coal Co. Ltd.* (1881) 9 R.225; *Clark* v. *West Calder Oil Co.*, (1882) 9 R.1017; *Bank of Scotland* v. *Liqrs. of Hutchison Main & Co. Ltd.*, 1914 S.C.(H.L.)1; *Liqr. of Style & Mantle Ltd.* v. *Prices Tailors Ltd.*, 1934 S.C.548. See also *Ayerst* v. *C. & K. (Construction) Ltd.* [1976] A.C.167; *John Mackintosh & Sons Ltd.* v. *Baker's Bargain Stores (Seaford) Ltd.* [1965] 1 W.L.R.1182.

41 *Clark* v. *West Calder Oil Co., supra., per* L.P. Inglis at p.1025.

42 *Ibid., per* Lord Shand at p.1031.

43 *Turnbull* v. *Scottish County Investment Co.*, 1939 S.C.5; *Smith* v. *Liqr. of James Birrell Ltd.*, 1967 S.L.T.(Notes)116; *Lord Advocate* v. *McInnes Textiles Ltd.*, 1978 S.L.T.(Notes)84. See Chap. 19, para. 2.

44 s.327(1)(*a*). See *Millar* v. *National Bank* (1891) 28 S.L.R.884.

45 s.327(1)(*b*).

46 *Gibson and Hunter Home Designs Ltd.*, 1976 S.C.23.

47 *Ibid, per* Lord Cameron at p.30.

48 *Crown Estate Commissioners* v. *Liqrs. of Highland Engineering Ltd.*, 1975 S.L.T.58.

winding-up which, if it had been made or done by an individual within six months before the petition for sequestration, would be deemed a fraudulent preference is invalid.[49] A fraudulent preference includes any alienation or preference which is voidable by statute or at common law on the ground of insolvency or notour bankruptcy. However, a floating charge cannot be invalidated under this provision.[50] Any conveyance or assignment by a company of all its property to trustees for the benefit of all its creditors is void to all intents.[51] The effect of liquidation on diligence has already been considered.[52]

Where there has been fraudulent trading, the court may direct that any persons who were knowingly parties to the fraudulent trading are to be personally responsible for all or any of the company's debts as the court may direct.[53] Sums recovered under such an order are dealt with as part of the general assets of the company.[54] Damages can be recovered from any promoter, past or present director, manager, liquidator or officer of the company in respect of misapplication of money or property or in respect of misfeasance or breach of trust.[55] Here again the claim forms part of the assets of the company.[56]

6. Contributories

In a liquidation, past and present members of the company may be liable to contribute to the assets of the company to an amount sufficient to pay the debts and the expenses of winding-up and to make adjustments of the rights of contributories *inter se*.[57] No member, past or present, of a company limited by shares can be liable for more than the amount unpaid on the share in respect of which he is liable. A past member is liable only if the present members cannot satisfy their contributions and he is not liable for

---

49 s.320(1).

50 s.322(3) added by Companies (Floating Charges and Receivers) (Scotland) Act 1972, s.8.

51 s.320(2).

52 See Chap. 15, para. 11 (poinding); Chap. 16, para. 13 (arrestment); Chap. 17, para. 4 (adjudication).

53 s.332.

54 *Re William C. Leitch Bros. (No. 2)* [1933] Ch.261; *Re Cyona Distributors Ltd.* [1966] Ch.462.

55 s.333.

56 *Re Park Gate Waggon Works Co.* (1881) 17 Ch.D.234.

57 1948 Act, s.212.

debts contracted after he ceased to be a member. He is not liable if he ceased to be a member more than a year before the commencement of the winding-up. The liability of a contributory creates a debt accruing due from him at the time his liability commenced but payable at the times when calls are made enforcing the liability.[58] The court makes orders enforcing the calls and such an order is conclusive evidence that the money ordered to be paid is due.[59]

If a company carries on business for more than six months with a number of members below the legal minimum of two everyone who is a member during the period and is cognisant of the illegality is severally liable for the debts contracted during the period.[60]

A member of a company whose liability to pay calls is decreased by a reduction of capital may be liable to a creditor who because of ignorance of the proceedings was not entered on the list of creditors in the reduction proceedings, if the company is later unable to pay the debt.[61] The liability is to the extent to which he would have been liable to contribute if there had been a winding-up commenced on the day before registration of the reduction minute and seems to be in addition to his liability to the company.

In the case of a company limited by guarantee, a member may be liable to pay a sum not exceeding the amount he undertook to contribute on winding-up together with any sum unpaid on his shares.[62]

In the case of an unlimited company, the contributories are liable to the full extent of their means. Persons registered as trustees are liable as contributories.[63]

7. Creditor's Claim

The creditor's remedy is to claim for his debt in the liquidation. The court may direct, on the application of the liquidator, that no action or proceeding shall be proceeded with or commenced against the company except by leave of the court and subject to such terms as the court may impose.[64] The debts which may be proved are all debts payable on a contingency and all claims against the company,

58 s.214.
59 ss.260, 262. See also s.275.
60 s.31.
61 s.70.
62 s.212.
63 *Muir* v. *City of Glasgow Bank* (1879) 6 R.(H.L.)21.
64 s.231.

present or future, certain or contingent, ascertained or sounding only in damages, a just estimate being made, so far as possible, of the value of such debts or claims as may be subject to any contingency or sound only in damages, or for some other reason do not bear a certain value.[65] Sections 45 to 62 (relating to voting and ranking for payment of dividends) and ss.96 and 105 (relating to the reckoning of majorities and the interruption of prescription) of the Bankruptcy (Scotland) Act 1913, apply *mutatis mutandis* to the liquidation.[66] The holder of a debenture secured by a floating charge is now required to value and deduct the security for voting purposes.[67]

An appeal can be taken to the court against any deliverance on claims to vote and rank within seven days of its date.[68]

The liquidator or any creditor or contributory may apply to the court to determine any question arising in the liquidation and the court may accede to the application if the determination would be just and beneficial.[69] This procedure is not appropriate for determining a claim for damages for breach of contract against the company; that should be done by a separate action for damages.[70]

If the assets are insufficient to meet the liabilities, the court may make an order as to the payment of the costs of winding-up in such order of priority as it thinks just.[71] All debts and liabilities incurred in the course of carrying on the business by the liquidator, being in the nature of salvage, rank for payment in priority to the general debts and liabilities of the company.[72]

8. Preferential Payments

The following debts are preferred and are to be discharged forthwith so far as the assets are sufficient to meet them subject to retention of the expenses of the winding-up.[73] They rank equally

---

[65] s.316.

[66] s.318.

[67] Companies (Floating Charges and Receivers) (Scotland) Act 1972, s.11(6).

[68] R.C.214.

[69] 1948 Act, s.307.

[70] *Crawford* v. *McCulloch,* 1909 S.C.1063; *Knoll Spinning Co. Ltd.* v. *Brown,* 1977 S.C.291.

[71] s.267.

[72] *Per* Cohen J., *Re S. Davis & Co. Ltd.* [1945] Ch.402 at 407.

[73] ss.267, 309, 319(6); *Re Barleycorn Enterprises Ltd.* [1970] Ch.465. A secured creditor whose debt is preferential only in part can apply the proceeds of his security to the non-preferential part: *Re William Hall (Contractors) Ltd.* [1967] 1 W.L.R.948.

inter se and abate in equal proportions if the funds are insufficient[74]:

(a) local rates due and payable within 12 months before the relevant date,[75] *i.e.* the provisional liquidator's appointment or the date of the winding-up order unless there has been previously a voluntary winding-up or, in any other case, the winding-up resolution.[76]

(b) taxes assessed up to 5 April next before the relevant date limited to one year's assessment[77] (the Revenue may select different years for each tax[78]).

(c) wages and salaries (whether or not earned by way of commission) of clerks or servants for four months before the relevant date but limited to £800 for any one claimant, and all wages (whether payable for time or piece work) of any workman or labourer in respect of services rendered during four months before the relevant date;[79] there is a limit of £800 but a labourer in husbandry paid in a lump sum at the end of the year of hiring has priority in respect of the whole sum, or a part thereof, as the court may decide to be due under the contract, proportionate to the time of service up to the relevant date.[80] Guarantee payments and certain other payments under employment legislation are treated as wages in respect of the period for which they are payable.[81] If the Secretary of State for Employment pays the employee arrears of pay (including guarantee and other payments under employment legislation) for eight weeks, payments in lieu of notice, holiday pay, compensation for unfair dismissal or reimbursement of apprentice's fees or premiums, at a rate not exceeding £120 a week, he obtains the same preference as the employee had and is to paid in priority to any other unsatisfied claim of the employee;[82] for purposes of computing limits, sums paid to the Secretary of State are treated as if they had been paid to the employee.

---

[74] s.319(5).
[75] s.319(1)(*a*). See also Chap. 21, para. 11.
[76] s.319(8)(*d*).
[77] s.319(1)(*a*). This includes tax deducted from employees' emoluments: Finance Act 1952, s.30.
[78] *Lord Advocate* v. *Liqrs. of Purvis Industries Ltd.*, 1958 S.C.338.
[79] s.319(1)(*b*). This includes holiday and sick pay: s.319(8)(*a*).
[80] s.319(2).
[81] Employment Protection (Consolidation) Act 1978, s.121.
[82] *ibid.*, s.125.

(d) accrued holiday remuneration[83] and sums due under the Reinstatement in Civil Employment Act 1944.[84]

(e) advances made for payment of the wages or accrued holiday remuneration of clerks, servants, workmen or labourers to the extent to which the employee's claim to a preference is reduced because of the advances.[85] A bank usually requires the opening of a special wages account to make advances for payment of wages but the preference can be obtained without such a special arrangement if the advances were in fact made to enable the company to meet its commitments including the payment of wages.[86] Where there was a wages account in debit and a current account kept in credit so that the credit always exceeded the debit it was held that the two accounts had to be regarded as one account which was in credit even although there was a larger debit on a third account which was "frozen".[87] On the other hand, a preference can be obtained for sums transferred to the wages account by debiting an overdrawn current account.[88] Where there is a credit account to be set off against two debit accounts of which one is preferential, the balance is treated as non-preferential except to the extent that the credit is insufficient to discharge the preferential claim in full.[87] Sums paid to a "labour only" sub-contractor are not wages.[89]

(f) certain payments due under the Workmen's Compensation Acts.[90]

(g) debts in respect of social security contributions and other debts specified in Social Security Act 1975, s.153(2), Social Security Pensions Act 1975, Sched. 3 and any corresponding Northern Irish provisions.[91]

---

83 1948 Act, s.319(1)(*d*). See also s.319(8)(*b*), (*c*).
84 s.319(1)(*c*).
85 s.319(4).
86 *Re Primrose (Builders) Ltd.* [1950] Ch.561; *Re Rampgill Mill Ltd.* [1967] Ch.1138.
87 *Re E. J. Morel (1934) Ltd.* [1962] Ch.21.
88 *Re James R. Rutherford & Sons Ltd.* [1964] 3 All E.R.137.
89 *Re C. W. & A. L. Hughes Ltd.* [1966] 2 All E.R.702.
90 s.319(1)(*f*), (*g*).
91 s.319(1)(*e*) (unless the company is being wound up voluntarily for reconstruction or amalgamation).

It seems that the landlord's hypothec is in the same position in a liquidation as it is in a sequestration.[92]

9. Voluntary Liquidation

A company can be wound up by a voluntary liquidation. This is initiated by a resolution of the company and notice of the resolution must be given in the *Edinburgh Gazette*. The date of commencement of the liquidation is the time of the passing of the resolution.[93] Before the date on which the notices calling the meeting at which the resolution is to be proposed are sent out, the directors may make a statutory declaration of solvency to the effect that they have made a full inquiry into the affairs of the company and have formed the opinion that the company will be able to pay its debts in full within such period not exceeding 12 months from the commencement of the winding-up as may be specified in the declaration. If such a declaration is made the winding-up is "a members' voluntary winding-up"; and if such a declaration is not made the winding-up is "a creditors' voluntary winding-up."[94] In the former, the liquidator is appointed by the company; in the latter, the company must summon a meeting of creditors on the day or the day next following the day on which the winding-up resolution is to be proposed. The directors must lay a full statement of the company's affairs before the meeting of creditors.[95] The creditors and the company at their respective meetings may nominate a person to be liquidator and if the same person is not nominated by both meetings, the creditors' nominee becomes the liquidator.[96] The creditors' meeting may also appoint a committee of inspection.

With certain exceptions, the liquidator may exercise without the sanction of the court all the powers of a liquidator in a winding-up by the court.[97] He must pay the debts of the company and adjust the rights of contributories among themselves.[98] The expenses of winding-up, including the liquidator's remuneration, are payable in

[92] See Chap. 7, para. 12; *Anderson's Trs.* v. *Donaldson & Co. Ltd. (in Liquidation)*, 1908 S.C.38; *Scottish Metropolitan Co. Ltd.* v. *Sutherlands Ltd.*, 1934 S.L.T. (Sh.Ct.)62.

[93] s.280.

[94] s.283.

[95] s.293.

[96] s.294.

[97] s.303.

[98] s.303(2).

priority to all other claims.[99] Thereafter, subject to the preferential payments, the property of the company is applied in satisfaction of its liabilities *pari passu* and, subject to such application, shall, unless the articles otherwise provide, be distributed among the members according to their rights and interests in the company.[1]

When the liquidation appears to be complete, the liquidator submits accounts and a return to the registrar and the company is dissolved three months from the date of registration of the return.[2] The court may defer the dissolution on the application of the liquidator or other person interested.

10. Dissolved Companies

After a company has been dissolved, previously unknown assets or debts may come to light.

If the company has been dissolved, the liquidator or other person interested may apply to the court within two years of the date of dissolution to declare the dissolution void and thereupon such proceedings might be taken as might have been taken if the company had not been dissolved.[3] This cannot be done to enable the company to receive a legacy to the prejudice of the heirs on intestacy.[4]

The registrar may strike a company off the register if the company is not carrying on business or in operation or if the affairs of the company are fully wound up. A member or creditor who feels aggrieved may apply within 20 years to have the company restored to the register. The court may give such directions or make such provision as seems just for placing the company and all other persons in the same position as nearly as may be as if the company had not been struck off.[5] An application may be made by a contingent creditor[6] but not by an assignee who acquired right to a debt after the dissolution.[7] In England, the court may order that the period between dissolution and restoration should not be counted

---

[99] s.309.

[1] s.302.

[2] s.290. See *Re Cornish Manures Ltd.* [1967] 1 W.L.R.807.

[3] s.352.

[4] *Re Servers of the Blind League* [1960] 1 W.L.R.564.

[5] s.353. The s.352 procedure can be used in this situation: *Re Test Holdings (Clifton) Ltd.* [1970] Ch.285.

[6] *Re Harvest Lane Bodies Ltd.* [1969] 1 Ch.457.

[7] *Re New Timbiqui Gold Mines Ltd.* [1961] Ch.319.

for limitation purposes[8] but this will not be done where the company was in liquidation.[9]

---

[8] *Re Donald Kenyon Ltd.* [1956] 1 W.L.R.1397.
[9] *Re Vickers and Bott Ltd.* [1968] 2 All E.R.264 n.

CHAPTER 24

ASSIGNATION OF DEBTS

1. Assignability

A debt is, in general, transferable by assignation.[1]

In particular the following are assignable: a *spes successionis;*[2] uncalled capital;[3] a shareholder's interest in the surplus assets of a company in liquidation;[4] a claim for damages (including *solatium*) in respect of personal injuries;[5] damages for breach of contract;[6] the share of a limited partner[7] (with the consent of the general partners); a floating charge.[8] Rights to damages for patrimonial loss and loss of society awards under the Damages (Scotland) Act 1976, are probably assignable but the right to the loss of society award is extinguished by the cedent's death.[9]

The following are not assignable: uncalled capital of a limited company where a resolution under s.60 of the Companies Act 1948 has been passed;[10] an amount payable under letters of guarantee by members of a limited company operative only on liquidation[11] (except where the guarantees are by non-members[12]); social security benefits[13] and supplementary benefit;[14] the wages of a seaman.[15] A policy under the Married Women's Policies of Assurance (Scotland) Act 1880 is now assignable.[16]

---

1 Bell, *Comm.*, II, 15.

2 *Wood* v. *Begbie* (1850) 12 D.963; *Trappes* v. *Meredith* (1871) 10 M.38. But see *McEwan's Trs.* v. *Macdonald,* 1909 S.C.57.

3 *Liquidator of Union Club Ltd.* v. *Edinburgh Life Assurance Co.* (1906) 8 F.1143; *Ballachulish Slate Quarries* v. *Menzies* (1908) 45 S.L.R.667.

4 *Jackson* v. *Elphick* (1902) 10 S.L.T.146.

5 *Cole-Hamilton* v. *Boyd,* 1963 S.C.(H.L.)1.

6 *Constant* v. *Kincaid & Co.* (1902) 4 F.901.

7 Limited Partnership Act 1907, s.6(5)(*b*).

8 *Libertas-Kommerz GmbH* v. *Johnson,* 1977 S.C.191.

9 Damages (Scotland) Act 1976, s.3. See *Traill* v. *Actieselskabat Dalbeattie Ltd.* (1904) 6 F.798.

10 *Re Mayfair Property Company* [1898] 2 Ch.28.

11 *Robertson* v. *British Linen Co.* (1891) 18 R.1225.

12 *Lloyds Bank* v. *Morrison & Son,* 1927 S.C.571.

13 Social Security Act 1975, s.87(1).

14 Supplementary Benefits Act 1976, s.16.

15 Merchant Shipping Act 1970, s.11.

16 Married Women's Policies of Assurance (Scotland) (Amendment) Act 1980, s.3.

Alimentary liferents and other periodical payments of an alimentary character are not assignable[17] but: (i) each term's payment when it falls due and is reduced into possession can be paid as the beneficiary directs,[18] (ii) arrears of payments can be assigned[19], (iii) the provision can be assigned in so far as it is excessive as aliment[20] but the court will not determine the excess for the future.[21]

There is little authority as to the effect of an express contractual provision that a debt will be non-assignable.[22] An assignation differs from an arrestment in that it may carry future or contingent debts.[23]

2. Form of Assignation

Mere delivery of the document of debt is not sufficient.[24] Although it has been said that writing is necessary to prove the transaction but not to constitute it, it is doubtful whether a verbal assignation is possible.[25] A form of assignation is given in the Transmission of Moveable Property (Scotland) Act 1862, which can be used for bonds, personal property or effects of every kind.[26] There is also a special statutory form for policies of assurance.[27] But it is clearly established that no special form is essential: "no words directly importing conveyance are necessary to constitute an assignation, but any words giving authority or directions, which if fairly carried out will operate a transference, are sufficient to make an assignation."[28] Accordingly, the following have been held valid: a letter containing the words "I . . . . hand over my life policy to my daughter" delivered with a certified copy of the policy;[29] a letter containing the words "I hand you two policies of insurance . . . . which I give you as an added security for the loan" which was

17 *Rennie* v. *Ritchie* (1845) 4 Bell's App. 221.
18 *Hewats* v. *Robertson* (1881) 9 R.175.
19 *Drew* v. *Drew* (1870) 9 M.163.
20 *Claremont's Trs.* v. *Claremont* (1896) 4 S.L.T.144.
21 *Cuthbert* v. *Cuthbert's Trs.*, 1908 S.C.967; *Coles, Ptr.*, 1951 S.C.608.
22 Gloag, p.413.
23 *Flowerdew* v. *Buchan* (1835) 13 S.615; *Carter* v. *McIntosh* (1862) 24 D.925; *Allan & Son* v. *Brown and Lightbody* (1890) 6 Sh.Ct.Rep.278.
24 *U.K. Life Assurance Co.* v. *Dixon* (1838) 16 S.1277.
25 Gloag, p.180; see *McCracken* v. *McCracken* (1928) 44 Sh.Ct.Rep.11.
26 Sched. A and B.
27 The Policies of Assurance Act 1867.
28 *per* L.J.-C. Inglis, *Carter* v. *McIntosh* (1862) 24 D.925 at 933; see also *McCutcheon* v. *McWilliam* (1876) 3 R.565; *International Fibre Syndicate Ltd.* v. *Dawson* (1901) 3 F.(H.L.)32.
29 *Brownlee* v. *Robb*, 1907 S.C.1302.

delivered with the policies.[30] Presentment of a bill of exchange or cheque operates as an intimated assignation of the sum for which it is drawn in favour of the holder.[31] Presentment of a bill of exchange accepted "payable at" a bank operates as an intimated assignation of the funds of the acceptor in the bank.[32]

It seems now to be established that a mandate by the creditor authorising the debtor to pay to a third party or authorising the third party to receive payment from the debtor may be equivalent to an assignation.[33] If the creditor is indebted to the third party it is a mandate *in rem suam* and cannot be unilaterally revoked by the creditor. The *tempus inspiciendi* is the time of intimation of the mandate and if the creditor was not indebted to the third party at that time the mandate does not become irrevocable by reason only of the subsequent creation of indebtedness. The intention of the granter must be determined from the terms of the document and the circumstances in which it was granted.[34] A mandate which is not a bill of exchange requires to be stamped as a "letter of attorney"[35] although there seems to have been dubiety or laxity about this at one time.[36]

A mere mandate which does not amount to an assignation is revocable by the granter and falls by his sequestration.[37]

3. Intimation: Form

Intimation of an assignation is necessary to complete the assignee's title and to put the debtor in bad faith to pay to anyone other than the assignee.[38] It is usually made by the assignee but can be made by the assignor on his behalf.[39] The Act of 1862 provides two methods of intimation.[40] The first is by a notary public delivering to the debtor a copy of the assignation certified as correct; a certificate by

30 *Caledonian Insurance Co.* v. *Beattie* (1898) 5 S.L.T.349.

31 Bills of Exchange Act 1882, s.53(2). See Chap. 6, para. 6.

32 *British Linen Co.* v. *Rainey's Tr.* (1885) 12 R.825.

33 *Carter* v. *McIntosh, supra; Executive Council for the City of Glasgow* v. *T. Sutherland Henderson Ltd.*, 1955 S.L.T.(Sh.Ct.)33.

34 *National Commercial Bank of Scotland Ltd.* v. *Millar's Tr.*, 1964 S.L.T. (Notes)57.

35 Sergeant & Sims, *Stamp Duties and Capital Duty*, 7th ed., p.163.

36 *Smith* v. *Paterson* (1894) 10 Sh.Ct.Rep.171.

37 *McKenzie* v. *Campbell* (1894) 21 R.904.

38 *per* Lord Young, *Grigor Allan* v. *Urquhart* (1887) 15 R.56 at 61.

39 *Libertas-Kommerz GmbH* v. *Johnson*, 1977 S.C.191.

40 Transmission of Moveable Property (Scotland) Act 1862, s.2.

the notary in the form of Sched. C to the Act is sufficient evidence of intimation. The second is by transmitting a copy of the assignation, certified as correct, to the debtor by post; a written acknowledgement by the debtor is sufficient evidence of intimation. The Policies of Assurance Act 1867 provides that an assignee shall have no right to sue on the policy unless a written notice of the date and purport of the assignation is given to the assurance company at its principal place of business and the date of receipt of this notice regulates the priority of the claims.[41] Upon request and payment of a 25p fee, the company must give an acknowledgement of receipt signed by a principal officer which is conclusive evidence against the company.[42]

Generally, however, intimation can be proved *rebus ipsis et factis*.[43] The terms must be such as to convey to the debtor that the debt has been transferred and that the transferee is asserting his claim to the debt from the debtor; general statements may not suffice; letters from the debtor to the intimator can be looked at.[44] It seems that intimation to the law agents of a trust is sufficient intimation to the trustees[45] although the general rule is that intimation to the debtor's factor is not sufficient.[46] Where one of two trustees was ill, intimation to the other who held the funds and administered the trust, was held sufficient.[47] Intimation to one of several co-obligants completes the assignee's right but it does not interpel the others from paying to the cedent.[48] Intimation to the principal debtor operates against the cautioner.[49] Intimation to a corporation is made at common law to the treasurer[50] but documents may be served on a limited company by delivering them at, or posting them to, the registered office.[51]

It should be noted that, where a debt has been assigned *ex facie* absolutely but truly in security, a further assignation of the re-

---

41 s.3.

42 s.6.

43 *Hill* v. *Lindsay* (1847) 10 D.78.

44 *Wallace* v. *Davies* (1853) 15 D.688; *Donaldson* v. *Ord* (1855) 17 D.1053; *Libertas-Kommerz GmbH, supra*.

45 *Browne's Tr.* v. *Anderson* (1901) 4 F.305.

46 Bell, *Lects.* i, 318; *E. of Aberdeen* v. *Merchiston's Crs.* (1729) Mor.867, seems to be an exceptional case.

47 *Jameson* v. *Sharp* (1887) 14 R.643.

48 Erskine, III, 1, 10.

49 *Mosman* v. *Bells* (1670) 2 Br.Sup.457.

50 *Keir* v. *Menzies* (1739) Mor.850.

51 Companies Act 1948, s.437.

versionary interest should be intimated to the prior assignee and not to the original debtor.[52]

4. Intimation: Equivalents

The following are equivalent to intimation: the raising of an action by the assignee for recovery of the debt;[53] the production of the assignation (not the lodging of a claim[54]) in a multiplepoinding for distribution of the fund assigned;[55] diligence by the assignee;[56] recording of the assignation in the General Register of Sasines;[57] the presentation of a bill of exchange for acceptance or payment.[58]

The following are *not* equivalent to intimation: registration of the assignation in the Books of Council and Session;[59] in the case of an assignation of uncalled capital, the reading of a report mentioning the assignation at a meeting attended by some of the shareholders.[60]

Intimation is unnecessary where the debtor is a party[61] (not a witness[62]) to the assignation as cedent[63] or assignee.[64] But where an assignation of his shares in a friendly investment society was granted by the society's manager it was held that his private knowledge did not make intimation to the society unnecessary.[65]

Otherwise the effect of the debtor's private knowledge of an unintimated assignation is doubtful. It is clear that it is of no effect in a competition with other creditors;[66] but it is not clear whether it even puts the debtor *in mala fide* to pay the cedent.[67] Certain actings

---

52 *Whittall* v. *Christie* (1894) 22 R.91; *Ayton* v. *Romanes* (1895) 3 S.L.T.203; in practice intimation will be made to both (Burns, *Conveyancing Practice,* 4th ed., p.679).

53 *Elphingston* v. *Ord* (1624) Mor.858; Erskine, III, 5, 4; *Watt's Trs.* v. *Pinkney* (1853) 16 D.279 at 288.

54 *M.P.-Mounsey* (1896) 4 S.L.T.46.

55 *Dougal* v. *Gordon* (1795) Mor.851; *Carter* v. *McIntosh* (1862) 24 D.925.

56 *Whyte* v. *Neish* (1622) Mor.854; Erskine, III, 5, 4.

57 *Paul* v. *Boyd's Trs.* (1835) 13 S.818; *Edmond* v. *Gordon* (1858) 3 Macq.116.

58 Bills of Exchange Act 1882, s.53(2).

59 *Tod's Trs.* v. *Wilson* (1869) 7 M.1100.

60 *Liquidator of Union Club Ltd.* v. *Edinburgh Life Assurance Co.* (1906) 8 F.1143.

61 *Turnbull* v. *Stewart & Inglis* (1751) Mor.868; see also *Crs. of L. Ballenden* v. *Countess of Dalhousie* (1707) Mor.865, where the assignation was *in gremio* of the bond constituting the debt.

62 *Murray* v. *Durham* (1622) Mor.855.

63 *Paul* v. *Boyd's Trs.* (1835) 13 S.818; *Browne's Tr.* v. *Anderson* (1901) 4 F.305.

64 *Miller* v. *Learmonth* (1870) 42 J.418; *Ayton* v. *Romanes* (1895) 3 S.L.T.203.

65 *Grigor Allan* v. *Urquhart* (1887) 15 R.56.

66 *L. Rollo* v. *Laird of Niddrie* (1665) 1 Br.Sup.510; *Dickson* v. *Trotter* (1776) Mor.873.

67 *Adamson* v. *McMitchell* (1624) Mor.859; *L. Westraw* v. *Williamson & Carmichael* (1626) Mor.859; *cf. Leith* v. *Garden* (1703) Mor.865.

on the part of the debtor, however, make intimation unnecessary—a promise to pay to the assignee proved *scripto*;[68] a written acknowledgement of indebtedness to the assignee;[69] payment of interest or of part of the debt to the assignee;[70] entering into a submission to arbitration relating to the debt with the assignee.[71] Mere "communings" with the assignee are not sufficient.[72]

5. Intimation: Importance

Intimation is not necessary to make the assignation effectual in a question with the cedent or his executors.[73] The executors are bound to warrant the assignation. The importance of intimation appears in questions with third parties:

(a) If the cedent is sequestrated before intimation the trustee in the sequestration is preferred to the debt.[74] Except in the case of registered titles,[75] the trustee does not require to intimate his title in order to obtain his preference because the sequestration itself is equivalent to an intimated assignation as at the date of the first deliverance.[76] The same principle holds in liquidations, the effective date being the date of presentation of the petition[77] or of the passing of the resolution.

(b) The debtor can safely pay to the cedent prior to intimation[78] and the cedent can treat with him and give him an effectual discharge.[79]

(c) If the cedent, after granting the assignation, assigns the same debt to a third party who takes in good faith and for value and whose assignation is intimated before that of the first assignee, the third party is preferred to the debt.[80]

---

68 *Home* v. *Murray* (1674) Mor.863.

69 *Wallace* v. *Davies* (1853) 15 D.688.

70 *Livingston* v. *Lindsay* (1626) Mor.860.

71 *Ritchie* v. *McLachlan* (1870) 8 M.815.

72 *Faculty of Advocates* v. *Dickson* (1718) Mor.866; *cf. L. of Dunipace* v. *Sandis* (1624) Mor.859.

73 *Grant* v. *Gray* (1828) 6 S.489; *Brownlee* v. *Robb,* 1907 S.C.1302; *Strawbridge's Trs.* v. *Bank of Scotland,* 1935 S.L.T.568.

74 *Tod's Trs.* v. *Wilson* (1869) 7 M.1100.

75 *Morrison* v. *Harrison* (1876) 3 R.406.

76 Bankruptcy (Scotland) Act 1913, ss.41, 97.

77 *Liquidator of Union Club Ltd.* v. *Edinburgh Life Assurance Co.* (1906) 8 F.1143; Companies Act 1948, s.229.

78 *McDowal* v. *Fullertoun* (1714) Mor.840.

79 *McGill* v. *Laurestoun* (1558) Mor.843.

80 *Campbell's Trs.* v. *Whyte* (1884) 11 R.1078.

(d) If a creditor of the cedent executes an arrestment in the hands of the debtor after the granting of the assignation but before intimation, the arrester is preferred.[81]

(e) The debtor can plead against the assignee any defence which he could have pleaded against the cedent provided that the defence was available to him prior to intimation. So, if the debtor acquired, prior to intimation, a debt due by the cedent, he can plead compensation on it against the assignee.[82] If, however, the debt was acquired by an assignation, this assignation must have been intimated to the cedent before intimation of the assignation granted by the cedent.[83] If the defence became available to the debtor after intimation it cannot be taken against the assignee.[84]

A person seeking to rely on a failure to intimate may be personally barred from doing so if, for example, he himself in another capacity was responsible, or partially responsible, for the failure. The trustee in his sequestration may be similarly barred.[85]

6. Title to Sue

If at the date of raising an action the pursuer has no title to sue, the defect cannot be cured by a subsequent assignation or retrocession.[86] It was thought at one time[87] that where a party granted an assignation and then raised an action he had a good title to sue if he obtained a retrocession during the course of the action, but this is not correct.[88] Apparently, the position is different where the pursuer's title to sue has been affirmed although it is not complete or is subject to some qualification. So, where the assignation of his interest granted by the pursuer before the raising of the action was rescinded in the English courts on the ground of misrepresentation

---

81 *Strachan* v. *McDougle* (1835) 13 S.954; for competition with an executor-creditor, see Chap. 26, para. 7.

82 *Shiells* v. *Ferguson, Davidson & Co.* (1876) 4 R.250.

83 *Wallace* v. *Edgar* (1663) Mor.837; *Alison* v. *Duncan* (1711) Mor.2657.

84 *Chambers' J.F.* v. *Vertue* (1893) 20 R.257; *Macpherson's J.F.* v. *Mackay*, 1915 S.C.1011.

85 *Graeme's Tr.* v. *Giersberg* (1888) 15 R.691.

86 *Symington* v. *Campbell* (1894) 21 R.434; Maclaren, *Court of Session Practice*, p.189. See also *Microwave Systems (Scotland) Ltd.* v. *Electro-Physiological Instruments Ltd.* 1971 S.L.T.(Notes)38.

87 Maclaren, *op. cit.*, p.219.

88 *Bentley* v. *MacFarlane*, 1964 S.C.76.

during the course of the action it was held that the pursuer had a good title to sue.[89]

An assignee can sue in the name of the cedent or in his own name; normally there is no objection to the assignee's suing in the name of the cedent and concluding for payment to himself.[90]

7. Assignee's Right

Assignatus utitur iure auctoris. The assignee has no better right than the cedent had and the debtor can take any defence against the assignee which he could have taken against the cedent and which was available to him prior to intimation. So the insurers can reduce a policy against an onerous assignee on the ground of the false statements made by the cedent in the proposal form;[91] there may be a duty on the insurers to communicate to the assignee any objection to the validity of the policy which comes to their knowledge.[92] Similarly, where a superior had not fulfilled his obligation to build streets and sewers, the vassal could retain the feuduty in a question with the superior's assignee.[93] The assignee of a gratuitous allowance cannot sue the donor.[94] A plea of compensation which could have been taken against the cedent can be taken against the assignee if it arose before intimation.[95] In this connection, it should be noted that the expenses of an action are deemed to arise at its commencement so that where an action was assigned the defender could set off against the assignee an amount awarded to him in respect of expenses.[96]

The nature of the right assigned, however, can be such that it is affected by the actings of the cedent or of other parties after the date of intimation. Where a husband assigned a sum which was to be paid to him by his antenuptial marriage contract trustees on the death of

---

89 *Westville Shipping Co. Ltd.* v. *Abram S.S. Co.*, 1923 S.C.(H.L.)68—distinguished in *Bentley* v. *MacFarlane, supra, per* L.P. Clyde at p.80, *per* Lord Guthrie at p.82.

90 *Blyth Dry Docks & Shipbuilding Co. Ltd.* v. *Commissioners for Port of Calcutta,* 1972 S.L.T.(Notes)7.

91 *Scottish Widows' Fund* v. *Buist* (1876) 3 R.1078; *Scottish Equitable Life Assurance Society* v. *Buist* (1877) 4 R.1076; affirmed (1878) 5 R.(H.L.)64.

92 *per* L.P. Inglis, *Scottish Equitable Life Assurance Society* v. *Buist, supra,* at p.1081.

93 *Arnott's Trs.* v. *Forbes* (1881) 9 R.89.

94 *Robertson* v. *Wright* (1873) 1 R.237.

95 *Shiells* v. *Ferguson, Davidson & Co.* (1876) 4 R.250; but obviously not a counter claim—*J.E. Binstock Miller & Co.* v. *E. Coia & Co. Ltd.* (1957) 73 Sh.Ct.Rep.178.

96 *Livingston* v. *Reid* (1833) 11 S.878.

his wife's father if the marriage then subsisted, and the husband was later divorced on the ground of adultery, the assignee obtained nothing.[97] If trustees have a discretion to restrict the cedent's interest to a liferent, or to reduce the amount of revenue payments, the exercise of the discretion—even after intimation—can affect the assignee's right.[98]

8. Warrandice

Where the assignation is for an onerous cause, there is an implied warrandice that the debt subsists.[99] In the case of a bond, this applies to the obligation of any cautioners as well as to that of the principal debtor. It is also implied that the cedent confers on the assignee everything necessary to make the assignation effectual.[1] There is, however, no implied warrandice as to the debtor's ability to pay. In assignations to a cautioner or co-obligant the implied warrandice is from fact and deed only.[2]

9. Bill as Transfer

Obviously, if the drawee accepts a bill presented to him there is, in the normal case, a transfer of a debt from the drawer to the holder but it is not clear that a drawee, even if he is indebted to the drawer, is bound to accept a bill presented to him.[3] The transfer of the debt is not dependent upon his acceptance, however, because, by s.53(2) of the Bills of Exchange Act 1882, in Scotland, where the drawee of a bill has in his hands funds available for the payment thereof, the bill operates as an assignation of the sum for which it is drawn in favour of the holder, from the time when the bill is presented to the drawee. Where a bill is accepted "payable at" a bank, presentment to the bank operates as an assignation of the acceptor's funds in the banker's hands to the extent of the sum in the bill.[4]

---

97 *Johnstone-Beattie* v. *Dalzell and Others* (1868) 6 M.333.

98 *Weller* v. *Ker* (1866) 4 M.(H.L.)8; *Train* v. *Buchanan's Trs.*, 1907 S.C.517; affirmed 1908 S.C.(H.L.)26.

99 Erskine II, 3, 27; *Reid* v. *Barclay* (1879) 6 R.1007.

1 *Miller* v. *Muirhead* (1894) 21 R.658.

2 *Russell* v. *Mudie* (1857) 20 D.125.

3 Thomson, *Bills of Exchange* (3rd ed.), p.228; *Encyclopaedia of the Laws of Scotland,* Vol. II, p.217.

4 *British Linen Co.* v. *Rainey's Tr.* (1885) 12 R.825.

CHAPTER 25

JOINT AND SEVERAL OBLIGATIONS

1. Kinds of Liability

Where an obligation is assumed by two or more parties, the liability may be *in solidum* or *pro rata*. If the liability is *in solidum,* any one party is liable, in a question with the creditor, for the whole amount of the debt. If the liability is *pro rata,* any one party is liable only for a *pro rata* (*i.e.* equal) share. Where liability is *in solidum,* the bankruptcy of one obligant does not affect the liability of each of the others for the whole debt. Where liability is *pro rata,* the bankruptcy of the co-debtor does not increase the liability of the others except in cautionary obligations.[1]

There is a presumption in favour of *pro rata* liability[2] but the liability is *in solidum* if the parties are bound "jointly and severally",[3] "conjunctly and severally",[4] "severally",[5] "as co-principals and full debtors",[6] "as full debtors".[7] The following prima facie indicate *pro rata* liability: "jointly",[8] "conjunctly",[9] "each for his own part".[10] *Pro rata* liability was inferred where A bound himself "along with B"[11] and also where the expression was "conjunctly and severally ilk one for his own part".[12]

In certain circumstances joint and several liability is implied. In partnership, each partner is liable jointly and severally for all debts and obligations of the firm incurred while he is a partner.[13] Co-acceptors and co-drawers of bills of exchange and co-makers of a promissory note are liable jointly and severally.[14] That is the

---

1 *Duke of Montrose* v. *Edmonstone* (1845) 7 D.759.

2 Stair, I, 17, 20; Erskine, III, 3, 374; Bell, *Comm.*, I, 361; *Prin.*, §51.

3 Bell, *Comm.*, I, 361; *Fleming* v. *Gemmill,* 1908 S.C.340.

4 *Dundee Police Commissioners* v. *Straton* (1884) 11 R.586; *Burns* v. *Martin* (1887) 14 R.(H.L.)20.

5 Montgomerie Bell, *Lectures,* I, p.262.

6 *Cleghorn* v. *Yorston* (1707) Mor.14624.

7 *Cloberhill* v. *Ladyland* (1631) Mor.14623.

8 *Coats* v. *Union Bank of Scotland,* 1928 S.C.711; the point seems to have been conceded in the House of Lords (1929 S.C.(H.L.)114); Bell, *Comm.*, I, 362, *Prin.*, § 57, is in error here.

9 *Campbell* v. *Farquhar* (1724) Mor.14626.

10 Bell, *Comm.*, I, 362.

11 *Alexander* v. *Scott* (1827) 6 S.150.

12 *Farquhar* v. *McKain* (1638) Mor.2282.

13 Partnership Act 1890, s.9.

14 Bell, *Comm.*, I, 363; *Prin.*, §61.

position at common law apart altogether from the statutory provision that if a promissory note in the form "I promise to pay . . . ." is signed by two or more persons they are deemed to have incurred joint and several liability.[15] Liability *in solidum* is also implied where several persons contract with an individual for a common object[16] and in particular where a number of persons grant a mandate to the same agent to appear in the same suit in a matter of common interest.[17] The creditors in a sequestration are not, however, liable to an agent employed by the trustee.[18] Joint wrongdoers[19] and, in certain circumstances, joint purchasers,[20] are liable *in solidum*. Co-obligants in an obligation *ad factum praestandum* incur joint and several liability[21] and this applies also to a claim for damages for failure to perform such an obligation unless the original obligation was clearly alternative.[22] The position of co-cautioners is dealt with elsewhere.[23]

If a joint and several obligation *ex contractu* has not been constituted by writing or decree, the pursuer in an action to enforce the obligation must call all the co-obligants as defenders if that is possible.[24] He need not call those outwith the jurisdiction.[25] If the obligation is constituted by writing the pursuer can bring his action against any one co-obligant; he need not call all the co-obligants.[26] The same holds with regard to joint wrongdoers including trustees sued for breach of trust.[27] In an action on a bond against two obligants bound jointly and severally, where only one remained in the process, it was held that the other could not in that process reduce the bond *ope exceptionis* on the ground of misrepresentation.[28]

---

15 Bills of Exchange Act 1882, s.85(2).

16 *French* v. *Earl of Galloway* (1730) Mor.14706.

17 *Walker* v. *Brown* (1803) Mor.App. '*Solidum et pro rata*' No. 1; *Smith* v. *Harding* (1877) 5 R.147.

18 Bankruptcy (Scotland) Act 1913, s.53.

19 Erskine, III, 1, 15.

20 *Mushet* v. *Harvey* (1710) Mor.14636; *Reid* v. *Lamond* (1857) 19 D.265.

21 Gloag, p.200.

22 *Darlington* v. *Gray* (1836) 15 S.197; *Rankine* v. *Logie Den Land Co.* (1902) 4 F.1074.

23 See Chap. 10, para. 1.

24 *Neilson* v. *Wilson* (1890) 17 R.608.

25 *Muir* v. *Collett* (1862) 24 D.1119.

26 *Richmond* v. *Grahame* (1847) 9 D.633.

27 *Western Bank* v. *Douglas* (1860) 22 D.447; *Croskery* v. *Gilmour's Trs.* (1890) 17 R.697; *Allen* v. *McCombie's Trs.*, 1909 S.C.710.

28 *Lucarelli* v. *Buchanan*, 1954 S.L.T.(Sh.Ct.)46.

On the other hand, where the obligation is *pro rata,* all the obligants must be called if possible[29] although where there were three co-cautioners liable *pro rata* it was held that the creditor could sue two of them for their shares without calling the representatives of the third.[30]

If two co-obligants are bound jointly and severally and decree in absence for the sum sued for is granted against one, the pursuer can continue the action against the other unless it is shown that the decree has been fully satisfied.[31] This does not apply where the taking of decree is an election between principal and agent.[32]

2. Right of Relief

Where there is a contractual liability *in solidum,* an obligant who had paid more than his *pro rata* share of the debt is entitled to recover the excess from the co-obligants;[33] but where the obligants are bound jointly and severally to the creditor but are in fact principal and cautioner, the cautioner is, of course, entitled to total relief from the principal and he may prove the true relationship *prout de jure*.[34] In a question of relief where all the co-obligants are solvent, each is liable only for his *pro rata* share and this is so even where the obligant seeking relief has obtained an assignation of the debt from the creditor.[35] In calculating the number of *pro rata* shares, it is a question of construction of the obligatory document whether or not a firm is to be treated as a co-obligant separate from its partners.[36] Where some of the co-obligants are insolvent, they are ignored in the calculation of the shares.[37] It seems that the obligant seeking relief need not prove the insolvency so long as there is a doubt as to solvency.[38] An obligant seeking relief may rank on the estate of a bankrupt co-obligant for the *pro rata* share unless the creditor has ranked for the same portion of the debt.[39]

---

29 Mackay, *Manual of Court of Session Practice,* p.172.

30 *McArthur* v. *Scott* (1836) 15 S.270.

31 *Royal Bank* v. *McKerracher,* 1968 S.L.T.(Sh.Ct.)77; *Hamilton Leasing Ltd.* v. *Clark,* 1974 S.L.T.(Sh.Ct.)95.

32 *Lamont & Co.* v. *Reid* (1926) 42 Sh.Ct.Rep.262.

33 Bell, *Prin.*, §62.

34 Bell, *Prin.*, §245; *Thow's Tr.* v. *Young,* 1910 S.C.588.

35 *Gilmour* v. *Finnie* (1832) 11 S.193; *Anderson* v. *Dayton* (1884) 21 S.L.R.787.

36 *Macbride* v. *Clark Grierson & Co.* (1865) 4 M.73; *Hamilton & Co.* v. *Freeth* (1889) 16 R.1022.

37 Bell, *Prin.*, § 62.

38 *Buchanan* v. *Main* (1900) 3 F.215; Gloag, p.208.

39 *Anderson* v. *Mackinnon* (1876) 3 R.608.

3. Right to Assignation

A co-obligant who has made payment in full is entitled to an assignation of the debt from the creditor.[40] He is also entitled to an assignation of any securities held by the creditor. This, however, applies only where there has been actual payment and not where the creditor has received only a dividend from the obligant's estate.[41] The creditor is entitled to refuse the assignation if he is prejudiced by granting it.[42] He is entitled to refuse to assign a security if another debt is due to him by the co-obligant who granted the security and that other debt was incurred prior to the debt paid by the co-obligant.[43] The co-obligant does not require an assignation in order to seek relief from his co-obligants and he cannot use the assignation to alter the right of equalisation *inter se* of all the obligants.[44] The assignation is, however, of advantage if there is a security for the debt, or if the debt has a preference, or if the debt is constituted by a document on which summary diligence can be commenced.

4. Co-obligants: Prescription

Where, by a probative writ, two or more persons are bound jointly and severally by an obligation to pay money to another party, the obligation as respects the liability of each of the co-obligants, is subject to the quinquennial prescription.[45] However, this does not apply to a co-obligant if the creditor establishes that he is truly a principal debtor or that, although he is not truly a principal debtor, the original creditor was not aware of that fact at the time when the writ was delivered.

5. Joint Delinquents

Where there are joint delinquents, the injured party may sue them all jointly and severally or recover all the damages from one if he so pleases.[46] If he sues one and obtains a decree against him upon

---

40 Bell, *Prin.*, § 255.

41 *Ewart* v. *Latta* (1865) 3 M.(H.L.)36.

42 *Russell* v. *Mudie* (1857) 20 D.125; *Bruce* v. *Scottish Amicable Life Assurance Society*, 1907 S.C.637.

43 *Sligo* v. *Menzies* (1840) 2 D.1478.

44 Gloag, p.213.

45 Prescription and Limitation (Scotland) Act 1973, Sched. 1, para. 3.

46 *Croskery* v. *Gilmour's Trs.* (1890) 17 R.697.

which no satisfaction[47] or less than full satisfaction[48] is obtained, he can sue the others whose right of relief against the discharged delinquent is not affected.[49] But where he has obtained a decree against one in respect of the full damage and that award has been obtempered, he cannot proceed against the others.[50]

It has been held that it is competent to sue two defenders jointly and severally where the pursuer has suffered a loss to which each defender, by breach of his separate contract with the pursuer, has contributed.[51]

Where it is sought to make two defenders liable for the wrong but it is possible that in the end of the day liability will be established against only one of them, the conclusion should be "jointly and severally, or severally".[52]

6. Relief between Joint Delinquents

If the wrongdoers are sued in the same action and both are found liable, the pursuer will be given a joint and several decree against them but the court will apportion their liability for damages and expenses *inter se* and if one pays to the pursuer more than the sum thus apportioned to him he may obtain relief from the other.[53]

Where only one wrongdoer is sued and has been found liable in damages or expenses, he is entitled to recover from any other person who, if sued, might also have been held liable in respect of the loss or damage on which the action was founded, such contribution, if any, as the court may deem just.[54] The action of relief must be brought within two years of the date on which the right to relief accrued.[55] The right of relief is not prejudiced by the pursuer abandoning an action against another delinquent.[56]

---

47 *Steven* v. *Broady Norman & Co.*, 1928 S.C.351; *Arrow Chemicals Ltd.* v. *Guild*, 1978 S.L.T.206.

48 *Dillon* v. *Napier, Shanks & Bell* (1893) 20 S.L.R.685; *Douglas* v. *Hogarth* (1901) 4 F.148; *McNair* v. *Dunfermline Corporation*, 1953 S.C.183; *Carrigan* v. *Duncan*, 1971 S.L.T.(Sh.Ct.)33.

49 *Corvi* v. *Ellis*, 1969 S.L.T.350.

50 *Balfour* v. *Baird & Sons*, 1959 S.C.64.

51 *Grunwald* v. *Hughes*, 1964 S.L.T.94.

52 *Ellerman Lines Ltd.* v. *Clyde Navigation Trustees*, 1909 S.C.690; *Arrow Chemicals Ltd.* v. *Guild*, 1978 S.L.T.206.

53 Law Reform (Miscellaneous Provisions) (Scotland) Act 1940, s.3(1).

54 s.3(2).

55 Prescription and Limitation (Scotland) Act 1973, s.20.

56 *Corvi* v. *Ellis*, *supra*, commenting on *Travers* v. *Neilson*, 1967 S.L.T.64.

A difficulty arises where one wrongdoer has made an extra-judicial settlement with the injured party and wishes to obtain a contribution from a joint delinquent. He has, it seems, no statutory or common law right of relief.[57] His only remedy seems to be to obtain an assignation of the injured party's right against the joint delinquent and sue him on the assignation for the full amount of the damages.[58] The second delinquent can then, presumably, recover a proportion from the first under s.3(2) of the Act of 1940.

7. Discharge of Co-obligants

Where the creditor obtains partial payment from one co-obligant, a distinction is made between a discharge and a *pactum de non petendo*. The effect of a discharge is to release the other obligants from any liability beyond their *pro rata* share.[59] The effect of a *pactum de non petendo* is that the creditor can make no further claim on the co-obligant who has paid but can recover the balance from the other co-obligants who in turn can still obtain *pro rata* relief from the first co-obligant. A document will be construed as a *pactum de non petendo* if the creditor expressly reserves his rights against the other obligants[60] and even where there is no such reservation it seems that this effect is presumed if the payment is a composition.[61] Where one co-obligant is sequestrated the others are not released if the creditor draws a dividend or assents to a composition or deed of arrangement.[62]

The position is different in the case of co-cautioners. The discharge of one without the consent of the others, discharges all.[63] The discharge of the debtor discharges the cautioner.[64]

8. Discharge of Co-delinquents

If a discharge is granted to one delinquent which appears to discharge the claims against all or which is given in return for a sum

57 *National Coal Board* v. *Thomson,* 1959 S.C.353; but see *Corvi* v. *Ellis, supra, per* Lord Guthrie at p.354.

58 *Cole-Hamilton* v. *Boyd,* 1963 S.C.(H.L.)1.

59 *Muir* v. *Crawford* (1875) 2 R.(H.L.)148; *Smith* v. *Harding* (1877) 5 R.147; *Morton's Trs.* v. *Robertson's J.F.* (1892) 20 R.72.

60 *Secretary of State for Scotland* v. *Coltness Industries Ltd.,* 1979 S.L.T. (Sh.Ct.)56.

61 Gloag, p.215; *cf. Delaney* v. *Stirling* (1892) 20 R.506, *per* Lord McLaren at p.509.

62 Bankruptcy (Scotland) Act 1913, s.52.

63 Mercantile Law Amendment (Scotland) Act 1856, s.9. See Chap. 10, para. 3.

64 *Aitken's Trs.* v. *Bank of Scotland,* 1944 S.C.270.

of money which is accepted as complete satisfaction for the wrong, the injured party cannot subsequently proceed against co-delinquents.[65] On the other hand, if the discharge is granted for a sum which is not accepted in full satisfaction for the wrong, the injured party can proceed against the co-delinquents. The sum received must, however, be taken into account in assessing the liability of the co-delinquents and, it seems, their right of relief is not prejudiced.[66]

---

65 *Delaney* v. *Stirling* (1893) 20 R.506.

66 *Western Bank* v. *Bairds* (1862) 24 D.859; *Dillon* v. *Napier, Shanks & Bell,* (1893) 30 S.L.R.685; *Douglas* v. *Hogarth* (1901) 4 F.148; *McNair* v. *Dunfermline Corporation,* 1953 S.C.183; *Cole-Hamilton* v. *Boyd,* 1963 S.C.(H.L.)1.

Chapter 26

DEATH

Creditor's Death

1. Transmissibility

As a general rule, debts transmit in the creditor's succession and on his death form part of his estate.[1] A right to damages in respect of personal injuries sustained by the deceased does not transmit to his executor in so far as it consists of *solatium* or compensation for patrimonial loss attributable to any period after the deceased's death; a claim in respect of patrimonial loss for a period prior to death, *e.g.* wage loss between injury and death, does transmit and the executor's claim for this is not excluded by the fact that a relative of the deceased is claiming damages in respect of the death.[2] Where the deceased died vested in a right to claim damages in respect of the death of another person, the claim in so far as it is for a loss of society award does not transmit but a claim for loss of support up to the death of the deceased does transmit.[3] An order for payment of periodical allowance to a divorced spouse terminates on the spouse's death except in relation to arrears.[4]

An annuity is prima facie for the life of the annuitant but the terms of the deed may show a different intention, as, for example, where the annuity was said by the grantor to be payable "during my lifetime".[5]

2. Heritable and Moveable

As the whole estate, heritable and moveable, now vests in the executor on confirmation,[6] the distinction between heritable and moveable debts is, in relation to the creditor's succession, of importance only with regard to legal rights. Most debts are moveable. In particular the following are moveable: personal bonds

---

1 Stair, III, 5, 5.
2 Damages (Scotland) Act 1976, ss.2, 4.
3 *ibid.*, s.3.
4 Divorce (Scotland) Act 1976, s.5(5).
5 *Reid's Exx.* v. *Reid,* 1944 S.C.(H.L.)25.
6 Succession (Scotland) Act 1964, s.14.

(unless executors are expressly excluded by the terms of the deed);[7] heritable securities in the form of a standard security or bond and disposition in security;[8] ground annuals;[9] an interest in a partnership[10] or joint adventure[11] even if heritage forms part of the partnership property; company shares;[12] an assignation in security of a lease.[13]

The following debts are heritable in the creditor's succession: feuduties and rents[14] (but arrears are moveable);[15] securities in the form of an *ex facie* absolute disposition;[16] an assigned *spes successionis* relating to heritage.[17] Rights having a tract over future time and not having a relation to any capital sum or stock are heritable.[18] So an annuity is heritable although each term's payment as it falls due is moveable.[19] Similarly, an assigned liferent is heritable,[20] as is a pension. The right to the annual interest of a capital sum is, however, moveable because the right has relation to a principal sum.[21]

The nature of an interest in a trust estate depends upon the nature of the property held by the trust and, possibly, upon the operation of the doctrine of constructive conversion.[22]

The doctrine of constructive conversion is also of importance in regard to sales of heritage. Where the deceased has contracted to sell heritage and the conveyance has not been effected at his death,

---

[7] The Bonds Act 1661 (c.32); Conveyancing (Scotland) Act 1924, s.22. See Meston, *The Succession (Scotland) Act 1964,* 2nd ed., p.47.

[8] Titles to Land Consolidation (Scotland) Act 1868, s.117; Conveyancing and Feudal Reform (Scotland) Act 1970, s.32; They remain heritable *quoad fiscum* and *quoad* legal rights.

[9] Titles to Land Consolidation (Scotland) Act 1868, s.117; Conveyancing (Scotland) Act 1874, s.30; Succession (Scotland) Act 1964, Sched. 3; they remain heritable *quoad fiscum* and *quoad* legal rights.

[10] Partnership Act 1890, s.22.

[11] *Lord Advocate* v. *Macfarlane's Trs.* (1893) 31 S.L.R.357.

[12] Companies Act 1948, s.73.

[13] *Stroyan* v. *Murray* (1890) 17 R.1170.

[14] Bell, *Prin.,* §1484.

[15] *Logan's Trs.* v. *Logan* (1896) 23 R.848; *Watson's Trs.* v. *Brown,* 1923 S.C.228.

[16] Gloag & Irvine, p.162.

[17] *Thain* v. *Thain* (1891) 18 R.1196.

[18] Erskine, II, 2, 6.

[19] *Reid* v. *McWalter* (1878) 5 R.630.

[20] *Allan* v. *Williamson* (1741) Elchies' Heritable No. 12; *Drummond* v. *Ewing* (1752) Elchies' Heritable No. 16.

[21] *Hill* v. *Hill* (1872) 11 M.247.

[22] McLaren, *Wills and Succession,* I, p.223.

the executor is bound to execute the conveyance but the price forms part of the moveable estate.[23]

3. Recovery

The only person entitled to collect debts due to the deceased's estate is the executor[24] and, in general, payment can be made to him only if he has confirmed to the debt; payment should not be made of an amount larger than that appearing in the confirmation.[25] However, under various statutes, there are certain small payments which can be made without the necessity of confirmation.[26] A person or corporation who, in reliance on any instrument purporting to be a confirmation (or any instrument purporting to be a probate or letters of administration issued by any court in England and Wales or Northern Ireland, as the case may be) has made or has permitted to be made a payment or transfer bona fide upon such document, is indemnified and protected in so doing, notwithstanding any defect or circumstance whatsoever affecting the validity of the document.[27] A debtor who has paid the executor is not concerned with the application of the money unless he knows of the executor's intention to misapply it.[28]

If the deceased has not pursued the debt and if it is transmissible, his executors may raise an action for its recovery. This may be done before they have confirmed to the debt but confirmation must be obtained before decree is granted.[29] A summons which was served by the deceased but had not been called, can be called in the name of his representatives.[30] If the deceased had raised an action for recovery of the debt which is in dependence, his executors are entitled to be sisted in his place,[31] even after judgment has been given.[32] If the deceased had obtained a decree which had not been

---

23 *Chiesley* v. *His Sisters* (1704) Mor.5531; *McArthur's Exrs.* v. *Guild,* 1908 S.C.743.

24 *Barnet* v. *Duncan* (1831) 10 S.128. See, as to a sole solicitor's client account, Solicitors (Scotland) Act 1980, s.46.

25 *Buchanan* v. *Royal Bank* (1842) 5 D.211.

26 The statutes are conveniently collected in the Administration of Estates (Small Payments) Act 1965. The present limit is £1,500: Administration of Estates (Small Payments) (Increase of Limit) Order 1975 (S.I. 1975/1137).

27 Confirmation and Probate Amendment Act 1859, s.1.

28 *Taylor* v. *Forbes* (1830) 4 W. & S.444.

29 *Mackay* v. *Mackay,* 1914 S.C.200.

30 *Gallie* v. *Lockhart* (1840) 2 D.445; Maclaren, *Court of Session Practice,* p.350.

31 *Martin's Exix.* v. *McGhee,* 1914 S.C.628.

32 *Scott* v. *Mills's Trs.,* 1923 S.C.726; *Cumming* v. *Stewart,* 1928 S.C.709.

extracted before his death, the executors, before they can proceed with diligence, must present in the Petition Department a bill for letters of horning and poinding together with proof of their title. On the bill being passed, the letters can be signeted and they then constitute a warrant for diligence.[33] If the deceased had extracted a decree in his favour, the executors present the extract together with the confirmation and a minute to the Petition Department.[34] A deliverance is written on the extract which then forms a warrant for diligence.[35] If a charge had been served prior to death, the execution of the charge is presented to the Petition Department in the same way. If a poinding had been executed, the executors can obtain a warrant for sale on production of the confirmation.[36] If the warrant had been obtained prior to death the executors may carry out the sale without further procedure.[37] Where an arrestment had been executed before death, the executors can raise a furthcoming.[38] An inhibition which has been served transmits to the executors if they sist themselves as pursuers in the relevant action.[39] If the deceased was creditor under a deed which could have been registered for execution, but was in fact not so registered, the executor must proceed by letters of horning and poinding.[40] If the deed had been registered, the executors present the extract together with the confirmation to the Petition Department and a deliverance is written on the extract which forms a warrant for diligence.[41]

DEBTOR'S DEATH

4. Diligence Commenced Before Death

Where the common debtor dies after execution of the arrestment, it is competent to bring an action of furthcoming against the representatives.[42] Similarly, where the debtor dies after execution of a poinding, the creditor can proceed with the sale.[43] These diligences

33 Graham Stewart, p.284.
34 In the case of a sheriff court decree, the sheriff clerk.
35 Debtors (Scotland) Act 1838, ss.7, 12.
36 Graham Stewart, p.363.
37 Graham Stewart, p.363.
38 Erskine, III, 6, 11; Graham Stewart, p.134.
39 Bankton, I, 7, 140; Graham Stewart, p.552.
40 Graham Stewart, p.284.
41 Debtors (Scotland) Act 1838, ss.7, 12.
42 Stair, III, 1, 26; Erskine, III, 9, 34; *Earl of Wemyss* v. *May* (1679) Mor.782.
43 Bell, *Comm.*, II, 80; Graham Stewart, p.363.

may, however, be affected by (a) confirmation to the asset by an executor-creditor,[44] (b) sequestration of the deceased's estate within seven months of death.[45]

It is not competent to commence diligence on a decree against the debtor after his death, although if another creditor has poinded or arrested, the decree can be produced in the process to obtain equalisation.[46]

5. Transmission: Debtor's Estate

The general rule is that debts transmit against the debtor's estate. The rights of creditors are not affected by any testamentary dispositions which the deceased may have made and the rights of beneficiaries do not open except to the free estate of the deceased *debitis deductis*.[47] In particular, the following transmit: claims *ex delicto*;[48] an order for payment of a periodical allowance to a divorced spouse (although the executor can apply for variation or recall).[49]

The children of the deceased have no claim for aliment against his estate if he had made provision for them.[50] Grandchildren have no claim if the deceased made provision for their parent and had not acknowledged their claim in his lifetime.[51]

An illegitimate child of the deceased has the like right to aliment out of the deceased's estate in respect of any period after the deceased's death as a legitimate child.[52] An adopted child is in the same position as a child of the adopter.[53]

The executor may be liable in damages to the landlord if he does not take up a lease.[54]

On the death of a contributory before or after he has been placed on the list of contributories, his personal representatives are liable

---

44 See *infra*, para. 7.
45 See *infra*, para. 12 and B.A., s.106.
46 Graham Stewart, Chap. XXXV.
47 *Heritable Securities Investment Association Ltd.* v. *Miller's Trs.* (1893) 20 R.675.
48 *Evans* v. *Stool* (1885) 12 R.1295.
49 Divorce (Scotland) Act 1976, s.5(5).
50 *Strathmore* v. *Strathmore's Trs.* (1825) 1 W. & S.402; *Ferguson* v. *Ferguson* (1899) 15 Sh.Ct.Rep.20.
51 *Gay's Tutrix* v. *Gay's Tr.*, 1953 S.L.T.278.
52 Law Reform (Miscellaneous Provisions) (Scotland) Act 1968, s.4.
53 Succession (Scotland) Act 1964, s.23; Children Act 1975, Sched. 2, para. 1.
54 *Bethune* v. *Morgan* (1874) 2 R.186; Paton & Cameron, *Landlord and Tenant*, p.187.

to pay calls in his stead and this liability is a debt due by the deceased at death even if the call was made after death.[55]

It is possible for a man to contract in such a way that the obligation is prestable from him during his life but does not bind his representatives; but the intention must be made clear.[56]

The personal obligation contained in any deed constituting a heritable security transmits against any person taking the security subjects by succession or bequest but the obligation is limited to the value of the estate to which the person succeeds and cannot be enforced by summary diligence unless an agreement to the transmission of the obligation has been executed by the person.[57]

Where a husband has gifted to his wife heritage which is burdened by a bond, the presumption is that the gift is taken *cum onere* and the husband's estate is not liable for the amount of the bond in a question with the wife even although the personal obligation in the bond has transmitted against the husband and wife jointly and severally.[58]

Certain property *in bonis* of the deceased may not pass to the executor as such and is not confirmed to. This occurs where property is disposed of by special assignation,[59] special destination,[60] nomination[61] or *donatio mortis causa.*[62] Such property is nevertheless available for payment of the deceased's debts.[63] The funds of an *inter vivos* trust constituted by the deceased may be available to creditors if the trust is revocable.[64]

6. Recovery

Where an executor has been confirmed to the estate of the deceased, the creditor's remedy is to intimate a claim to him. The executor is *eadem persona cum defuncto* and in relation to the deceased's creditors is a debtor with a liability limited to the amount

---

55 Companies Act 1948, s.215; *Galletly's Trs.* v. *Lord Advocate* (1880) 8 R.74.

56 *Gardiner* v. *Stewart's Trs.*, 1908 S.C.985.

57 Conveyancing (Scotland) Act 1874, s.47; Conveyancing (Scotland) Act 1924, s.15; *Welch's Executors* v. *Edinburgh Life Assurance Co.* (1896) 23 R.772.

58 *Ballantyne's Trs.* v. *Ballantyne's Trs.*, 1941 S.C.35.

59 Confirmation Act 1690.

60 A deposit receipt has no testamentary effect: *Dinwoodie's Exix.* v. *Carruther's Exor.* (1895) 23 R.234.

61 *Gill* v. *Gill,* 1938 S.C.65; *Ford's Trs.* v. *Ford,* 1940 S.C.426.

62 *Morris* v. *Riddick* (1867) 5 M.1036.

63 *Renouf's Trs.* v. *Haining,* 1919 S.C.497, *per* Lord Dundas at p.507.

64 See *Scott* v. *Scott,* 1930 S.C.903; *Ross* v. *Ross's Trs. (sub. nom., Rose* v. *Rose's Trs.)* 1967 S.L.T.12.

of the deceased's estate.[65] The executor is not entitled, and cannot be obliged, to make payment of a debt until the expiry of six months from the date of death.[66] An action to constitute the debt can be brought within that period[67] but an action of accounting cannot be.[68] Payment can be made before the six months of privileged debts—deathbed and funeral (including cremation) expenses, the widow's mourning allowance[69] (which need not be claimed before the funeral[70]) the current term's rent of the house occupied by the deceased, domestic servants' wages for the current term and rates and taxes for one year.[71] By universal practice aliment for the family of the deceased is provided from the date of death from all estates not manifestly insolvent.[72]

After the expiry of the six months period the executor is bound to pay any just debt *primo venienti*.[73] He is not obliged to make provision for contingent debts. If it appears that the estate may be insolvent, he should not make any payment and should merely give notice of the possible insolvency. The creditors must then proceed by sequestration of the estate.[74] If the executor pays ordinary debts without providing for privileged debts, or pays the beneficiaries without providing for debts, he is personally liable.[75] An executor can make payment of a claim in safety even although he has not been made to pay by legal process but if the estate is small, and the amount of claims uncertain and the existence or amount of the alleged debt doubtful, he is entitled to protect himself and the estate by requiring formal constitution.[76] The rule that the creditor constitutes the debt at his own expense is not absolute.[77] If the executor puts forward an unreasonable defence he may be held personally liable in expenses with a right of relief against the estate.[78] Where an

65 *Stewart's Tr.* v. *Stewart's Exix.* (1896) 23 R.739.
66 Bell, *Prin.*, §1900; *Sanderson* v. *Lockhart-Mure,* 1946 S.C.298.
67 *McPherson* v. *Cameron* (1941) 57 Sh.Ct.Rep.64.
68 *Brown* v. *Wallace* (1894) 10 Sh.Ct.Rep.142.
69 *Griffiths' Trs.* v. *Griffiths,* 1912 S.C.626.
70 *Morrison* v. *Cornfoot* (1930) 46 Sh.Ct.Rep.74.
71 Bell, *Prin.*, §§1402-1405.
72 *Barlass* v. *Barlass's Trs.*, 1916 S.C.741.
73 *Taylor & Ferguson Ltd.* v. *Glass's Trs.*, 1912 S.C.165.
74 See *infra*, para. 12.
75 *Lamond's Trs.* v. *Croom* (1871) 9 M.662; *Heritable Securities Investment Association Ltd.* v. *Miller's Trs.* (1893) 20 R.675.
76 *McGaan* v. *McGaan's Trs.* (1883) 11 R.249.
77 *Barclay's Bank Ltd.* v. *Lawton's Trs.*, 1928 S.L.T.298.
78 *Law* v. *Humphrey* (1876) 3 R.1192; *cf. Harper* v. *Connor's Trs.* (1927) 43 Sh.Ct.Rep.138.

action for payment has been raised against the executor a formal action of constitution is not necessary.[79] In some circumstances he may be justified in raising an action of multiplepoinding.[80] The executor can be sued even although he has not been confirmed.[81] The executor is entitled to make payment of sums due to himself, as an individual, unless the estate is apparently insolvent or there is a serious dispute about the validity of the claim.[82] A creditor who has received payment of his debt in good faith is not obliged to refund it if it subsequently transpires that the estate is insolvent.[83]

If, after the expiry of the six months, the executor, in the reasonable belief that all debts have been satisfied, makes payment of the balance of the estate to the beneficiaries he is not personally liable to a creditor who has not intimated a claim before the payment.[84]

If the estate is sequestrated, the executor may be ordained to convey any assets in his possession to the trustee.[85] The assets in the possession of the executor may also be attached by the completion of diligence commenced before the debtor's death.[86] Where the executor dies in the course of the administration of the estate, the creditor's ultimate remedy is to sequestrate the original debtor's estate; he cannot proceed against the executor's executor unless he has intromitted with the debtor's executry estate.[87]

Where the creditor proceeds against the executor or the beneficiary and the estate of the executor or beneficiary is sequestrated, the creditor has, it seems, in competition with the creditors of the bankrupt, a preference over the assets of the deceased which can be distinguished and identified. As regards heritable estate, this preference was conferred by the Act of 1661, c.24 but, as that statute has now been repealed,[88] the preference as regards the whole assets now depends on the common law,[89] as the Confirmation Act 1695 applies only where an executor has not been

[79] *Galloway* v. *MacKinnon* (1936) 52 Sh.Ct.Rep.135.

[80] *Jamieson* v. *Robertson* (1888) 16 R.15; *cf. Mackenzie's Trs.* v. *Sutherland* (1895) 22 R.233.

[81] *Emslie* v. *Tognarelli's Exrs.*, 1967 S.L.T.(Notes)66.

[82] *Salaman* v. *Sinclair's Trs.*, 1916 S.C.698; *Watson* v. *British Linen Bank*, 1941 S.C.43.

[83] *Cathcart* v. *Moodie* (1804) Mor. "Heir & Executor" App. I. No. 2.

[84] *Stewart's Trs.* v. *Evans* (1871) 9 M.810; *Beith* v. *Mackenzie* (1875) 3 R.185.

[85] Bankruptcy (Scotland) Act 1913, s.28.

[86] See *supra*, para. 4.

[87] *Hutcheson & Co.'s Administrator* v. *Taylor's Exix.*, 1931 S.C.484.

[88] Succession (Scotland) Act 1964, Sched. 3.

[89] Bell, *Comm.*, II, 85; McLaren, *Wills and Succession*, II, pp. 866, 1299; Graham Stewart, p.681; *Menzies* v. *Poutz*, 1916 S.C.143.

confirmed. This preferential right was subject to the long negative prescription and may be extinguished in a shorter period by personal bar or acquiescence.[90] Where the executor has properly paid over the funds to the legatees or beneficiaries the creditor's remedy is to sue them.[91] It seems that the claim must be constituted against the executor first.[92] The beneficiary is not liable if at the time the payment was made to him there remained sufficient funds in the hands of the executor to meet all claims.[93]

Where testamentary trustees have carried on a business and thereby contracted debt, they can be sequestrated as trustees.[94]

7. Confirmation as Executor-Creditor

If no executors have been confirmed, there has been no vitious intromission,[95] and no third party has obtained possession of the estate,[96] the creditor's remedy is to confirm to the deceased's estate as executor-creditor. This is a species of diligence by which the creditor satisfies his debt out of the estate to which he confirms.[97] Formerly, this had to be moveable estate but it seems that the effect of s.14 of the Succession (Scotland) Act 1964, is to allow an executor-creditor to confirm to heritable estate of the deceased. The creditor must hold a decree or a liquid document of debt.[98] An appointment as executor-creditor is null if executors *qua* next of kin have already been confirmed.[99] A foreign title does not exclude an executor-creditor.[1] It is possible to confirm as executor-creditor to estate which has not been confirmed to by an executor *qua* next of kin. The procedure is to apply for decerniture and then obtain confirmation. The domicile of the deceased is immaterial.[1] Notice of the application must be inserted in the *Edinburgh Gazette* immediately after its presentation.[2] The inventory must include the whole estate of the deceased but the confirmation may be restricted to certain assets.[2] The effect of confirmation is to create a *nexus* on

---

90 *Traill's Trs.* v. *Free Church of Scotland,* 1915 S.C.655.

91 *Poole* v. *Anderson* (1834) 12 S.481; *Stewart's Trs.* v. *Evans* (1871) 9 M.810; *Beith* v. *Mackenzie* (1875) 3 R.185.

92 *Clelland* v. *Baillie* (1845) 7 D.461.

93 *Magistrates of St. Andrews* v. *Forbes* (1893) 31 S.L.R.225.

94 *J. & W. Campbell & Co.* (1899) 6 S.L.T.406.

95 See Wilson & Duncan, *Trusts, Trustees and Executors,* p.448.

96 *Irvine* v. *King's and Lord Treasurer's Remembrancer* (1949) 65 Sh.Ct.Rep.53.

97 *Smith's Trs.* v. *Grant* (1862) 24 D.1142.

98 For the procedure where the debt is not liquid see next paragraph.

99 *Lees* v. *Dinwidie* (1706) 5 Brown's Sup. 35.

1 *Smith's Trs.* v. *Grant, supra.*

2 Confirmation of Executors (Scotland) Act 1823, s.4.

these assets which is limited by (a) the amount of the debt, and (b) the value in the confirmation.[3] The executor-creditor must use due diligence to ingather the assets in the confirmation and must account for any surplus.[4] If there are two successive confirmations to the same asset and the asset is included at a higher value in the second confirmation, the creditor first confirming has no preference beyond the value in his confirmation.[5] The confirmation gives a complete title to the creditor.[6] He may sist himself as a party to an action begun by the deceased to recover an asset included in the confirmation.[7] If an executor-creditor dies without having received payment of his debt, his representatives can proceed with its recovery.[8]

It is necessary that the assets to which the executor-creditor confirms should be *in bonis defuncti*. So if an *inter vivos* assignation granted by the deceased has been intimated prior to confirmation, the assignee is preferred.[9] Similarly, if a special assignation or disposition falling under the Confirmation Act 1690 has been made by the deceased and intimation or possession has followed thereon, confirmation is incompetent.[10] A decree of preference in a multiple-poinding,[11] or consignation,[12] does not take assets *ex bonis defuncti*.

The position as to competition is as follows:

(a) *Privileged Debts:* the right of the executor-creditor is postponed to these.[13]

(b) *Other Creditors:* any other creditor holding a liquid document of debt or a decree may apply to be conjoined in the application for decerniture and thereafter ranks *pari passu* with the original applicant.[14] Moreover, any creditor who cites the executor-creditor within six months of the death is ranked *pari passu* but he must bear a proportion of the expenses of confirmation.[15] After the expiry of the six months, an executor-creditor who has confirmed within the

---

3 *per* Lord Curriehill, *Smith's Trs.* v. *Grant, supra,* at p.1169.
4 *Lee* v. *Donald,* 17 May 1816, F.C.
5 *Smith's Trs.* v. *Grant, supra.*
6 *Dickson* v. *Barbour* (1828) 6 S.856.
7 *Mein* v. *McCall* (1844) 6 D.1112.
8 *Mitchel* v. *Mitchel* (1737) Mor.3935.
9 *Sinclair* v. *Sinclair* (1726) Mor.2793; *Cust* v. *Garbet & Co.* (1775) Mor.2795.
10 *Bell* v. *Willison* (1831) 9 S.266.
11 *Anderson* v. *Stewart* (1831) 10 S.49.
12 *Smith's Trs.* v. *Grant, supra.*
13 Stair, III, 8, 64; *Crawford* v. *Hutton* (1680) Mor.11, 832.
14 *Willison* v. *Dewar* (1840) 3 D.273.
15 Act of Sederunt, 28 February 1662; *Ramsay* v. *Nairn* (1708) Mor.3139.

six months is preferred to other creditors who have not cited him by that time. Similarly, if no creditor has confirmed within the six months, the first to do so thereafter obtains a preference. Creditors who cite the executor-creditor after the six months are ranked *pari passu inter se* if the one has not obtained decree before citation by the other.[16] If one has already obtained decree he is preferred.

If an executor-nominate or executor-dative *qua* next of kin is also a creditor he obtains the same preference as an executor-creditor after the six months period.[17]

(c) *Diligence commenced before Death:* the executor-creditor is preferred if his confirmation is prior to the date of sale[18] or the decree in the furthcoming.[19]

(d) *Sequestration:* it is not competent for a creditor to be confirmed as executor-creditor after the date of the first deliverance in the sequestration.[20] If the deceased is sequestrated within seven months after his death, a confirmation as executor-creditor expede prior to the sequestration is of no effect in a question with the trustee but the creditor has a preference for the expenses bona fide incurred in obtaining confirmation.[21]

8. Decree cognitionis causa tantum

In the case where the debt is not liquid, the creditor must proceed against the *hereditas jacens* by raising an action against the deceased's next-of-kin for a decree *cognitionis causa tantum*.[22] It is not now necessary to charge the next-of-kin before raising the action.[23] All the known next-of-kin must be called for their interests whether or not they are subject to the jurisdiction of the Scottish courts.[24] Executors who have not confirmed need not be be called.[25] It is competent to bring an action against two defenders jointly and severally and to restrict the decree sought against one to a decree

---

16 *Graeme* v. *Murray* (1738) Mor.3141.

17 *Macleod* v. *Wilson* (1837) 15 S.1043.

18 Graham Stewart, p.452.

19 *Wilson* v. *Fleming* (1823) 2 S.430.

20 Bankruptcy (Scotland) Act 1913, s.29.

21 s.106.

22 The Confirmation Act 1695.

23 *Forrest* v. *Forrest* (1863) 1 M.806; *Ferrier* v. *Crockhart,* 1937 S.L.T.205.

24 *Smith* v. *Tasker,* 1955 S.L.T.347. See *Davidson Pirie & Co.* v. *Dihle's Reps.* (1900) 2 F.640; *Stevens* v. *Thomson,* 1971 S.L.T.136.

25 *Smith's Trs.* v. *Grant* (1862) 24 D.1142; *cf. Emslie* v. *Tognarelli's Exrs.,* 1967 S.L.T.(Notes)66.

cognitionis causa tantum.[26] Once decree *cognitionis causa tantum* has been obtained, the debt, being now liquid, can be the basis of an application for confirmation as executor-creditor.

9. Creditors of Next-of-Kin

If there has been no confirmation, the creditors of the deceased's next-of-kin may confirm as executors-creditors.[27] The deceased's creditors doing diligence within a year and a day of the death are, however, preferred to the diligence of the creditors of the next-of-kin.

10. Heritable and Moveable Debt

Although a creditor is entitled to payment of his debt from any part of the debtor's estate, in questions between the debtor's representatives heritable debts must be paid from the heritable estate and moveable debts from the moveable estate.[28] As a general rule debts resting *in obligatione* are moveable *quoad debitorem*. The following moveable debts require special mention: the unpaid price of heritage;[29] arrears of feuduty[30] and rent;[31] and obligations of warrandice.[32]

The following are heritable—debts secured over heritage and real burdens.[33]

Where the security subjects are insufficient in value to satisfy the heritable debt secured, the other heritable estate is liable for the balance.[34]

11. Judicial Factors

If the deceased left no settlement appointing trustees or other parties having power to manage his estate or part thereof, or if such parties do not accept or act, one or more creditors or persons interested in the succession may petition the court to appoint a

---

26 *Smith* v. *Tasker, supra*.

27 The Confirmation Act 1695.

28 McLaren, *Wills and Succession,* II, p.1305; Succession (Scotland) Act 1964, s.14(3). The distinction is still important where there are legal rights and in cases of partial intestacy.

29 *Clayton* v. *Lowthian* (1826) 2 W. & S.40; *Ramsay* v. *Ramsay* (1887) 15 R.25.

30 *Johnston* v. *Cochran* (1829) 7 S.226.

31 *Kinloch's Exrs.* v. *Kinloch* (1811) Hume 178.

32 *Duchess of Montrose* v. *Stuart* (1887) 15 R.(H.L.)19.

33 *Breadalbane's Trs.* v. *Jamieson* (1873) 11 M.912.

34 *Bell's Tr.* v. *Bell* (1884) 12 R.85.

judicial factor on the estate.[35] The procedure is not competent where the deceased left no assets[36] nor where nominated but unconfirmed executors are acting.[37] The application is to the Court of Session or to the sheriff court where the deceased resided or carried on business during the year immediately preceding the date of the petition or where heritage belonging to the deceased at his death was situate.[38] In the Court of Session, procedure is regulated by Rule of Court 201. Intimation is made to the creditors and other persons interested in the estate and in the *Edinburgh Gazette*. The court's power to appoint is discretionary.[39] The factor advertises for claims within 14 days of the issue of the first certified interlocutor of his appointment.[40] He examines the claims and may call for further evidence thereof or require the creditor to constitute the debt.[41] For purposes of ranking and payment the date of his appointment is equivalent to the date of sequestration.[42] He administers the estate subject to the Judicial Factors Acts and under the supervision of the Accountant of Court[43] but he has no title to reduce gratuitous alienations by virtue of the Bankruptcy Act 1621.[44] Within six months of the issue of the first certified interlocutor of his appointment he must prepare an inventory of the estate, a state of the debts and a scheme of division amongst the creditors which is laid before the Accountant of Court who reports thereon to the court.[45] If the estate is insolvent, it is to be divided among the creditors in accordance with the rules as to ranking obtaining in sequestrations.[46] Notice of the scheme must be given to the creditors who may lodge a note of objections thereto which is disposed of by the court.[47] If the

---

35 Bankruptcy (Scotland) Act 1913, s.163 (amended by the Law Reform (Miscellaneous Provisions) (Scotland) Act 1980, s.14(2)).

36 *Dunn* v. *Britannic Assurance Co. Ltd.*, 1932 S.L.T.244.

37 *Emslie* v. *Tognarelli's Exrs.*, 1967 S.L.T.(Notes)66.

38 It seems that, if there is no heritage, the petition is competent only within a year of death: Lewis, *Sheriff Court Practice,* 8th ed., p.298; Dobie, *Sheriff Court Practice,* p.394.

39 *Masterton* v. *Erskine's Trs.* (1887) 14 R.712; *Youngson Ptrs.*, 1911 2 S.L.T.448; *London & Brazilian Bank* v. *Lumsden's Trs.*, 1913 1 S.L.T.262.

40 R.C.201(*d*).

41 R.C.201(*e*).

42 R.C.201(*e*).

43 B.A., s.163.

44 *Reid's J.F.* v. *Reid,* 1959 S.L.T.120. See, however, N.M.L. Walker, *Judicial Factors,* p.46.

45 R.C.201(*f*), (*g*).

46 B.A., s.163.

47 R.C.201(*h*)-(*k*).

scheme is approved payment is made to the creditors in accordance therewith. Out of the first funds realised the factor reserves the estimated cost of administration of the estate and he may, without waiting for the expiry of six months from the date of death, pay the deathbed and funeral expenses, rent, taxes, such servants' wages as are privileged debts and interest becoming due or past due to creditors having preferences over the estate.[48] If there is a residue after payment of the creditors the factor submits a statement of the amount, the parties claiming and the grounds of claim. He then pays over the residue to the parties found entitled thereto by the court.[49] In the sheriff court, the procedure is regulated by the Judicial Factors (Scotland) Act 1880.[50] The appointment of the factor has the effect of an intimated assignation of the deceased's rights.[51] It does not prevent a subsequent sequestration.[52]

12. Sequestration of Estate of a Deceased Debtor

It is possible to sequestrate the estate of a deceased debtor who at the date of his death was subject to the jurisdiction of the supreme courts of Scotland. The petition must be at the instance of a mandatory to whom the debtor had granted a mandate to apply for sequestration or of one or more creditors qualified as in the case of a living debtor.[53] The petition is presented in the Court of Session or in the sheriff court of the sheriffdom in which the debtor resided or carried on business for 40 or more days during the year before presentation of the petition.[54] Where sequestration is awarded in the Court of Session it is subsequently remitted to such sheriff court as is deemed expedient for further procedure.[55] The petitioning creditor's oath must specify the place where the debtor resided or had a dwelling-house or carried on business in Scotland at the time of his death, and whether he was then owner of estates in Scotland.[56] The petition may be presented at any time after the debtor's death. It is not necessary to show that the debtor was notour bankrupt at the time of his death but, if this was not the case, sequestration cannot be awarded until the expiration of six months from the death

48 R.C.201(*n*).
49 R.C.201(*o*).
50 Act of Sederunt, 16 July 1936, s.I(B), adding S.C.R.170.
51 *Campbell's J.F.* v. *National Bank*, 1944 S.C.495 *(ex concessione)*.
52 *Arthur* (1903) 10 S.L.T.550.
53 Bankruptcy (Scotland) Act 1913, s.11.
54 s.16.
55 s.17.
56 s.23.

unless the debtor's successors concur in the petition or renounce the succession in which event sequestration may be awarded forthwith.[57] A judicial factor may be appointed *ad interim* to administer the estate until the expiry of the six months.[58] "Successors" include all persons who have succeeded to any property which was vested in the debtor at the time of his death, whether as heirs, heirs apparent, trustees under voluntary conveyances, representatives by deed or otherwise, executors, administrators or nearest of kin, or as assignees or legatees, and shall also include singular successors where they have acquired the right.[59] It is thought that, where the petition is presented by a mandatory, sequestration can be awarded forthwith.[60]

On presentation of the petition the court orders citation of the debtor's successors.[61] If a successor does not appear at the diet of appearance and show cause why sequestration cannot competently be awarded, the court awards sequestration and ordains any successor who had made up a title to or is in possession of any part of his property to convey the same to the trustee.[62] A successor who has not renounced the succession and has not concurred in a creditor's petition may petition for recall of the sequestration.[63] Where a successor has made up title to heritable estate the trustee may petition the court for a declaration that the estate is transferred to and vested in him.[64]

The subsequent course of the sequestration of a deceased debtor does not differ in its general features from that of a living debtor.

It is not competent for any creditor, after the date of the first deliverance on the petition for sequestration, to be confirmed executor-creditor.[65] The sequestration of a deceased debtor is merely a process for the distribution of the estate and the court will not recall the sequestration on the application of the executor unless he shows that he has sufficient funds to pay the creditors or that there would be some advantage in having the estate administered by him.[66]

---

57 s.13.
58 *J. & G. Stewart Ltd.* v. *Waldie,* 1926 S.L.T.526.
59 s.2.
60 Goudy, p.117.
61 s.25.
62 ss.28, 29.
63 s.30.
64 s.101.
65 s.29.
66 *McLetchie* v. *Angus Brothers* (1899) 1 F.946.

CHAPTER 27

SPECIAL DEBTORS

AGENTS

1. Agency

A contract may be entered into through an agent. This may be done in three ways: (a) where the agent enters the contract expressly as agent for a named principal; (b) where he enters expressly as agent for a principal whose name is not disclosed; (c) where he enters the contract nominally as principal without the existence of the agency being disclosed.

In general, in all three cases the principal can sue on the contract[1] but there are certain exceptions: (i) where the principal's title to sue is expressly excluded,[2] (ii) where evidence of the existence of an undisclosed principal would contradict the terms of a written contract,[3] (iii) where the other party to the contract entered the contract "with reference to the known personal capabilities or character" of the agent acting on behalf of an undisclosed principal.[4]

In general the agent can sue on the contract only if he is liable thereon but there are exceptions: (i) where there is an express term of a contract that the agent has a title to sue although he is not liable on the contract,[5] (ii) where the agent has a lien for his charges and commission.[6]

2. Liability of Agent

As a general rule, the principal is liable on a contract made by the agent when acting within his actual or ostensible authority. The onus of proving the authority is on the third party attempting to enforce the contract.[7] There may be exceptions to the general rule where it is clear that the parties entering the contract did not intend

---

1 Bell, *Comm.*, I, 526; *Bennett* v. *Inveresk Paper Co.* (1891) 18 R.975.
2 *Ransohoff & Wissler* v. *Burrell* (1897) 25 R.284.
3 *Drughorn Ltd.* v. *Rederiaktiebolaget Transatlantic* [1919] A.C.203.
4 Bell, *Comm.*, I, 527.
5 *Bonar* v. *Liddell* (1841) 3 D.830; *Levy & Co.* v. *Thomsons* (1883) 10 R.1134.
6 *Mackenzie* v. *Cormack*, 1950 S.C.183.
7 *Wylie & Lochhead Ltd.* v. *Hornsby* (1889) 16 R.907.

that the principal would be liable.[8] Where the agent has contracted ostensibly as a principal without disclosing the existence of the agency, the agent is liable on the contract but, once the principal's name is disclosed, the third party may elect to hold liable either the principal or the agent.[9] In these circumstances the liability of the principal and the agent is alternative and not joint and several; once the third party has elected to hold the one liable he cannot proceed against the other. The obtaining of a decree against one,[10] or the acceptance of a dividend in his bankruptcy,[11] constitutes election; in other cases election is a question of fact.[12] Even where the third party does not become aware of the existence of the agency until after he has obtained decree against the agent he cannot proceed against the principal.[13] If the third party elects to sue the agent, the agent can enforce a counter claim due to the principal.[14]

Where an agent has expressly contracted on behalf of a named principal, as a general rule he incurs no liability under the contract.[15] There may, however, be circumstances showing that the parties intended that the agent would be personally liable on the contract,[16] and the general rule is also affected by a custom of trade.[17] There seems to be no absolute rule that an agent contracting on behalf of a foreign principal is personally liable.[18]

Where the agent has contracted expressly as agent for a principal whose name is not disclosed, the position is not altogether clear but it seems that the agent may be liable.[19] It seems that it is not

---

8 *Lamont, Nisbett & Co.* v. *Hamilton,* 1907 S.C.628.

9 *Bennett* v. *Inveresk Paper Co.* (1891) 18 R.975.

10 *Meier & Co.* v. *Küchenmeister* (1881) 8 R.642.

11 *David Logan & Son Ltd. & Liquidator* v. *Schuldt* (1903) 10 S.L.T.598; a claim for ranking may be sufficient: Gloag, p.141.

12 Gloag, p.141.

13 *Ingram Clothing Mfg. Co. (Glasgow) Ltd.* v. *Lewis* (1960) 76 Sh.Ct.Rep.165.

14 *Craig & Co.* v. *Blackater,* 1923 S.C.472; *James Laidlaw & Sons Ltd.* v. *Griffin,* 1968 S.L.T.278.

15 Bell, *Comm.,* I, 536; *Millar* v. *Mitchell* (1860) 22 D.833; *Livesey* v. *Purdom & Sons* (1894) 21 R.911; *Armour* v. *Duff,* 1912 S.C.120; see, as to the relationship between the terms of the contract and the form of the signature, *Universal Steam Navigation Co. Ltd.* v. *James McKelvie & Co.* [1923] A.C.492; *Stone & Rolfe* v. *Kimber Coal Co.,* 1926 S.C.(H.L.)45. An agent who has opened a bank account for a named principal is not liable for an overdraft: *Royal Bank of Scotland* v. *Skinner,* 1931 S.L.T.382. Contrast *Bank of Scotland* v. *McNeill,* 1977 S.L.T.(Sh.Ct.)2, where the agency was not fully divulged.

16 *Lamont, Nisbett & Co.* v. *Hamilton,* 1907 S.C.628; Gloag, p.136.

17 *Meier & Co.* v. *Küchenmeister, supra.*

18 Gloag, p.139.

19 Gloag, p.138; Gloag & Henderson, p.295.

competent for the agent to prove by parole evidence that he is in fact the principal.[20]

Where the agent contracts ostensibly as a principal without disclosing the existence of the agency, he is, as has already been explained, liable on the contract and, once the principal's name is disclosed, the third party may elect to hold liable either the principal or the agent.[21] This, however, does not apply, and the agent is not liable, where the third party knew of the agency at the time the contract was made,[22] but it is incompetent to prove such knowledge by extrinsic evidence if the contract is in writing.[23]

Where the agent has entered a contract outwith his authority, he is not personally liable thereon but he may be liable in damages for delict or misrepresentation.[24]

3. Ostensible Authority

There may be circumstances in which a general agent has an implied power to borrow money.[25]

The onus is on the other party to prove the agent's authority.[26]

4. Praepositura

A wife or other relative[27] who is managing the household—*praeposita rebus domesticis*—is presumed to purchase necessaries as the agent of the master of the household.[28] Necessaries are food, clothing, furniture and medical attendance.[29] The husband is liable for such purchases and the wife is not liable[30] even if she has a

---

20 *Hill Steam Shipping Co.* v. *Hugo Stinnes Ltd.*, 1941 S.C.324.

21 Bell, *Comm.*, I, 536; if the agent signs the contract in his own name without qualification he is deemed to be contracting personally unless it appears from other parts of the document that he did not intend to bind himself as principal: *Stewart* v. *Shannessy* (1900) 2 F.1288; where a firm of brokers gave an order to supply a named ship it was held that they made the contract as agents for a disclosed principal, the owner of the ship: *Armour* v. *Duff & Co.*, 1912 S.C.120.

22 *Bank of Scotland* v. *Rorie* (1908) 16 S.L.T.21.

23 *Lindsay* v. *Craig*, 1919 S.C.139.

24 Gloag, p.155; *Anderson* v. *Croall & Sons Ltd.* (1903) 6 F.153.

25 *Paterson* v. *Banks*, 1958 S.L.T.(Sh.Ct.)33.

26 *Blackwood & Tinto Ltd.* v. *Gascoines Ltd.*, 1950 S.L.T.(Sh.Ct.)5.

27 *Hamilton* v. *Forrester* (1825) 3 S.572.

28 Erskine, I, 6, 26.

29 *Kinfauns* v. *Kinfauns* (1711) Mor.5882.

30 *Aiton* v. *Lord Halkerton* (1629) Mor.5952; *Scougall* v. *Douglas* (1630) Mor. 5953; *Howieson* v. *Lady Laurieston* (1631) Mor.5954.

separate estate.[31] The husband is not liable if the goods were not used for the family.[32] It is thought that the husband cannot avoid liability by proving that he paid the wife a sufficient allowance.[33] The husband may avoid liability by giving express notice to tradesmen that he will not be liable for his wife's debts.[34] An advertisement is effectual for this purpose only if the tradesman has read it. The most effective method is to take out Letters of Inhibition. The procedure is by an application to the Petition Department of the Court of Session which is granted as a matter of course. The Letters are then signeted, served on the wife, and registered in the Register of Inhibitions and Adjudications. The Inhibition formally prohibits the wife from incurring debt and is effectual against "all mankind". The husband is not liable even if the tradesman extending credit did not know of the Inhibition.[35] He may, however, still be liable for necessaries for the wife's maintenance if he does not give her an allowance.[36] He may also be liable if he ratifies his wife's contracts by acquiescence after the date of the Inhibition.[37]

A wife has no implied authority to borrow money[38] or grant bills.[39]

A wife who contracts with her husband's express authority may nevertheless be liable if the tradesman did not know she was a married woman.[40]

When the husband and wife separate, the implied mandate arising from a course of dealings is not necessarily terminated.[41] A wife living apart from or deserted by her husband in buying goods or furnishings for herself or her children binds her own estate as if she were unmarried without prejudice to any right of the seller to recover from the husband.[42]

---

31 *Mitchelson* v. *Lady Cranston* (1780) Mor.5886; *Robertson* v. *Haldane* (1801) Hume 208.

32 *London Clothing Co.* v. *Bremner* (1886) 2 Sh.Ct.Rep.116.

33 See Clive, *Husband and Wife*, p.254.

34 *Buie* v. *Gordon* (1827) 5 S.464.

35 *Topham* v. *Marshall* (1808) Mor.App. *s.v.* 'Inhibition' No. 2.

36 *Auchinleck* v. *Earl of Monteith* (1675) Mor.5879; *Campbell* v. *Ebden* (1676) Mor.5879; *Gordon* v. *Sempill* (1776) Mor.App. *s.v.* 'Husband and Wife' No. 4.

37 *Ker* v. *Gibson* (1709) Mor.6023.

38 *McIntyre* v. *Graham* (1795) Hume 203.

39 *Forrest* v. *Earl of Sutherland* (1749) Mor.6019.

40 Walton, *Husband and Wife*, 3rd ed., p.203.

41 Clive & Wilson, *Husband and Wife*, p.260; see also *infra*, para. 19.

42 Married Women's Property (Scotland) Act 1920, s.3(2).

PARTNERSHIP

5. Authority of Partners

Partnership is the relation which subsists between persons carrying on a business in common with a view of profit.[43] If the business is limited in purpose and duration the partnership is sometimes known as a joint adventure.[44] A partner is an agent of the firm and his acts for carrying on in the usual way business of the kind carried on by the firm bind the firm, unless he has in fact no authority to act for the firm in that particular matter and the person with whom he is dealing either knows that he has no authority, or does not know or believe him to be a partner.[45] Consequently, if there is an agreement between the partners restricting the power of one or more of them to bind the firm, an act done in contravention of that agreement does not bind the firm in a question with a person having notice of the agreement.[46] If a partner pledges the credit of the firm for a purpose apparently not connected with the firm's ordinary course of business, the firm is not bound unless he was in fact specially authorised by the other partners.[47] If a contract is not binding on the firm, it binds the partner personally even if he signed the firm name.[48] An act or instrument relating to the firm's business and done or executed in the firm's name or in any other manner showing an intention to bind the firm, by any person thereto authorised, whether a partner or not, is binding on the firm and all the partners.[49]

6. Liability of Firm

The firm is liable for any wrongful act or omission of a partner acting in the ordinary course of the firm's business which causes loss or injury to a person who is not a partner in the firm.[50] The firm is also liable to make good the loss where a partner acting within the scope of his apparent authority receives money or property of a third person and misapplies it and where a partner misapplies the money

---

43 Partnership Act 1890, s.1(1).
44 *Mair* v. *Wood,* 1948 S.C.83.
45 1890 Act, s.5.
46 1890 Act, s.8.
47 1890 Act, s.7.
48 *Fortune* v. *Young,* 1918 S.C.1.
49 1890 Act, s.6.
50 1890 Act, s.10.

or property of a third person which has been received by the firm in the course of its business and is in its custody.[51] If a partner who is a trustee improperly employs trust property in the business or on the account of the partnership no other partner who has no notice of the breach of trust is liable for the property but the trust money can be followed and recovered from the firm if still in its possession or under its control.[52]

7. Liability for Firm Debts

A partner is liable jointly and severally with the other partners for all debts and obligations incurred by the firm while he is a partner.[53] The estate of a partner who dies, or is sequestrated, is not liable for firm debts contracted after the date of death or sequestration but it is liable for debts contracted before that date.[54] A retiring partner remains liable for firm debts contracted before his retirement unless he is discharged by an express or implied agreement between himself, the members of the firm as newly constituted and the creditors.[55] Moreover, the retiring partner may, in certain circumstances, be liable for firm debts contracted after his retirement because a person dealing with a firm after a change in its constitution is entitled to treat all apparent members of the old firm as still being members of the firm until he has notice of the change.[56] It seems that the creditor need not elect to hold liable either the old firm including the retired partner or the newly constituted firm; the liability is joint and several.[57] An advertisement in the *Edinburgh Gazette* is sufficient notice to persons who had no dealings with the old firm. In other cases individual notice is required but it is always competent to show that the creditor knew of the change although he was not given formal notice thereof.

A person who is admitted as a partner does not thereby become liable for debts contracted before he became a partner.[58] Whether liability exists depends on the facts. If the whole assets of a going concern are transferred to the new firm there is a presumption that

---

[51] 1890 Act, s.11.
[52] 1890 Act, s.13.
[53] 1890 Act, ss.9 and 12.
[54] 1890 Act, s.36(3).
[55] 1890 Act, s.17. As to liability for delict, see *Welsh* v. *Knarston*, 1973 S.L.T.66.
[56] 1890 Act, s.36.
[57] *Blacks* v. *Girdwood* (1885) 13 R.243; Gloag & Henderson, p.310.
[58] 1890 Act, s.17(1).

the new firm, including the new partner, has assumed the liabilities of the old. This presumption may be rebutted if the new partner has paid in a large sum of capital and the other partners have put in the going concern as their shares and also if the basis is that the new firm is not liable for the debts of the old and has no right to collect debts due to the old firm.[59] These principles apply equally where an individual carrying on a business has taken in a partner.

A person who is not a partner may render himself liable for firm debts by "holding out", *i.e.* representing himself by words or conduct, or knowingly suffering himself to be represented, as a partner in the firm. He is liable as a partner to any one who has on the faith of the representation given credit to the firm, whether or not the representation was communicated to the person giving credit by or with the knowledge of the person holding out.[60]

8. Enforcement of Liability

If the debt has to be constituted, the action must be brought against the firm and not against one partner alone.[61] If the firm debt has been constituted by bill, bond or decree, any partner may be sued alone or charged.[62] A decree against the firm is a warrant for diligence against the partners whether they are named in the decree or not[63] but it is not a warrant for diligence against a person liable for the firm debts in respect of "holding-out".[64] The remedy of a person who is not a partner is to suspend the charge. When an obligation is granted by all the partners without mention of the firm, there is a rebuttable presumption that it was granted for the firm's purposes and the firm's property can be poinded even if only the partners have been charged.[65] The prescriptive period runs against the liability of the partner from the date of decree against the firm.[66]

---

59 *McKeand* v. *Laird* (1861) 23 D.846; *Miller* v. *Thorburn* (1861) 23 D.359; *Heddle's Exx.* v. *Marwick & Hourston's Tr.* (1888) 15 R.698; *Thomson & Balfour* v. *Boag & Son,* 1936 S.C.2; *Miller* v. *John Finlay MacLeod & Parker,* 1974 S.L.T.99.

60 1890 Act, s.14(1).

61 Kilkerran *s.v.* 'Society' No. III, Feb. 26, 1741; *Reid & McCall* v. *Douglas,* 11 June 1814, F.C.

62 *Wallace* v. *Plock* (1841) 3 D.1047.

63 Partnership Act 1890, s.4(2); S.C.R.11; *Ewing & Co.* v. *McClelland* (1860) 22 D.1347.

64 *Brember* v. *Rutherford* (1901) 4 F.62.

65 *Rosslund Cycle Co.* v. *McCreadie,* 1907 S.C.1208.

66 *Highland Engineering Ltd.* v. *Anderson,* 1979 S.L.T.122.

9. Instance

Where the firm name consists of personal names—whether these are the names of the partners or not—the firm can sue and be sued in the firm name in the Court of Session and the sheriff court.[67] If the firm name is descriptive, (*e.g.* "Antermony Coal Company") the firm can sue or be sued in that name in the sheriff court but in the Court of Session it is necessary to add the names of three of the partners (or of two, if there are only two).[68] In all cases, however, the firm can sue in the names of the whole partners provided that words are added to show that the action is for a partnership debt.[69] An action cannot proceed in the name of the partnership if a majority of the partners disclaim it.[70] If the firm has been dissolved, the former partners can sue and be sued together as such former partners or as individuals but in an action against the dissolved firm all the former partners within the jurisdiction must be called.[71]

It is hardly necessary to say that where an individual carries on business under a firm name, the business does not constitute a separate *persona* and there is no distinction between the assets of the business and the private assets of the individual even if he styles himself by the legal illiteracy "sole partner".[72] The appropriate instance is "XY carrying on business under the name of AB & Co." The Registration of Business Names Act 1916, applies.[73] The individual's executor can sue for debts due to the business.[74]

10. Registration of Business Names

Where an action is raised by a partnership it is sometimes important to ascertain if the firm name is registered with the Registrar of Business Names under the Registration of Business Names Act 1916.[75] The following are required to register: (a) a firm carrying on business under a business name which does not consist of the true surnames of all partners who are individuals and the corporate

---

67 *Forsyth* v. *Hare & Co.* (1834) 13 S.42.

68 S.C.R.11; *Antermony Coal Co.* v. *Wingate* (1866) 4 M.1017.

69 *Plotzker* v. *Lucas,* 1907 S.C.315.

70 *Hutcheon and Partners* v. *Hutcheon,* 1979 S.L.T.(Sh.Ct.)61.

71 *Muir* v. *Collett* (1862) 24 D.1119; *McNaught* v. *Milligan* (1885) 13 R.366; *D. Forbes Smith & Johnston* v. *Kaye,* 1975 S.L.T.(Sh.Ct.)33.

72 *Reid* v. *Chalmers* (1828) 6 S.1120; *Road Haulage Executive* v. *Elrick,* 1953 S.L.T.112. But, as to the illiteracy, see *Allen & Son* v. *Coventry* [1980] I.C.R.9.

73 See *infra,* para. 10.

74 *Mills* v. *Hamilton* (1830) 9 S.111.

75 Amended by Companies Act 1947, s.116.

names of all partners who are corporations without any addition other than the true Christian names of individual partners or initials of such Christian names, (b) an individual carrying on business under a business name which does not consist of his true surname without any addition other than his true Christian names or the initials thereof,[76] (c) a company as defined in the Companies Act carrying on business under a business name which does not consist of its corporate name without any addition.[77] The following do not make registration necessary: an addition merely indicating that the business is carried on in succession to a former owner of the business; the addition of an "s" at the end of a surname where two or more individual partners have that surname.

A person need not register the title by which he is known if it is different from his surname.[78] "Initials" include any recognised abbreviation of a Christian name. It has been held that the surname with the addition of only one Christian name out of the several Christian names of an individual is registrable.[79]

One effect of failure to register is that the rights of the defaulter under or arising out of any contract made or entered into in relation to the business at any time while he is in default[80] are not enforceable by action or other legal proceeding either in the business name or otherwise.[81] A default existing at the raising of the action has no effect if there was no default at the time the contract was made.[82] The defaulter is not disabled from enforcing a counter claim or set-off arising out of the contract.[83] A contract entered into in the name "X trading as Y" when X is an individual and Y an unregistered name is affected.[80]

The defaulter may apply to the court for relief against the disability and the court, on being satisfied that the default was accidental, or due to inadvertence[84] or some other sufficient cause,

---

76 s.1; as to an individual who has changed his name, see s.1(*c*) and Companies Act 1947, s.116(4). As to overseas companies, see Companies Act 1976, s.32(1).

77 Companies Act 1947, s.58.

78 1916 Act, s.22.

79 *Limond* v. *Bernthal*, 1953 S.L.T.(Sh.Ct.)97; *Brown* v. *Thomas & Burrows* (1922) 39 T.L.R.132.

80 *Kinnear* v. *Paper Shavings Co. Ltd.*, 1967 S.L.T.(Sh.Ct.)75.

81 1916 Act, s.8.

82 *Halliday* v. *Watt & Co. Ltd.*, 1950 S.L.T.(Sh.Ct.)58; *Mackinnon* v. *McIntosh*, 1955 S.L.T.(Sh.Ct.)69; see also *John and Francis Anderson* v. *Balnagown Estates Co.*, 1939 S.C.168.

83 1916 Act, s.8.

84 See *Watson* v. *Park Royal (Caterers) Ltd.* [1961] 1 W.L.R.727; *Thomas Montgomery & Sons* v. *W.B. Anderson & Sons Ltd.*, 1979 S.L.T.101.

or that on other grounds it is just and equitable to grant relief, may grant relief generally or as respects particular contracts on such conditions as it thinks fit but relief is not given if a party to the contract proves that if the Act had been complied with, he would not have entered into the contract.[85] The application is to the Court of Session but if a proceeding to enforce any contract is commenced in the sheriff court, the sheriff may grant relief as respects that contract.[86] It is for the petitioners to satisfy the court that they are entitled to relief.[87] Conditions as to service and publication of notice of the application, and as to expenses, may be imposed. The relief, when granted, operates retrospectively and validates the contract *ab initio*.[88]

The entry in the Register of Business Names may have an effect on the onus of proof where a person avers that he was not at the material time a partner in a firm.[89]

11. Compensation

Questions of compensation arising from the existence of a partnership are regulated by the principle that a partner is a debtor in debts due by the firm but is not a creditor in debts due to the firm.[90] So, where a creditor of a firm is also a debtor of a partner, either the creditor or the firm can plead compensation.[91] But where a debtor of the firm is also a creditor of a partner neither the firm's debtor nor the partner can plead compensation[92] unless the firm has been dissolved when solvent in which event the partner's share of the debt due to the firm can be set-off against the private debt.[93] If a former partner is sued for a debt due by a dissolved firm he can set-off a debt due to him personally by the pursuer.[94] It has not been

---

85 1916 Act, s.8; see as to relief, *Clydesdale Motor Transport Co.*, 1922 S.C.18; *J.J. & P. McLachlan,* 1929 S.C.357.

86 *Clydesdale Motor Transport Co.* v. *McCosh & Devine* (1922) 38 Sh.Ct.Rep.109; *Kennedy Contractors* v. *Connell,* 1977 S.L.T.(Sh.Ct.)32.

87 *J. & H. Cook* v. *Alban Expanded Metal and Engineering Co. Ltd.*, 1969 S.L.T.347.

88 *Re Shaer* [1927] 1 Ch.355.

89 *Smith* v. *Virgo,* 1946 S.L.T.(Notes)29.

90 Gloag & Irvine, p.325.

91 *Russell* v. *McNab* (1824) 3 S.63; *Christie* v. *Keith* (1838) 16 S.1224; *Scott* v. *Hall & Bissett,* 13 June 1809, F.C.; *Salmon* v. *Padon & Vannan* (1824) 3 S.406; *Hill* v. *Lindsay* (1847) 10 D.78; *Thomson* v. *Stevenson* (1855) 17 D.739.

92 *Mackie* v. *McDowal* (1774) Mor.2575; *Morrison* v. *Hunter* (1822) 2 S.68.

93 *Oswald's Trs.* v. *Dickson* (1833) 12 S.156; *Heggie* v. *Heggie* (1858) 21 D.31; Bell, *Comm.*, II, 553.

94 *Lockhart* v. *Ferrier* (1842) 4 D.1253.

decided whether, if two separate firms have the same partners, a debt due to one firm can be set-off against a debt due by the other.[95]

12. Sequestration of Firm

Sequestration may be awarded of the estates of a firm, either jointly with those of the partners or separately or without sequestration of the individual estates of the partners.[96]

If two firms, although consisting of the same partners, carry on separate and distinct businesses—having a real and perceptible distinction of trade and establishment—they cannot be treated as one firm for bankruptcy purposes.[97] A dissolved firm is not a "deceased debtor" for bankruptcy purposes.[98] Where an individual carries on business under a trade name, no distinction is made between his business assets and his private assets for bankruptcy purposes.[99]

The partnership must be notour bankrupt, notour bankruptcy being constituted either in one of the ways applicable to an individual or by any of the partners being rendered notour bankrupt for a company debt: "one which the company as a company have to pay."[1] The petition may be at the instance of the partnership. There is a sufficient citation if a copy of the petition and warrant is left at the place where the firm's business is or last was carried on provided that a partner, clerk or servant of the firm is there. If this cannot be done the alternative is to leave the copy at the dwelling-house of any of the partners or, if such a house cannot be found, at the office of edictal citations.[2] It seems that citation of the firm does not warrant sequestration of the estates of the partners as well as those of the firm if citation of the individual partners has not been effected.[3]

Where the firm is sequestrated but the partners remain solvent, the partners are liable jointly and severally for the debts of the firm. It has been doubted whether the trustee on the estate of the firm can sue a solvent partner for payment of debts by the firm; it seems that any action against the solvent partners must be at the instance of the

95 See *Mitchell* v. *Canal Basin Co.* (1869) 7 M.480.
96 Bankruptcy (Scotland) Act 1913, s.26.
97 *Commercial Bank of Scotland* v. *Tod's Tr.* (1895) 33 S.L.R.161.
98 *Stewart & McDonald* v. *Brown* (1898) 25 R.1042.
99 *Reid* v. *Chalmers* (1828) 6 S.1120.
1 B.A., s.6; *Mullen Ltd.* v. *Campbell,* 1923 S.L.T.497.
2 B.A., s.26.
3 *Central Motor Engineering Co.* v. *Galbraith,* 1918 S.C.755.

creditors individually.[4] A partner who pays a debt is entitled to a proportionate relief from the other partners.

Where the firm and the individual partners are sequestrated, the primary rule is that the creditors of the firm rank on the estate of the firm to the full amount of their debts to the exclusion of the private creditors of the partners.[5] The firm creditors can also claim on the estates of a partner but the trustee on the partner's estate must put a valuation on the estate of the firm, deduct the estimated value from the creditor's claim and rank the creditor only for the balance.[6] The ranking here is of course *pari passu* with the partner's private creditors. Moreover, the firm's trustee can also rank on the partner's estate for debts due by the partner to the firm on capital account but the dividend drawn on this claim is taken into account in estimating the value of the firm's estate for purposes of the deduction from the creditors' claims on the partner's estate.[7]

A creditor is not bound for purposes of voting on the firm's estate to deduct from his claim the value of his claim against the partners' estates but in claiming against a partner's estates he must put in his notice of claim a specified value on his claim against the firm's estate and also his claim against the other partners in so far as they are liable to relieve such partner. The specified value is deducted from the debt and the creditor can *vote* only for the balance without prejudice to the amount of his debt in other respects.[8] There is an absence of authority as to the method of valuing the claim against the estates of the other partners for this purpose.[9]

A wife of a partner who has lent money to the firm is not a postponed creditor.[10]

13. Limited Partnerships

A limited partnership must be registered under the Limited Partnerships Act 1907 and if it is not so registered it is deemed to be a general partnership.[11] It consists of one or more general partners

---

4 *Laing Brothers & Co.'s Tr.* v. *Low* (1896) 23 R.1105; *cf.* Goudy, p.578, n.(c).

5 Bell, *Comm.*, II, 550.

6 B.A., s.62.

7 Goudy, p.578; *Dunlop* v. *Spiers* (1776) Mor.14610, affirmed 1777 (H.L.) Mor. *s.v.* 'Society' App. No. 2.

8 B.A., s.57.

9 See the discussion in Wardhaugh, *Scottish Bankruptcy Manual,* p.122; Goudy, p.190.

10 *Lumsden* v. *Sym* (1912) 28 Sh.Ct.Rep.168.

11 s.5.

and one or more limited partners. A body corporate may be a limited partner.[12] The total number of partners cannot exceed 20 except in the case of solicitors, accountants, stockbrokers and other types of business specified by regulations.[13] General partners are liable for all debts and obligations of the firm. Limited partners contribute to the partnership a sum of money as capital or property valued at a stated amount and are not liable for the firm's debts beyond the amount of that contribution. If he directly or indirectly draws out or receives back any part of his contribution during the continuance of the partnership, the limited partner becomes liable for the firm's debts to the amount taken back.[14] A limited partner cannot take part in the management of the business and if he does so he becomes liable for the debts incurred while he is taking such part.[15] He has no power to bind the firm. The Registration of Business Names Act 1916 applies to a limited partnership. The rules of the Partnership Act 1890, and the general law relating to partnerships apply to limited partnerships subject to the provisions of the Act of 1907.[16]

When the limited partnership is dissolved its affairs are wound up by the general partners unless the court orders otherwise.[17] The court may order a winding-up by a judicial factor.[18] If the partnership has not less than eight members, the court may order a winding-up under the Companies Acts.[19]

14. Clubs and Associations

An unincorporated association is not a legal person.

A member of a club or association does not, in the absence of a special provision in the constitution, become liable for the debts of the body and is liable only for his subscription.[20]

---

12 s.4(4).
13 Companies Act 1967, s.121.
14 1907 Act, s.4(3).
15 1907 Act, s.6(1).
16 1907 Act, s.7.
17 1907 Act, s.6(3).
18 *Muirhead* v. *Borland,* 1925 S.C.474.
19 Companies Act, 1948 ss.398, 399. The position is not completely clear—see Gow, *Mercantile and Industrial Law of Scotland,* p.561; Lindley on *Partnership,* 14th ed., p.857. In England, limited partnerships are subject to the Bankruptcy Act 1914 and the Bankruptcy Rules, 1952—see *Re Barnard* [1932] 1 Ch.269. In Scotland the Limited Partnerships (Winding-up) Rules 1909 (S.R. & O. No. 327/L.14) apparently still apply.
20 *Wise* v. *Perpetual Trustee Co. Ltd.* [1903] A.C.139.

The liability for debts depends on principles of agency and is a question of circumstances.[21] There may be personal liability on the part of a manager but as a rule he contracts as an agent for the committee or for the whole membership. Individual committee members may be personally liable if they personally gave orders or signed cheques for specific accounts. Where the system of orders and payments was such that members of the committee had general knowledge that supplies were being obtained from a particular tradesman and his accounts were passed for payment by the committee as part of its ordinary business, the members of the committee were held jointly and severally liable. The whole membership of the club may be liable if they gave the committee a mandate to pledge the credit of the general body of members.

In the Court of Session the association should sue or be sued in its own name with the addition of the office-bearers;[22] in the sheriff court the association can sue and be sued in its name alone but the addition of the names of the office-bearers is desirable.[23] However, if the constitution prescribes a mode of suing, that should be used.[24]

An extract decree against the association is a warrant for diligence against the association but not against office-bearers or members not called in the action.[25]

An unincorporated association cannot be made notour bankrupt and cannot be sequestrated.[26]

15. English Debtor

Sequestration will not normally be awarded if there has been a receiving order in England.[27] A sequestration may be recalled within three months if it appears that a majority of the creditors reside in England or Northern Ireland and that the estate ought to be distributed under the insolvency laws of one of these jurisdictions.[28]

---

21 *Thomson & Gillespie* v. *Victoria Eighty Club* (1905) 13 S.L.T.399. See also *Bryson & Co. Ltd.* v. *Glasgow Civil Service & Mercantile Guild* (1916) 32 Sh.Ct.Rep.23.

22 *Bridge* v. *South Portland St. Synagogue,* 1907 S.C.1351; *Pagan & Osborne* v. *Haig,* 1910 S.C.341.

23 S.C.R.11; *Whitecraigs Golf Club* v. *Ker,* 1923 S.L.T.(Sh.Ct.)23.

24 *Whitecraigs Golf Club* v. *Ker, supra.*

25 S.C.R.11; *Aitchison* v. *McDonald,* 1911 S.C.174.

26 *Pitreavie Golf Club* v. *Penman,* 1934 S.L.T.247.

27 *Bank of Scotland* v. *Youde* (1908) 15 S.L.T.847.

28 B.A., s.43. The corresponding English provision is Bankruptcy Act 1914, s.12.

Once there is an adjudication of bankruptcy in England the bankrupt's property, whether real or personal, and whether situate in England or elsewhere, vests in the trustee.[29]

It seems that a discharge in an English bankruptcy is recognised in Scotland in respect of a debt contracted in England; whether it is recognised in respect of a Scottish debt is more doubtful.[30]

16. "Sole Partner"

Where an individual carries on business under a name which is not his own, he is obliged to register under the Registration of Business Names Act 1916.[31] On his sequestration, no distinction is made between the assets of that business and his other assets.[32] On the sale of such a business to another individual, the purchaser incurs no liability for the debts of the business in the absence of any special agreement.[33] Where the "sole partner" assumes a partner, however, the new partner may incur liability for the business debts.[34]

17. Scottish Companies

Securities granted by companies[35] and the liquidation of companies[36] are dealt with elsewhere. A company is not liable for a debt incurred prior to the date of its incorporation; so a company is not liable for a debt incurred prior to its incorporation by another company, later dissolved, which had the same name, some of the same directors, and carried on the same type of business.[37] A contract binds the company if it is signed by any person acting under its authority.[38] Where a document is signed by a person "as director" it is a question of circumstances as to whether he is personally bound or is to be treated as an agent. A deed is validly executed on behalf of the company if it is executed in accordance

---

29 Bankruptcy Act 1914, ss.53, 167; see *Salaman* v. *Tod,* 1911 S.C.1214.

30 Anton, *Private International Law,* pp.443-444.

31 See *supra,* para. 10.

32 *Reid* v. *Chalmers* (1828) 6 S.1120.

33 *Turnbull & Kay* v. *Chisholm & Co. and Blair* (1887) 3 Sh.Ct.Rep.379.

34 *Miller* v. *Thorburn* (1861) 23 D.359. See *supra,* para. 9.

35 Chap. 9.

36 Chap. 23.

37 *F.J. Neale (Glasgow) Ltd.* v. *Vickery,* 1973 S.L.T.(Sh.Ct.)88.

38 Companies Act 1948, s.32(1). As to the secretary's authority, see *Panorama Developments (Guildford) Ltd.* v. *Fidelis Furnishing Fabrics Ltd.* [1971] 2 Q.B.711; *McLean* v. *Stuart,* 1970 S.L.T.(Notes)77. See, as to bills, Chap. 5, para. 13.

with the provisions of the Companies Act (which includes in the manner provided by the company's articles[39]) or if it is sealed with the company's common seal and subscribed by two directors or by a director and a secretary, whether attested by witnesses or not.[40]

An unregistered company may be wound up in Scotland even although it has never carried on business in Great Britain; the court has a discretion to exercise its winding-up jurisdiction and the fact that the company's only asset is in Scotland favours the exercising of the jurisdiction.[41]

18. English Company

The requirements as to registration of charges created by a company registered in England differ slightly from those applicable to a company registered in Scotland.[42] A floating charge created by an English company is given effect in Scotland. The view has been expressed that s.1(1) of the Companies (Floating Charges and Receivers) (Scotland) Act 1972 applies to a company whether registered in England or in Scotland,[43] but there is a theoretical difficulty that the floating charge referred to in s.1 can be only a floating charge as defined by the other provisions of the Act. An English receiver may exercise his powers in Scotland so far as their exercise is not inconsistent with the law applicable there.[44]

In the liquidation of an English company the English court can restrain proceedings against the company in Scotland.[45]

19. Married Persons

Apart from cases of agency,[46] one spouse is not in general liable for the debts of the other. Where the spouses are living apart, if the husband is not adequately supporting the wife and if the wife has no

---

39 *Clydesdale Bank (Moore Place) Nominees Ltd.* v. *Snodgrass*, 1939 S.C.805.

40 1948 Act, s.32(4).

41 Companies Act 1948, s.399; *Inland Revenue* v. *Highland Engineering Ltd.*, 1975 S.L.T.203; *Banque Des Marchands de Moscou (Koupetschesky)* v. *Kindersley and Another* [1951] Ch.112; *Re Compania Merabello San Nicholas S.A.* [1973] Ch.75.

42 See Chap. 9, para. 1.

43 *Gordon Anderson (Plant) Ltd.* v. *Campsie Construction Ltd. and Anglo Scottish Plant Ltd.*, 1977 S.L.T.7.

44 Administration of Justice Act 1977, s.7.

45 Companies Act 1948, s.226; *Re Dynamics Corporation* [1973] 1 W.L.R. 63. As to the effect of Scottish diligence in the liquidation of an English company, see *Inshaw Seamless Iron and Steel Tubes Ltd.* v. *Smith Roberts, & Co. Ltd.* (1912) 28 Sh.Ct.Rep.171.

46 See *supra*, para. 4.

means of her own, the husband is liable on the principle of recompense to those who have supplied necessaries to the wife.[47] This liability cannot be terminated by inhibition or notice to traders. By statute, a husband has a liability for the ante-nuptial debts of his wife limited to "the value of any property which he shall have received from, through, or in right of his wife at, or before, or subsequent to the marriage."[48]

---

[47] *Neilson* v. *Guthrie & Gairn* (1672) Mor.5878. *Moore Taggart & Co.* v. *Kerr* (1897) 14 Sh.Ct.Rep.10; *Buie* v. *Gordon* (1827) 5 S.464; (1831) 9 S.923.

[48] Married Women's Property (Scotland) Act 1877, s.4; *Kennedy* v. *Peebles* (1921) 38 Sh.Ct.Rep.80. See Clive, *Husband and Wife*, p.265.

INDEX